Studia Fennica
Historica 3

To Bea and Bob

with warmest greetings
from the Finnish friend
Perti

DECEMBER 2002

The Finnish Literature Society was founded in 1831 and has from the very beginning engaged in publishing. It nowadays publishes literature in the fields of ethnology and folkloristics, linguistics, literary research and cultural history.

The first volume of Studia Fennica series appeared in 1933.

Since 1992 the series has been divided into three thematic subseries: Ethnologica, Folkloristica and Linguistica. Two additional subseries were formed in 2002, Historica and Litteraria.

In addition to its publishing activities the Finnish Literature Society maintains a folklore archive, a literature archive and a library.

Editorial board
Anna-Leena Siikala
Rauno Endén
Teppo Korhonen
Pentti Leino
Auli Viikari
Kristiina Näyhö

Editorial office
Hallituskatu 1
FIN-00170 Helsinki

Pertti Pesonen & Olavi Riihinen

Dynamic Finland

The Political System and the Welfare State

Finnish Literature Society • Helsinki

Cover picture:
Mari Rantanen,
Competitive Codes
© Kuvasto 2002

ISBN 951-746-426-6
ISSN 1458-526x

Tammer-Paino Oy,
Tampere 2002

Contents

Barents Sea

NORWAY

SWEDEN

Arctic Circle

Rovaniemi

Gulf of Bothnia

Oulu

FINLAND

RUSSIA

Vaasa

Kuopio

Joensuu

Jyväskylä

Pori

Tampere

Lappeen-
ranta

Lake
Ladoga

Lahti

Turku

HELSINKI

Gulf of Finland

ST. PETERSBURG

Baltic Sea

TALLINN

100 km

Geodoc 2002
© Tuija Jantunen

Foreword

Dynamic Finland is a welcome addition to political science. To those of us interested in the comparative analysis of politics – the only effective way to analyze politics! – Finland is an especially important case. It combines several phenomena in ways seen nowhere else, and in fact anchors the scale on many important aspects of politics:

– The process of building the Finnish state was relatively recent, and it is of special interest. Among other things, because its international position during its early decades as a state was contested and delicate, Finland offers a fascinating case of the impact of international politics on the domestic politics of states.

– Perhaps partly because of this history, its party system and the Finnish approach to resolving political conflict is of great interest on the broader canvas of cross-national comparison. Finland was one of the few European democracies with a large and active Communist Party during the post-war period, and was the only one to combine this with an essentially consensus-based society. All other West European states with a large Communist presence were stalemated polities; Finland was not.

– In the last sentence above, I called Finland "West European", but that is not really true. Another virtue from the standpoint of the comparative scholar is that it is not exactly "Western" or "Eastern", either geographically or historically. One puzzle for comparative scholars, for instance, is to assess the extent to which democratic institutions in Western Europe in the post-war years were shaped by American influence, by the emerging pan-European institutions of the Common Market, and by mutual imitation. None of these applied in the same way to Finland, so Finland serves as a very useful control.

– Finland's political institutions are unique and interesting; more about this below.

– Finland has perhaps the most equal income distribution in the world.

– Finland has perhaps the least corrupt system of public administration and politics in the world.

– Much has been made of the pressures on the modern welfare state, from global competitive pressures and other economic dislocations that make it difficult for states to maintain comprehensive support for their citizens. In the 1990s Finland experienced greater economic dislocation and pressures than any other mature welfare state has ever experienced. The Finnish case is very important for understanding the resilience of welfare states.

I could have added many more examples, but I hope these are enough to make the picture clear: Finland provides unique phenomena of great importance in comparative political analysis.

But there is another reason why Finland is of special interest in comparative politics. The science of politics is a science of design; the reason we study politics comparatively is to assess the impact of different designs for governance, so that we can improve our political lives. It should be no surprise that, just as Finland is a leader in industrial and material design, so is it a leader in political design. Finland pioneered early in the twentieth century in the experiment of combining elements of presidential government and parliamentary government in one system, something that has been picked up and used in dozens of states in the latter part of the twentieth century, starting with France in 1958.

Finland embarked in the late 1990s on a plan of reorganization and reform that is intended to balance the president and cabinet in the way that France and many other imitators intended, but have never achieved. Perhaps because the model of hybrid executive power has so often been adopted in stalemated societies like France's, it has usually evolved into a system in which President and cabinet compete for power rather than sharing power. In France, for instance, Presidents wholly dominate cabinets unless they are forced into a situation of *cohabitation*, at which time the situation flips to one of domination by the cabinet.

In Finland, too, political leaders are not oblivious to power. Through much of the first several decades there was a polite tug-of-war between president and cabinets for power with some presidents, like Kekkonen, gathering the reins largely into their own hands. Over the last couple of decades, though, as is admirably laid out in *Dynamic Finland*, a redesign of the powers of the president and cabinet has been carried out that should leave the relationship much like what DeGaulle and his advisors originally intended for France: a president with great residual power and responsibility for the security and intergrity of the state, but removed from most immediate political conflicts. As we see in the pages of this book, power has been fine-tuned in innumerable ways to produce a redesigned presidency.

For all these reasons, Finland is a case of very special interest in the comparative study of politics. But, political scientists are human too. Everywhere in the world there is a great affection for Finland, which we share. Finland is a plucky nation that has managed to thrive in a cold, forbidding climate, off the major trade and communication lines, and in an international situation throughout the twentieth century that was fraught with danger and hardship. Somehow this people have managed despite the rigors of their environment to produce a renaissance in music, success in athletic enterprise far beyond what one could expect of such a small country, leadership in industrial design – and an original, superbly functioning democracy. In reading this book, pleasure mingles with intellectual stimulation.

The book presents a very clear exposition and introduction to the politics of Finland, and as such it is a real boon to the field of comparative politics. But fortunately for us, the authors also go beyond plain exposition to add a great deal of very accessible but nonetheless original and useful analysis of politics to the book. Their analysis of how Finnish nationalism developed, or their assessment of how effectively the Finnish welfare state decommodifies society, are but two examples of how they build on their excellent exposition and introduction to Finnish politics. And finally, just as this reader combined pleasure with intellectual stimulation in reading the book, it is good to see that Professors Pesonen and Riihinen, also, could not resist showing their admiration for the way Finns have built their state. It is clear as one reads this book that it was as much a pleasure for the authors, as for the reader, to reflect on the politics of this remarkable state.

W. PHILLIPS SHIVELY

Minneapolis, August 23, 2002

Preface

Finland is small and little known. Even where the name is familiar, recent changes may have passed unnoticed. But we have also observed a rising interest in Finland. And we have seen how difficult it can be to obtain a general presentation, written for an international audience, that would outline our country's political system and civil society, its development, and the services it provides for the wellbeing of its citizens.

This was our motivation in writing a book for a foreign audience about Finland and the Finnish experience. We had a variety of readers in mind: university students engaged in area studies or comparative politics, people whose professional interests create an interest in Finnish society or a need to grasp its essentials quickly, and friends of Finland who desire more knowledge about the country.

We aimed to offer a view of Finland's presence and dynamic development from political and social points of view. This is not to deny that it was enjoyable to set down our country's achievements and uniqueness and it was encouraging that Finland ranks so high among the countries of the world in cross-national comparisons, but we have sought to remain objective. We have no illusions of Finland as a model society, free of error or pressing problems.

Our general approach is descriptive and analytic. Theoretical considerations are added if they could help the reader understand certain points, but the material is not viewed through a systematic frame of analysis. The goal is to offer a description of the basis and functioning of democracy in Finland, and to present selected policy areas that are essential in a welfare state.

The book contains 17 chapters. We divided our task keeping in mind that Pesonen's academic background is in political science and Riihinen's in social policy. Pesonen wrote chapters 1, 4, 6 to 13, and 15, and Riihinen chapters 3 and 5. Four chapters (2, 14, 16, and 17) were co-written, as designated by the initials at the end of each section. As coauthors we assume responsibility for the entire text. Pesonen wrote in English, and texts by Riihinen were translated by Mikko Pitkänen, Nina Tuominen, and Pesonen. We thank Patrick Humphreys for his able and creative editing of the manuscript.

Kaisa-Riitta Puttonen assisted us in many ways and prepared the indexes and the list of references. The Research Institute for Social Sciences of the University of Tampere has kindly provided working facilities for Pesonen, and the University of Helsinki offered a place for our joint meetings.

Our work would not have been possible without the cooperative attitude of the people who have provided us with specialist information. We encountered the same willingness to help at government offices, research outfits, organizations, and companies. Without mentioning by name the many individuals to whom we are indebted, we would like to express how inspiring it was to meet such positive understanding of our aims.

Special thanks are due to the Alfred Kordelin Foundation for financial support that covered our expenses. And we are pleased to have this book published by the Finnish Literary Society, particularly because it launched the rise of Finland's civil society 171 years ago.

At one time the authors attended the same sociology seminar at the University of Helsinki. We enjoyed working together as students. Having observed our country's changes and stability through half a century, it has been a pleasure to work together once more.

Tampere and Helsinki, July 17, 2002

Pertti Pesonen and Olavi Riihinen

1 Finnish Features

Finland, or, as the natives call it in Finnish, Suomi, is a country of lakes and islands. It is a vast continent about which strangers until lately hardly knew anything, beyond such rude facts as are learnt in school, viz., that "Finland is surrounded by the Gulfs of Finland and Bothnia on the South and West, and borded by Russia and Lapland on the East and North," and yet Finland is larger than our own England, Scotland, Ireland, aye, and the Netherlands, all put together... Finland is not the home of barbarians, as some folk then imagined; neither do Polar bears walk continually about the streets, nor reindeer pull sledges in summer – items that have several times been suggested to the writer.

Tweedie 1913, pp. 11–12

This quotation is no longer news. It is from a travel book on Finland written before the First World War. Its British author, Mrs E. Alec Tweedie, closed her various observations with a political survey that included the following crucial facts of those days:

It is a fundamental principle of the Finnish Constitution that the country shall be governed with the assistance of native authorities only... The people of Finland are awaiting with grave anxiety further developments in the present Russian policy.

Op.cit., pp. 461, 476

Indeed, Finland had developed a political identity of its own; largely because it had been an autonomous state with its own "home rule" since 1809. For a century its head of state was an authoritarian ruler in other parts of his Russian empire, but with constitutionally limited powers in Finland. Then, in 1917, quite unexpected "further developments" dethroned Russia's emperor, the Tsar. Finland seized the opportunity and declared its independence on December 6, 1917. Soon thereafter, in the aftermath of World War I, several more states in Europe gained independence or adopted a new constitution but, before three decades had passed,

Finland remained the only one among those states that had kept the same constitution in force without interruption.

In 1997, the eightieth year of Finland's independence, there were no fewer than 186 independent countries in the world. One of them, and since 2000 two, had more than a billion inhabitants. Forty-eight had at least 20 million, while the population of thirty-five countries was below a million. Such a comparison ranks Finland near the median of all countries. In Europe Finland is typically classified as one of the small states. Its population of 5,181,000 (in 2000) makes it smaller than Switzerland or Denmark but larger than Ireland or Norway.

Finland's area of 338,145 square kilometers (130,558 sq mi.) means that the country is relatively spacious, being 46 percent larger than Great Britain and 12 percent larger than Italy. A comparable area in the United States would cover New York, Pennsylvania, "aye," and Indiana "all put together," but it would be smaller than California.

In August 1975, the Final Act of the Conference on Security and Cooperation in Europe (CSCE) was signed in Helsinki. The number of European heads of state or government who participated in the conference was 33, and the participation of Canada and the United States increased the number of signatories to 35. Later, when Finland began to organize the fourth follow-up conference of the CSCE in 1991-1992, facilities were being prepared for only 34 delegations, because the unification of Germany had recently reduced the number of European states. But before the opening of the conference, the number of participating states had increased to no less than 51. So many newly independent states had suddenly made their appearance on the European scene. In 2000, the revamped Organization for Security and Cooperation in Europe (OSCE) included 55 states.

Such a change illustrates the fact that the number of independent countries was flexible throughout the 20th century. Some were, forcefully or otherwise, annexed by a neighbor, some disengaged themselves from an undesired ruler, and former colonies gained independence. In the entire world, there were 129 independent countries in 1965. Political scientists, as well as the leaders of great powers, had a general tendency to predict that the number would decline. What actually happened, however, was a rapid increase to 186 states by 1997, and to 194 by the year 2000.

Among the countries of the world, and even among the small European democracies, Finland is unique in many respects. It does not conveniently meet all the expectations and stereotypes of cross-national comparisons. While it is one of the five Nordic countries of Europe, often jointly called the Scandinavian countries, most Finns do not speak a Scandinavian or even an Indo-European language. It is the northernmost country in the world after Iceland – but its agriculture produces more than the country consumes.

Having gained independence, Finland shared a 1566-kilometer long land border (973 mi.) with the newly established communist superpower, the Soviet Union (1922–1991). This did not prevent Finland from developing its advanced free-market economy, and the life of Finnish citizens was firmly based on Western traditions, a democratic political system, a market economy, and full respect for human rights.

In November 1939, Finland met a concerted attack by the Soviet Union quite alone. However, "David" was able to repulse the "Goliath" and to prevent the Red Army from occupying its territory, and thus defend its national independence. Finland – with Great Britain and the USSR – was one of the three European countries engaged in World War II that were not occupied by a foreign army.

After the war, Finland did not accept Marshall aid and did not join a military alliance. It belonged to the group of Europe's neutral "N-countries," lived in "peaceful co-existence" with its communist neighbor, and cultivated good relations with all countries.

The Finns have some tendency to believe, even "beyond rude facts," that their relative visibility in world culture and sports, as well as in international organizations, exceeds their meager 0.1 percent of the world population, possibly even their 0.7 percent of the world trade. Should the Finns really want to feel big, they could at least think of themselves as almost one-third of the world's population who live north of the 60th parallel. But they take much more pride in entering the 21st century as a well-developed, modern country, in being one of the world's foremost users of information technology, and also in having been the first nation in the world to hold democratic elections with universal and equal suffrage and eligibility during the early part of the 20th century, and the only country that paid back its World War I debt to the United States.

Finland's location between west and east has brought fruitful influences from both directions, while also causing severe problems. Indeed, geostrategic location has made survival Finland's most essential national goal. Culturally, however, Finland is strongly oriented toward the west and is relatively less influenced by the east. The country has created a strong and seemingly self-confident identity of its own.

The last decade of the 20th century again brought drastic changes in the international environment. The cold war ended and the Soviet Union collapsed, and the processes of globalization and European integration advanced significantly. Finland, conscious of its identity and proud of its independence, became one of the fifteen countries in Western Europe that yielded some of their independence to the supranational organization called the European Union in 1995. Although the union is not, and is not intended to be, a federal state, some visionaries have been hoping or predicting since the 1950s that deeper integration will eventually lead western Europe toward the federal goal.

During the 1990s, Finnish politics needed to adjust to an unpredicted domestic difficulty. Finland was by no means the only country that faced economic problems in those years and was, therefore, compelled to trim its public expenditure and reconsider the benefits and services a country can provide for its citizens, but the sudden economic slump that hit Finland in the early 1990s was exceptionally severe, being worse than the great depression of the 1930s.

The following pages will describe various features of Finland's politics and policies, such as they were at the turn of the 21st century. The governance of Finland involves unique features, but also features that are familiar from country to country. Moreover, many aspects of the political system can only be understood against their historical background; nor would it be possible to account for the basics of how Finland is governed without constantly alluding to quite recent transformations of the system. The 1990s, with the economic crisis and the new international environment, were an exceptional decade. The political system was tested in various ways over quite a short time span. What was essential was the interplay between stability and change.

Democracy is an ideal that permeates or is intended to permeate the entire political system. Although the ideal is not easy to define in uniform and exact terms, it serves as a highly valued guideline for governance, in Finland as in numerous other nations. Sevenscore years ago *Abraham Lincoln* defined it concisely as "government of the people, by the people, for the people." Accordingly, this book on Finnish democracy describes the people, their political institutions, and what the political system does for them. The functions of authorities and official decision-makers occupy an obvious place in the picture, but so do the roles and organization of civil society and non-governmental actors, the political involvement of individual citizens, and the conflicts caused by differences in social structure and ideologies.

Concerning the system's output "for the people," particular attention will be directed to the social benefits the country provides for its individual citizens. The characteristics of the Finnish welfare state, its ability to meet its established goals, and its effectiveness in protecting less fortunate persons against the unexpected economic hardships of the 1990s, are of obvious interest here. In retrospect, it seems fair to say that the social security network has provided successful protection for the Finnish people. However, new circumstances and modified values have necessitated some rethinking of the general structure and affordability of the country's public services.

In the latter part of the 1990s, some small member countries of the European Union – notably *Ireland, Portugal* and Finland – again experienced unusually rapid economic growth. Indeed, Finland's recovery from the slump was unusually rapid. However, what was the normal state of affairs before the slump will obviously never return unaltered. Irreversible changes have occurred both domestically and in the political and economic environment and, possibly, in the prevailing values. Finland entered the 21st century with many new adjustments in how the country governs itself.

Consequently, this book is not only about Finnish institutions and practices, and not only about the political system's inputs and outputs; it is also about stability and change. It is obvious that the text would have been considerably different if it had been written in the late 1980s. Soon thereafter, the general view would have been far more cautious and pessimistic than it again appears at the very beginning of the 21st century.

However, before embarking on the account of Finland's governance, both its stable patterns and its recent flexibility, its environment and institutions, a broad outline of the history of the country is in order. The following chapter will also include a more specific list of topics that concern the functioning of democracy in Finland (on page 37), and specific questions about the Finnish welfare state (on page 51).

2 Pathways to Modern Finland

Swedes we are not; Russians we do not want to become; so let us be Finns.

A. I. Arwidsson 1791–1858

I believe...that Finland has emerged a winner from the ordeals of the twentieth century.

Max Jakobson 1998, p. 1

Roots, Autonomy, and Independence

Because Finland and Sweden were united for more than 600 years, their shared history had a deep impact on Finnish society and left durable traces on the governance of modern Finland. For example, one historical paradox is that the constitution of 1772 and 1789, which lived only until 1809 in Sweden, remained effective in Finland 110 years longer, until 1919.

Sweden's constitution swung like a pendulum. From Finland's point of view, its power relations were quite convenient in 1809, when Finland broke away from Sweden. During the late 17th and early 18th century the regime had become an absolute monarchy. The estates then reversed the system in 1719, and in 1720 the Form of Government abolished absolutism even more categorically. What followed then was the "Age of Freedom" with all political power in the hands of the Diet of Estates. The next swing of the pendulum was the bloodless coup d'état of King Gustavus III in 1772. The Form of Government adopted in 1772 and followed in 1789 by the Act on Union and Security again made the monarch the very powerful ruler of the country, albeit one whose powers were constitutionally limited. The next swing, the more balanced constitution of 1809, no longer affected Finland.

In much earlier times, almost a millennium ago, the Finns had been less organized politically than the Swedes and the Danes. Their land was thinly populated and they lived in isolated settlements. However, they had some trading contacts all the way to Mediterranean Europe. They became a tempting target for the power politics of the Swedes and also of the Danes and the German Hansa League, whereas the Finns living in Karelia became the allies of Novgorod (later Russia). Christianity spread into Western Finland in the early twelfth century, and the Popes were anxious to conquer all Finns for the realm of the Roman Catholic Church. Swedish kings and warlords and English missionary bishops served as the Church's tools.

The first crusade took place in 1157 (or in 1155), and eastbound expansion from the west continued. In 1293 the Castle of Vyborg was built about 100 miles west of what would become, centuries later (in 1703), the site of St. Petersburg. The Peace of Pähkinäsaari (Schlüsselburg) in 1323 defined for the first time the border between Sweden and Novgorod. It also confirmed the division of Karelia and its Finnish population between Sweden and Russia and, at the same time, between the Catholic and Orthodox versions of Christianity.

Finland gradually became a part of Sweden. Although the two peoples spoke different languages, Finland gained hardly any identity of its own. There was also some migration from Sweden to the coastal areas of Southern and Western Finland, as well as westbound migration from Finland. The Baltic Sea was a unifying rather than a separating factor. In 1362 the right of Finnish representatives to participate in the election of the king was confirmed, and King Magnus Ericson's National Code of Laws in 1347 and the common law of the land in 1442 applied to Sweden's "Eastland" as much as to its "Northland" and its more central provinces. Formally, the king was elective until 1544 and hereditary after that.

During the late Middle Ages the one administrative unit that covered Finland as such, and actually had a dominating position in the governing of the country, was the Diocese of Turku. Originally it was guided directly by the pope, not by the Church of Sweden. In 1291 a native Finn was for the first time appointed to the office of bishop. Even in those days, Finland kept in close contact with European cultural developments. Many Finns studied at the University of Paris as members of the English nation and two served as rectors of the university. Prague was an early alternative and, especially in the fifteenth century, Finns studied in German universities.

The centralization of the Swedish state after the Lutheran reformation in the sixteenth century, the role of Sweden as a great power in the seventeenth century, and Sweden's reformed laws and social developments particularly in the 18th century, all concerned Finland as much as they concerned the rest of the kingdom. For example, in the 1600s the expansion of Swedish rule tempted Lutheran Finns to settle *Ingria,* an area east of Estonia and south of eastern Karelia. The Swedish General Code of 1734 remains effective in some fields of law even in today's Finland.

However, during the 18th century Finland also began to grow apart from Sweden. Sweden's declining strength touched Finland much more than the rest of the kingdom. Central Sweden was unable or unwilling to defend Finland against the Russians, who occupied the country both in

1710 and in 1741. As the consequence of wars, famine, and disease, Finland's population declined dramatically at the turn of the eighteenth century.

In 1807, Tsar Alexander I of Russia and Napoleon made peace at Tilsit, East Prussia. The two rulers also agreed to exercise complete political control in central Europe, and the Russian emperor promised to persuade the Scandinavian countries to join the Continental System (the boycott of British goods). Because Sweden did not comply, Russia punished it by forcing it to surrender all of Finland after the Finnish War of 1808–1809.

This war was still going on in the north when Tsar Alexander I summoned the Finnish Diet of the Four Estates to convene in March 1809 in Porvoo, on the southern coast of Finland. Fortunately for Finland, King John III of Sweden had in 1581 added to his titles that of Grand Duke of Finland, and this was conveniently transferred to the Russian emperor's long list of titles. He ratified "the religion and fundamental Laws of the Land" and the privileges and rights which each estate and all the inhabitants of Finland "have hitherto enjoyed." Thus the emperor, who was an authoritarian ruler elsewhere, became a monarch with constitutionally limited powers in Finland. The Diet, in turn, pledged the Finnish people's oath of allegiance to their new ruler. Only later, in September 1809, was Finland formally ceded to Russia in the peace treaty signed in Hamina.

Thereby Finland was "elevated" to the status of an autonomous "state among states" with its own legal system, its own representative body (the Diet), its government (called the Senate) and civil servants. It also had its own postal service and, later, state railways and even its own army (until 1904) and own currency, the *Finnish markka* (from 1860).

The Imperial Finnish Senate included two divisions, economic and judicial. Later, in independent Finland, the economic division became the government, which is called the *Council of State*, and its administrative departments[1] continued their functions as the *ministries* of the government. The judicial division, in turn, was the forerunner of the *Supreme Court* and the *Supreme Administrative Court.* Chairmanship of the Senate belonged to the governor-general, who was the emperor's personal representative in Finland, and in St. Petersburg the minister state secretary presented the emperor with matters about Finland that required his decision. There was a gradual retreat in Finland from the principle of concentrating all governmental affairs in the Senate, so that by 1881 the country had set up 24 national boards or other separate national offices (Savolainen 1999, p. 123).

Further steps toward independence presupposed a conscious national identity. Finnish had become a written language in the 1540s when the ABC book, the prayer book, and the New Testament were published.

---

1   At the beginning of the 20th century, there were nine administrative departments, dealing with ecclesiastical affairs, financial affairs, justice, transport, the treasury, internal affairs, trade and industry, agriculture, and (until 1903) military affairs.

A true Finnish identity and a sense of the Finnish nation began to gain importance rather late, only after 1809. The growth of nationalism will be discussed more in the next section of this chapter but, as milestones in its growing strength, one could mention here the publication of the national epoch *Kalevala* in 1835 and the first public performance of Finland's national anthem in 1848. Nationalist feelings dominated Finland's cultural life increasingly toward the end of the nineteenth century. The domestic political processes that led to independence were hastened in the 1860s. The *Diet of the Estates* began regular sessions and the 1860s became an important decade of political, administrative, economic, and cultural reforms in Finland.

At the very end of the nineteenth century Finland's position was endangered by the growing force of pan-Slavism and the growing power of the nationalists in Russia. What was called a policy of unification in St. Petersburg meant a policy of Russification at the country's edges and among its minorities. In 1899 the Finns, as well as wide circles of west-European intellectuals, were shocked by the "February Manifesto," which declared and concretely commenced attempts to Russify the country, in gross violation of Finland's legal rights.

These measures provoked passive resistance. "Within a few weeks, three million of the Czar's most faithful subjects began to despise him" (Jutikkala with Pirinen 1996, p. 355), and the desire for full independence was strengthened. Defeat in the war with Japan and the general strike in November 1905 weakened Russia, which in turn enabled Finland to democratize its popular representation. The traditional Diet of the Four Estates was replaced by the most democratic *representative body* the reformers could imagine: a parliament characterized by universal and equal suffrage, universal eligibility, unicameralism, and proportional representation. At the 1904 election only 125,000 men had the right to vote but in 1907 the electorate numbered 1,273,000 persons.

A second period of Russification started in 1909. Russia itself experienced internal unrest again, and Nicholas II, the Emperor and Grand Duke, was dethroned in 1917. Four weeks after the October Revolution, on December 6, 1917, Finland declared itself independent. On January 4, 1918, Finland's independence was recognized by Russia's new Central Executive Committee and by France and Sweden, and soon also by Germany. A War of Liberation was still fought from January to May 1918, between the "White" forces of the government and rebellious "Red" socialist forces. Russian troops stationed in Finland participated on the side of the rebel Red Guard and, in April, the White army received support from a German expeditionary force. Primarily, however, it was fought as a bitter *civil war*, in which the Reds were defeated. Peace with Soviet *Russia* was concluded in 1920 in Tartu, Estonia.

The nonaggression pact that Finland and the *Soviet Union* signed in 1932 did not prevent the USSR from invading Finland on November 30, 1939. The Russian aim was to gain possession of the whole country, but it failed because of Finland's unexpectedly strong defense. The Winter

War ended in March 1940 with the cession of 12 percent of Finland's land area to the Soviet Union. The entire population of the lost area was evacuated to other parts of Finland. *The Continuation War* of 1941–1944 was terminated by the armistice in September 1944, later confirmed in the Paris peace treaty of 1947, where the area lost in 1940 and some extra land was ceded. In the two wars Finland lost the lives of 91,000 soldiers. In addition, 122,500 were wounded, of whom 93,000 remained permanent invalids (Honkasalo 2001, pp. 10-11). A third war was fought in 1944-1945 against German troops in Lapland.

In 1997 Finland celebrated eighty years of independence. It is the only state to have gained national independence in 1917, when World War I was still going on. At the time of World War II Finland was still young among the world's independent states but it is no longer young today. Its economic, political, and social development was rapid and in many respects quite successful during the two decades after 1918, but the Finns also tend to feel that the final confirmation of their independence was their successful armed defense of their country during World War II.*[PP]*

Emerging National Identity

As mentioned above, Finland's independence would not have been possible without the conscious national identity that emerged during the 19th century. More generally, the birth of nation states is considered to be a typical 19th century development, although in some countries national identity began to emerge a century or two earlier. The "nation state" concept has been defined as an entity consisting of a homogeneous people having its own political system, common culture and language, and shared interests. It is also obvious that no nation in the world does completely fulfill these requirements of homogeneity.

Values influencing the birth of national identity have included, on the one hand, a common language and literature, and on the other hand, a generally felt loyalty toward the legal and political authority. To this one should add religion, which has been a paradoxical factor. The history and present day of Europe have proven how religious tradition can unite, or how it can sharply divide people who inhabit the same area. There is good reason to consider language and religion to be the central elements of culture. In Europe the impact of a common religion has been much more powerful than in the USA, for example.

Western culture spread into Finland with Christianity in the 12th century, but the people also preserved their heathen habits and beliefs. When the pagan peasant Lalli killed Finland's first bishop Henry, he defended very concretely what was Finnish some eight and a half centuries ago. Christianity became Lutheran during the 16th century, and this became one of the solid cornerstones of the Finnish value structure. Together with Lutheranism, some typically German ways of thinking and German ideals spread into Finland, while the political connection with Sweden stabilized western governmental institutions. An essential element of Lutheranism is the protestant work ethic, which emphasizes both zealous work and social trust. Even nowadays it provides an obvious contrast to Finland's eastern neighbor, Orthodox Russia.

The *Lutheran church* offered its sermons and instruction in the people's native language. Thus the Church, together with western institutions, helped to initiate among the Finns a consciousness of their own identity. There was a problem, however. Having reached a great power position in the 17th century, Sweden lost some interest in Finland. The central administration became unresponsive toward the needs and desires of the Finnish people, and officials in Finland were more and more of Swedish origin. Administration both in religious and in secular offices, and to some extent even in the courts, was conducted in a language that was foreign to the majority of the population. This was opposed by the Early Fennophiles in the 1660s, and the intellectuals of Turku (Åbo) Academy continued to criticize Swedish policies throughout the 18th century, until such criticism was combined with the Fennoman movement of the 19th century. During the 18th century there also were political and partly revolutionary endeavors to separate Finland from Sweden and, for the first time, some members of the educated class referred to the Finns as a nation.

While Finland's position between Sweden and Russia made Finland a battle field, it became obvious that, when Finland's vital interests were at stake, it was much more important to take Russia into consideration than seemed necessary from the point of view of Sweden proper, still dreaming of its great power status. Already during the 1740s, the officers of some military units in Finland contacted the Russian ruler without Sweden's permission, and Russia even offered independence for Finland in order to create a convenient buffer against Sweden.

The idea of national independence emerged more distinctly during the 1780s. Some military officers who had been influenced by the French enlightenment philosophy strongly criticized the king and the government of Sweden. The most central figure of the independence movement was Göran Magnus Sprengtporten (1740–1819), who was called "Finland's Washington" by many of his contemporaries. He even outlined a constitution for Finland: the country was to become a federal republic, characterized by liberalism, tolerance, and equality. The time was too early to realize such a plan, but the idea of independence stayed alive and gave strength to Finnish identity.

Simultaneously with the birth of the Fennoman movement, the European *Geistesleben*, or spiritual life, adopted new values and ideas that later became known as romanticism. This turned the attention of educated persons inward: to their own nation, its language and literature, and the nature and history of the country. Such ideas introduced new dynamics into nation building, particularly because they connected the upper classes with ordinary people. In Finland, an essential precondition for national awareness and national identity was research on the Finnish language and on the origin of the Finns. Romanticism appeared effectively through research done by Henrik Gabriel Porthan (1739–1804) on Finnish poetry and Finland's history and language.

National identity was also greatly strengthened by the political change resulting from the Napoleonic wars. The Russian ruler promised to maintain the laws of the country and its religion. The civil servants and the military personnel could remain in their positions, with the exception of those born in Sweden who might, the Tsar thought, tempt Finns to favor Sweden. Thus Finnish identity was strengthened in the governing of the country.

However, the language of the educated class of people had become Swedish, although most of them originated from Finnish-speaking homes. Many young educated persons looked with disapproval on the prominent position of Swedish among the educated class; they had been influenced by romanticism, and the national values of the majority were central in their thinking. Finland's autonomy opened opportunities for fomenters of nationalism, the main figures being Elias Lönnrot (1802–1884) and J.V. Snellman (1806–1881). Following the romantic heritage, Lönnrot took it upon himself to assemble the folklore of Finland. His work became known in 1835 as the *Kalevala* and in 1849 he published a new version of this national epic of Finland. Snellman, in turn, was a philosopher who had adopted ideas from Friedrich Hegel; he was troubled by the lack of nationalism and patriotism and he considered it important to save Finland's national uniqueness.

Without Lönnrot's and Snellman's input there might not have occurred such a strengthening of national identity during the 19th century. The *Kalevala* made the Finns realize that they possessed an old culture of their own: poetry and literature that so far had remained unpublished. Thanks to Snellman, people began to understand the importance of their own language and of Finnish governmental institutions for maintaining Finnish culture. Furthermore, Snellman was influential in obtaining for Finland its own monetary unit in the 1860s. With some exaggeration it has been claimed that Finland became independent already when it obtained its own Finnish markka, separate from the Russian ruble.

By the end of the 19th century Finnish society became a new type of arena for ideological conflicts. The new ideas emphasized international values, which could potentially weaken Finland's national identity. At the same time, the class structure, in politics known as the estate-society, was subjected to three kinds of pressure, namely liberalism, Finnish nationalism, and socialism.

The impact of liberalism became visible from the 1860s onward. Emphasis on personal freedoms, industrial freedom, and freedom in general, evoked the importance of the individual person. Such a change in thinking was a necessary precondition for modernization, especially for the birth of modern manufacturing. Liberalism was an ideology that emphasized internationalism more than national viewpoints. It also began to tear apart the unified Christian culture that had been prominent in Finland.

But alongside liberalism arose the Finnish cultural movement, which attempted to improve the position of the Finnish language and Finnish-speakers in general. An additional aim of this movement was to further national unity and catalyze a broad political and educational awakening. This became quite successful. In order to further national unity the movement resisted the prevailing class society, which was for its part hindering the goals of the masses, especially because class society strengthened the position of the Swedish language. However, Finnish and Swedish speaking Finns agreed on the necessity of preserving the social system of Nordic origin, in spite of Finland being an autonomous part of Russia. Thus the Russian connection strengthened Finland's Nordic-type social system as one element of Finnish identity.

The development of Finnish culture began to reach realization from the 1880s onward. A national romantic orientation was most visible in painting, in architecture, and in music. *Akseli Gallen-Kallela* (1865–1931), possibly the most noted Finnish pictorial artist, created an impressive production of Kalevala themes, and was followed by artists inspired by the same national origins. Eliel Saarinen (1873–1950), who later worked in the USA, based his world-famous Finnish architecture on national romanticism. Jean Sibelius (1865–1957) is perhaps the best-known representative of Finland's national romanticism. Several of his compositions were based on Kalevala themes. The artistic orientation represented by Gallen-Kallela, Saarinen, Sibelius, and many others, was known as Karelianism, because Karelia had preserved many of the old cultural characteristics that no longer could be found elsewhere in Finland.

Sibelius published his Finlandia, the famous musical expression of Finland's desire for independence, in 1899, some months after the Russian government had launched its policy of Russification. The strongest expression of Finnish nationalism up to that point had been to collect, very quickly and in secret, 522,931 signatures to an address strongly opposing the Russian February manifesto. However, Tsar Nicholas II did not receive the 500-member delegation that traveled to St. Petersburg to present the address to him.

Russification attempts were continued under Governor General Nikolai Bobrikov's leadership, until a Finnish patriot assassinated him in 1904. The pan-Slavistic policy of Russification greatly strengthened Finnish identity, awareness of the country's own national interests, even though Bobrikov made use of political disagreements among the Finns. Such disagreements concerned three issues: how to resist Russification; conflicts of interest between the growing workers' movement and the 'old' parties; and the language cleavage. The February manifesto was repealed during the general strike in 1905, in conjunction with the events that led in Finland to the world's most advanced body of popular representation. In a country located next to reactionary Russia, a modern parliament became a symbol of Finland's national identity. It differentiated the Finns sharply from the Russians, and even from the people of Sweden, who did not yet have comparable political rights.

The Russian government recovered quickly from the shock caused by defeat in the Russo-Japanese war and by the rebellious actions of 1905–1906. A new period of oppression started in Finland and the attempts to Russify the country lasted until the World War. Although democratic freedoms facilitated internal political struggles, all Finns opposed the emperor's power politics. Thereby the Finnish identity grew stronger in every part of the nation. This is well illustrated by the Olympic Games in Stockholm in 1912. During the opening ceremonies the Finns could not use their own flag, but they also refused to follow the flag of Russia. They marched as a separate group and carried only a sign bearing the name of their country. Finland's athletes emerged as the third most successful national team at the games, a success that helped to strengthen Finnish self-esteem.

The unity of Finnish identity was tested when independence was gained in 1917–1918. Disagreement on social conditions and the proximity of the Russian revolution provoked portions of the workers and tenant farmers to rebel against the legal government of the new republic. Obviously the people's political and social rights were mutually inconsistent: large parts of the nation were frustrated because the promises attached to broader democracy did not lead to desired social reforms.

Because the Whites won the civil war, Finland was spared the kind of development experienced in the Soviet Union. Instead, it now became possible to develop independent Finland with democratic rules of play and in accordance with the Nordic model. Two decades later, in 1939-1940, the same rebellious reds and their descendants fought against Stalin as a vital part of Finland's field army. Not only did the Finnish people succeed in their defensive fight but, during the extreme danger, their Finnish identity also won a great victory over the nation's internal political cleavages.*[OR]*

The Rise of Civil Society

Political democracy can hardly develop in the absence of a functioning civil society. The birth and development of the democratic system in Finland support this claim. In the 19th century there were increasing numbers of people joining popular movements, associations and organizations, paving the way for the political reform of 1906. A legislative precondition for the trend was the realization of freedom of trade, freedom of migration and freedom of association from the 1850s to the 1880s. What makes this more interesting is that Finland was a part of Russia, a very conservative country.

The foundations of civil society were being laid throughout the 19th century. Its building materials were liberal ideas about individual rights and, on the other hand, thoughts awakened by nationalism on the possibilities to influence society and the state. The elite of the autonomous grand duchy also quickly learned what John Stuart Mill wrote about civil liberties in his book On Liberty (1859). There were ideological contrasts between liberalism and Fennomania, but both ideologies promoted the civil society: the liberals by conveying ideas on liberties, and the Fennomans by drawing in the Finnish-speaking majority and by emphasizing equality and solidarity between the educated class and the common people (Alapuro and Stenius 1987, pp. 8–39; Pulkkinen 1987, pp. 54–69).

The founding of the *Finnish Literature Society* (Suomalaisen Kirjallisuuden Seura) in 1831 was the true starting point of organized civil activity. The Society developed Finnish cultural life and pioneered the increase in organizational activity. As early as the 1840s, it started to accept women and peasants in addition to educated men as its members, which helped to clarify the idea of civil society and to broaden ideas towards democracy.

The revolutionary movement in Europe in 1848 made the Russian authorities cautious and, in 1849, freedom of association was restricted by forbidding common people from participating in the Literary Society's activities. It became the emperor's prerogative to approve or reject the rules of various associations, and associations were ordered to strengthen governmental authority. Freedom of association was not expanded until 1893, when the task of confirming of association rules was transferred to the Finnish Senate; four years later it became the duty of provincial governors. However, the early signs of Russification did not take long to surface: at the beginning of the 1890s, confirmation of association rules was made dependent on the will of the Russian governor general.

Despite all this, several associations were founded between the 1860s and 1880s that played a major role in the development of civil society and the idea of the state. The pressure to organize was so strong that many new associations kept their true aims secret in order to circumvent the restrictions and be allowed to exist. For example, many volunteer fire-brigades were set up that had their goals in educational matters and class fellowship rather than fire fighting. They became forerunners in establishing libraries, choirs, orchestras and theater groups. From the 1880s, as the literacy rate increased, more and more representatives of the lower classes assumed leading roles in associations (Alapuro and Stenius 1987, pp. 31–35). This served the needs of the new parliament from 1907 onwards.

A good example of an association with national goals is the *Society for Popular Education* (Kansanvalistusseura), founded in 1874. It was a project of leading Fennomans and a loose political group called the Finnish Party. Its leadership wanted to steer clear of language conflicts and keep the doors open to both Finnish and Swedish speakers. The Society's goals included raising the education and well-being of the people, which in practice meant the educational interests of the Finnish-speaking majority. The conscious goal was to give the people the necessary tools to meet the spiritual and material challenges of a new kind of society and state. The Fennomans saw to it that the Society stayed in their hands although the language question was kept in the background (Inkilä 1969).

The Society for Popular Education in its early days was the biggest and most influential contact network independent of state and church. Starting from the 1870s, Fennomania evolved in a more liberal direction, stressing the demands of social fairness. As early as 1880, the head of the Society, professor E. G. Palmén, described its mission in accordance with the principles of a modern civil society: "The autonomy of the people, its right to participate in decisions on how to proceed, requires that the represented follow the work of those who represent them, in order to call the representatives to account for how the task was carried out" (Liikanen 1987, pp. 126–134). The sentence defines one of the basic functions of civil society: its role in determining a state's legitimacy. Palmén presented his view twenty-six years before the democratic parliament was created and thirty-eight years before Finland's independence.

Membership of the Society reached 5300 by the end of the century. Yet the combined membership of the temperance movement, the youth society movement, and the labor movement overtook it. The influence that the Society for Popular Education had lay in its publishing operations and the patriotic song festivals it organized, rather than in its membership numbers. Decades after Finland had become independent, the Society continued to publish a very popular almanac with articles on national questions and all-round education. By the end of the 19th century the song festivals had already grown into massive patriotic manifestations that reflected Finnish identity and the urge for national independence (cf. op. cit., pp. 136–141). Finland's civil society was organizing rapidly, which was a precondition for the political turning point of the next decade.

The goals of the *Friends of Temperance*, founded in 1884, were similar to those of the Society for Popular Education: it aimed to improve the morals, manners, and sense of responsibility of the people. Halfway through the 1890s, it was the biggest organization until youth societies overtook it. At the beginning of the 20th century, its membership increased manifold reaching 40,000. The members were primarily working-class.

The role of the Friends of Temperance, from both a societal and political viewpoint, developed into a historical one that the founders could not have foreseen. Its ideology included a strong political message, an accusation that the state was pursuing the wrong policy towards alcohol. It allowed financial profits to be made through the production and sale of alcohol, while numerous people, especially among the workers and the poor, suffered from the consequences of alcohol consumption. This message helped working-class people see the societal connections of their alcohol problems. That the faults were to be eliminated by legislation was something that fitted like a glove the state-centered ideas of the Fennomans in the organization.

The temperance ideology also provided important support for the radical labor movement that was rising to its feet. Its aim was to recruit working-class people to support major reforms in society. At the end of the

19th century, the leaders of the labor movement organized an alcohol boycott, the radical mass nature of which was emphasized by mass meetings, demonstration marches and popular petitions. Soon active working-class people started to demand a prohibition law, and that demand was included in the program of the Social Democratic Party, founded in 1899 and originally called the Finnish Labor Party. The temperance movement realized that an effective expansion of its ideology required cooperation with the growing labor movement; otherwise the masses could not be attracted to stand behind the movement (Sulkunen 1986, pp. 249–253).

The Fennoman dream of improving the people's morals and manners may have been realized in a surprisingly successful way, but it also played an unexpected role in the organization of the labor movement. The reciprocal effects of the temperance movement and the labor movement show what kind of connections the organization of a civil society may have with political activity and the development of a state.

The Society for Popular Education, the Friends of Temperance, and the labor movement are part of a historically essential phase in the cultural and political modernization of Finnish society. They do not, however, constitute the whole picture of that modernization process. The 1870s and 1880s had already seen the emergence of other popular movements that strengthened civil society. They included the youth society movement, the cooperative movement, the sports movement and the trade union movement within the labor movement. The *women's movement* was also an integral part of the modernization process; its significance is reflected by the fact that Finnish women gained the right to vote in 1906, at the same time as men. However, women participated, above all, in other mass movements. For example the Finnish Women's Association, established in 1884, did not have many members, but like other ideological organizations had an impact based more on the message than the numbers. The women's association to attract the largest membership was the Martha Association, born in the aftermath of the February Manifesto in 1899. Its home economics extension work has been significant (cf. Jallinoja 1983, pp. 32–50; Sulkunen 1987, pp. 162–172).

The goals of the *youth society movement* were largely similar to those of the Society for Popular Education and the Friends of Temperance: to civilize the people, improve their morals and teach them a proper way of life. With its aim on self-education and on upbringing of decent human beings, the movement also emphasized national ends. Its central organization, the Finnish Youth League, was founded in 1897. As a politically independent organization it was able to influence a high proportion of young people in Finland, even in the most remote areas (Numminen 1961).

Sports and physical exercise corresponded to the youth society activity in the field of physical culture. There had been gymnastics and sports within various associations for decades before the foundation of the Finnish Gymnastics and Sports Federation (SVUL) in 1900. The mental state and pressing values of the Finnish society also surfaced in the formation process of this central sports organization, with national motives rising to the fore. Physical exercise was seen as a means to improve the fitness of threatened people and unite their resources in the struggle against oppressive Russian rule and against unhealthy habits, such as drinking (Halila 1960, pp. 5–30).

As for *cooperative action*, it has, in a sense, been part of the traditional popular culture of Finland for hundreds of years: neighborly help, the purpose of which is to provide assistance in demanding tasks, such as building and harvesting, has been characteristic of an agrarian society. Perhaps this was why cooperation in its more modern form also suited Finnish society. Ever since the 1860s, various trades and worker groups had created cooperative associations and various predecessors of cooperatives, such as stores and common means of production (Mauranen 1987, pp. 179–180). The first central organization, the Pellervo Confederation, was founded in 1899. Its name refers to the old Finnish god of tilled fields and its ideology combined cooperation and nationalism. It has been said that the Pellervo Confederation was born in a spring of great sorrow, awakening, and hope. The saying refers to the coincident existence of Finnish nationalist enthusiasm and Russian oppression (Henttinen 1999, pp. 32–56).

National ends did not manifest themselves in the same manner at the outset of the *labor movement* as in other old movements. The initiative was usually taken by the upper social classes. In the 1880s they tried to establish politically independent workers' associations, which would have functioned as meeting places for the propertied and working classes. The upper social classes also aimed at keeping Finnish workers apart from the radical doctrines of European socialism. Nevertheless, the labor movement underwent radicalization in the 1890s, putting an end to the activity that stressed class unity.

This was the beginning of a labor movement that emphasized collective values and, at the time, had no parallel outside Europe. In 1899, with the Russification attempts intensifying, the newly founded political party became the core of the labor movement. Its program contained many demands, including freedom of association, freedom of assembly, freedom of speech, freedom of the press, universal suffrage, equality between men and women, compulsory education, and an eight-hour working day (Soikkanen 1961, pp. 21–72). The demands were influenced by the 1891 Erfurt program of the German Social Democrats. They seemed particularly radical in a dark phase of Finland's history when the conservative Russian regime was trying to abolish most of the existing rights. During the Great Strike of 1905, with the grip of the Russian regime slipping, this radical program was paving the way for the democratic reform of 1906.

The labor movement grew stronger at the beginning of the new century. In common with other old movements, its aim was to improve the economic conditions and education of the ordinary people. At the same time, it strongly emphasized equality and economic, educational, and civil rights. In 1905–1906, inspired mainly by the Great Strike, workers joined trade unions in great numbers. The bipolar field of the Finnish labor market also took its early shape when employers saw it necessary to form their own central organization. The establishment of the Confederation of Finnish Employers (STK) in 1907, two weeks before the first parliamentary elections, foreshadowed the formation of a new kind of organizational field; six weeks later, unionized workers set up their central organization, the Trade Union Organization of Finland. However, the labor market did not begin to function as a centralized system until decades later, after the Second World War.

Unionization was encouraged by the success of the Social Democratic Party in the first parliamentary elections, the party winning eighty of the 200 seats. Yet, in 1907, the membership of the Trade Union Organization of Finland did not rise much above 23,500 even though the number of unionized workers may have been many times higher. Many trade unions had not yet joined the central organization. In the following years, unsettled conditions with numerous strikes prevailed in the labor market, which was marked by workers' great expectations and by the employers' refusal to make collective agreements (Ala-Kapee and Valkonen 1982, pp. 176–210, 792–793). There was disappointment in the air arising from unchanging working conditions and the weakness of parliament.

The various organizations had already been trying to influence national and local decision-making under the old Diet of the Estates and pursued their attempts after the new Parliament had come into existence. They collected popular petitions, which was one way to express the public will. For example, the Friends of Temperance organized the collection of several petitions to change the licensing laws during 1885-1900, and the small Finnish Women's Association presented to the Diet a petition with 5700 names to suppress prostitution in 1888. Many other means were also used to influence the Diet and the new Parliament (Tuominen 1974).

Finnish civil society emerged mainly during the latter half of the 19th century and, after the parliament reform of 1906, organizations were rather numerous, diverse and strong. What was special about the emergence of civil society was the fact that the values that promoted national identity and state formation were central in very different types of associations and organizations.

Without this activity the parliamentary reform of 1906 would have been impossible. The reform was essential for Finnish democracy but much effort and many sacrifices were still required. Society became stagnant due to conservative Russian rule and, as a consequence, civil society soon split in two. One side did not regard the prevailing system as legitimate, which resulted in the tragic civil war in 1918. There are many viewpoints about what caused the war. One explanation could be the contradiction between an active civil society and a non-functioning political democracy. *[OR]*

The Democratic Republic

When all the countries of the world were reviewed in 1980, only 21 of them were identified having been continuously democratic since the time of World War II. They included the five Nordic countries, ten other countries in Europe and two in North America, plus Australia, New Zealand, Israel, and Japan. (Raymond D. Castil, according to Lijphart 1984, p. 38). All 21 countries also entered the 21st century as stable democracies. Furthermore, by 1980 the total number of democracies around the world already was much larger, and a very important new wave of democratization started in the early 1990s.

Finland, on the other hand, is one of the 13 countries that have been democratic continuously since the time of World War I. National independence was the final step to be taken before it was possible for Finland to adopt a democratically functioning political system. On the other hand, it is obvious that democracy cannot be introduced instantly. In Finnish society some of its foundations had prevailed for centuries, and others had appeared during the 19th century and at the beginning of the 20th century. Important among those were personal freedom, the rule of law, and participation in local decision-making, followed by the emergence of a civil society, democratically structured political institutions, and a unifying national identity that was connected to the basic legitimacy of the government of the country.

There had been a tradition of personal freedom throughout Finland's known history. The farmers were independent. Unlike most parts of Europe but like England, Switzerland, and some parts of the Netherlands, Sweden-Finland had no serfdom. Neither was there personal authoritarian rule without legal-constitutional limitations of power (with the exception of the short period from 1680 to 1718). As described above, a civil society was being activated during the 19th century. Political parties were also emerging.

When Finland was separated from Sweden, Finland's negotiators were unwilling to discuss the country's position in Russia without obtaining the formal consent of the people. Tsar Alexander I summoned the Finnish estates, which assembled in the coastal town Porvoo in March, 1809. At this Diet of Porvoo the Emperor and the Estates exchanged the sovereign pledge and oath of allegiance. The focal role of Finland's own legislature in the country was thus recognized, although the Diet did not actually meet again until September 1863. Thereafter the legislature was elected and convened at regular intervals and the representation of the people became firmly established in the country.

The Diet represented various elements of Finnish society, as well as the country as a whole, but it did not have a democratic base. The big change was accomplished at the beginning of the 20th century. Soon after the first period of attempted Russification, the Finnish people invested great hopes in their democratically based parliament, the Eduskunta, which replaced the Diet of the Estates and was elected for the first time in March 1907.[2] Before that election, political parties were reorganized so that they could appeal to the newly enfranchised mass electorate. The Social Democrats established the first party organization with a large mass membership. They were, with their devoted "agitators," the most effective election campaigners. A lively party press also emerged in all regions of the country to support party activity. The new electorate had high expectations and was mobilized so well that 71 percent turned out to vote.

Finland's modern parliament was reformist and passed important new legislation. But even the most democratic representative body did not suffice when the right to veto the bills and to dissolve parliament was in the hands of an outside monarch. The Eduskunta was elected for a term of three years, but its dissolutions were so frequent that it needed to be elected no fewer than eight times between 1907 and 1917. For example, parliament was dissolved instantly after the opening session in February 1909, because the speaker's remarks contained "impertinent criticism." Indeed, nothing short of full national independence could have made it possible to realize in practice the potential of democratic government.

In 1918 the form of government was a crucial political issue. When Norway became independent in 1905, it followed the Scandinavian monarchical tradition and invited a king from Denmark. When Finland declared independence twelve years later, it specifically decided to break away from the monarchical tradition and to give the new state a republican constitution.

However, due to the chaotic conditions in 1918, there grew a desire for strength and continuity in the political system. The parliament that had been elected in July 1917, but in which 80 socialist members no longer participated, proceeded to elect Prince Friedrich Karl of Hessen as king of Finland in October 1918. Due to Germany's collapse soon thereafter, he relinquished his crown and never went to Finland. Iceland, too, became a republic after its independence from Denmark in 1944. Consequently, the five Nordic countries of Europe consist of two republics (Finland and Iceland) and three monarchies (Denmark, Sweden, and Norway).

Although Finland's monarchists lost their cause, their goal had some impact on the Form of Government Act that was passed by the newly elected parliament in July 1919. This constitution became a dualistic one, adding a strong elected president (of the American type) to the parliamentary form of government (of the British type). Later, in 1958, the Fifth Republic of France made use of a similar dualistic idea.

Finland, in turn, made use of the French type of direct elections in 1994. Originally the Finnish president was chosen by a popularly elected electoral college of 300 members (301 in 1982 and 1988). The important

2   The Parliament Act was passed by all four estates (two of them unanimously) in May 1906 and it became effective in October 1906.

point, also concerning indirect elections, was the detachment of presidential from parliamentary elections. The president's direct mandate from the people, as well as the relatively long term of six years, highlights his or her independent position.

However, in the political life of the country the president is very dependent on the parliamentary prime minister and his cabinet. The president does send the government's bills to parliament and he promulgates the laws passed by it, but ordinarily that is only a formality and the prime minister's cabinet assumes the political responsibility. The president's power to dissolve parliament and order new elections has been applied six times (in 1924, 1929, 1930, 1962, 1972 and 1975), but a constitutional amendment in 1991 made parliament's dissolution conditional upon the prime minister's initiative. The president leads foreign policy, has wide powers of appointment and is supreme commander of the armed forces, whereas parliament's right to overrule a presidential veto was simplified in 1991. The reformed new constitution, effective since 2000, weakened the powers of the president further, making the head of state cooperate still more closely with the parliamentary cabinet, in Finland called the Council of State.

Voting age in Finland was originally 24 years. That was lowered in 1945 to 21 years, then to 20 years in 1970, and to 18 years in 1975. Eligibility has involved the same age requirements, no more. The most recent change took place in 1996. Until then the age requirement had to be met by the end of the preceding year, but now the youngest voters reach the minimum age on election day.

Voter turnout is one indication of how democracy functions. In Finnish elections it has not reached the highest European levels. However, turnout in Finland's election of 1907, (71 percent) was exceptionally high for a newly enfranchised electorate. In the fifth election in 1913 the turnout was down to 51 percent. It remained below 60 percent during the 1920s and was less than 70 percent during the 1930s.

In the election of 1945 turnout rose to 75 percent and the record for parliamentary elections was 85.1 percent in 1962. It began to decline again during the 1970s; in 1991 and in 1995 it was down to 72 percent, in 1999 to 68.3 percent. The elections of the president (actually, the electoral college) mobilized 40 percent of the electorate in 1925, but such elections became the most active ones during the 1980s. In 1982 voter turnout was 86.8 percent, and in both rounds of the first direct elections in 1994, 82 percent participated. The turnout remained rather high in 2000 as well, being first 77, then 80 percent.

Voting behavior of the Finnish electorate is but one of the many aspects of the democratic governance of the country. Democratic rules of play are firmly established and internalized in Finland. This book attempts to describe various aspects of Finnish democracy:

- what are the political institutions like and how do they function and interact;
- what is their social environment, and how do citizens and civil society support and influence democratic governance;
- what other factors influence Finnish politics;
- how are the goals and the output of the decision-makers implemented in the governance of the country, and how does this influence society and the lives of ordinary citizens; and
- how has the political system reacted to change and changed itself? *[PP]*

From Preindustrial to Postindustrial Economy

Compared with the leading industrial nations, isolated Finland long remained a backward country in terms of its economic structure. It is true that some industries developed rather early; for example, the first iron blast furnace was built in 1616 and the manufacture of glass began in 1681. Founded in 1793, Finland's oldest glass factory still in operation is Nuutajärvi Glass, which is one of the major art glass manufacturers in the world. The textile industry emerged in the 1730s and the spinning machine and weaving machine, which mark the beginning of the Industrial Revolution, came to Finland as the forerunners of modern industry around 1800.

However, the turn towards a modern industrial society dates back to about 1860. In 1856, the new emperor, Tsar Alexander II, dictated into the records of the Senate a statement that called for special attention to the development of trade, maritime commerce, industry and traffic routes, and to the establishment of primary schools. The statement clearly revealed liberal ideas, which were easier to put forward in Finland than in conservative Russia. In 1860, 82 percent of Finns earned their living in agriculture and forestry and only 5 percent in industry, handicrafts and construction. Typical of the age of mercantilism, this economic structure and the values associated with it did not suit a society that was aiming for economic growth.

A very remarkable reform that was to serve the increasingly liberal economy was Finland's independent monetary unit, despite suspicions about Finnish separatism on the part of Russian authorities. It was bound to release the Finnish economy from its many ties to the Russian economy and the rouble, and to bring it closer to the European economy. The change in the monetary system did not disturb trade with Russia to any significant extent, and Finland's economic independence was further increased when it, along with several other European countries, switched to the gold standard in 1870.

Liberal legislation reflecting new values was implemented in Finland from the late 1850s onwards. There was a desire to bring into effect three essential freedoms concerning economic life: freedom of occupation, freedom of contract and freedom of ownership. These were supported by some other freedoms, such as freedom of migration. Historically, liberalism was connected to technical development, which at first was most clearly seen in a considerable improvement of communication. For example, the Saimaa Canal, an important connection particularly for the transport of timber, was completed in 1856, and Finland's first railway was opened to traffic in 1862. In 1870, the train service was extended from Helsinki to the capital of the Russian Empire, St. Petersburg, where a Finnish-owned railway station was established.

The earliest stage of industrialization in Finland was the emergence of the sawmill sector. It started the exploitation of forests, the most abundant of Finland's natural resources, and expanded rapidly although it was restricted by a lack of ports that remained unfrozen throughout the year (cf. Rasila 1982, pp. 13–26). For the next hundred years, forest products were to be the backbone of Finnish industry. Sawn goods were the single main export group from 1860 until World War I, reaching 45 percent of the total value of exports in 1913. However, the fastest expanding branch of industry was paper, which between 1860 and World War I increased more than thirty fold in the number of its personnel, and hundredfold in the volume of its output. Other sectors also grew during that first period of industrialization; in 1860–1913, the annual output growth of industry and handicrafts averaged as much as 5.2 percent.

Most of the exports were directed to Russia, the railway connection to St. Petersburg being an essential prerequisite for them. Exports to the west increased in the early 1900s, but exports to Russia totaled 60 percent as late as the onset of the World War I. The separateness of autonomous Finland from Russia is reflected by the fact that Russia levied tariffs on Finnish goods, if not usually as high as those on goods from other countries (Heikkinen and Hoffman 1982, pp. 60–84).

By the First World War, the forest sector's share of the total value of exports rose to over 70 percent. Sawmills faced great difficulties after the outbreak of the war, while the war had quite an opposite influence on paper mills, which experienced a sharp increase in demand for their products from Russia. The situation was, however, revolutionized by the transformation of Russia into the Soviet Union: Paper exports to the east, which constituted 80 percent of Finland's paper production, ended completely. Therefore, independent Finland had an urgent need to expand its export markets. New trading partners were found in western and central Europe in the early 1920s. It was a successful decade, above all, for mechanical woodworking. Particularly sawmills captured new markets. Again, this development was held back by the onset of the Great Depression at the turn of the 1930s. Now, if not before, the Finns realized that sawn goods were very sensitive to economic fluctuations, whereas the economically well-organized paper sector, based on modern technology, was able to expand into new markets even during the depression (Seppälä 1990, pp. 34–35).

The 20th century was a time of intense change for Finland, and the speed of the change was exceptional. For example, the decline from 50 to 15 percent of the people working in agriculture and forestry, which lasted approximately 80 years in Norway (1882–1963) and 50 years in Sweden (1909–1959), took only 26 years in Finland (1946–1972). As tertiary production simultaneously grew rapidly, Finland moved almost directly from an agricultural to a post-industrial society and passed through the phase of industrial society quite briefly (Karisto et al. 1999, pp. 63–65). Between 1900 and 1995, the proportion of the working population engaged in primary production (mostly agriculture and forestry) was reduced from 68 percent to only 6 percent. During the same period, secondary production rose from 11 to 27 percent and tertiary production from 13 to 65 percent of the working population. The rest, 8 and 2 percent, had miscellaneous jobs or their occupation was unknown (Myrskylä 1999, p. 108; SYF 2000, p. 83). Such an enormous change in the economic structure in less than a hundred years illustrates most of the factors that explain the development of living conditions in Finland.

The relative share of primary production decreased from 60 percent in 1860 to 40 percent at the beginning of the World War I. In the end of the 1920s, tertiary production grew to be the biggest sector, measured by output, for the first time. This was partly due to the public sector's expansion, required by the functions of an independent state. By World War II, the exports of the forest industry reached approximately 85 percent of the total value of exports. However, primary production remained the biggest employment sector until the 1950s (Hjerppe 1989, pp. 64–65; Seppälä 1990, p. 35), partly due to the agrarian reforms that had started in the 1920s and continued until the post-war resettlement of the Karelian people and the settlement of war veterans.

The number of farms began to decline in the 1960s, reaching 80,000 by 2000. The scale of the change is illustrated by the fact that the number of milk suppliers fell by over 90% in those forty years. However, larger farms with better herds were more productive, and the volume of milk sent to dairies hardly changed at all. In the 1990s alone, the number of farms exceeding 100 hectares (250 acres) rose some 240 percent.

Employment in secondary and tertiary production did not outnumber that in primary production until the end of the 1950s (Figure 2.1). However, due to higher productivity, the output of these modern sectors grew more rapidly: Secondary production exceeded primary production at the end of the 1940s, while tertiary production had exceeded it since before the Great Depression. Finland turned into an industrial society around 1960. At that stage, the structure of industry also became more diversified as the value of metal production and engineering reached that of forest products. Since the end of the 1960s, the value of metals and engineering output has increased approximately twice as fast as forest products although the value of its exports did not exceed forest product exports until the mid-1980s.

Figure 2.1

Distribution of employment from 1860 to 2000 (in %).

Sources: Hjerppe 1989 and Statistics Finland.

In Finland's case, industrialization involved a significant rise in productivity. Finland was in the position to utilize the catch-up effect: it could adapt innovations developed by the forerunners of industrialism. The preconditions for catching-up included expanding the number of educated people, increasing foreign connections, bolstering the country's own central administration, and so on. The change is clearly visible in a comparison of gross national income per capita in 16 industrialized countries from 1870 to 1970. This comparison includes the major west European countries and Australia, Canada, Japan, and the United States. In 1870, Finland was in fifteenth place before Japan. In 1970 Finland ranked 12th. Its productivity had risen the third fastest after Sweden and Japan, to 14.3 times that of 1870. At the same time, the productivity of the top-ranking country of 1870, Australia, had risen to 3.9 times that of 1870.

As long as Finland remained a typically industrial society in the 1960s and the 1970s, the productivity growth rate of the business sector was rather similar to that of the other European OECD countries. After the 1970s, Finland's development has been remarkable: both overall productivity and labor productivity have risen twice as fast as the European average.[3] In some comparisons Finland's productivity has even ranked as the world's highest. At least two essential factors can be mentioned as reasons for this new development: differences in the way economic structures have changed and in the pace of technical development. Finland

---

3   Between 1970 and 1995 the average annual growth in overall productivity in Finland was 2.5 percent and in the OECD 0.8 percent, labor productivity in Finland rose 3.5 percent annually, in the OECD 1.8 percent (Vartia and Ylä-Anttila 1996, p. 221).

experienced great changes in the last two decades of the 20th century: The economy shifted to a post-industrial stage and the society to late modernism.

The structural changes of industry are usually caused by three different factors: demand, international trade, and technological changes. The favorable development of Finland's industry in the past couple of decades is primarily due to changing technology. These changes are largely the result of intensifying research input, which has been growing faster in Finland than in any other OECD country. Overall productivity has developed rapidly and the share of high technology products in Finland's exports has more than doubled. But, starting from the end of the 1980s, the structural changes of demand and international trade have also been remarkable and Finland's industry has been able to respond. Although forest products are no longer the leading branch of industry, they have had a positive effect on industrial development in cooperation with other industries. Finland has become the leading paper machine manufacturer with a 30 percent market share, as well as a producer of electronics and automation connected with process control. Other new sectors born from the needs of the forest products sectors have been harvesters and harvester technology, and some fields of chemistry. (Cf. Vartia and Ylä-Anttila 1996, pp. 54, 77-83, 222.)

Table 2.1

Employed persons by occupation in 1970, 1980, 1990, and 1995 (in %)

Occupation	1970	1980	1990	1995
Technical, natural, and social science; humanistic and artistic work	11.9	16.8	24.0	28.1
Administrative, managerial, and clerical work	9.9	13.7	14.5	14.8
Services	10.5	11.7	12.3	12.5
Military work	0.4	0.4	0.5	0.6
Sales work	8.2	7.3	8.5	8.5
Transport and communications	7.2	6.9	6.5	6.1
Industrial and other production work	31.2	28.3	22.6	21.3
Mining and quarrying	0.3	0.3	0.2	0.1
Agriculture, forestry, fishing	20.1	12.5	9.0	6.6
Unknown	0.3	2.1	2.1	1.4
Total	100.0	100.0	100.0	100.0

Source: Statistics Finland, Population Statistics.

The shift to a post-industrial economy and a late modern society is also reflected in the development of the major sources of employment. (Table 2.1). In the areas of employment that show the expansion of information technology and the growth of education input, the change between 1970–1995 was dramatic: employment more than doubled. On the other hand, employment in primary production dropped by two-thirds and employment in secondary production by one-half (Riihinen 1998, p. 38). [OR]

The Arduous Road to Welfare State

Economic development is a necessary precondition for improvements in social conditions, which, in turn, influence economic development. In the global context, all welfare states are rich countries, but the historical roots of welfare states can be found in their poor past. Finland was just like the rest of Europe, a poor country before the period of industrialization.

In the Middle Ages and during early modern times, the standard of living fluctuated in Europe because of three factors: weather, wars, and epidemic diseases. The so-called small Ice Age from the beginning of the 17th century to the mid-nineteenth century made agriculture difficult, especially in the north. As a part of Sweden, Finland also had to contribute to several wars Sweden fought both on Finnish soil and abroad. After the mid-eighteenth century, it seems that fluctuations of mortality were caused by epidemic diseases, primarily smallpox and measles, rather than by periods of famine (Jutikkala 1988, pp. 128–129). The Swedish era was economically unfavorable for Finland: the Finns could not have a strong enough influence on the decisions that were made in Stockholm.

Autonomy, with its important domestic institutions, opened up new opportunities. However, towards the end of that era, the Russian government slowed down the pace of reforms, particularly those of a social kind, because it apparently feared that they would set an example for the rest of its vast empire. In this social sense, the Swedish connection would have been an obviously better choice for Finland than autonomy as a part of Russia.

Industrialization brought capital and even wealth to the country in the latter half of the 19th century, but the wealth was unevenly distributed. Many employees, whom liberalism set free of their traditional ties, ended up in an even worse situation as they lost their communal security. Furthermore, in those days the ordinary people still lived at the mercy of uncertain weather conditions, with an undeveloped transport system. Food supplies from abroad were very limited, if not impossible, during winter. The 1860s was especially difficult. The severe weather conditions reached their worst in 1867 and the consequences were fatal. Infant mortality rose to 392 deaths per 1000 children in 1868, the highest in the known history of the country (Turpeinen 1987, p. 377).

Poor relief, built largely after the English model and partly conveyed by Sweden, formed the basis of social policy. It became the municipalities' duty to look after the disabled, elderly, orphans, and other persons who could not manage on their own or with their families, but this care was insufficient, and the state began to assume more responsibility for those who needed care. Universal suffrage accelerated the process (Haatanen 1992, pp. 90–102). Although the measures were modest in terms of social policy, the stronger role of the state from the end of the 19th century should be noted. It marked the beginning of a vast line of development.

What was also typical of Finland's early industrialization period was the polarization of social differences in rural areas. A peasant proletariat had been forming from the 18th century onwards, consisting mainly of tenant farmers and farm workers. Social inequalities were polarized because land prices went up when the value of forest increased and because the population grew rapidly. The number of those who did not own land grew and the position of tenant farmers worsened. Around 1880, rural areas were overpopulated by an estimated 40 or 50 percent, and the majority of the surplus population were farm workers and tenant farmers (Kaukiainen 1981, p. 55). To some extent this problem was eased by the expansion of towns and by emigration, above all to the United States. By 1914, 2.2 times more people were employed in Finnish industry than in 1890, which also relieved the problem (Vattula 1983, pp. 133–134). However, a sufficient solution, the agrarian reform, was achieved only after agrarian problems had helped spark the civil war of 1918.

Looking at Finland's 20th century, it is possible to distinguish some fundamental factors that have had a great influence on the living conditions of the people. In addition to industrialization and the change in economic structure in general with subsequent urbanization, the most influential factors include independence, democracy, and the building of a welfare state.

The long-term rise in productivity, described above, enabled Finland to grow wealthier and to achieve social reforms despite the wars and other setbacks. The catch-up effect also applied to social reforms: it was possible to observe the advantages gained by others, as well as the mistakes they had made. The news of the birth of a new kind of social policy in Bismarck's Germany quickly reached Finland. The German system of workers' insurance, constructed in fear of socialism in the 1880s, included sickness insurance, accident insurance and disability and retirement insurance. Finland soon adapted accident insurance (1895) but for various reasons the other reforms were put on hold. In the meantime, the German model of workers' insurance was, especially in Scandinavia, molded into a national insurance, the ideals of which included universalism: social security covering all citizens. This ideal later played a major part in the building process of the Finnish welfare state.

The new parliament made it possible to transmit the preferences of citizens to decisionmakers in the form of constant reform initiatives. However, the reforms progressed slowly because of Russian obstruction. After 1917, the pace of reforms picked up. Already in the summer of 1917, before Finland's independence and also before any other European country, parliament passed a bill on an eight-hour working day. It had long been one of the demands of the international labor movement. The law was approved by Lev Trotsky's Russian government. This temporary government also approved prohibition, which had been repeatedly agreed upon by the Finnish Parliament, and it approved changing the organization of the Senate so that a department of social affairs was founded. In independent Finland the name of the department was changed to the ministry of social affairs. In 1918 came a significant law on the redemption of leased land, which made independent farmers of almost 100,000 tenant farmers. The reforms greatly strengthened the legitimacy of the young republic.

Between the world wars, the agrarian economic structure seemed to change slowly, although Finland was paradoxically industrializing relatively faster than any other country in Europe. Most people earned their livelihood in agriculture, but its share of the gross domestic product had already sunk to less than one-half in the early 1920s. Before World War II, Finnish values, reflected also in the party structure and the support of different parties, favored agrarianism characterized by small farms. The unfavorable climate kept the productivity of agriculture low. Nevertheless, in the long run the country grew wealthier quite fast. Because of an ideological antithesis with the former mother country, now the Soviet Union, foreign trade was directed almost entirely to the west and south.

Compulsory education in 1921 was one of the early independence period reforms, but it did not mean any radical change. Already in the 1680s, the Lutheran Church had ordered that the people be taught to read so that they could familiarize themselves with the Bible. An extensive network of basic education had been developed starting from the 1860s but, despite its autonomy, Finland had not been able to implement compulsory education during Russian rule. Nevertheless, the Finnish people were already among the most literate in the world at the end of the 19th century.

The most far-reaching social policy reform in the period between the world wars was the *National Pensions Scheme* in 1937. The enactment of general disability and retirement insurance was an important revision of the social contract and a step towards a welfare state.[4] At the beginning of the 1920s labor legislation was also reformed and in 1924 the first bill on collective labor agreements was passed. Due to the opposition of employers, it did not become effective until 1944. At that time the employers had accepted an equal agreement system in principle, because the majority of the field army in the Winter War consisted of workers who were determined to defend their country and society.

The hard war years of 1939–1944 and the cessions of territory which followed, together with the settling of evacuees and the war reparations, made the country poorer. But they also forced the nation to reform. The

---

4   Actually, the original funding system would have been all too slow to offer immediate protection.

level of pre-war total production had already been regained by 1946 and an exceptional growth period began: until the mid-1970s the annual growth of gross national product was almost 5 percent (Vartia and Ylä-Anttila 1996, pp. 66–67). At the same time, an intensive period of building the welfare state was experienced. Economic growth contributed to the social building process. Besides, Finland had a particular motive in developing the living conditions of its people. The communist superpower behind the border tried to influence Finland ideologically, and the people's democracies in central Europe set a warning example. Great care had to be taken of the legitimacy of the political and social system.

Already during the Second World War (1942), an extensive program of social reforms was introduced in Great Britain. Called the Beveridge Plan, its aim was described by its planner as a fight against five giants: want, disease, ignorance, squalor and idleness, by which he meant unemployment. This program had two goals: raising well-being and upholding the legitimacy of the society, which would be promoted by increasing the equality of the citizens. The plan, the economic views of which were based on the theoretical thinking of John Maynard Keynes, included the essential principles of a modern welfare state. William Beveridge's description of the aims of his plan influenced European countries on their way to a welfare state.

Finland's post-war social policy began in 1945 with the extensive measures taken to organize the living arrangements of the evacuees and soldiers who returned from the war, and to help them acquire land. The number of the evacuees was approximately 12 percent of Finland's population at that time, which, if scaled up to the population of the United States in 2000, would have meant resettling some 33 million people. Another immediate task was to organize the welfare and rehabilitation of disabled war veterans.[5]

In the peace treaty, Finland lost 10 percent of its arable land and forest resources, 12 percent of its total area, 13 percent of its national wealth, and 20 percent of its railway network. In addition, one-quarter of the pulp production capacity and one-third of the hydroelectric capacity were lost (Myllyntaus 1992, p. 46). The war reparations, paid in total by 1952, added to Finland's difficulties. At their highest in 1945, they were 61 percent of exports and 6.4 percent of the GDP, but their proportional share decreased as exports grew and national income increased (Auer 1956, pp. 243–245). Finland's losses also included its second largest city, Vyborg. Being a neighbor to the Soviet Union was a heavy burden on Finland, a small nation struggling to preserve its freedom.

In this situation, the Finns started building their country's future with three goals: securing independence and democracy, and providing welfare for the people. The total war, with its comprehensive planning, taught

---

5   Proportioned to the U.S. population, the 94,000 permanently disabled veterans would equal 6.7 million.

the Finns, as so many other peoples, a new way of thinking: the country could be developed by planning. During the war, Finland had had to rely on an unprecedentedly large public sector, which rose to 20 percent (excluding the military), although such an increase in the public sector employment remained temporary.[6] Organizing the welfare and rehabilitation of the disabled veterans was started ahead of the Act on Military Injuries of 1948, and Finland has received a great deal of international recognition for its disabled veteran policy. At the same time, the veterans themselves have taken responsibility for their own wellbeing in an exemplary fashion. (Honkasalo 2000.)

As had been agreed during the Winter War, the law on the collective labor agreement system was reformed in 1946. In addition, a holiday law that granted a right to three weeks' annual leave with pay, was passed. Because the birth rate was on the rise and large families were hard pressed under the tough conditions of continued rationing, attention was drawn to family policy. A law was passed in 1948 on child allowances, and a year later on maternity benefits. In these laws, the Nordic principle of universalism was followed: every child under 17 years was entitled to child allowances and every woman giving birth was entitled to maternity benefits. Also, it was necessary to expand housing production. Three laws were passed in 1949: on housing loans and benefits, on promoting housing production in population centers, and on subsidizing building with state money. The reforms were an effort to bring some improvement in the nearly chaotic situation in post-war Finland. Despite the reforms, social expenditures did not rise very high in retrospect; they amounted to approximately 8 percent of the gross domestic product in 1950 (Sosiaaliturvan kehitys Suomessa 1950–1977. 1978, p. 37). But considering the circumstances of the time, they were a heavy burden.

The war had delayed the development of social security. *National Pension Insurance*, which was intended as basic security to all citizens, was reformed in 1957, and a corresponding system for employees, the *Employees' Pension Scheme*, was created in 1962. National Pension Insurance was based on a flat-rate pension system, the Employees' Pension Scheme on earnings-related pensions.

The 1960s was a time of growing radicalism in all democratic states. In Finland, radicalism furthered the development of social policy since it included a strong pathos of equality. The rapidly growing economy created resources for reforms. During the decade, the Finnish trade union movement quickly became stronger as social democrats and communists agreed on cooperation, as social democrats settled their internal differences, and as unionization gained further popularity among white-collar workers. One of the major aims of the trade union movement was the

---

6   The corresponding level of public sector employment was only reached in the middle of the 1980s, now as the consequence of the developing welfare state. The growth of the public sector continued until the beginning of the 1990s; in 2000 it amounted to 27.3 percent. (Vartia and Ylä-Anttila 1996, p. 280; *SYF 2001,* p. 366.)

development of a welfare state. Employers also adopted rather positive attitudes to social policy: they realized that improving the know-how, health, and motivation of the population would increase human capital.

Cooperation between labor market organizations became clearly evident when the *Employees' Pension Scheme* was being prepared and implemented (cf. Suonoja 1992, pp. 441–457). While parliament had the final word in enacting social policy laws, labor market organizations greatly contributed to the development of the welfare state and influenced the content of its laws, beginning from the early 1960s and especially from the end of that decade. The development that began at that time seemed to foreshadow a later claim that a welfare state means a working society, an essential element of which is a fully employed wage earner. There was much truth in that statement before the 1990s.

The evolving Finnish welfare state had its problems. One of them was a high incidence of various diseases in the 1960s. Life expectancy at birth, however, had risen greatly. In 1911–1920 male life expectancy was 43.4 years and female 49.1 years; in 1961–1965 the figures were 65.4 for men and 72.6 for women (The Yearbook of Population Research in Finland XXXIII. 1996, p. 347). The health care of young children and expectant mothers was of a high standard, which was shown by low infant mortality. In this respect, Finland had its place among the elite countries of the world. The hospital system had been developed especially in the 1950s, with the number of beds being of average European level. However, there were few doctors per capita and a high mortality rate among working-age men. These factors and their uneven regional distribution remained a great problem, and in this regard Finland belonged to the most problematic countries in Europe (Kuusi 1961, pp. 254–267).

The problems of national public health were taken up with determination. In 1963, *National Sickness Insurance* attempted to bring health services within the reach of all citizens. At the same time, medical education was substantially increased. It was soon noted that the high mortality of men was connected to circulatory diseases. Extensive follow-up research on public health showed that Finns needed to change their lifestyle to reduce these diseases, and Finns have proved to be adept at this: since the late 1970s, they have changed their diet and the differences in dietary habits between various socio-economic groups have diminished or disappeared.

By 1993, the age-standardized mortality of women from circulatory diseases had fallen below that of most European countries, and men, too, had almost reached the average European level. In 2000, women's life expectancy at birth was 81.2 and men's 73.7. The figure for women was higher and that for men slightly lower than corresponding estimates in the United States, but life expectancy was shorter in both countries than, for instance, in Sweden or France *(SYF 2001, p. 593)*.

Obviously, better health is due to many other factors besides health care; a general improvement in living conditions affects health. A higher standard of living in Finland is reflected, for example, by the fact that the proportion of food in all private consumption was 52.1 percent in 1900, but only 12.5 percent in 1997. Correspondingly, more was spent for health care, transport, recreation, leisure time, foreign travel, etc. (Tennilä 1999, p. 202). The quality of life improved as a result of a number of factors.

From the late 1960s until the late 1980s, employers' and workers' organizations had such a strong influence on social policy reforms that, in the opinion of some critics, they were dictating parliament's decisions. But during those decades Finland realized the characteristic features of Nordic welfare states that it had lacked previously. They included the forty-hour working week (1965); five-week annual leave with pay (1978); the Employment Act, including a reform of unemployment benefits (1972); the Public Health Act, which also transformed the traditional hospital organization into municipal health centers (1972); day care for all children (1973); an increase of the private sector's full employment pension from 40 to 60 per cent (1975); the Social Welfare Act (1984); and several revisions of the National Pensions Act.

The oil crises of 1973 and 1979 put strain on the economies of nearly all industrialized countries and, for example, in Great Britain led to criticism of the welfare state and a reduction in social expenditures. In Finland, the ensuing slump lasted for a shorter time than elsewhere, partly because Finland benefited from its position as a neighbor of the Soviet Union. Bilateral trade agreements guaranteed Finland advantageous access to Soviet oil, which was bartered for Finnish goods.

Housing conditions improved particularly in the 1970s and 1980s. In 1960, the average number of rooms in Finnish homes was 2.7, reaching 3.7 in 1997. At the same time, the average number of people living in a household decreased from 3.3 to 2.3, which added to more spacious living.[7] In addition, amenities in Finnish homes increased significantly (Juntto 1999, p. 135). Nowadays many Finns have both a bath and a sauna; in recent decades it has been quite common to build a sauna in modern urban flats and the estimated total number of saunas in Finland exceeds 2 million (equivalent to over 100 million in the U.S.). Besides, 800,000 Finns, about 16 percent of the population, live in households that also have a holiday home.[8]

Finland is one of the most equal societies in the world, but differences remain in housing conditions. Finnish social policy has long struggled to solve the problem. Numerous factors, such as high building and housing costs due to the northern climate and the high price of land – surprising in a country large in area – have hindered progress. On the other hand, Finland has few homeless people, who in many other countries pose a typical problem. Further, the safety of living is raised by an internationally high

---

7   Between 1960 and 2000, the number of rooms per person increased from 0.76 to 1.68, and floor space per person from 14.3 to 35.3 square meters (*SYF 2001,* p. 229).

8   The number of summer cottages in Finland rose from 252,000 in 1980 to 451,000 in 2000 (*SYF 2001,* p. 232).

proportion of owner-occupied homes, which totaled 59 percent of all homes in 1999, having been as high as 67 percent in 1990 (*SYF 2001*, p. 231).

The quality of housing depends, above all, on domestic conditions and policies. The causes of another significant social problem, *unemployment*, include both domestic structural factors and international factors. In the early 1900s, Finland's unemployment was mainly caused internally, relating to the economic structure of the country. In the countryside, unemployment arose largely from issues connected to land ownership and in the cities from seasonal variations in construction. However, the Great Depression of the 1930s already showed how easily international economic conditions affect employment. In the winter of 1931–1932, the number of unemployed people rose to over 90,000 (Figure 2.2), which led to extensive arrangements for relief work.

Figure 2.2

Unemployment from 1900 to 2001

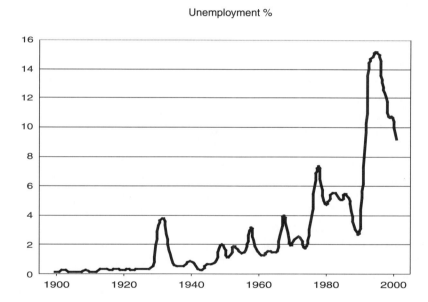

Unemployment %

Source: Statistics Finland.

Finland recovered from the depression quite fast, and the war and the following years were a time of labor shortage rather than unemployment. But from the 1960s, structural factors as well as international economic conditions increased unemployment. Since Finland at the time adopted the ideology of a welfare state, which included the aim of full employment, unemployment began to be seen as a serious defect. At first, structural factors played an important role. Although large numbers of Finnish women had traditionally participated in the labor market, growth in the number of working women during the 1960s and 1970s came unex-

49

pectedly. In 1960, 24 percent of family mothers were wage earners or entrepreneurs; by 1975, the percentage had risen to 60 (Suominen 1979, p. 51). In addition, the large post-war generations were reaching working age. Hence, the supply of labor leapt to a new level, and this resulted in a wave of migration from the countryside to population centers, considerable emigration to Sweden, and increased unemployment.

As a result of the international oil crisis, the number of unemployed rose to 180,000 in 1977, corresponding to over 7 percent of the labor force. The fact that president Urho Kekkonen wanted to appoint an emergency government because of unemployment and that a goal was set to lower it again by the 1980s to 2.5 percent – virtually full employment – reflects the values of the welfare state and the fears that political legitimacy would be shaken. The political decisions were typical of a welfare state: the Unemployment Pension Scheme (1981) meant, before long, that wage earners unfit for work could retire; the Unemployment Security Act (1985) improved earnings-related security for the jobless; the Employment Act (1987) obliged the state and municipalities to create employment for the young and the long-term unemployed (cf. Keinänen 1999, pp. 74–76).

However, the welfare state was confronted with quite another type of challenge when Finnish society entered the deep recession of the early 1990s. This subject will be dealt with in Chapter 15. At that stage, the ability of the welfare state to take care of the wellbeing of its citizens was put to a severe test.

The proportion of social expenditure in the gross domestic product has often been used as a criterion in determining which countries can be regarded as welfare states. In Finland, the percentage was below the EU average until the turn of the 1990s, but jumped significantly above it after the exceptional rise in unemployment and the exceptional fall in the GDP in the early 1990s. In 1999, social expenditures were estimated at 26.5 percent of the GDP, which was again below the average in EU countries (*Sosiaaliturvan suunta 1999–2000*. 1999, p. 13). Economic growth, which has been faster in Finland than in most EU countries since 1994, reduced unemployment, and cuts in social expenditures also contributed to the falling proportion of social spending.

Thanks to its advanced social welfare legislation and high level of wellbeing, Finland has fulfilled the criteria of a welfare state since the mid-1970s at the latest, but did not reach the level of the Nordic welfare states before the 1980s. And the proportion of public sector employees among all employed persons exceeded 15 percent at that time (Vartia and Ylä-Anttila 1996, p. 280).

The diversity of the welfare state is also evident in the wide scope of legislation dealing with social policy. It has been concluded in jurisprudence that the legal paradigm of the constitutional state has been replaced, to a large extent, by that of the welfare state. This reflects a deep change in values and even in culture. The fundamental rights of the citizens have been enlarged to include their social rights in order to safeguard their ability to utilize their rights to freedom and participation in practice. (Habermas 1996; see also Ilveskivi 2000, pp. 12–19.) The Finnish constitution was influenced by the new emphasis when a comprehensive list of economic, social, and educational rights was added to its text in 1995 (see Chapter 14).

This book attempts to provide answers to various questions about the welfare state:

- What is the structure of the Finnish welfare state;
- how does Finland implement the goals of the welfare state, including the citizens' economic, social, and educational rights;
- what impact did these rights have on Finland's efforts to build an information society;
- what are the roles of civil society in the welfare state;
- how did the welfare state survive the consequences of the serious recession of early 1990s; and
- can the welfare state maintain its goals under the pressure of globalization and increased international competition?[OR]

Foreign Relations

The 20th century brought about unforeseen technical advances and social progress, but it has also been called Europe's "century of violence." Autonomy within the Russian empire protected Finland from World War I, but two decades later the country was deeply involved in World War II. Because of its geographic location between east and west, the relations with Finland's eastern neighbor have been of constant importance and the collapses of the Russian regime in 1917 and in 1991 greatly shaped Finland's international environment. During the latter half of the 20th century Finland was able to remain outside the Soviet power block, maintaining its democratic form of government, strengthening its economy, and cultivating its lively cultural and trade contacts around the world.

Finland declared its independence in December 1917 and adopted the new constitution in July 1919, but some additional time went by before the international borders were clearly established. Peace with Soviet Russia was concluded in October 1920. On the west side, Sweden made attempts, both at the Versailles peace conference and in the League of Nations, to gain possession of the Åland islands. This issue was referred in 1920 to the League of Nations, which in 1921 pronounced Åland historically, geographically, and economically a part of Finland.

In March 1922, Finland's foreign minister negotiated a defense pact with three other newly independent neighbors of Soviet Russia (Poland,

Latvia, and Estonia), but parliament refused to ratify the treaty. Rather, Finland believed in the collective security provided by the League of Nations. This belief was severely shaken in 1935, when the League did not react to Germany's unilateral abrogation of the Versailles Peace Treaty. From the middle of the 1930s, Finland's principal foreign policy orientation was one of neutrality, leaning toward Scandinavian cooperation. However, the USSR and Germany agreed in August 1939 in a secret protocol to their Molotov-Ribbentrop pact that Finland would belong to the Soviet sphere of influence, a pact which the Finns did not let the USSR consummate.

In the postwar world the main characteristic of the international environment was global balance between two military alliances. The North Atlantic Treaty Organization (NATO) was started in 1949 and the Warsaw Pact followed suit in 1955. Europe was effectively divided by an "iron curtain," and Finland needed to adjust its foreign policy to the cold war situation. Like Ireland, Austria, Sweden, and Switzerland, Finland stood outside both military alliances. Among the five neutrals, Finland was the only direct neighbor of the USSR[9] and very carefully guarded its relations with Moscow. For example, in order to safeguard its neutrality Finland declined Marshall aid for postwar reconstruction. Instead, Finland built bilateral economic ties with the western countries and, for example, reconstruction of Finnish export industries received support from the United States.

Finland signed a Treaty of Friendship, Cooperation and Mutual Assistance with the USSR in April 1948. The FCMA treaty was drafted by the Finns and differed from the ones the USSR had with the Warsaw Pact countries. It also was, implicitly at least, interpreted differently by the two countries. The Finnish interpretation stressed not only friendly relations between the two countries but also the neutrality clause in the preamble.[10] On the other side, only Nikita Khrushchev, in 1956, referred to Finland's neutrality in public, until Mikhail Gorbachev finally acknowledged it in October 1989 when speaking in Finland.

In 1955 Finland joined the Nordic Council and also became one of the 16 new member states of the United Nations. Thus a good opportunity was obtained to demonstrate the policy of neutrality, and Finland's links to its primary foreign reference group, the Nordic countries, were illustrated. Finland was striving for a clear recognition of its neutral position. The cautious opening up to West European integration coincided with that goal.

The elements of the Finnish model of becoming involved in integration policy included the protection of essential trade interests and guaranteeing its exporters the same benefits as were offered by competitors

9   Finland's land border with Russia is 1269 km (789 miles), with Norway 716 km (445 mi), and with Sweden 536 km (333 mi).
10 Regarding mutual assistance, Finland agreed to enter negotiations about the need for Soviet assistance in the event that Finland was attacked by Germany or its allies.

(e.g., Sweden), and doing both of these in harmony with the policy of neutrality. Finland sought separated solutions, avoided political commitments, guaranteed to the USSR same trading benefits as to its Western partners and, in addition, sought to protect the adjustment of domestic industries. A convenient solution was Finland's association with the European Free Trade Association (EFTA) in 1961.

During the 1960s Finland's foreign policy became more active. Since 1963 an oft-repeated Finnish suggestion was that a nuclear-free zone should be created in northern Europe. In 1969 Finland proposed the Conference on Security and Cooperation in Europe (CSCE) and, at the same time, was a member of the UN Security Council and hosted the SALT negotiations. In 1975 Finland hosted the signing of the "Helsinki Accords," the Final Act of the CSCE, by thirty-five heads of government. During the 1980s, relationships between the European Community and EFTA grew closer, and Finland participated actively in the integration process, but within the limits set by its neutrality policy.

The fall of the Berlin Wall in November 1989, the unification of Germany in October 1990, and the breakup of the Soviet Union in December 1991 represented dramatic changes in the international environment. Finland was involved in launching in January 1994 the European Economic Area, consisting of EFTA and the European Community, but Austria and Sweden had quite early taken one step further, applying for membership of the European Community. In March 1992 Finland, in turn, applied for membership of what has been called since November 1993 the European Union. The accession treaty was signed in June 1994, and after an affirmative referendum on October 16, 1994, Finland joined the EU from January 1, 1995, together with Austria and Sweden. In 1999 it was Finland's turn to assume responsibility for the rotating presidency of the EU.

Because the EU-countries had long been Finland's most important trading partners, Finnish industries had already become integrated in the economic system of Western Europe. For several decades the policy of neutrality had been the most important element in Finland's foreign policy. Now Finland declared that it fully accepted the goals and policies of the EU, including the formation of a common foreign and security policy. The presidency of the European Council also engaged Finland in 1999 in the formulation of common EU policies and, in addition, made Finland the EU's spokesman in various international contexts. However, in its own security policy Finland wanted to remain nonaligned. Its doctrine has been national security based on nonalignment and a credible national defense.

Although Finland has bound itself to the policies of the EU, it also pursues numerous other foreign interests, both bilaterally and through international organizations. It continues its small-state approach to foreign policy with a certain regional emphasis. In the EU Finland has emphasized the importance of the northern dimension – the Baltic Sea area and the Barents Sea area – and common policies toward Russia, as well as stressing the role and the position of small member states in the structural reforms of the European Union. Finland continues to take an active part in the United Nations and to provide troops for peace-keeping operations. Other forums of active participation include the Nordic Council, the Organization for Security and Cooperation in Europe, the Council of Europe, the Organization for Economic Cooperation and Development, and the World Trade Organization.

In a small symposium, arranged in Porvoo in May 1999 to commemorate the 190th anniversary of the Finnish diet's meeting in that coastal town, Prime Minister Paavo Lipponen drew broad conclusions about Finland's current international role: "Today Finland is living through the most significant period in its international relations... In joining the European Union and the economic and monetary union EMU, we have fully utilized the opportunities open for us... In the 15-member union, emphasizing relations with Russia before the next enlargement, our influence is at the maximum." He also referred to President Martti Ahtisaari's participation in international attempts to settle the crisis in Kosovo: "Finland has made a clear choice in favor of the type of policy which tries to participate closely in the structures of European and international cooperation." *[PP]*

3 Finnish Nationalism

People are very stubborn there [in Finland]. We were smart not to annex Finland. It would have been a festering wound.

Former Soviet foreign minister Vyachesvlav Molotov twenty years after World War II. Chuev 1993, p. 10

Sisu, Sauna, and Sibelius.

Finnishness defined by Finnish Americans

As was outlined in Chapter 2, Finnish identity grew strong enough to prompt Finland to declare its national independence in 1917. From then on, strong and healthy nationalism remained a necessary prerequisite for survival next to an imperialistic superpower. When Finland's existence was at stake during the Winter War of 1939–1940, nationalism was one of the factors uniting the people and healing the wounds of the civil war of 1918. And the success story continued: After the war Finland remained the one European neighbor of the USSR that preserved its independence and democratic social system. At the beginning of the 21st century nationalism may face a new problem: how to retain national identity as a member of the European Union and pressured by ever stronger globalization?

Early Nationalism

Nationalism contains explicit or implicit ideas about a nation's characteristics as compared with those of other nations or ethnic communities. It is based on slowly changing values that touch people's identity. Nationalist attitudes vary greatly: they may appear as a slight attachment to one's own nation and as tolerant attitudes towards foreign peoples and races. But they may also include strict views according to which one's own people are seen as superior to other peoples, which are classified as inferior, even in terms of their race.

Doctrines such as Fascism and National Socialism, or the sad events in former Yugoslavia and in Rwanda and Burundi, are examples of exceptions in which such an ideology and ethnic feelings are taken to extremes. But even strong nationalism can be sane: recall the Greek triumph against the Persians at Marathon, Joan of Arc's heroism against the English, and the Finnish Winter War 1939–1940.

State and nation-state are concepts that help to understand nationalism, even though it can exist irrespective of these institutions. A common language and shared history are among nationalism's underlying factors. Various narratives about the past describe how a nation or an ethnic group perceives its own essence or what concepts it identifies with. As a reflection of common values, nationalism helps a nation create and strengthen the legitimacy of its societal and political system.

The rise of nationalism has been linked to modernism by most scholars who have analyzed this topic. It appears to have proceeded in two ways. Earlier, it was born within strong, already existing states: a strong state created opportunities for the rise of nationalism, even regardless of the ethnic composition of the nation. In the more slowly developing conditions of Eastern Europe, contrary development was experienced: the rise of nationalism gave birth to a state. In developing conditions, a prerequisite for nationalism is an ethnic community that people want to identify with. The desire for national attachment results, above all, from a common culture, the central elements of which are a common language and religion and shared historical experiences.

However, neither model suits adequately the rise of Finnish nationalism, because in Finland the rise of nationalism was neither state-centered nor ethnic-centered. When nationalism rose in Finland, the country was an autonomous part of the Russian empire having its own distinct administrative system. The culture belonged to Western Europe but the language was sharply different from West European languages and even more from Russian. The religions were different in Finland and Russia. The economy was less developed in Finland than in most of Western Europe, but overdeveloped if compared with the rest of the Russian empire. Finland had a non-feudal class structure, and although the upper class spoke Swedish, it soon began to feel Finnish. By the end of the 19th century Finnish had already achieved a strong or even a predominant position in central institutions.

Due to the exceptional growth of civil society (see Chapter 2), the patriotic message of numerous associations was accepted by a large majority of the people. Finland's independence in 1917 was an awaited consequence of the developments of its civil society, nationalism, and democracy. But the Finns did not agree about the kind of societal system that ought to be chosen: capitalist or socialist. The civil war broke out in January 1918, causing tragic human destinies and bitterness, and tearing the nation in two. There is reason to ask how nationalism was able to survive and develop in a young state whose population was ideologically divided. How was it possible that, two decades later, a field army comprised mainly of workers and small farmers defended its fatherland as one – in a manner that reflected strong nationalism?

Chapter 2 presented some of the factors that strengthened Finnish identity and nationalism particularly in the late 19th century: a common language spoken by the great majority of the population, very dissimilar to other European languages (except for Estonian and to some extent Hungarian); the northern area that Finns had inhabited for thousands of years; old popular culture, manifested in many ways in spiritual and material folklore; the rise of modern culture, and pride in Finnish achievements. The Fennomans' dream came true when the Finnish language made its breakthrough in the most significant social institutions by the beginning of the 20th century, which created a link between the elite and the mass of the people.

Several institutions, for example religion, united the Finns with Western Europe. Lutheranism originated in Germany, and when Finland became independent, the Evangelical Lutheran Church was a state church comprising virtually the entire population. As a continuing cultural undercurrent, religion unified the people and created a strong tradition. During the Second World War, the Finns said that they were fighting for their "home, religion, and fatherland."

Another strong institution, local self-government, was of Nordic origin and became firmly established in Finland during the period of Swedish rule. It derives from ancient Germanic and Nordic conceptions: from the right and duty of free men to engage in decision-making on public issues. Even though this right came into conflict with state absolutism at some stage in history, it remained and grew stronger again after the mid-nineteenth century, drawing its inspiration from romanticism, liberalism, and Hegelian thought. This happened because these ideologies preferred the local government system (Soikkanen 1966). Strong local government has become an essential part of the Finnish political culture, and in its background one finds a cultural ethos that is in harmony with a more common feature of Finnish culture, namely, the Nordic tradition that emphasizes the importance of liberty and self-determination. Such cultural uniformity fortifies both legitimacy and positive attitudes towards own country.

At the level of national government, the parliamentary reform of 1906 was bound to raise hopes among the majority of the population of ever-stronger democratic development and of a state that people could identify with. The radical Marxist wing of Finland's old labor movement, which rejected rather than favored nationalism, grew stronger when the parliamentary reform showed few immediate results. On the other hand, the Social Democratic Party had strong leaders who stressed the importance of national ends. These leaders, together with non-socialist politicians, smoothed the path of independent Finland toward a legitimate society in which healthy nationalism strengthened. The historical conflict between international Communism and Finnish nationalism presents a series of interesting events that were also linked to the extreme nationalist tendencies troubling the young republic.

Nationalism vs. Communism

The revolutionary Marxist tradition and the bitterness caused by the civil war prepared the ground for Communism. The Finnish Communist Party was founded back in August 1918, not in Finland but in Moscow, where Red émigrés together with Russian communists began to make plans on a new revolution in Finland.

In Finland, communist action was centered in the Socialist Workers' Party, founded in May 1920. Soon the Moscow-based group of the Finnish Communist Party took up the reins in the Workers' Party, and in the parliamentary elections of 1922 the Communists received fifteen percent of the vote. In 1923, the Socialist Workers' Party was outlawed, which ever tightened the grip of Moscow-stationed communists on the party's former members. During the civil war, both Whites and Reds had exercised terror, which was typical of such a war, but it can be said that the terror campaign was continued by the victorious side after the war. This added to the bitterness and helped the communists. There were, however, supporters of moderate nationalism in Finland, the most visible of whom was K.J. Ståhlberg, the first president of the republic (1919–1925). By 1930, the ban on communist activities was tightened, and the underground operations of the Finnish Communist Party were increasingly run from Moscow (cf. Rentola 1998, pp. 159–163). But the struggle between moderate nationalism and the extreme movements was still to continue for decades.

The Communists sought to weaken Finnish nationalism and the will of the people to defend their country. Nevertheless, in the early 1920s sentiments of nationalism rose among young people with an academic background. Their concern was mainly to support the national and cultural interests of the Finnish population across the border in the Soviet Union. The Academic Karelia Society also aimed at strengthening the patriotic defensive will and nationalist thinking in Finland. Some members, however, carried their ideologies to such extremes that many resigned from the Society. The society was dissolved by the 1944 armistice treaty. Although extreme rightist in a sense, the Society, nevertheless, aimed at national integration and at repairing the division caused by the civil war. It particularly stressed that the duty of the educated class was to remain close to the common people (cf. Soikkanen 1975; Alapuro 1973.)

Another extreme rightist organization, the Lapua Movement, was formed in 1929. Unlike the Academic Karelia Society, it was a popular movement. One of its aims was to eliminate Communism in Finnish society, but it failed to see the crucial difference between moderate and revolutionary leftists. The movement organized a peasants' march, which was joined by some 12,000 rural people from Ostrobothnia, to pressure parliament to pass anti-communist laws. Such laws were actually ratified in 1930. In 1932, the unrest provoked by the Lapua Movement culminated in a coup attempt, which the conservative president P.E. Svinhufvud was able to avert with a determined radio speech. When the movement began to direct its operations against normal Finnish parliamentarism, it was suppressed in 1934.

The early 1930s thus saw the suppression of two extreme movements that both were preparing revolution: a leftist one which put both democracy and independence in danger, and a rightist one which endangered democracy. Restraining these movements benefited the development of healthy nationalism and social life. In 1932 a party was founded, named the Patriotic People's Movement (IKL), whose objectives were essentially similar to those of the Lapua Movement, but it did not receive much support; in 1939 it had only eight seats in Parliament.

The relationship of Finnish communists to their own nationality and nationalism turned out to be interesting in a tragic way. The Finnish Reds who had fled to Soviet Russia in 1918 faced a terrible fate there: they were suspected and persecuted and a large proportion of them, especially from the mid-1930s onwards, became the victims of expanding purges. This was also to be the fate of large numbers of Finnish immigrants who had moved to East Karelia from the Midwestern United States and Canada. News of the atrocities of Stalin's regime quickly reached Finland, and those who managed to escape brought concrete evidence of what was happening across the border. The mentality of Finnish communists was twofold from the outset, and the persecution of minority nationalities strengthened their awareness of being Finnish both in Finland and the Soviet Union. Some communists were ready even to take up arms to defend the Republic of Finland. Hence, Stalin on his part had been preparing the ground for "the miracle of the Winter War" (Rentola 1998, pp. 163–169). Insofar as there existed Communism in Finland, it formally opposed nationalism and put emphasis on the international solidarity of the working class.

How attached citizens are to their fatherland, is after all largely dependent on the conditions provided by society. It was important for the new republic that independence in 1917 be followed by significant social reforms. An eight-hour working day was already achieved and soon other reforms that met a long-time need were passed (see Chapter 2). The interwar period also gave faith in favorable economic development. Independent Finland had itself become a concrete object of identification.

The Soviet offensive in 1939 and the Winter War that followed made Finnish national solidarity stronger. It was reinforced by the territorial cessions after the war in 1940, which were regarded as a heavy loss and an act of infamy. The Finns were now prepared for a new war. The fate of the Baltic States lay before their eyes: the Soviet Union had invaded them in the summer of 1940 and annexed them to the Soviet empire, had begun to terrorize their population and had transformed their societal system into Communism. The Soviet Union's intention was to extend the invasion to Finland, as its Foreign Minister Molotov informed Adolf Hitler in November 1940 (Jakobson 1998, p. 35). Such factors and a desire to recover lost areas motivated Finland to join a new war against the Soviet Union in 1941.

At first, the Continuation War proved a success but in the end was a difficult experience. Finland managed to keep its independence and political and societal system, but again lost Finnish Karelia and various other territories. War-weariness, the territorial cessions, the war indemnities, resettlement of evacuees, and some bitterness were shown in the people's political reactions. In the general elections in March 1945, the Finnish People's Democratic League, an umbrella organization set up by the Communists, won forty-nine seats in parliament (see Table 8.1). At that stage, many countries adopted a skeptical attitude toward the future of independent Finland and to the nation's likelihood of retaining its identity.

However, most Finns did not lose their sense of nationalism as a result of the war. There were large projects ahead that had to be coped with: the settlement of evacuees, the acquisition of land and housing for war veterans, reconstruction, the welfare of disabled war veterans and the payment of war indemnities. In retrospect, Finland managed to handle the projects very well. While many other countries were left with a great refugee problem, this was not the case in Finland, although twelve percent of the population had to be evacuated and resettled. Finland's success in dealing with the problems caused by the war was the key factor in maintaining the legitimacy of its political system and true nationalism.

Nevertheless, Communism sought ways to increase its influence in Finland. The Soviet Union was transforming countries of Eastern Europe into people's democracies and, with the aim of doing the same in Finland, tried to gain more ideological influence in Finland. In a letter in February 1948 to President Paasikivi, Stalin stressed that Finland was the only European neighbor of the Soviet Union that did not have a defense agreement against a recurrence of German aggression. The letter was dated the same day that the communist attempt to seize power in Czechoslovakia culminated. It was a determined Finnish aim to eliminate the possibility of Soviet troops entering the country on some excuse. The FCMA treaty that Finland concluded with the Soviet Union was mainly based on a Finnish draft, designed with this aim in mind (Jakobson 1998, pp. 55–59; see Chapter 2, page 51).

The destinies of Finland and Czechoslovakia took different paths in a way that also describes the differences in the nationalism of these two countries. The Winter War had taught Stalin to respect the Finnish people's will for independence. This was apparent in the Tehran conference in December 1943. In a discussion about Finland, Stalin told Roosevelt and Churchill that "any nation that fought with such courage for its independence deserved consideration." The Czechs and the Slovaks, on the other hand, regarded Russians as their friends and allies, the one people that had expressed the will to help Czechoslovakia in 1939. Most Finns saw the USSR as Finland's archenemy. Soviet leaders had a clear view of how hardheaded the Finns were, as revealed by Molotov in an interview twenty years later (see the citation above). The communists also held a stronger position in Czechoslovakia than in Finland in 1948. Despite this, a Communist coup was feared in Finland; the army and the police were on the alert (op. cit., pp. 47, 61–62). The will for independence and Finnish nationalism did not fail when the survival of the country was on a razor's edge.

In addition to parliament and political parties, the trade union movement, standing in a decisive position because of its economic and other potentially disruptive effects, was the main battlefield for ideological dissension. Although less than a quarter of the population supported the communists, many unions were led by them. If they had reached a majority in the movement as a whole, the situation would have become critical. Much of the credit for their lack of success goes to the "companions-in-arms socialists", Social Democrats whose ideology was in line with the majority, emphasized both their own war experience and national aims. In terms of Finland's future, the battles between the Communists and the Social Democrats, fought on every level from the local branches to the central organization of the trade union movement, were just as important as governmental negotiations with the neighboring great power. The Social Democrats, as representatives of moderate nationalism, emerged the winners from these battles.

The aim of upholding good relations with the great power was quickly established as the main line of Finland's foreign policy, but at the same time the importance of national cohesion was stressed. This policy, known as the "Paasikivi-Kekkonen Line," ritually assured the Soviet Union of Finland's desire for peace and the will for good neighborly relations, at the same time as realistically pursuing national aims. Finland tried to emphasize its neutrality in every chance it got, whereas the Soviet Union preferred to remain silent about it.

Although Finnish nationalism was no longer as evident as in the 1920s or the 1930s, it lived on strongly among both the Right and the moderate Left. The Communist Party split in two already in the 1960s, into a "blue and white" wing with national ideas and a "Stalinist" minority closer to the Soviet Union. The former, the majority in the party, was an example of Eurocommunism. It seems that since the 1960s the Finnish Communist Party was never a real domestic or foreign political threat because of its moderate and even nationalist majority.

The development of the welfare state since the 1960s fortified not only citizens' welfare but also the legitimacy of the state. The strong if quiet nationalism of the Finns is perhaps best illustrated by their patriotic defensive will, which, in international comparison, has remained at a very high level ever since the Second World War. Those who talked about "Finlandization" in the 1960s–1980s disregarded the most significant matter: the will to defend the country had not diminished over the years.

According to surveys, in Finland it remained on a clearly higher level than in any of the countries in which "Finlandization" was discussed. This fact was also well known among the Russians.

Nationalism and Globalization

Currently nationalism exists in a totally different cultural environment than in its early days during the rise of modernism. The era described as postmodern involves an enormous change in the pace of communication and information, an epoch-making increase in international cooperation and relations, shortening of distances, expansion of trade of goods, of services and, above all, of capital transfers, growing tourism, and so on. These changes as a whole have been called globalization, which refers to a global strengthening of the dependencies between individuals and peoples and especially the effects of a market economy transcending all national borders. It will be discussed more in Chapter 16 below.

Some are of the opinion that globalization evens out the differences between cultures or at least creates multicultural communities. Cultural diversity incorporated in postmodernism points to the kind of new identities in which both national and various international cultural elements are combined. However, there are differences in the emphases of the concepts of postmodernism and globalization: the former stresses diversity and heterogeneity, whereas the latter emphasizes the power of economics.

Governmental relations and ties between nations also change their nature in the course of time. After the Soviet Union collapsed, Finland immediately repudiated the FCMA treaty. The existence of the Soviet Union had been, however, a factor strengthening the Finns' will to emphasize their own identity: they had to ensure that the communist aim of ideological infiltration would not affect their will for independence. In January 1995, three years after the collapse of the USSR, Finland, together with Austria and Sweden, joined the European Union with a large majority of the people in support of it. The main motives were economic or related to national security.

As a member of the European Union Finland is committed to following a number of governmental and administrational norms that are aimed at harmonizing policies with the other EU countries. Another great change that has led to internationalization is linked to multinational enterprises. At the dawn of the new millennium, Nokia was the largest company in Europe measured by market capitalization and a Finnish-led paper manufacturer was the biggest in its sector in the world, another paper company placing third. The international operations of these companies and many smaller ones mean that despite their Finnish management more and more of their business is done outside Finland. In a small country like Finland, the position of companies is very different from that in the United States, for example, and their actions are more likely to affect the preconditions of economic and national balance.

Are national cultures and, above all, the cultures of small nations – and with them national identities – changing their nature as globalization and postmodernism proceed and, in Finland's case, as the unification of Europe proceeds? A country rather isolated for so long has, thanks to its developed information technology, come into closer contact with universal cultural trends in a very short period of time. How will Finnish identity and nationalism live through this?

A unique foundation of the Finnish culture is the language. Finnish is, however, under the growing influence of foreign languages, now especially English, and when it comes to other aspects of cultural change, it has been claimed that Finland is the most Americanized country in Europe. Despite all this, purist measures, like those taken in France to preserve the country's own language from Americanisms, have not been regarded as necessary. Many are concerned about the survival of regional dialects and the changes in intonation and accent typical of Finnish, changes that are mostly due to the role of the media in everyday life. The development of languages has been a continuing process: their structure and vocabulary change as a result of cultural influence. Despite the changes, the disappearance of the distinctive Finnish language, which is so characteristic of the Finnish identity, is nowhere in sight.

Finns have many other distinctive cultural features as part of their identity, such as persistence and the characteristic described by the Finnish word "sisu" (perseverance, guts). The subcultures that are reflected in a strong identification with local tradition and units of local government form an important part of the foundation of Finnish national identity. Finns are also proud of the old tradition of personal freedom. Equality, exceptional by international standards, is present in today's Finland in many ways: in the division of labor between the sexes, in the great number of women actively taking part in working life and social life in general, and in perhaps the most even distribution of wealth in the world. One part of the Finnish identity is the memory of the successful defensive battle against the communist superpower. Finns have great interest in books and films about the wars that Finland fought; thus the battles for national survival continue to create cultural narratives for generations to come.

The material culture reflects some very old features. For example, the sauna illustrates the affection a Finn of the 21st century has for a very old institution. Another reflection from old times is the Finns' love for summerhouses and for a rural environment. Summerhouses are usually built by lakes and, if possible, far away from permanent residential areas. When a Finn, after a sauna bath, speaks on his mobile phone on the porch of his summer house, the act combines age-old and ultra-modern national phenomena: there are more saunas and mobile phones per capita in Finland than anywhere else in the world.

The Finnish culture is quite homogenous, for some concepts and values seem to be commonly held. In a comparison of characteristics of the

Dutch, Americans, Hungarians and Finns, Finnishness was found to be defined by such concepts as homeland, state, independence, work, school, and national defense, and that especially the first three concepts were emphasized. The unity of the Finnish culture seems to enable a good mutual conceptual understanding. Low-context cultures such as this are typical of the Nordic countries: they are well integrated and homogenous, which is largely based on ethnic, linguistic and religious unity (Anttila 1993, pp. 114–115).

Some researchers have claimed that Finns are inclined to suffer from inferiority complexes. Surveys paint a different picture. In 1984, when the claim "It is good luck and a privilege to be a Finn" was presented to Finnish respondents, the percentage of those who agreed was 90. In 1992, during deep economic recession, the percentage dropped to 61 but rose back to 68 in 1994 and to 79 in 2000 (EVA 2001a, p. 74). The strong patriotic defensive will illustrates an affection for one's own country and Finnishness. At the turn of 1994–1995, Finnish people were asked to list characteristics typical of Finnish mentality; the most typical characteristic given was the will to defend the country (82%). Patriotism and national spirit were in second place (81%) in this "self-portrait," the following being industriousness and entrepreneurship, a feeling of insecurity and concern for the future, sisu (perseverance), respect for work and honesty, and xenophobia. The feeling of being part of Western Europe and the EU (32%) and an interest in other countries and cultures (29%) were ranked among the last characteristics on the list (EVA 1995, pp. 32–33).

Behind the above-mentioned beliefs lie values and narratives typical of the Finnish culture that reflect nationalism. The feeling of insecurity was probably partly due to the point of time when the interviews were carried out: the deep economic depression was only just easing. The estimated level of xenophobia is rather surprising since there have been no racist movements in Finland, let alone racist parties. The few and scattered racist phenomena, above all skinheads, have met determined opposition. On the other hand, many refugees that have entered Finland have reported Finnish prejudices towards foreigners. Whether the negative side of Finnish nationalism is reflected in these prejudices remains unclear.

The change towards an information society will probably lay the way into the Finnish society for forces of globalization and will affect the Finnish consciousness. Empirical studies indicate a change. In 1994, clear tendencies were observed: the younger the generation, the more education and the more exposure to news from abroad there was and, consequently, the more international the people felt themselves to be. In addition, occupation was of significance: those working in agriculture considered themselves the least international. The results concerning people's spatial identification were hardly surprising. Those who identified the strongest with their own locality were the most opposed to EU membership and the most parochial, while an identification with international or global phenomena was connected to international and cosmopolitan attitudes. Those who regarded the country as their foremost object of identification were placed midway between weak and strong internationalism. (Sänkiaho and Säynässalo 1994, pp. 114–116.)

The Eurobarometer survey on the EU countries in autumn 2000 showed that the share of those who are very attached to their own village or town was the smallest in Finland (30 percent) and the greatest in Greece (75 percent), whereas the Finns were more attached to their own country than the average. Citizens in eight countries, particularly Luxembourg, Sweden, and Spain, were more attached to Europe than the Finns were. When asked about European and national identity, the majority of Finns identified with only their own nation, while no more than 5 percent felt more European than Finnish (Eurobarometer 54, pp. 13, B13–16).

The years ahead will show how Finnish nationalism changes as young generations who have always known an environment of internationality define their own relationship with Finnishness under the influence of globalization and the European Union. Renouncing one of the national symbols, Finland's own monetary unit, in 2002 may have an impact on this. The Finns are attached to their own country, but in the future the objects of identification will be increasingly international. Because information technology is especially multinational, the rapid growth of jobs in this sector will probably have influence on the way the Finnish people feel and think.

4 Social Structure and Bases of Conflict

We have had fierce internal disagreements and conflicts, but it has been possible to bridge them and to unite our nation.

Mauno Koivisto in December 2000

Issues and cleavages derivative from those of industrial society... remain the more important source of policy division and electoral choice.

Seymour Martin Lipset 2001, p. 7

The Population

During the 20th century the world experienced an unforeseen population explosion: from 2 billion people in 1930 to 6 billion in 2000, and the growth is predicted to continue. The European countries, however, face an opposite trend. They will no longer have natural growth. For a while their growth may still be sustained by longer life expectancies, but soon it will be based only on the number of immigrants they receive from outside countries.

In Finland the population has grown for almost three centuries, but a projected downturn is now approaching. In the early eighteenth century tragic events reduced numbers to only 390,000. It then reached 1 million in 1812, which equaled 13 percent of the population of the United States in those days. But the 3 million Finns of 1920 and the 4 million of 1950 equaled only 3 percent, and the 5 million Finns in 1991 equaled 2 percent of the U.S. population. In 1995–1999, Finland's average annual population growth was only 0.3 percent, low compared with the entire world's 1.6 percent but rather typical of Europe.[11]

Consequently, at the turn of the 21st century the age structure of the population is a major social problem in Finland, as it is in other Euro-

11 Finland's total fertility rate in 1999 was 1.74 (Sweden 1.50, Britain 1.68, France 1.73, and Germany 1.36, but USA 2.06 (in 1997) and India 3.13 *(SYF 2001, p. 592).*

pean countries. More children were born in Finland during the six years between 1945 and 1950 (619,300) than during the ten years 1991-2000 (616,700). In 1960, only 7 percent of Finland's population was sixty-five years and older, but in 2000 the corresponding percentage was 15 and growing fast: 20 percent is predicted in 2015 and 25 percent in 2026. Longer life expectancies have kept the total population growing, but the net production rate of 83 percent foreshadows a sharp decline after the 2020s. (See Table 4.1.)

Table 4.1

Population and projected population by age from 1950 to 2030 (in %)

| Year | Population* | Age groups | | | | Total |
		0–14	15–34	35–64	65–	
1950	4,029,800	30.0	30.1	33.2	6.7	100.0
1960	4,446,200	30.1	28.9	33.6	7.4	100.0
1970	4,598,300	24.4	32.2	34.1	9.3	100.0
1980	4,787,800	20.2	34.2	33.6	12.0	100.0
1990	4,998,500	19.3	28.1	39.1	13.5	100.0
2000	5,181,100	18.1	25.3	41.6	15.0	100.0
2010	5,267,900	16.2	25.0	41.5	17.4	100.0
2020	5,317,400	15.7	23.3	38.1	22.9	100.0
2030	5,290,600	15.2	21.9	36.6	26.3	100.0

* Actual from 1950 to 2000, projected from 2010 to 2030.

Source: *SYF 1961*, p. 28; *1962*, p. 28; *1972,* p. 41; *1981*, p. 39; *1992*, p. 70; and *2001*, pp. 76, 121.

Some tension has already developed between Finland's active and retired people, but so far the retirees have not been a strong interest group politically. Although they are active voters and have formed several pensioners' organizations, and the party register contains two pensioners' parties, the political parties of the aged have not gained any weight and their organizations have not exerted effective political pressure. Relatively speaking, retired persons even lost some of their benefits during the 1990s, such as their monthly pension payments from the Social Insurance Institution in case they are covered by another pension. The pressing political problem is, how and to what extent does the reduced active population protect or intend to protect the interests of the increasingly numerous elderly.

Twice during Finland's rapid population growth there was considerable emigration, which eroded the number of inhabitants of the "old country." The first such wave peaked more than a century ago, the other one mainly in the 1960s and 1970s. Emigration to America in the late 19th and early 20th century involved about 350,000 persons, quite a large number from a small country, although relatively less than from many other European countries, such as the Scandinavian countries and, particularly, Ireland. The second big wave was the post-war emigration of Finns to Sweden, which peaked in 1951, in 1965, and, most strongly, in 1969–1970.[12]

During the 1980s Finns returning from Sweden were already compensating for emigration from Finland. In other respects, Finland has received fewer immigrants than most other European countries. In public discourse there has also been some tendency to confuse two different groups of foreigners: the immigrants with the refugees and asylum seekers. Out of Finland's total population of 5,181,000 in 2000, only 136,000 (2.6 percent) were born in a foreign country and 91,000 (1.8 percent) were foreign citizens. Such numbers seem very small when compared with other European countries. Yet the number of foreign-born persons had actually doubled and the number of foreign citizens had more than tripled since 1990 (*SYF 2001*, pp. 104, 110).

The numbers and treatment of foreigners, both the immigrants and the refugees, have become salient political issues in Finland. However, negative mass attitudes are not prevalent, nor have they led to populist political movements with xenophobic leanings that could be compared with the Freedom Party of Austria, the Progressive Party of Norway, and so on. Very few Finns would go as far as to approve "skinhead" actions against foreigners, and in 1998 only one out of six Finns thought that "if unemployment grows, some foreigners should be sent back." Such an opinion had been held more widely five years earlier, during the highest mass unemployment. (Jaakkola 2000, pp. 138, 147.)

Finland is a thinly populated country and its population is unevenly distributed. The region called Uusimaa covers 6366 square kilometers and had 1,305,000 inhabitants in 2000, whereas North Karelia of 17,782 sq. km. had 172,000 inhabitants and Lapland of 93,003 sq. km. had 192,000 inhabitants (*SYF 2001*, pp. 78–96). These figures translate to two hundred, ten, and just two inhabitants per square kilometer of land area. The country's central regions have grown due to net movement in two directions: to the south, and to urban centers. Industrialization catalyzed unusually vigorous internal migration during the 1960s, and so did the post-industrial economic development of the 1990s.[13] Differences between the regions will be discussed more below (pages 77–81).

---

12 According to one estimate, some 700,000 to 800,000 Finns moved to Sweden between 1945 and 1994, and about 250,000 of them remained there permanently (Reinans 1996, p. 66).

13 In the 1990s about five percent of the population moved annually from one municipality to another. In 2000 their number was 260,000, including 119,000 persons who moved from one province to another (*SYF 2001*, pp. 145–146).

Language

The arrival of the Finns in their country belongs to distant pre-history, undocumented in writing. The earliest remains of any human activity in Finland since the Ice Age are from approximately 7200 B.C., and archeological finds indicate various phases of the Stone Age, each with a different culture and some characterized by contacts with distant peoples. Then the Bronze Age lasted one millennium from about 1500 B.C. onward. The pre-Roman Iron Age, in turn, began two millenniums ago. That was long believed to be the time when the forebears of today's Finns settled in Finland. More recently, this so-called resettlement theory has been replaced by the continuity theory: what really arrived in Finland 2000 years ago was a new culture that was adopted by the people who already lived there. Possibly the proto-Finns inhabited both sides of the Gulf of Finland as early as the beginning of the Bronze Age and, thus, before Finnish and Estonian developed into two different languages. (Jutikkala with Pirinen 1996, pp. 11–24.)

It is easy to detect the close linguistic relationship of Finnish and Estonian. The Finno-Ugric group also includes Hungarian, although the Finnish and Hungarian are not as close to each other as are, for example, English and Russian within the Indo-European language group. Among the several other peoples of the Finno-Ugric language group are *the Sami* (who have been commonly known as Lapps), the indigenous minority of northern Europe. They have their recognized territorial base. About 5000 Sami live in Finland (40,000 in Norway, 17,000 in Sweden, and 2000 in Russia).

Table 4.2

Population by language from 1900 to 2000

Year	Finnish	Swedish	Sami	Other	Total
1900	2,353,000	349,700	1,300	8,500	2,712,500
1920	2,754,200	341,000	1,600	8,300	3,105,100
1940	3,027,500	354,000	2,300	11,800	3,695,600
1960	4,108,300	330,500	1,300	6,100	4,446,200
1980	4,476,800	300,500	1,300	9,100	4,787,800
1990	4,675,200	296,700	1,700	24,800	4,998,500
2000	4,788,500	291,700	1,700	99,200*	5,181,100

* "Other" in 2000 included Russian 28,200; Estonian 10,200; English 6900; Somali 6500; Arabic 4900; Vietnamese 3600; German 3300, Albanian 3300, Kurdish 3100, Chinese 2900, etc.

Source: *SYF 2001*, pp. 112, 114.

In 1973 a government decree demarcated almost 10 percent of Finland's territory as the Sami's homeland region and, in fact, their traditional reindeer husbandry extends even further south of the designated region (Sillanpää 1994, pp. 3, 183). Only 1700 persons in Finland now speak Sami (Lappish) as their mother tongue (see Table 4.2), but literature and schooling are available in it and Sami Radio is operated by the Finnish Broadcasting Company.

In 1995 a constitutional amendment guaranteed the cultural autonomy of the Finnish Sami[14] and a new law was passed that reorganized Finland's Sami Assembly. This 21-member body is elected for a term of four years and represents the four major areas of Sami population, and the government is required to consult the assembly in matters relating to the Sami. In October 1999, there was some controversy regarding the exact definition of Sami origin: 5000 persons had the right to vote in the election, but a court refused the petition of another 800 persons, who could not prove Sami origin at least three generations back in their family tree.

In the future the courts may face a bigger problem. A study published in 2000 came to the conclusion that some Sami can claim legal rights of ownership to much of the forestland in Lapland, which the state has owned since the end of the 19th century (Korpijaakko-Labba 2000). Such a conclusion may raise the possibility of complicated court proceedings in which the state and Sami groups fight over large land areas.

Ordinarily the few Sami people do not receive much national attention in Finnish politics, whereas relations between the Finnish speakers and the *Swedish-speaking minority* are of a completely different magnitude. This language cleavage has even dominated the political scene in the past. Finland's Swedish speakers are numerous enough to explain the country's official bilingualism, which was stipulated by the Constitution Act of 1919 and repeated in the Constitution of 1999 as follows: "The national languages of Finland are Finnish and Swedish. The right of everyone to use his or her own language, either Finnish or Swedish, before courts of law and other authorities, and to receive official documents in that language, shall be guaranteed by an Act." (Constitution of 1999, Section 17).

The Swedish language became established in Finland during the six centuries of shared history, but the proportion of Swedish-speakers apparently never reached as high as 20 percent of the population (McRae 1997, p. 86). The Finns who spoke Swedish were largely concentrated along the western and southern coastal regions. At the turn of the 20th century, 350,000 Finns or 13 percent of the population spoke Swedish as

14 The amendment also concerned other minorities: "The Sami, as an indigenous people, as well as the Roma and other groups, have the right to maintain and develop their own language and culture. Provisions on the right of the Sami to use the Sami language in their dealings with the authorities are laid down by an Act. The rights of persons using sign language and of persons in need of interpretation or translation aid owing to disability shall be guaranteed by an Act." (Constitution of 1999, Section 17).

their native language. The following one hundred years reduced their absolute number by only 58,000, but the growth of the total population lowered their proportion to less than 6 percent (see Table 4.2).

After the separation in 1809, Swedish remained the official language of Finland's administration, courts, and higher education, until the Language Ordinance of 1863 declared Finnish "to be on a footing of complete equality with Swedish in all matters that directly concern the Finnish-speaking part of the population." Actually it took longer than was intended, until 1902, before the system of equality between Finnish and Swedish was implemented. In public life and in the economy of the country, Swedish long continued to be relatively more significant than plain numbers would indicate.

During the 1870s, the position of these two domestic languages also caused the country's first political cleavage. Two estates of the Diet (nobility and burgesses) were controlled by the Swedish party, and two (clergy and peasantry) by the Finnish parties. Universal suffrage, which was granted in 1906, motivated Swedish-speaking politicians to organize the Swedish People's Party, a mass membership party with the ability to reach out to the enlarged electorate. Linguistic strife was very salient in Finland's politics during the half century from the late 1880s to the late 1930s.

However, as mentioned above, the basic settlement was written in the Constitution Act of 1919. It also emphasized equal principles in meeting the cultural and economic needs of the two language groups. The constitutional provisions were supplemented by detailed legislation in 1922 (amended in 1935, 1962, and 1975). The language legislation sought to accommodate two conflicting aims, namely, the need of the individual citizen to use his or her own language in dealings with the authorities, and the practical problems caused by the regional concentration of Swedish-speakers, which left most of the country almost entirely Finnish speaking (Jansson 1985, pp. 78–83).

Thus, the Language Act implements Finland's principle of bilingualism on the level of municipal administration so as to let most municipalities function in Finnish only. Unilingual municipalities can contain a minority that is smaller than 8 percent (a bilingual municipality becomes unilingual if its minority declines below 6 percent). If the minority in a unilingual municipality grows larger than 8 percent, or if the minority consists of at least 3000 persons, local administration becomes bilingual.

The language that municipalities use in their administration is determined for ten-year periods on the basis of the latest census results. Table 4.3 summarizes how the language situation has grouped the municipalities since the 1950s. Fewer than 50 municipalities have been required, at any given time, to conduct their local administration in two languages, while the number of unilingual Swedish municipalities has gradually declined. From 1993 to 2002, they have numbered only 21. Of those, 16 are in the province of Åland and 5 on the west coast.

Table 4.3

Official language of Finland's municipalities from 1953 to 2002

	1953–1962	1963–1972	1973–1982	1983–1992	1993–2002
Finnish	458	457	407	396	391
Bilingual, Finnish majority	12	13	18	21	21
Bilingual, Swedish majority	32	34	25	20	22
Swedish	47	44	31	24	21
Total*	549	548	481	461	455

* The numbers concern the beginning of the ten-year period; they may have changed during subsequent years, primarily as the result of mergers of municipalities.

Source: *SYF 1953*, p. 26; *1963*, p. 46; *1973*, p. 11; *1983*, p. 12; *1994*, p. 78.

The language conflict between Finnish and Swedish speaking Finns is one of the social tensions that were mollified by the war experience. Also, it became easier to cater to the special interests of the linguistic minority when the language of the majority had reached an unquestioned dominance in public life. Nowadays a large majority (75 percent) of the Finns support treating the Swedish language equally as the country's second national language, and almost all the Swedish speakers in the country (96 percent) identify with the Finnish people (Allardt 1997, pp. 26, 30). Nevertheless, over 40 percent of the Finns also think that there still remains at least some conflict between the two language groups (see Table 4.5 below).

Actually, opinion surveys have recorded disparities in how the Finnish speakers and Swedish speakers have felt about each other, or about various other groups in Finland and abroad. When sympathy scores were used in 1983 to compare people's feelings toward selected ethnolinguistic groups, both the Finnish and the Swedish speakers placed their own language group at the very top and they shared warm feelings toward the Sami and the Norwegians, whereas Swedish-speaking Finns were more sympathetic toward Finland's (but not Sweden's) Finnish speakers than were Finnish-speaking Finns toward Swedish speakers, whether in Finland or in Sweden (McRae 1997, p. 156).

Finland's Swedish-speakers developed their own network of voluntary associations very early on, active in different cultural fields, as well as in economic activities, sports, and recreation. During the 1990s some of them were integrated with the larger Finnish-speaking associations, for example, the Swedish-speaking cooperatives with the Pellervo Movement. There is also an umbrella body that attempts to link general Swedish interests in politics, culture, and the economy. Called Svenska Finlands Folkting, it was established in May 1919. It has functioned on a more regular basis since 1941 and was restructured in 1977 to an assembly of 75 members, who represent different regions and different political parties in proportion to the votes cast for Swedish-speaking candidates in municipal elections. It can be seen "as a pragmatic substitute for the autonomous Swedish-speaking province that was dreamed of by a few visionary leaders but never achieved" (McRae 1997, p. 217).

There is also some pressure from a small but vocal ultra-Finnish movement, which has compared the rights of the Swedish minority in Finland with the position of the Finnish minority in Sweden. It has advocated either reduced minority rights in Finland or thorough improvements for Finnish speakers in the neighboring country. The most current language debate, however, concerns primary education. The issue is known as "compulsory Swedish," in other words the required teaching of Swedish as the second new language (if not already chosen as the first one).

In his comparison of three multilingual societies, Kenneth McRae pointed out the low level of linguistic conflict in Switzerland, but he also emphasized the fact that neither in Finland nor in Belgium has the linguistic conflict ever "degenerated into mass violence but has been fought politically." What distinguishes Finland is its linguistic instability, which is "to a degree unmatched by Switzerland or Belgium or Canada." (Op. cit., p. 361.) This refers particularly to the declining proportion of Swedish speakers in Finland, as noted above: the fall of their relative share from 14.3 percent in 1880 to only 5.6 percent in 2000.

Social Class and the Red-White Cleavage

Next to the language issue Finland's most pervasive political division, the conflict between social classes, arose a century ago. It had two origins. One was the inability of the economy and the legislature to correct the poor social conditions of the time, and the other was the rapid dissemination of radical socialist ideology. The division has many names. For historic reasons it is called the red-white cleavage, and ideologically it is known as the left-bourgeois or the socialist-nonsocialist (or socialist-bourgeois) division. "Left-right" would not be accurate because of the strong political center that belongs on the white, or nonsocialist-bourgeois, side of the dividing line.

The official statistics of the 2000 municipal elections recorded detailed results not only by party but also in the traditional manner by the socialist-nonsocialist summary: the socialist parties had 33.4 percent and nonsocialist parties 54.6 percent of the national vote. The former group included the Social Democratic Party, the Left Alliance, and two small communist parties, while in the latter group were the Center Party, Conservative Party, Swedish People's Party, Christian League (now Christian Democrats) and the True Finns (former Finnish Rural Party). However, the dichotomy did not suffice, because it left 12 percent of the votes unaccounted for. There was also a third group, "others," containing the Green League, a pensioners' party, and various small political groups and independents, unwilling to declare for either the socialist or the nonsocialist camp. The Greens became the first such political group in parliament in 1983. The party system will be described in Chapter 8.

In political rhetoric the left side of the party spectrum has been identified with the working class; the Social Democratic Party and the parties further to the left have been traditionally called the working-class parties. This had solid empirical grounds in the formative years of the mass parties and much later as well. In 1966, Robert R. Alford's "index of class voting" led to the following simplified picture: the three socialist parties were supported by 79 percent of blue-collar workers (excluding the nonpartisans), but by 24 percent of farmers and white-collar groups, so that the index measure was 79–24 = 55. In cross-national comparisons it represented a high degree of class voting (Pesonen 1974, p. 294).

However, because changes have occurred in both the objective social structure and in people's subjective ideological attachments, the dominance of the class cleavage appears somewhat outdated. Farm laborers have almost disappeared and other blue-collar workers have declined in numbers. From 1981 to 2000 the share of unskilled workers dropped from one-half to one-third, while the percentage of skilled workers (26%) remained unchanged (Blom and Melin 2002, p. 45). The total population in 1995 could be divided into the following socio-economic groups:

18.7 percent:	blue-collar workers (including .7 percent in agriculture)
2.9 percent:	farmer employers and farmers on own account
4.7 percent:	other employers and self-employed workers
29.1 percent:	white-collar workers (including 11.1 percent upper level)
22.2 percent:	pensioners
8.1 percent:	students and pupils
14.2 percent:	others (*SYF 2001*, p. 102).

The effect of socioeconomic background on party choice has weakened, but it still remains significant: 58 percent of the workers and only 24 percent of the white-collar group voted in 1991 for one of the two leftist parties, and three-quarters of the farmers were loyal to the Center Party. The Greens, in turn, got relatively more support among students than from other social groups. (See Table 4.4.)

Table 4.4

Distribution of votes in 1991 among six social groups (in %)

Parties	Workers	Farmers	White Collar	Retired	Students	Others	Total
Left Alliance	24	–	6	11	4	7	10
Soc.Dem.Party	34	–	18	27	10	25	22
Center Party	21	74	17	28	26	25	25
Rural Party	3	–	6	5	5	6	5
Christ.League	3	–	2	4	7	3	3
Swedish	1	4	8	5	7	5	5
Conservative	5	19	30	14	23	17	19
Greens	5	3	9	1	15	7	7
Others	4	–	3	3	33	4	3
Total	100	100	100	100	100	100	100
(n)	(186)	(53)	(314)	(155)	(77)	(180)	(994)

Source: Adapted from Pesonen, Sänkiaho, and Borg 1993, p. 108.

However, very little remains of people's subjective class identification, which provided the basis for the ideological "class struggle" not so long ago. According to a study in 1991, only 11 percent of the Finnish people identified spontaneously with the working class, while 17 percent identified with the middle class and 16 percent with something else. A 56-percent majority said that they do not belong to any class (Pesonen et al. 1993, p. 115). Since then, working-class identification has declined even further.[15] Even so, perceptions of group conflicts in general, or the class struggle in particular, have not disappeared from people's thoughts and discourse.

In 1991, 31 percent of the Finns were of the opinion that there is a strong conflict between the rich and the poor, and three-quarters thought the conflict is either "strong" or "rather strong" (in 1972, 85 percent thought so). Two-thirds thought that employers and employees are in conflict (in 1972, 73 percent). Table 4.5 summarizes how many perceived the existence of these and eight other social conflicts. Surprisingly, the most generally recognized conflict was, in 1991, the new one between the environmentalists and the industry's decision makers. Two additional conflicts appeared strong: the old one between farm producers and consumers, and a more recent one between the politicians and the people.

15 Responses to a structured (non-spontaneous) survey question have shown that the percentage choosing working class declined from 26 to 17 percent between 1984 and 2001. Those choosing middle class increased from 40 to 54 percent, while 34 and 28 percent chose "no class" (EVA 2001a, p. 22).

A factor analysis extracted three general factors out of the ten social conflicts listed in the survey, but the three factors explain only 33 percent of the total variance.[16] Indeed the strongest perceived conflict emerged as the "class conflict" (defined by blue-collar vs. white-collar workers, employers vs. employees, the rich vs. the poor, and socialists vs. bourgeoisie). The second general conflict can be given the more diffuse label "new conflicts" (the unemployed vs. employed, men vs. women, and politicians vs. the people). The third factor is the "nature-conflict" (environmentalists vs. the industry's decision-makers).

Table 4.5

Perceived existence of group conflicts in 1991 (% saying "strong" or "rather strong"), and factor loadings (varimax-rotation)

The Conflicts	Conflict exists	Factor 1 "Class"	Factor 2 "New"	Factor 3 "Nature"
Blue collar/ White collar	45%	.65	.37	−.02
Employers/ Employees	68%	.54	.23	.24
The Rich/ The Poor	74%	.46	.17	.28
Socialists/ Bourgeois	55%	.43	.20	.32
Farm Producers/ Consumers	67%	.27	.18	.21
Unemployed/ Employed	57%	.17	.56	.14
Men/ Women	32%	.33	.46	.11
Politicians/ The People	65%	.21	.38	.25
Finnish/ Swedish-speakers	44%	.25	.31	.28
Environmentalists/Economy	82%	.12	.13	.58
Explained variance (cumulative %)		27.2	30.8	33.2

Source: Pesonen et al. 1993, pp. 124, 543.

Of the three conflict dimensions the strongest one, the extended idea of the class struggle, is also clearly reflected in Finland's party system on the level of the mass electorate: the supporters of the Left Alliance tended to think that this is a strong conflict, and the supporters of the Swedish People's Party and the Conservatives felt that it is relatively weak. The Social Democrats leant toward the strong estimate, and supporters of the Center Party were closer to the Conservatives. The two other factors also

---

16 *Factor analysis* is a statistical technique to see whether a larger number of disparate objects (ten social conflicts in this case) can be summarized by a smaller number of variables, which help to discover underlying patterns. Rotation is the position in which each item loads on as few factors as possible. The higher the "variance" explained by the factors, the more fully they account for the objects.

differentiated the party groups to some extent and placed parties in a different sequence, but they were less party politicized. For example, the existence of a nature conflict was perceived the strongest by the Greens and the weakest by Rural Party supporters. (Pesonen et al. 1993, p. 129.)

Regional Differences

Finland's land area is located between the 60th and the 70th parallel (67 being the arctic circle). Unlike neighboring Sweden, which extends close to the 55th parallel in the south, Finland does not have any milder and more fertile areas, reminiscent of north-central Europe. Even so, the geographic differences and the long distance between northern and southern Finland offer very different economic opportunities and have caused big regional differences. In the south the country faces the Gulf of Finland, part of the Baltic Sea, which provides direct links to central Europe and the oceans of the world. The country's economic development has been guided by proximity to energy, raw materials, and markets.

The dissimilarities of Finland's regions obviously cause conflicting interests. Many of these are related to the economy, but additional differences are more the result of political tradition and differences in people's values and attitudes. Active farms are being discontinued while centralized services and modern production draw people toward the south and to a few central cities. There has been some such mobility ever since industrialization started, and the process accelerated in the 1990s. The loss of rural population was offset by higher rural birth rates, but now the situation is becoming critical because birth rates are low and the population is aging. Emptying areas are more than a demographic problem. It has long been possible to identify the vicious circle in which population, economy, and culture interact (Riihinen 1965). Now Finnish poverty means most of all poverty in the peripheral countryside. The loss of rural population has already created a shortage of forestry workers and even led to worries about national defense.

The map of Finland in Figure 4.1 presents the country's twenty formally defined regions that also perform certain governmental functions. They have distinct cultural identities and they vary greatly in area and the number of residents. As the comparisons in Table 4.6 indicate, their social situations are not similar: the center fares better than the peripheries.

Figure 4.1

Finland's regions and municipal boundaries

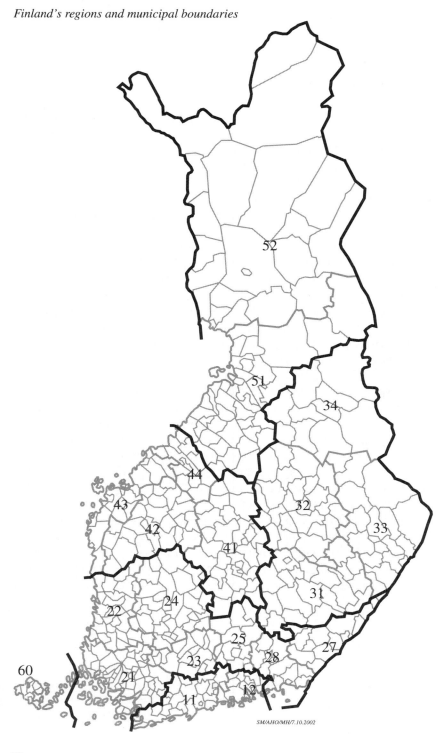

SM/AHO/MH/7.10.2002

Table 4.6

Regions in 2000: Population; population change in 2000; degree of urbanization; gross value added per capita (in 1999); rate of unemployment; and mean disposable income of households

Major Ragions* and Regions	Population %	Change %	Urbani- zation (index)	Value added %	Unemp- loyment (FIM)	Income
Whole country	5,181,000	0.2	82	100	10	155,000
Uusimaa	1,395,000	1.1	93	138	6	174,000
11. Uusimaa	1,305,000	1.1	94	142	6	
12. East Uusimaa	90,000	0.6	76	83	6	
Southern Finland	1,819,000	0.0	83	92	10	149,000
21. Varsinais-Suomi	447,000	0.4	82	101	8	
22. Satakunta	237,000	−0.7	81	71	11	
23. Kanta-Häme	165,000	0.1	80	78	9	
24. Pirkanmaa	447,000	0.6	85	87	10	
25. Päijät-Häme	197,000	0.0	85	81	12	
26. Kymenlaakso	187,000	−0.6	86	100	12	
27. South Karelia	137,000	−0.2	80	92	10	
Eastern Finland	681,000	−0.7	70	74	14	135,000
31. South Savo	167,000	−0.8	67	71	14	
32. North Savo	252,000	−0.7	73	77	12	
33. North Karelia	172,000	−0.5	68	75	15	
34. Kainuu	90,000	−1.4	68	69	19	
Mid-Finland	704,000	0.2	75	82	11	154,000
41. Central Finland	264,000	0.2	68	85	19	
42. South Ostrobothnia	196,000	−0.6	69	70	14	
43. Ostrobothnia	173,000	−0.2	83	94	11	
44. Central Ostrobothnia	71,000	−0.5	75	75	16	
Northern Finland	557,000	0.1	76	85	14	151,000
51. North Ostrobothnia	365,000	0.8	81	87	12	
52. Lapland	192,000	−1.3	74	82	18	
60. Åland	26,000	0.3	58	136	1	149,000

* Major regions correspond to level 2 of the statistical classification system of the EU. Numbering of the regions refers to the map in Figure 4.1.

Source: *SYF 2001*, pp. 78-98, 100, 310, 373, 400.

Between 1960 and 2000 Finland's population increased by 16.5 percent, but Helsinki and two neighboring cities grew by 71 percent. Population changes within one year, shown in Table 4.6, illustrate the country's regional variation. Uusimaa region in the south grew by 1.1 percent in 2000, while all small eastern regions lost population. Lapland in the north and Kainuu in north-east lost relatively the most. In addition, Finland's declining area includes four regions on the west coast and two regions in south east.

People have been attracted to the most urbanized areas and the less urbanized are losing population. The winning region had the most productive economy and the lowest unemployment, whereas the added gross value was much lower in the less urbanized regions. They also suffered from the worst unemployment. The mean disposable income of households was fairly close to national average in four major regions, but average households in Uusimaa earned 12 percent more, and those in Eastern Finland 13 percent less than national average in 2000. Differences in disposable income would have been even greater without current income transfers, which flattened regional differences. Chapter 14 will discuss the issues of regional support and reallocation of resources.

The magnitude of internal migration is illustrated by the fact that of the 200 members of parliament (MPs), the two southern election districts (Helsinki and Uusimaa) elected 31 MPs in 1948, but 52 MPs in 1999. On the other hand, it is illustrative of regional political differences that in 1999 the Center Party received only 9 percent of the votes cast in these two southern districts, but 43 percent in the two most northern districts (Oulu and Lapland).

Because most Swedish speakers live near the coasts or in the archipelago, the language issue involves a regional element too. Such a concentration of voters benefits the Swedish People's Party in parliamentary elections, because it makes the party relatively strong within four election districts. On the other hand, the political power of the Swedish speakers as a social group is weakened by regional variations between their different living areas. They are also connected to the center-periphery dimension: some Swedish speakers live in the center, i.e. the capital city area, while others live in economically declining areas, and the Swedish-speakers are a minority both in the center and in the periphery (Allardt and Miemois 1982).

Another example of regional variations in people's political thinking is evident in differences in opinions concerning the European Union. In the consultative referendum on Finland's membership of the EU in October 1994, a 57 percent majority voted yes, but of the 15 election districts, a majority of voters in the six northern districts opposed it. The affirmative votes varied from 74 percent in Helsinki and 68 percent in the surrounding Uusimaa district, to only 44 percent in two districts (Vaasa and Oulu). Both the region and population density had an independent influence on voting in all three Nordic EU referenda in 1994, in Norway somewhat more so than in Finland and Sweden (Ringdahl and Valen 1998, pp. 176–178, 185–188).

An international aspect was also linked to the regional conflicts when Finland joined the EU: Finland's regions were organized for the purpose of more effective lobbying, and they began to compete for the resources that are returned to Finland from the EU in what the EU calls "the Europe of Regions." In this activity the regions compete less with each other than with areas that are located far away, mostly in the peripheries of western Europe.

As mentioned above, the prevailing paradox in Finnish society was that families in the country's peripheral and poor regions produced the most offspring and thus took care of the growth of the nation's population. Only slight traces of such a difference still remain. By now the average household size has become small everywhere. Three-generation households are rare, children are few, and they leave the nest early.

Other Conflicts and Cleavages

The center-periphery cleavage is not as apparent in Finnish politics and culture as it is in Norway, and the difference between private and public employment is not as significant as in Sweden. But both conflicts exist, and many other differences in the social structure cause permanent or periodic political conflicts.

Retirees worry about the level of current and future pensions, students worry about study support and employment prospects, young families find child care and children's allowances inadequate, patients and the aged need more attention, the unemployed focus on their problems, and feminists find women to be underprivileged. Many such issues became increasingly salient because of difficulties in public finance and attempts to balance the budget. This has also caused additional tension between the state and local self-government. When the state pruned the support it pays to the municipalities, it did not relax local responsibilities for schools and welfare.

Increasing public attention has been directed to the cleavage that exists between the society's included and excluded members, the "ins" and the "outs". An important reason for the division's current significance is unemployment, which became a difficult problem in the 1990s. Not only did many people lose their jobs temporarily, but number of permanently unemployed also began to rise. This is the main reason why unemployment has led to serious social and political problems: a small segment of the population is becoming more and more alienated. The situation will be discussed more in Chapter 17 below.

Not all conflicts are based on structural differences. It is also possible to speak of non-structural social cleavages, as many ideological cleavages and various disagreements on current issues can be virtually unrelated to social structure. Historic examples of nonstructural cleavages include the conflict between the constitutionalists and the compliers and subsequent disagreements concerning Finland's foreign policy, or the 1918 struggle between the monarchists and the republicans. A very important ideological cleavage separated the communists and the majority of the people, also dividing Finland's political labor movement into communists and social democrats, as described in Chapter 3 above. For a long time it split the left side of the party system and the trade unions, and was a sharp divider of people in places of work.

The Social Democrats returned to normal parliamentary life after the civil war, but the radical leaders of the red rebellion founded the Finnish Communist Party. Originally, both leftist orientations aimed at socialism, but they were divided by the ideological conflict between democracy and democratic procedures, on the one hand, and "the dictatorship of the proletariat" through revolution, on the other. In the 1960s the Communist Party modernized its program, declaring that it aimed at a socialist revolution through peaceful and democratic means: through parliamentary decisions and changes in ownership. Its Moscow-oriented and more uncompromising wing could not accept this and organized an internal opposition to the more moderate wing. Later the end of the Soviet Union and the financial bankruptcy of the Finnish Communist Party, for all practical purposes, terminated the entire history of the party. Since 1991 the Left Alliance has continued its tradition, but denies any linkage to the communist past. In a modified form, traces of the cleavage remain relevant, especially in some trade unions.

Different approaches to Finland's foreign policy, and in particular the relationship toward the Soviet Union, were debated more intensively soon after the Second World War than in the 1970s, when the official foreign policy line was quite generally accepted. In the 1990s, Finland's role in the integration of Western Europe became a salient issue. As was mentioned above, when the basic decision, membership of the European Union, was decided in a national referendum in October 1994, regional differences in EU support were considerable. As an EU member Finland again had conflicting opinions on the next step, the common European currency and membership of Economic and Monetary Union. The EU issue continues to separate the antagonistic farmers from the favorable business world and even from most trade unions. Political parties differ on it, and some are internally divided about the EU questions (see Table 16.2 on page 269). In some parties, the rank-and-file also tend to disagree with the party leaders.

Other new confrontations have appeared. Protection of the environment was the strongest conflict in the minds of the people in 1991 (Table 4.5). Actions by small "eco-activist" groups have been directed against fur farming and the forest industry, and the "Natura 2000" environmental program of the EU caused much controversy. Increased nuclear energy has been an issue and in 2001 again returned very much to the fore as a major political conflict. And the typical Finnish belief in a conflict between politicians and the people was not at all muted by the slowness of the government in curing the serious unemployment problem.

Some structural and political differences that are familiar in many other countries are not salient in Finnish society. Most notably, the people are not divided by a religious cleavage, as people in the Netherlands, Austria, and Italy have been; nor are there currently divisive moral issues, such as the questions of abortion and death penalty in the United States.

A Case Story: The Nuclear Power Issue

According to Table 4.5, the most commonly perceived group conflict in Finland in the 1990s was more ideological than structural, as most people viewed the environmentalists and the industry's decision-makers as two groups that strongly opposed each other. This "nature conflict" was not related to the "class" and the "new" dimensions of social conflict. One aspect of the perceived nature conflict had to do with nuclear energy, which first became widely debated by the very end of the 1970s. Even some political parties were divided on this issue while the environmentalist movement focused on it as one of their most central goals.

In Finland the state-owned electric power company IVO started a nuclear reactor in 1977. The Olkiluoto company that was founded cooperatively by privately owned industrial companies, followed suit in 1978. The second nuclear reactors of both power stations began to operate in 1980, and for a while Finland was relatively the most nuclear-powered country in the world (to be soon overtaken by France). In 2000, when nuclear power was the source of 17 percent of the world's electricity generation, the percentage was 32.2 in Finland and 76.4 in France. Many countries were more dependent than Finland on nuclear power.[17]

The opponents of nuclear energy could draw some arguments from events abroad. Warnings about potential dangers included the Harrisburg accident in the USA in 1979 and, worst of all, the catastrophe in Chernobyl in 1986. Nuclear energy was losing political support. In Austria, a closely fought referendum blocked the start-up of the country's brand new reactor in 1978. After a referendum the Swedish government, too, decided in 1980 that the country would close all its nuclear power stations by 2010 (nine active ones and two under construction).[18] Both sides in the debate have made use of an environmental argument: radiation and nuclear waste vs. air pollution and the greenhouse effect.

Thus the opposing groups in the Finnish debate have been, on the one hand, the energy dependent and energy producing sectors of industry and, on the other hand, the environmentalist movement. To a very large extent their fight has involved an attempt to influence public opinion

---

17   31 countries had nuclear power stations in 2000. The percentage of nuclear power in electricity generation was 74 in Lithuania, 57 in Belgium, 53 in Slovakia, 47 in Ukraine, 39 in Sweden, 38 in Switzerland, and 34 in Japan, but 31 in Germany, 22 in Britain, 20 in the USA, 15 in Russia, and 12 in Canada (*SYF 2001*, p. 604).

18   In fact, the Swedish government is not acting in accordance with this decision. It plans to close nuclear reactors in about 2040 or 2050.

which, in turn, has influenced politicians. The decision to build a fifth reactor was first postponed to 1982. The "Energy Policy Association" EVY campaigned against nuclear power but did not gain enough public support to stop the two power companies from jointly applying in March 1986 for permission to build Finland's fifth nuclear reactor. If the application had been submitted a couple of months earlier (or if the Chernobyl accident had happened a couple of months later), the license would have been granted. But now public opinion changed sharply, the anti-nuclear movement gained strength, and politicians became very hesitant. A new law on nuclear energy made construction of a nuclear power station subject to a decision in principle by the government and by parliament.

Eventually, the opinion climate mellowed enough to warrant presenting the issue for a decision in parliament. The vote in September 1993 was very exciting and, unexpectedly, went against increased nuclear power. Thereby the environmentalist movement defeated the forest industry, the biggest labor unions, and many leading politicians. The power industry suffered its second big setback. The new government, which took office in 1995, refused to tackle the issue at all. In the meantime, the circumstances had changed somewhat after the country's economic slump: reasonably priced imported electricity had become easily available, and doubts were expressed about whether the new economy would consume as much energy as had been predicted.

When the Greens joined the new five-party coalition government in 1999, they demanded that nuclear power should not be dealt with again by this government. Elsewhere, Germany decided in 2000 that its 19 reactors would be closed by the end of the 2020s (but the issue was again debated in 2002). What cannot be doubted is Finland's need to secure additional electricity in the future. How to generate it is the salient issue. Even inside the government, the Green Minister of the Environment and the Social Democratic Minister of Trade and Industry disagreed sharply on the nuclear energy issue, while the nuclear industry, having carefully observed the dynamics of public opinion and the opinions of members of parliament, made its move in November 2000 and asked for parliament's permission to build a new reactor.

The new debate concerned the need to arrange a consultative referendum on this issue. According to a survey of MPs in November 2000, a majority did not want to refer the issue to a referendum (*Helsingin Sanomat* daily, 30 November 2000). Obviously, it was the MPs who were against additional nuclear power who wanted a consultative referendum, especially because public opinion was known to be adverse and a large majority of the people wanted to have a referendum (HS, 18 November 2000). The government was against any referendum but two unsuccessful private member's motions in parliament requested it. In January 2002 the government voted in favor of permitting the construction of more nuclear generating capacity and the members of parliament were given a free hand without party guidance in their vote in May. For both the proponents and the opponents of more nuclear power the situation was "now or never," because, obviously, whatever parliament decided would no longer be on the agenda of the new parliament elected in 2003.

The mass media intensively followed what MPs were deciding; the commerce committee reported in favor of the license in early May, and on May 24 Parliament decided in principal to allow construction of a fifth nuclear reactor. The winning margin was larger than expected, 107 to 92. Because both sides had pressured politicians and public opinion more quietly and with more factual information than in 1993, open reactions were not very emotional. Only a Greenpeace vehicle disturbed the forecourt of the parliament building with its loud siren. The Green League resigned from the five-party government and some environmentalists maintained that upcoming bureaucratic, political, economic, and technical problems would offer additional opportunities to block a new reactor's operation in 2008 or 2009, as is now projected.

One might say that the issue was exaggerated, because the permit merely gives private companies the right in principle to raise the proportion of nuclear power in Finland's total energy supply from 30 to 35 percent. For the environmentalist movement, however, this was an important issue of principle. Besides, Finland's decision may reverse the anti-nuclear trend that has prevailed in western Europe. The case suggests a few general observations:

– While many conflicting political interests are based on cleavages in social structure, others are more ideological and only remotely, if at all, linked to social differences; in this case age, sex[19] and engagement in industrial production are of minor significance.

– Decision-makers can be influenced both directly and through public opinion, and effective lobbying requires time, skill, and persistence. Threats from either side are less effective than presentation of factual information.

– Domestic decisions have international connotations and may activate interested outsiders, in this case both Greens in official positions in the EU as well as environmentalist activists, including the Greenpeace organization, which sent its ship to Helsinki in December 2000 to monitor the situation.

– While it is the duty of the representatives of the people to make political decisions, the referendum is a desired tool not only for those who emphasize direct democracy in principle, but also for those who want to use it as a strategic tool to prevent change.

19 Male members of parliament voted 85–40 in favor, female MPs 22–52 against. The cleavage between government and opposition was not very visible in this case, as all party groups except the Greens were split and 8 of the 17 government ministers voted against the government's proposal. – A gallup survey also showed the sex difference: more men than women approved parliament's decision (66% and 44%) while more women disliked it (23% and 40%). The old liked it better than the young.

5 Civil Society

Society is one half of an antithetic tandem in which the other is the state.
Immanuel Wallerstein 1987, p. 315

In Finland the state permeates civil society and civil society permeates the state.
Jussi Simpura in 2001

As was described in Chapter 2, Finland's functioning civil society originated in the 1830s, emerged during the latter half of the 19th century, and
was varied and relatively strong in the eve of independence. When Finland still was part of the Russian empire, civil society served the essential function of strengthening Finland's position and Finnish identity. Independence opened a new era, differentiating civil society more distinctly
to serve the goals of interest groups. Individual citizens felt that the state,
as the counterpoise of civil society, was closer to them and more useful
than before, and their role in the state became emphasized and concret-
ized. They assumed more responsibility as citizens.

This chapter carries the picture into the 21st century, dealing first with
trade unions and the other old organizations, then with more recently
born organizations, and especially with those active in the field of social
welfare and health care. For a fuller picture of the democratic system it
seems appropriate here to begin with a conceptual analysis of how civil
society relates to the state.

The Concepts

The state may be viewed as the antithesis of civil society. The state uses
power and is grounded on the rule of law. As a system built on law it
consists more of offices and tasks than of persons; rights and responsibilities are closely defined in the law. What is important is the imperson-
ality of power and the justifiability of measures. But the justification of

the state should also be viewed from the side of the citizens: they need to accept the state, regard it as credible, and find it trustworthy, in other words, they need to legitimize it. That goes beyond the obligations connected to power and legality. The state has to justify its power and prove its usefulness in practice (cf. Dyson 1980, pp. 101–118).

Thus, a democratic state links the citizens to the state through the law with a degree of independence and the authorities must be able to justify their measures. Legitimacy, in turn, ties the state and civil society more firmly together: the state's legitimacy implicitly includes the concept of civil society. Civil society cannot exist without the freedom of assembly and the freedom and opportunity of expression, which enable citizens to criticize the use of power and to attempt to influence it, while a democratic state cannot exist without a functioning civil society. Legitimacy also requires transparency, because confidence cannot be born if the citizenry and civil society are not aware of how power is being used.

Globalization expands the problems of civil society. Multinational organizations influence people's lives. Critical reactions from the citizens may focus on multinational corporations, or on the consequences of international treaties, or the lack of appropriate agreements. In a globalizing world also the functions of civil society internationalize. Numerous cross-national or worldwide movements have been born. For many of them the primary legitimacy target is the nation-state, but for perhaps a larger number it is an international organization.

Two principal lines of thought have concerned the relationship between individual citizens and the state, namely, the liberal and the communitarian. The *liberal* way of thinking that started with John Locke defines the citizen's role as individualistic and instrumental. It sees citizenship as membership of an organization; individuals, in a sense, work for the state in return for the benefits they get from their organizational membership. Citizens are private persons with pre-political or non-political interests.

The other way to look at citizenship is based on *communitarian* and ethical interpretation, tracing via political philosophy back to Aristotle. In it the model of citizenship is earned membership in a self-determining ethical community and citizens are integrated into the political community as parts of the entity. They can only form their personal and social identity in close contact with the other traditional and commonly acknowledged institutions.

Charles Taylor is a communitarian who has criticized the liberal view because it structures citizenship in a totally instrumental way and does not value participation and the feeling of unity as such. Jürgen Habermas pointed out that the holistic model of the communitarians, which considers every citizen fully bound, is insufficient because of the many aspects of modern politics. He admits, however, that it has its merits when compared with the organization model of the liberals, which leaves isolated individuals alone against the state apparatus, although private persons cannot realize their political autonomy only by looking after their special interests.

Habermas added that according to Taylor's remarks the universal principles of democratic states need to be anchored to the political culture typical of each country, whereas, in Habermas' own opinion, a political culture rising above different cultural backgrounds must function as a common denominator. To prove the one-sidedness of Taylor's view, he mentions multicultural democracies such as the United States and Switzerland as examples of countries where the principles of the constitution have been successfully implanted in anything but a uniform linguistic and cultural background. (Habermas 1994, pp. 24–28; Taylor 1989, p. 178.)

In reality the liberal and the communitarian models are hardly mutually exclusive. Individuals have interests that are at the same time related to themselves and the community. Social structures and situations influence the different emphases of these interests. A civil society cannot consist of individuals totally independent of each other, nor can it be a totally monolithic, normative entity. The fact alone that individuals are often forced to look after their own interests in cooperation with others, as is the case with interest organizations, means that the two models are ideal types rather than true descriptions of reality. When associations, organizations, and social movements are seen as central parts of civil society, what is emphasized implicitly is that autonomous citizens need cooperation in order to influence the state and society. On the other hand, a functioning civil society requires that the political culture adheres to the values and norms related to human rights and civil liberties.

Although civil society is more than the sum of associations, organizations, and social movements, it is normally studied using these kinds of collectives: they reflect the actions based on the freedom of association and other freedoms. The difference between associations and organizations and, on the other hand, social movements, concerns the degree of formality of structures. Social movements are born to pursue certain ideological, social, or international aims and they may evolve into associations and organizations, and associations may also be born without the movement phase. Associations, organizations, and federations have confirmed rules that define their goals and lines of action. The birth of associations and organizations does not necessarily end the existence of the movement, but usually it brings about some bureaucracy, as was pointed out by Max Weber as early as the beginning of the 20th century (cf. Siisiäinen 1998, p. 220).

A large number of associations and organizations and active participation in them are typical features of democratic countries. A civil society of course allocates its influence in conferring legitimacy through conventional democratic channels too, first and foremost through the election process. Ideal voting follows the liberal behavioral model: the citizens should decide themselves. Political socialization, the mass media, and various social contacts and ties, however, direct people's behavior in a way that blends in ingredients of the communitarian model.

Labor Market Organizations

Finns like to talk of their country as the promised land of associations. International comparisons seem to justify that image: there are very few countries where citizens have more association memberships than in Finland (Inglehart 1997, p. 190). Unionization is especially extensive; Sweden is probably the only country where the density of labor union membership is approximately as high as in Finland (Borg 1990, p. 314; Mansner 1999, p. 342). There are three major labor union confederations: the Central Organization of Finnish Trade Unions (SAK) with 1,071,000 members in its 31 unions in 2000, the Finnish Confederation of Salaried Employees (STTK) with 625,000 members, and the Confederation of Unions for Academic Professionals in Finland (AKAVA) with 391,000 members. Table 5.1 presents a list of their largest member unions in 2000.

The history of unionization remained multi-phased and colorful after the early stages described in Chapter 2. In 1917, when social contrasts became acute, the membership of the Trade Union Organization of Finland rose from 42,000 to 160,000. That year, employees organized almost 500 strikes and the general strike in November was clearly a new development on the road to the 1918 civil war. After the Whites had won the war, membership of the Trade Union Organization dropped to approximately 20,000 in March 1919. For the union movement, the 1920s was a period when the Finnish Communist Party had a strong background influence. Employers responded by selecting their employees on political grounds and by using strikebreakers. The Trade Union Organization, with a membership of approximately 90,000 in 1928, started to dissolve after the moderate social democrats were left outside the radical movement. It was abolished in October 1930 and only weeks later the moderate social democrats founded the Confederation of Finnish Trade Unions (SAK) (Haatanen 1998, pp. 35–51). As mentioned earlier, this organization earned its legitimacy during the Winter War of 1939–1940.

The history of the organization of government employees has not been so exciting. There had been various kinds of activity already before the First World War, but actual interest organization activity did not truly exist at all until Finland's independence. Organizations of officials from various fields founded the Partnership of Intellectual Work in 1922. Its birth reflected many social changes: democratization, growth in the number of civil servants, weakening of the status of officials from the elite to the middle class, and the loss of the financial privileges enjoyed in class society (cf. op. cit., pp. 56–57). The true occupational interest organization activity of government employees did not begin until the second half of the 20th century.

Table 5.1

Membership of employee organizations in 2000

Organizations	Number of members
Central Organization of Finnish Trade Unions (SAK)	1,071,000
Trade Union for Municipal Sector (KTV)	208,000
Service Unions United	201,000
The Finnish Metalworkers' Union	170,000
Construction Trade Union	79,000
Finnish Transport Workers' Union (AKT)	51,000
The Wood and Allied Workers' Union	50,000
Paperworkers' Union	49,000
Finnish Foodstuff Workers' Union	41,000
Affiliated Unions of the Joint Organization of State Employees (VTY)	36,000
Chemical Workers' Union	35,000
Finnish Electrical Workers' Union	30,000
Ten others	119,000
Finnish Confederation of Salaried Employees (STTK)	625,000
Union of Salaried Employees	126,000
Union of Health Care Services (Tehy)	121,000
Pardia - Confederation of State Employees' Unions	88,000
Federation of Municipal Officers (KVL)	74,000
The Finnish Union of Practical Nurses	60,000
Financial Sector Union SUORA	39,000
Sixteen others	117,000
The Confederation of Unions for Academic Professionals in Finland (AKAVA)	391,000
Trade Union of Education in Finland (OAJ)	108,000
The Finnish Association of Graduate Engineers	51,000
Union of Professional Engineers in Finland	49,000
The Finnish Association of Graduates in Economics and Business Administration	37,000
The Finnish Medical Association	18,000
Twenty-seven others	128,000

Sources: *SYF 2001*, p. 380; www.sttk.fi.

The strong social and political influence of the trade union movement was felt immediately after the Second World War. Society became more radical and the political Left gained electoral support (cf. Table 8.1 on page 146). Membership of the SAK reached 340,000 in 1947. The density of union membership was now at 40 percent, having been at 7 percent before the war. The period of 1944–1948 in Finnish history has been called the "years of peril." As was described in Chapter 3, the communists aimed at taking over the trade unions. Power struggles between communists and social democrats were raging in most parts of Europe, and Finland's geopolitical location was especially vulnerable. However, the communists failed in their attempt to conquer the commanding heights of the trade union movement. Finland's slide toward a people's democracy definitely ended in 1948. The communists suffered a defeat in the parliamentary election, and the social democrats were victorious in that year's trade union election.

The first general agreement between the Confederation of Finnish Trade Unions (SAK) and the Confederation of Finnish Employers (STK), concerning the whole country, was reached in 1944. It determined not only wage levels but also forbade striking without advance warning. Nevertheless, the Communists kept organizing wildcat strikes until the 1950s in order to stir up workers and to cause disturbance in society. In addition to several strikes, the SAK threatened a general strike as many as four times by 1950. These were avoided because the employers agreed to the wage claims. But the recession that started in the middle of the 1950s made the employers unwilling to accept the wage demands of the SAK and a general strike began on 1 March 1956, joined by more wage-earners than there were SAK members. The strike, the largest in the history of independent Finland, lasted 19 days but proceeded in a surprisingly peaceful way. The government, however, considered the situation dangerous and tried to arbitrate. Finally, the employers conceded the wage rises. For the workers the achievement was a Pyrrhic victory: wage rises triggered inflation that cancelled out the increase in purchasing power by autumn that year. Taking into consideration the pay foregone for the duration of the strike and the empty state of strike funds, it clearly turned into a bitter defeat.

The 1956 general strike was a lesson to remember for the trade union movement. Two changes became visible in the strategy of the movement. Firstly, if strikes became unavoidable, the tendency was to plan them carefully so as to stop all activity in the most important sectors while other sectors could continue to operate and generate resources to support the strike. Secondly, it was realized that fighting for money alone is not wise because financial achievements were vulnerable to inflation. The quality aspects of working life had to be considered as well.

Attitudes towards communism were among the factors that split the trade union movement and the Social Democratic Party in the period from the late 1950s to 1969. A great majority of SDP members remained in the more traditional (right-wing) party, whereas the minority formed a more left-wing Social Democratic League (TPSL). In the trade union movement the situation was quite the reverse: the new Trade Union Organization of Finland (SAJ) was far more right-wing than the bigger Confederation of Finnish Trade Unions (SAK), whose large membership included communists. The Communist Party of the Soviet Union had long had some influence on the Finnish trade union movement via the large communist minority. Now the CIA stepped in and supported the SAJ financially. The disintegration of the SDP ended before the mid-1960s and the division of the trade union movement was over by the end of the decade. A formally new organization, the Central Organization of Finnish Trade Unions (SAK) united the two competing groups and its membership reached 600,000, more than ever in the history of the Finnish trade union movement. It was obvious that foreign forces would hardly play any role in the Finnish trade union movement in the future.

Harmonization initiated the growth of the trade union movement and its very significant role. The SAK had already expanded into a large organization of over one million people by the mid-1970s. Despite reduced employment in the secondary sector, the SAK has remained an organization of approximately 1,100,000 union members, establishing its position as the biggest and most influential organization.

However, the organizations of those with a higher education have grown immensely. The Central Organization of Salaried Employees (TVK), founded in 1957 and consisting primarily of women in the public sector, expanded to close to 400,000 members at the beginning of the 1990s. The Finnish Confederation of Salaried Employees (STTK) has grown even faster: from less than 50,000 members in 1970 to 625,000 members by the beginning of the new millennium. A great change took place in 1992, when the TVK dissolved due to economic difficulties. Most of its members switched to the STTK, leaving Finland with three trade union confederations. The AKAVA of academic professionals grew from over 40,000 members in 1970 to 391,000 in 2000. While the number of university graduates has risen fast, the fact that their income level in comparison to other groups dropped motivated them to organize.

The trade union movement faces three employers' organizations in the private sector, two of them big and one small. In addition there are a few public sector employer organizations. None of them has experienced bitter, ideological power struggles similar to those of the employees' organizations. However, there have often been clashes between the different interests of large and small companies. The above-mentioned Confederation of Finnish Employers (STK) was founded in 1907 and was regarded as the central organization of large-scale industry. In 1992 it merged with the Confederation of Finnish Industries, which did not add members but rationalized operations. The new Confederation of Finnish Industry and Employers (TT) represents employers of approximately 545,000 workers and salaried employees, only 20 percent of whom work in small companies. The Employers' Confederation of Service Industries (PT) was founded in 1996. It came to replace a central organization that had primarily represented companies in commerce. In 2000 its member companies employed 349,000 people. The public sector, which employs 540,000 people, has two employer organizations, namely, the Commission for Local Authority Employers and the State Employers' Office.

At the end of 1994 there were 2,064,000 members in Finnish trade union organizations, including small, independent organizations. Because the number of wage earners was 2,137,000, the density of union membership appeared as high as 96.5 percent. However, in addition to wage earners the member listings included many others (pensioners, students, non-paying members). Actual density of union membership was 78.5 percent, which still is internationally high. Sweden reported its density to be 82.5 in 1990, but it was not announced whether this percentage included others than wage earners. Elsewhere in Europe the percentages are much lower, normally 30–50, and in France the rate was only 9.8 percent in 1990. (Haatanen 1998, pp. 105–108.) In the United States union membership was 13.9 percent in 1999 (*The World Almanac 2001*, p. 171).

The fundamental reason for the success of the trade union movement in Finland is that it has managed to acquire a major role in social and economic policies. A system of incomes policies has been created since the end of the 1960s. In it the central interest organizations and the state together with the other public administration institutions negotiate on the important decisions of economic policy. An organizational prerequisite of this change was the above-described harmonization of the trade union movement.

In addition, the change contributed to wise economic policy. Inflation had been at a high level almost continuously since the Second World War. The damage to foreign trade had been solved by repeated devaluations. According to Keynesian economic theory, the aim now was to apply an incomes policy so as to control both demand inflation and cost inflation. It was in the state's interest to use agreements that would commit the big organizations to adhering to both wage and price discipline. Incomes policies truly started in 1968, after a large devaluation the previous year. The agreement of 1968, signed by all central interest organizations, has been a frame of reference in later incomes policy agreements, although inflation was not successfully prevented until the 1990s. Difficulties have been caused by individual unions, which have not always adhered to the general agreements made by the central organizations, and by wage rises that have exceeded agreements (Pekkarinen and Vartiainen 1993, pp. 310–317).

Among the state's interests in the incomes policy agreements are economic growth, a reasonable interest rate level, creating more jobs, and raising general welfare. This is why the government has been ready to negotiate about the taxation of wage-earners and companies, social policy benefits, the laws on working conditions, and so on. The incomes policy negotiations after the mid-1970s have also settled the size of income tax adjustments due to inflation. It is in the employers' interest to uphold a good working atmosphere and competitiveness. The incomes policy system apparently increases social solidarity, although in collective bargaining, unions may express very different views. The Finnish system seems relatively successful. It is also explained by the country's unique historical and geopolitical factors.

The unions continued to grow in the 1990s despite the changes in ideological, economic, and social structures, which in many other countries have caused problems to the trade union movement. The Finnish system may indeed be regarded exceptional. The political space of the labor movement has narrowed because the central source of social conflicts, relations of production, has lost some of its significance. This narrowing is due to many reasons. A growing proportion of the labor force works in the private and public sector service industry, in which the problems of relations of production are not as clear as in traditional blue-collar work. Employees have also reached a new understanding of the interests they share with employers, such as the aim of preserving jobs by upholding competitiveness. It has even been claimed that the foundation of the labor movement – that is, collective identification with a workplace – is falling apart (Ilmonen 1998, pp. 26–27).

There are also groups other than the labor market organizations that have influence on incomes agreements. The most notable of the organizations not part of the labor market sector proper, but having a significant impact on incomes policy, is the Central Union of Agricultural Producers and Forest Owners (MTK). It was founded as early as 1917. Until the Second World War its primary function was to act as an educational organization, but when the number of farms increased greatly after the war, the organization expanded rapidly and adapted new tasks: It became a typical interest organization and, at the same time, pursued national objectives that were important when the country was threatened by the dangers of Soviet Communism. The organization has been controlled by the Agrarian Union, since 1965 the Center Party. It had influence in economic policy especially when it was still possible to restrict the import of agricultural products by tariffs and when the Agrarian/Center Party had significant political power.

A new era began when Finland joined the European Union. The MTK still influences incomes policy because many of its members are forest owners, who can jointly affect the price of timber. There are over 440,000 private forest owners in Finland, nearly 330,000 of whom are members of Forest Management Associations. Since approximately 80 percent of the domestic wood purchased by industry comes from small privately owned forests, these statutory associations also influence incomes policy. The Forestry Council of the MTK works closely together with the Forest Management Associations, which explains the significant influence of the MTK (cf. Henttinen 1999, pp 166–169; www.mmm.fi/metsatalous).

Incomes policy alone does not explain the high density of union membership; some features of the Finnish employment model also influence it. Since 1968, employers have, as a gesture of social harmony, agreed to deduct the union membership fees directly from wages.[20] Consequently, the unions have become wealthier and have been able to offer various benefits to their members. Another factor is that union membership fees are tax deductible in personal taxation. By making this concession in 1968, the state helped the parties to reach agreement and since then the practice has remained permanent. Thirdly, the 1971 law on unemployment funds made the administration of the funds a task of the unions. To be entitled to unemployment benefit from an unemployment fund, a wage earner has to pay unemployment insurance. Although it is possible to belong to the fund without being a union member, in practice joining the fund has also meant joining a union.

One more explanation of the high density of union membership is that, in Finland and the other Nordic countries, membership by women is just as common as by men. Besides, in Finland, unlike countries of lower union membership, the unionization of salaried employees has risen to an even higher level than that of workers (Haatanen 1998, pp. 75–77, 109).

So there are several reasons why the disintegration of people's collective identification is not leading to a loss of members from the trade union movement. A study of the values of central organization members, made in the mid-1990s, classified values into two categories: collective and individualistic.[21] In the trade unions of the SAK, age divided the members into two relatively clear-cut parts: those born before the end of the 1950s were collectively oriented while younger members were individualistic. The line of business had similar effects: those in the private service sector were individualistically oriented; and there are relatively many young workers in this sector. In the confederation of salaried employees (STTK) no similar distinction between different age groups was found. Within the unions for academic professionals (AKAVA) the difference was the reverse of the SAK: the young had the strongest collective orientation, the old were individualistically oriented. (Jokivuori et al. 1996.)

It is surprising that the attitudes of young workers and young people with a university degree differ greatly from those of the older members in their respective organizations. The collective orientation of young salaried employees with university degrees, however, does not seem to be connected to communitarian solidarity, as is the case with the old employees in the SAK, but rather to their lower wages and more insecure position in working life. The collectivity of young salaried employees

20 This gesture of goodwill has also been explained by reference to the personal relationship between Päiviö Hetemäki, managing director of the employers' STK and Niilo Hämäläinen, chairman of the employees' SAK. They were companions-in-arms in the Second World War and had great respect and trust for each other.

21 Members with collective values emphasize equalized income, equality between men and women, workplace democracy, and decisions on benefits made by organization representatives. Individualistic values prefer individually agreed terms of employment and more limited tasks for organizations.

illustrates an instrumental attitude, while the collectivity of the older employees is an indication of internalized values and solidarity (cf. Ilmonen and Jokivuori 1998, pp. 156–159). The young university-educated salaried employees represent the fastest growing part of the labor force.

Since the mid-1990s, Finland's labor force has grown faster than union membership. Thereby the level of unionization went down from 78.5 percent in 1994 to an estimated 72 percent in 2002. Although unionization still ranks exceptionally high in international comparisons, the new trend suggests that wage earners are losing interest in joining unions. The unions themselves explain this as a consequence of the economy's structural change that has made short-term jobs increasingly numerous, because temporary workers are not as motivated to join unions as permanent ones. Furthermore, wage earners can join an unemployment fund without becoming union members. Despite recent difficulties in recruiting new members, labor unions remain very influential in Finnish society.

In the political system the Finnish pattern may be regarded as an example of corporatism. If observed from this point of view, it is a case of bargained corporatism, in which free collective agreements and directive measures of the state are combined (cf. Ponton 1984, p. 150).

Other Old Movements

While the labor market organizations have become a part of Finland's daily politics and social life, some old movements have not kept their traditional social position. The tasks that once powered them are no longer of interest and do not inspire Finns. The achieved goals may be treasured, but cherishing is not the same as an uplifting aspiration towards goals. Thus, the *Society of Popular Education* is still operating, but its importance is not what it was a century ago, even though it has adapted its program to such modern functions as adult education, language training, education for international understanding, etc.

The temperance movement is also operating but its tone of voice does not carry the same weight as it did at the beginning of the 20th century. Its values have long influenced the thinking of the Finnish people. When the first parliament in 1907 passed the prohibition law, the importance of the temperance movement was decisive. The law was not, however, implemented until 1919. Just as in the United States, it proved a failure and after a consultative referendum in 1931 the law was annulled with the alcohol law of 1932. Even after that, the influence of the temperance movement has remained in the values of many people and, as a result of the ideology of the movement, Finland's policy towards alcohol remains more restrictive than policies in Southern or Central Europe. Currently, alcohol policy and related educational information emphasize public health work and its basis, scientific research, while average Finns are less and less conscious of the influence of the temperance movement in their own culture.

The *youth society* movement has also lost the very important position it had until the mid-twentieth century. Back then, it was mainly based on activities organized by young people from rural areas. Urbanization and modern mass communication have narrowed its arena. It still organizes significant art events for the young on a yearly basis, and cultural organizations such as the Finnish Folk Music Association and the Association for Free Cultural Activities are part of it. But the movement no longer has its previous status.

The 1944 armistice treaty led to the dissolution of some movements that were claimed to be fascist. The most notable ones were the *Civil Guard* defense organization and its sister organization, the *Lotta Svärd*. The Civil Guards were formed in the autumn of 1917 when disagreements between the Whites and Reds came to a head. In January 1918, they were appointed as government troops and for a while they formed the majority of the Finnish White Army. The ideological scale of their local units varied from the political center to extreme rightism. The status of the Civil Guard Organization became official with its incorporation into the Finnish armed forces in 1927. Thus the president of the republic became its supreme commander. At the same time, it was brought under tighter state control. Left-wingers were not admitted to the organization until February 1940, when some thousand social democrats joined it. At its highpoint, total membership topped 100,000. There is no doubt it was one of the factors that allowed Finland's successful defensive battle in the Winter War of 1939–1940.

The wartime role of the Lotta Svärd also turned out to be remarkable, for its members significantly contributed to national defense in air surveillance, war hospitals and even field hospitals, communication, etc. In 1944, the membership of the organization reached 220,000. This women's organization was largely responsible for the total involvement of Finnish society in the war. Now it is reservist organizations, which do not have any ideological preconditions for membership, that extol patriotic defensive spirit.

Two old movements have continued their activities. These are the cooperative and sports movements, both influential in today's society. In the *cooperative movement,* similarities to the labor movement, and particularly to the trade union movement, can be observed. Even the memberships of these three movements overlap to a great degree. Both the cooperative and the trade union movement are tormented by the weakening of collective identification. This is also true for the one core group of cooperative movement supporters, the rural population. The growth of average farm size and the transition to a demanding, competitive economy have altered *agriculture* in a way that has been described as a profound change of values, or a transformation from a way of life into a form of business.

The cooperative movement continues to operate strongly despite all the factors that are presumed to weaken the motivation of the membership in a late modern society. Cooperation remains one of the mainstays of Finnish civil society. Its activities cover a number of different fields: commercial cooperation between producers and consumers, cooperation between agricultural producers and forest owners, dairy and slaughterhouse production, banking, communication (telephone cooperatives) and water supply and sewerage, etc. The memberships of these cooperatives are large: in 2001 the Finnish Co-operative Wholesale Society, SOK, had 787,000 members and the Cooperative Tradeka Corporation, which has its origins in the old left-wing cooperative movement but no longer has ideological ties, was owned by 370,000 consumers. The Okobank Group Central Cooperative has the largest relative influence; in March 2002 its number of owner-members topped one million. Its market share of euro-denominated deposits was 33 percent. These three memberships totaled 2,357,000, making Finland one of the most "cooperative" countries in the world and perhaps the most cooperative market economy country.

In the early days of the cooperative movement, the activities of small cooperatives had features similar to those of the communitarian model. The large cooperative central organizations typically developed into economic bureaucracies and their membership became alienated. Recent years have seen the emergence of a new type of cooperative activity that aims to restore the original ideals of the movement and at the same time to create activities that meet people's needs in a modern society. The economic slump of the early 1990s added to this. For example, various marketing and purchasing cooperatives and those providing welfare services have been formed (Hänninen 1995, pp. 67–69). Fresh ideas may enliven activities and restore the enthusiasm of the good old days.

The *sports movement* has undergone many changes over the decades. Already in the early 20th century, competitive sports began to dominate this large movement, and the Finnish Gymnastics and Sports Federation (SVUL, the Finnish Central Sports Federation as of 1962), which was licensed in 1906, represented competitive sports above all. After the civil war, political disagreements led to the foundation of the Finnish Labor Sports Federation (TUL) in 1919. Thirdly, the Swedish speakers wanted to safeguard their linguistic identity and founded the Swedish Central Sports Federation of Finland (CIF) in 1946. The Sport for All Association, which focuses on recreational sports, is considerably younger and more moderate in its sphere of activities than the above-mentioned organizations.

Sport and various sports organizations attract masses of people from all strata of society. Apparently they have unifying effects as there are no major disagreements between various organizations with different ideological backgrounds. Competitive sports unites people: When Finns watch their compatriots compete in international events, what counts is how the athletes perform, not which sports organization they are members of. Political barriers have also broken down among the memberships of sports organizations. A report from the 1970s showed that the membership of the "bourgeois" SVUL was comprised as follows: the working class (42 percent), white-collar employees (32 percent) and farmers (28 percent). In the 1980s, 9 percent of bourgeois party supporters who belonged to a sports organization were members of the "leftist" TUL, and that proportion was on the rise (Hentilä 1992, pp. 366–367). This kind of organizational behavior, in which politics and sports are not dependent on each other, has become more general since the 1980s as the old left-bourgeois cleavage has increasingly lost significance in Finnish politics.

In 1993 the independent central organizations joined forces and founded the Finnish Sports Federation (SLU) that consists of the three central organizations, national associations of different kinds of sports, and some regional associations and special sport clubs, altogether 127 societies with 1,100,000 individual members. Of them, 338,000 belong to the TUL and 120,000 to the CIF, and the rest, some 640,000 people, are members of the associations that belonged to the SUL. The aim of joining forces was to increase the influence of sports upon the public sector, because that is where most of the sports' funding comes from. This is especially true when new facilities are built. The state has reciprocating interests, such as the favorable impact of sports on public health. (Heikkala 1998; www.cif.fi; www.slu.fi; www.tul.fi.)

The New Movements

The old movements in Finland were also characterized by their unique, historical role in nation building. And, as in other countries, their influence has been based on large memberships. Typical of new movements is their involvement in international, even global questions and their influence through the media rather than through large memberships.

New movements have been a consequence of changes in western culture. One of the major changes is the increasing dominance of economy in today's society. In the United States, dominant economic values have left a lasting mark on society, and such values came under criticism in that country as early as the beginning of the 1960s. *Social Indicators,* a US publication issued in 1966, states on its cover page that "economic indicators have thus far dealt not with how good but with how much, not with the quality of our lives but rather with the quantity of goods and dollars." The importance of the quality of life was given prominence in a NASA publication (sic!) by the researchers of the American Academy of Arts and Sciences. The study stressed that new kinds of "measures of social performance are all the more important in a 'postindustrial' society, one in which the satisfaction of human interests and values has at least as high a priority as the pursuit of economic goals." (Gross 1966, p. viii.)

The contradiction between economic ends and the quality of life is only one, if essential, example of the contradictions that began to emerge in the 1960s. Already from the late 1950s, the Beat Generation presented new views about man's subjectivity. Similar cultural criticism was presented somewhat later by the hippie movement. Rebellion against the prevailing culture was shown in attempts to penetrate the roots of human experience, in a desire to seek ecstasy even in drugs, and in a conscious emphasis of rootlessness. The Beat Generation was interested in eastern religions and also openly brought out the possibility of sexual deviation. Many favored leftist ideas but it was impossible for the beatniks to identify with systems such as communism, which did not tolerate deviation (Burner 1996, pp. 113–125).

Another movement that started in the United States and rejected the dominant culture was the student movement. Its protests continued throughout the 1960s. It has been explained, in part, by the exploding numbers of university students and by their widening social backgrounds from the late 1950s, but these are certainly only one aspect in the complex phenomenon. The themes included the status of racial minorities, opposition to the Vietnam War and rejection of university administrations. The radical students protested against mainstream capitalist culture without acknowledging its pluralism. (Op. cit., pp. 134–166.) In Europe the movement adapted themes that were much the same as those in the United States. Students, also in Finland, included environmental problems in their programs. These were regarded as resulting from capitalism and many saw the solution in the Soviet system.

In the sixties and seventies, the programs of the new movements in Finland included pacifism and equality, with specific issues such as feminism, the rights of sexual and other minorities, the problems of developing countries, and economic exploitation. Other themes were tolerance, liberal sexual behavior, the Vietnam War, and later on, environmental questions (cf. Konttinen 1998, pp. 187–195). These movements had an interest in rational societal planning, which was not as apparent in their American counterparts.

The ideals of rational planning received great support in Finland. This can be largely traced to a plan of a welfare state by Pekka Kuusi, a senior administrator and researcher in social policy. His publication in 1961, "The social policies in the 60s" (*60-luvun sosiaalipolitiikka*), was a most remarkable book. It includes a strong message of the applicability and indispensability of rational planning. Kuusi and many other Finnish experts were unaware that such planning had been already criticized with good reason at the end of the 1950s and replaced mainly by a strategy of disjointed incrementalism (cf. March and Simon 1958; Myrdal 1958; Braybrooke and Lindblom 1963).

Since the new movements tried to bring about immediate far-reaching social changes, the model of rational planning seemed very promising. More realistic options to reform society would hardly have been equally inspiring. The model had utopian elements, such as comprehensiveness and the idea that it was possible to make use of perfect information. In Finland, rational planning inspired not only the politically radical youth, who connected it to the development of socialist countries, but many others as well. What was essential was the strong belief that societies could be changed.

However, reforming a society is not merely a matter of reason and rationality; it requires morality too. It is not surprising that modern ethics deals with similar issues to many of the new movements: poverty in the world, environmental questions, problems of crime and criminal policy, fundamental questions involved in sexual behavior, human relations, equality, discrimination, treatment of animals, ethics of business and economy, and issues of war and peace (cf. e.g. Singer 1994, pp. 273–395).

Pacifism is one of the central areas of morality. Founded in 1920, the Peace Union of Finland, tinged with liberal and Christian ideas, stood for traditional pacifism in Finland. Its aim was to promote the views of the League of Nations and later the United Nations, in solving conflicts. In 1949, the supporters of the extreme left and the Agrarian Union (later the Center Party) created an organization named the Finnish Peace Committee. It was a member of the communist-led *World Peace Council* and undertook to cherish Finnish-Soviet relations (Litmanen 1998, p. 284). However, the organization seemed to consider political "expediency," which meant largely agreeing with Soviet views, to be more important than true pacifism.

Modern pacifism began to spread to Finland from the West in the early 1960s. In England, the Committee of 100 was founded as a result of the criticism that Bertrand Russell directed towards nuclear armament. Finland followed suit and an organization of the same name was created. Its purpose was to function as a provocative pacifist forum that questioned the prevailing defense doctrines and even demanded unilateral disarmament. In West Germany, for example, the equivalent organization encountered severe criticism, whereas in Finland the organization's provocativeness was interpreted as peaceful activity. It was a discussion forum, above all, for young academic intellectuals. Only the student organization of the Conservative Party wanted to steer clear of the activities of the Committee of 100, and to make its stand it adopted the name "Committee of 1000" (Tuhatkunta).

The Committee of 100 participated in demonstrations for the peace cause but at the same time urged social reforms. Several of its members took part in single-issue movements. The leaders of Finnish foreign policy in the 21st century were members of the organization in their youth: President Tarja Halonen, Prime Minister Paavo Lipponen, and Foreign Minister Erkki Tuomioja. They all were members of the Social Democratic Party, which took a cautious view of the organization, fearing that it would fall into communist hands. The Committee of 100 even inferred that the then-President of Finland, Urho Kekkonen, was a member of their organization (Suominen 1997, pp. 165–167).

In a number of countries anti-war movements and environmental movements were connected by their mutual interest in opposing nuclear energy. In Finland, however, their values came into conflict when the Finnish Peace Committee took a stand in favor of nuclear plants because nuclear energy was favored in the USSR. Other organizations promoting pacifism did not take part in the discussion about nuclear energy to any significant extent. In 1977 the environmental activists set up their anti-nuclear organization (Energy policy society – Alternative to nuclear power) (cf. Litmanen 1998, pp. 289–291).

The Committee of 100 functioned as an example for the formation of a number of movements whose origins went further back in history than those of the Committee of 100. One such organization was the Tricont, which was founded in 1968 to support the developing countries. The United Nations paid attention to Third World problems, which were already sparking discussion among the academic youth in the early 1960s. The name Tricont referred to the Tricontinental symbol used by the OSPAAL – a solidarity organization of Asian, African and Latin American peoples. In the Finnish organization, political barriers were becoming blurred, which has become characteristic of late modern society. The membership included people from nearly all political parties and, in addition, independents and religious persons. Often the members criticized their own parties and assumed the political line of the New Left. The Tricont represented itself as anti-imperialistic, criticizing the politics and policies of the United States, the Soviet Union, and China (Tuominen 1991, pp. 216–222).

One typical single-issue movement of the age was the "November Movement", born in 1967, whose aim was to achieve a rational and humane control policy. The movement's membership overlapped with the Committee of 100. It saw that people who were different in some respect were often treated arbitrarily and harshly because they were different (op. cit., pp. 229–235). Soon the revolutionary left wing of the movement gained the upper hand and control policy came to be seen as part of a socialist revolution. Thereafter the movement began to decline. However, its propagation and vast publicity helped to soften the existing strict attitudes towards deviation.

The overall image of the new movements that were born in the 1960s–1970s involved the *student movement*, mentioned above. As in the United States, the Finnish movement attacked the power structure of universities. The student organizations aimed at a system in which the administration of universities would be elective, on the "one man - one vote" principle. The idea was to achieve an equal opportunity for all, from first-year students to professors, to have their say about the composition of administrative organs. The professors and most of the staff found the demand unviable because they considered universities to be expert organizations. However, in 1970 a reform bill based on the "one man - one vote" principle was nearly passed in parliament. MPs who were familiar with how universities functioned saw the danger and, by filibustering, managed to defer the proposed reform bill past the March 1970 parliamentary elections (see Pesonen 1982).

Even though the objectives of the student movement were overambitious and unrealistic, they probably prepared the way for an administrative reform in the 1970s. The adopted quota system brought representation of students and staff to the administrative bodies of the universities.

Earlier the Finns had seen how students could fall under the spell of fanatics. Such fears did not prove unfounded when the Soviet-oriented "Stalinists" gained a strong foothold in many Finnish student organizations at the beginning of the 1970s. However, this radicalism rapidly came to an end, not the least because the students were able to get a closer view of Soviet conditions. History has proved that student movements are not long-lived and that students change their minds quickly. Their organizations, on the other hand, are well established in Finland. Students' interests are represented on the national scene by the National Union of Students (SYL), founded in 1921, and some student organizations own valuable property, including dormitories.

The *women's movement* has survived since the 19th century. Nevertheless, a qualitative transition took place when the task of women's emancipation was taken up by an organization called the "Association 9," founded in 1966. It was the only women's organization that managed to increase its membership in that radical decade. Instead of equal rights the organization began to speak about gender roles in the effort to make women's and men's roles more similar. It also wanted to alter the role of men. Almost one-third of the members were men, which further illustrates that the organization was not merely a women's interest organization; its goal was to change the whole culture (Jallinoja 1983, pp. 123–190).

Neo-feminism proper – as distinguished from traditional feminism and its striving for emancipation, in which economic status and political power were essential questions – has not received strong support in Finland. Women have long participated in political organizations within the party system, and this traditional and established channel seems to have curbed the feminist movement. Ever since the early 20th century, the proportion of women in various political fields has been internationally high. Until the 1970s, the percentage of women in parliament was higher in Finland than in any other west European country. It was not until the end of that decade that the other Nordic countries, except for Iceland, caught up with Finland. Neo-feminists' theses on women's social and sexual rights and physical integrity have not caused any major public stir because the demands have been channeled into the political arena and the official equality policy. It is justifiable to characterize Finland as the home of "state feminism" (cf. Bergman 1998, p. 170–181).

Women's participation in social activities through the trade union and cooperative movements and party organizations has been tens of times higher than that through the women's movement. The importance of the women's movement has been based on its role as the societal vanguard and, especially since the 1960s, on its extensive use of publicity. One of the remaining problems is economic inequality, mainly concerning the wage differential between men and women, but in fact the most efficient group to urge improvement in the issue is the large body of trade union women. Another problem, if a diminishing one, is the small number of women occupying top positions in businesses and public administration.

Modern civil society covers such a wide range of activities that it would not be possible to outline all of them here. What need to be emphasized, however, are the *environmentalists*. They attract plenty of publicity and, as was shown in Table 4.5, are regarded by most people as conflicting with the economy. The Greens began to inspire young people in the 1970s, won their own representation in parliament in 1983, and thereafter founded their political party. But they form only a part of the picture. The Nature Society was founded in 1938, and in 1969 it helped to establish the Finnish Union for Natural Protection, which does nationwide education work and participates in environmental planning. The World Wildlife Fund has had a Finnish branch since 1972. *Greenpeace*, a radical although nonviolent international organization that fights polluters, also has active members in Finland. Some nature groups are prone to advance their goals through illegal acts. A notorious example were the "fox girls," activists who have damaged fur farms.

ATTAC was founded in Paris in 1998 to protect democracy against undesirable consequences of the globalized economy. The Finnish ATTAC started in 2001; it wants the Tobin tax imposed on speculative transfers of capital and opposes the privatization of health services, education, and government enterprises. Other international organizations advocating high moral principles include the Friends of the Earth Finland, which was founded in 1996 (internationally in 1971) to further "the creation of a democratic and economically sustainable society" and "social, economic, political and intergenerational equality."

Amnesty International, established in 1961, has been active in Finland since 1967. It is a global organization working to protect human rights. Paying special attention to autocratic systems, it focuses on "grave abuses of the rights to physical and mental integrity, freedom of conscience and expression, and freedom from discrimination." It is a sharp opponent of recent limitations or attempted limitations of citizens' personal freedoms in connection with anti-terrorist government activity. Amnesty attracts plenty of publicity in Finland but has only about 9000 members. The one area where it has been in disagreement with the Finnish government concerns conscientious objectors who refuse military training.[22]

The anti-globalization activists are international movements that are typically held together through intensive Internet contacts. The Finnish activists have taken part in big international demonstrations, but apparently not at all in the related violence. Certain other new international movements have not gained mentionable foothold in Finland. For instance, there have been hardly any neo-Nazis comparable to those found in Germany and Sweden.

---

22 Compulsory military service lasts 180, 270, or 360 days, the alternative and easier option of civilian service 395 days. A majority of Finns regard civilian servicemen as freeloaders, while Amnesty claims that civilian service lasts too long. It is particularly critical of Finland for having "prisoners of conscience," those who refuse to do even civilian service.

The significance of the new movements has no doubt been greater than what could be inferred from the number of their members. They have often exposed to the public problems which political parties and state institutions have neglected. At the same time, they have been pioneers in adapting new values, which has paved Finland's way to a late modern society.

Social Welfare and Health Care Organizations

The grouping into old and new movements does not apply to most social welfare and health care organizations. Their objectives and lines of action differ from those of the movements discussed above. The Finnish Red Cross was formed as early as 1877 and the Finnish Association for Mental Health in 1897, whereas organizations such as the Center of Expertise in Child Welfare and the Association for Care-Giving Relatives and Friends were founded in the 1990s. However, approximately 35 percent of these organizations date back to the 1960s–1970s (Social Welfare and Health Care Organizations in Finland. 1999). During those decades, Finland's fast modernization process included extensive political reforms on social welfare and health care. The new winds in setting sociopolitical goals illustrate that one aim was to develop civil society at the same time as the state was given new obligations to take care of its citizens.

The objectives of social welfare and health care organizations are usually clearly defined and do not include general political aims or aims intended to change the culture, which are typical of most old and new movements. They are service or voluntary organizations, in legal terms associations or foundations. However, there exist some organizations that are conceptually close to the new movements. For example, the Sexpo Foundation was formed in 1969 to promote healthy sexuality, and the Finnish Lesbian and Gay Organization was founded in 1974. These organizations indicate a reaction to attitudes against sexual minorities and aim at changing prevailing values ond norms.

Finland has three central organizations of social wellfare and health. The Association of Voluntary Health, Social and Welfare Organizations (YTY) consisted of 115 organizations with some 9500 local associations and 1,600,000 individual members in 2000. Another big central organization is the Finnish Federation for Social Welfare and Health (STKL), which generally shares its membership with the YTY but in addition has most of Finland's municipalities as its members. This illustrates close connections between the local government units and civil society. The third central organization is the Finnish Center for Health promotion (TEK).

These central organizations, as well as their large member organizations, are influential in social and health care policy. Some of their functions coincide, but they also emphasize individual aims. The YTY concentrates upon the cooperation of voluntary organizations and furthers cooperation between its members and public authorities. One scholar has characterized it as the trade union of social and health care organizations. The more policy-oriented STKL is interested in promoting social and health policy on local, regional, and national levels. It is active in education and research and its concrete activities are performed mainly by member organizations. TEK's obvious role contains preventive health care information and activity. (Poteri 1998, p. 23; Myllymäki and Tetri 2001, pp. 118-123.) The three central organizations also disseminate knowledge on social policy in the third world.

The Disabled War Veterans Association of Finland is a typical Finnish organization, which has proved successful. It was founded after the Winter War in 1940. Its membership has been above 100,000 but naturally decreases year by year. In the past the state took care of disabled war veterans by providing them with education, work, and housing. The veterans have striven for their cause with the help of their association, in line with the principle of not deserting a comrade-in-arms. Without the veterans' own efforts, supported and encouraged by their socially influential association, it would not have been possible to take care of their welfare in a way that has received international recognition. (Honkasalo 2000.)

The Slot Machine Association is an institution unique to Finland. It supports voluntary, non-governmental social welfare and health care organizations, which set up the association in 1938. At the beginning of the 21st century it has ninety-six member organizations. The association, whose board of directors consists of representatives of state administration and social welfare and health care organizations, has a legal monopoly on slot machine games in Finland. The profits are allocated yearly to charity. Its specific purpose is to support civil society, the so-called third sector, and not to finance the tasks of the government or municipalities. There is one exception to this: within limits set by the state budget the association's profits can be used to improve the condition of war veterans and to treat military injuries. In 2001, its profits were 2060 million markkas (346 million euros), of which 546 million markkas went to the government and 1513 million markkas (254 million euros) were allocated to 1075 organizations and foundations. Formerly, some of them had received support from the state budget. (Myllymäki and Tetri 2001, pp. 163, 293–294.)

After Finland joined the European Union, some private entrepreneurs claimed that there was a contradiction between the monopoly and free competition. The result of a series of trials, the final one in the EU court, was that the Slot Machine Association could carry on as before. What influenced the decision was that the monopoly reduces the possibility of misusing slot machines and that the association is more efficient than private businesses in controlling the problems caused by cases of compulsive gambling.

It is worth noting that in a welfare state, in which the state and the municipalities spend much of their tax revenue on social welfare and health care services, voluntary action promotes such a wide range of the welfare of the citizens. In 1998, the proportion of voluntary organizations in total social expenditure was about 5 percent, that is 6.3 billion markkas (1.1 billion euros). Nevertheless, their actual share in advancing the welfare of citizens was considerably larger as it includes much voluntary activity, which cannot be measured in money. What the voluntary organizations can contribute is years of experience and expertise, cooperation with customers and intensive group work. They operate in such a wide area that only few examples can be mentioned here: the maintenance of rehabilitation centers and hospitals, vocational guidance, housing services for the disabled, day care for children, shelter homes for children and adolescents, sheltered work centers, and holiday activities for the sick and disabled. At the beginning of the new millennium, issues of special concern are young people and the unemployed, housing of the elderly, mental health problems, and drug problems. The task of voluntary organizations is to complement the measures taken by the welfare state's government in all these areas.

The Finnish example illustrates that a welfare state and voluntary help are not mutually exclusive, quite the contrary. There is a dense local government network in Finland (see Chapter 12), which as an institution resembles civil society. This is concretely shown in cooperation between municipalities and social welfare and health care organizations. For example, the municipalities pay most of the expenses that the organizations incur in rehabilitation, and the organizations for their part provide a considerable part of the necessary workforce. Also, they have become major initiators and operators of various projects funded by the EU. In the future the role of voluntary organizations in social welfare and health care is likely to grow stronger, a development that does not conflict with the idea of retaining the welfare state. It is perhaps justifiable to talk about moving from a welfare state to a welfare society, which, however, does not mean that the state can renounce its role as the highest guardian of its citizens' welfare.

Political Influence

Citizens' organizations and social movements form an essential part of any democratic society, and an active civil society is particularly characteristic of established and stable democracies. A great deal of their influence occurs outside the political system, but most political decisions also concern the interests of some organizations, groups, or businesses. Politics can be of great importance for various organizations, and all associational interest groups complement representational democracy by providing citizens with alternative channels for political influence.

In Finland, as in other Nordic countries, trade unions and business organizations have become the strongest political actors outside the conventional representative system. Their impact covers the entire society. For example, the development of social legislation, described above in Chapters 2 and 5, can provide numerous examples of the political influence of labor market organizations.

In the turbulent spring of 1917 the length of working days in industry was shortened to eight hours, and trade unions, which were growing stronger and more radical, soon pressured parliament to pass the law that made the eight-hour working day a legal requirement (excluding farming and domestic work). During the inter-war period the trade unions were not strong politically, but the Second World War added much to their strength. A period of efficient influence was launched. In 1946 alone, legislation on working life developed more than it had during the twenty inter-war years. The law on collective agreements was renewed, a system of shop stewards was created, and the Labor Court was established. Even a law on production committees was legislated, but such committees did not gain real influence in the shops. On the other hand, collective agreements became an established pattern and relationships in the shops changed into a situation that was, with some exaggeration, described as relations of equal parties. (Haatanen 1998, pp. 141–143.)

In the 1940s and 1950s, political pressure was seen as a very central feature in trade union activities, which were now often called extra-parliamentary. Thus, after the general strike of 1956 there followed a debate that pitted the interest organizations and the constitution against each other; even the unconstitutionality of the strike was discussed (Borg 1990, p. 321). Organizational pressure seems to have been called extra-parliamentary pressure because, on the one hand, the more conservative groups were not accustomed to the new role of the unions and, on the other hand, especially the communist members of trade unions organized illegal actions and disrupted the functioning of society. The use of organizational pressure has become less frequent, but it has not been discontinued. And the power of different unions does not depend on their size only. In the mid-1900s the government had to yield to the small Locomotive Engineers Union despite the threat to order the engineers to run trains as military reserve training; the longshoremen are in a strategic position to block foreign trade, and the Paperworkers' Union of under 50,000 members have had a stronger voice in labor negotiations than the Trade Union for Municipal Sector with 208,000 members.

In the 1960s and 1970s labor legislation advanced the era of rapid change in Finnish economy. Mutual antagonisms of the negotiating parties began to fade away: they saw more and more advantages that could only be gained through cooperation. The employers and the employees, corresponding in politics to the conservatives and the social democrats, found the basis for consensus in labor policies, which later developed into one of the foundations of Finland's national consensus and legitimacy. In this spirit, laws were passed on working time (1962, 1964) and health insurance (see Chapter 2, p. 47). The labor market organizations participated in governmental commissions when the reforms were being prepared. A new approach to social policy in the employers' central organization was related to the arrival of the "comrades in arms" generation in positions of leadership (Suonoja 1992, pp. 441–457).

A parliament with a socialist majority, elected in 1966, and the New Left that swept through the society, were the background for many initiatives to develop labor legislation. Workshops got their extensive systems of labor protection, drawing the following ironic comment from one expert: "One would have thought that this mighty-looking reform would have lowered the internationally high work accident numbers and curtailed work-related illness, but the statistics do not show any essential change. Each year about the same 200,000 work accidents were reported to the insurance companies, before as well as after the reform" (Haatanen 1998, p. 143). But even though working safety could not be improved, the labor market organizations had a decisive influence on large social policy reforms in the area of pensions and insurance.

In 1968 there was a thorough change in the opportunities for labor market organizations to influence national policies, when the broadly based comprehensive incomes policy agreements started. These organizations became able to influence a great deal of Finnish legislation (Myllymäki 1979, pp. 190–197). Government bills concerning the welfare state system were combined with agreements on incomes policy, and it was difficult to make changes to any proposals because rejecting one law would have blocked the entire agreement and been fatal for economic development. Such a strong influence continued up to the turn of the 1990s (Piirainen 1992, pp. 300–301). One observer concluded that "the labor market organizations became, in a way, a part of the formal decision-making machinery, although no judicial change had happened in their position" (Borg 1990, p. 321).

The strong role of the labor market organizations, especially in the social policy area, has not escaped criticism. Soon it was no longer called extraparliamentary activity. It became customary to call parliament a rubber stamp, the role of which was to formalize the laws that had been actually decided in the "smoke-filled rooms" of the organizations. It is true that the influence of the organizations was strong from the 1960s to the end of the 1980s, in other words, during years when the Finnish welfare state was created. Their voice was heard because they had close connections to the parliamentary groups of the relevant parties. Many members of parliament had also personally held important positions in labor market organizations.

The growing influence of the organizations can be seen in their increased representation in governmental commissions; they had 76 memberships in 1946 and 87 memberships in 1950, but 499 memberships in 1970 and about 1660 in 1987. For example, in 1975 only 16 percent of government commissions functioned without representation of labor market organizations. About one-half of the memberships in 1980 had to do with social policy. The Confederation of Finnish Industry was efficiently represented in bodies dealing with industry, and the agricultural producers were in those dealing with agriculture. Already at the end of the 1980s some signs indicated a lessening role of organizations in governmental planning (op.cit., pp. 323–326). It is also possible that the economic slump of the 1990s halted the growth of their influence.

Active attempts to reform societal policies continued. The red-blue coalition government of the Conservatives and Social Democrats (1987–1991) aimed at "managed" structural change, in which as many citizens as possible would benefit from the economic growth and nobody would suffer (Haatanen 1998, p. 144). The slump reversed these plans, and the bourgeois government in 1991–1995 openly resisted the trade unions. The recession showed that the power of organizations is dependent on the economic situation. In times of rising unemployment trade unions lose power and their cooperation with the employers becomes more troubled.

The bourgeois government was forced to cut some social expenditures when tax revenue declined and, still more expensively, unemployment grew. The reform plans of the young prime minister Esko Aho of the Center Party aimed at discontinuing comprehensive trade agreements and moving income negotiations to the union level. The negative reaction of the trade unions may have been one reason why the election of 1995 changed political power relations. In the very close election of 1999, too, the Social Democrats were able to remain the largest party and hold on to the premiership. Obviously the experience of the 1990s proved that large trade unions can influence national politics.

Attempts to influence public opinion are an indirect way to influence politics, while assisting the campaign work of party organizations is a more direct method. Both of these were at work during the 1990s. Naturally, the organizations are active also when particular political decisions are planned; the role of labor market and business organizations in social reforms was mentioned above, and so was the role of organizations when new legislation is prepared. They are invited to have their representatives take part in planning commissions, and a variety of group representatives are normally invited for questioning in parliament's committees when government bills are being handled. In these cases their influence is largely based on the expertise that they can add to the preparation process.

The labor market organizations are also consulted in directing national economic policies. For example, essential interest organizations, and not only the labor market organizations, are represented in the Economic Council, which is chaired by the prime minister. In it members of the government, together with organizational representatives, make plans for economic policy. This council is assisted by the Incomes Policy Information Commission, which comprises experts from interest organizations and representatives of the Ministry of Finance, the Bank of Finland, and economic research institutes.

Large organizations are conscious of their power. In 2002 the Confederation of Finnish Industry declared that it "plays, together with its branch organizations, a major role when political and economic decisions which influence companies' activities and this economic operating environment are prepared." Its "expertise is engaged in drawing up legislation and agreements" and it is represented on some 300 committeess, boards and working groups. (www.tt.fi/english/tarinat.shtml#pkt-asiat.) The organizations of wage earners hardly lag behind in the willingness and opportunity to influence politics and decision making.

Many studies have shown that making special expertise available for politicians is, in fact, the most efficient method of pressure politics. It is also possible that some speeches read by MPs in parliament were actually written inside interested organizations. But the popular expression "there is no such thing as a free lunch" sounds somewhat irrelevant in Finland, at least as far as senior civil servants are concerned, because the country is strictly opposed to any corruption and personal gain in public office.

Mass demonstrations are the most visible form of political pressure via public opinion. However, the character of demonstrations has changed. They have become less massive and their primary purpose is to obtain maximum exposure in the mass media. Many demonstrations are organized in front the parliament building, because it is a background to which it is relatively easy to attract television news crews. There were times when the labor movement organized annual massive May Day parades, but very few people want to march today and outdoor speeches are the only remaining part of the tradition. Public demonstrations do happen, but they are few and typically quite peaceful. Besides, there are more direct links to the attention of political decision-makers. The sports organizations provide a good example: The SLU has formed within parliament a network of 42 MPs from different parties who hold leadership positions in sports organizations and, therefore, can be expected to react favorably to goals of the sports movement.

Many organizations also approach the authorities in their organizational self-interest, because money can be obtained for good causes from the state and local government and from the Slot Machine Association. Even political parties discovered long ago that public funding could help to support their organizations, with government subsidies for temperance, youth, and pensioner work, as well as general adult education.

6 The Mass Media

The relations between politicians and the press have been bad. They are getting even worse. We must definitely see to it that they get no better.
Lord Sydney Jacobson in 1978

I can remember I went to a pizzeria, I don't need to read about it in a tabloid paper.
Pentti Arajärvi, husband of President Halonen, in 2001

No political system can exist without communication, and no democratic system can function without free communication. Finland's constitution states this as follows: "Everyone has the freedom of expression. Freedom of expression entails the right to express, disseminate and receive information, opinions and other communications without prior prevention by anyone" (Section 12). Naturally, opinions are communicated to wider audiences via the mass media, which have essential roles within civil society as well as the political system.

A great deal of publicly disseminated opinions consist of the elite's political discourse, and politicians use the media as a tool to influence public opinion. This they can do as long as they are newsworthy. Through their news reporting the mass media keep audiences informed about essential events, thereby contributing to the awareness of the citizenry. At the same time, the media can be independent actors on behalf of their own political goals. They can even lobby in their own self-interest.

The Press and Other Print Media

The growth of radio and television changed mass communication dramatically in the 20th century, but Finland's printed press does not feel much threatened by the growth of the electronic mass media. The total circulation of daily newspapers has remained one of the highest in the world. Counting the dailies that appear 4–7 times a week, the number of printed copies was 558 per 1000 inhabitants in 1990. By 1998 it had declined to 451 copies per 1000 persons, but was again 544 copies in 2001. Only Norway and Japan boasted higher total circulations in 2001. Sweden printed 543 newspaper copies per thousand inhabitants, the United Kingdom 383, Germany 371, the United States only 274, and Italy 127 copies. (*Finnish Mass Media 2000*, p. 270; *World Press Trends 2002*, p. 11.)

The oldest continuously published newspaper in the country, Åbo Underrättrelser, was founded in 1824. Twenty-five other papers of the 21st century have been published since the 19th century. The total number of newspapers was 85 in 1900 and rose to 122 in 1910. In 1930 it was 176, in 1970 the number was 237, and in 1990 it reached 252. Thereafter the number declined to 200 in 2001. But obviously this number depends on how frequently published papers are counted as daily newspapers. In international comparisons, such as the one above, it is customary to count only the newspapers that come out four or more times a week. Among Finland's 200 newspapers in 2001, only 54 met this definition, but these accounted for 72 percent of the total circulation, which was 3,208,000. Among them, seven-day papers numbered 28, and 10 papers appeared six times a week.

The economic slump on the 1990s had severe consequences for the sale of newspapers. Having been 4,080,000 in 1990, total circulation sank to 3,680,000 in 1993. It did not pick up when the economy improved again but continued to decline to the above-mentioned total of 3,208,000 in 2001. (Finnish Mass Media 2000, p. 200; *Suomen Lehdistö* 6/2002, p. 6.)

Yet the economic situation of the press as a whole has remained relatively strong. The total turnover of all Finnish mass media amounts to approximately 3 percent of the gross domestic product; it remained at this level throughout the 1980s and 1990s, although a slight decline since the mid-80s can be detected (see Table 6.1). Of this cake of 21 billion Finnish markkas (3.52 billion euros), the slice of the newspapers was 31 percent in 2001, in other words the same percentage as in 1980. The newspapers fared better than printed advertising, book publishing, or magazines through the slump years of the early 1990s, but nationwide television and radio managed even better than the press. However, commercial television did not do as well as had been expected, and it has encountered difficult economic problems at the beginning of the 21st century.

Advertising in the Finnish media has amounted to 1.0 percent of the GDP; it was FIM 7.1 billion (1.2 billion euros) in 1999 and 1.1 billion euros in 2001. Of that cake, the share of newspapers has remained considerably larger in Finland than in many other countries. The proportion of all advertising revenue going to newspapers sank from 65 to 57 percent between 1980 and 1998, but even this was above the European average and much higher than the 16.5 percent in the United States (Finnish Mass Media 2000, pp. 29),

Table 6.1.

Breakdown of annual mass media turnover from 1980 to 2000 (in %)

Mass Media	Year 1980	1985	1990	1995	2000
Daily newspapers*	26.5	27.6	27.8	28.3	27.4
Non-dailies	4.1	4.4	4.2	3.8	3.2
Magazines, periodicals	21.8	20.1	18.4	17.9	18.0
Free sheets	1.5	2.2	2.0	1.7	2.4
Books	15.7	12.7	13.7	12.4	12.7
Printed advertising	9.9	11.6	9.7	7.9	8.7
Print media total	79.5	78.6	75.8	72.0	72.4
Nationwide tv & radio	13.2	13.1	12.5	15.3	14.7
Local radio, cable tv	0.2	0.5	3.4	3.2	2.8
Online info. services	0.0	0.5	1.1	2.2	1.8
Electronic media total	13.4	14.1	17.0	20.7	19.3
Recorded media** total	7.1	7.3	7.2	7.3	8.3
Total %	100.0	100.0	100.0	100.0	100.0
Total, FIM million	5,533	10,566	16,102	16,418	20,910
As percent of GDP	2.9	3.2	3.1	2.9	2.7

Sources: *Finnish Mass Media 2000*, pp. 26–27; Statistics Finland Mass Media and Culture statistics.

 * *Dailies 7–4 times a week, non-dailies 3–1 times a week.*
** *Phonograms, videos, cinemas, and CD-Rom.*

269).[23] In 2001 the newspapers received 56 percent, television and radio together only 22 percent of Finland's total advertising revenue (YLE 2002).

Although economic considerations are a necessary element of newspaper publishing, the Finnish press was started and developed primarily for ideological rather than business reasons. Increasing nationalist feelings and loosely defined political orientations motivated the founding of papers in the 19th century, and a party press became quite normal at the time of the democratic parliament reform of 1906. Political parties tried to have one of their own newspapers published in each election district, and political agitation among the people and the selling of newspaper subscriptions became two interlinked activities that reinforced each other at the grass roots level. For example, of the 122 newspapers published in

---

23 Between 1988 and 2001 the share of newpapers of global advertising expenditure fell from 40% to 31%, while the share of television rose from 33% to 40%; *World Press Trends 2001*, p. 2.

1910, only 25 were non-affiliated while 97 were published as an organ of one of the five political parties.[24]

During the latter part of the 1920s the total number of newspapers grew mainly because small local papers began to complement the national and regional press. There were 70 non-affiliated Finnish-language papers in 1930, while 82 were affiliated with one of seven different parties. The latter included the 7 communist papers that ceased publication soon thereafter, in 1931. In addition, 24 papers that were published in the Swedish language supported the bourgeois side of the political arena. Very few party papers were directly attached to the party's membership organization, with the exception of the non-profitable regional papers of the political left; more typically the party organs were published by a printing company that was owned by a group of individuals or even by a single family that supported the party (Salokangas 1987, pp. 207, 328).

The pattern of evenly strong regional papers did not last: typically one paper began to outgrow the others of its area and was aided by the spiral from broader news coverage, more readers, more advertising revenue, and improved technical possibilities, to broader news coverage, more readers, more advertising, etc. Thereby the other papers were weakened, relatively at least, and many were eventually discontinued. The non-party press finally emerged as the winners on two fronts: many independent papers were more competitive than party papers, and they became more numerous because party-affiliated papers, one after another, detached themselves from their party connection. No more than 12 Finnish language party papers remained in 2001, eight of them supporting the Social Democratic Party, three the Center Party, and one the Left Alliance. In addition, a few papers defined themselves as "independent centrist" or "independent left wing."

Finland continues to be well covered by regional newspapers. The country is divided into twenty regions (see Table 4.6), and each has at least one daily paper that is published seven times a week (except Åland, where the regional papers come out five and four days a week). Table 6.2 has a list of 16 seven-day papers, two afternoon papers (six times a week), and three largest papers specializing in economy. The biggest newspaper, called *Helsingin Sanomat*, is published in the southern Uusimaa province and ranks as the biggest paper of all Nordic countries, with a daily circulation of 454,000 in 1999 and 446,000 in 2001.

Domestic and international politics get quite good coverage in the Finnish press, but they do not dominate its contents, and the overall balance of space allocated to different kinds of editorial material has been fairly stable. Articles (editorials and columns) covered 5 percent of the material both in 1991 and 1998, while home news declined slightly from 34 to

24 Among the 97 party papers in 1910, the Young Finns had 34, the Finnish Party 27, Social Democratic Party 20, Swedish People's Party 10, Agrarian Union 4, and Christian Workers' Party 2 papers (Nygård 1987, p 21).

32 percent, entertainment rose from 11 to 14 percent and radio and tv pages from 8 to 10 percent. The relative space for culture (7 %), international news (6 %), the economy (8 %), sports (14 %), and letters to the editor and cartoons (totaling 5 %) hardly changed at all during those years (*Finnish Mass Media 2000*, p. 210). What is of significance in this connection is the attention paid by the newspapers to politics and civil society in both the articles and the home news section.

Table 6.2

Largest newspapers in 2001: Circulation, readership, founding year, and place and region of issue

Newspapers	Circulation (weekdays)	Readers	Year founded	Place of issue	(Region)*
Leading morning papers:					
Helsingin Sanomat	446,000	1,150,000	1889	Helsinki	(11)
Aamulehti	135,000	335,000	1881	Tampere	(24)
Turun Sanomat	115,000	288,000	1905	Turku	(21)
Other 7-day morning papers:					
Kaleva	83,000	224,000	1899	Oulu	(51)
Keskisuomalainen	77,000	194,000	1871	Jyväskylä	(41)
Savon Sanomat	67,000	186,000	1907	Kuopio	(32)
Etelä-Suomen Sanomat	62,000	148,000	1900	Lahti	(25)
Satakunnan Kansa	57,000	146,000	1873	Pori	(22)
Ilkka	56,000	148,000	1906	Seinäjoki	(42)
Hufvudstadsbladet	53,000	133,000	1864	Helsinki	(11)
Karjalainen	48,000	129,000	1874	Joensuu	(33)
Lapin Kansa	35,000	96,000	1928	Rovaniemi	(52)
Etelä-Saimaa	34,000	89,000	1885	Lappeenranta	(27)
Pohjalainen	33,000	110,000	1903	Vaasa	(43)
Hämeen Sanomat	30,000	81,000	1879	Hämeenlinna	(23)
Kouvolan Sanomat	30,000	77,000	1909	Kouvola	(26)
12 others	249,000	–	–	12 places	
Afternoon papers:					
Ilta-Sanomat	219,000	855,000	1932	Helsinki	(11)
Iltalehti	135,000	699,000	1980	Helsinki	(11)
Specialized newspapers:					
Kauppalehti	85,000	318,000	1898	Helsinki	(11)
Taloussanomat	31,000	84,000	1997	Helsinki	(11)
Maaseudun tulevaisuus	89,000	319,000	1916	Helsinki	(11)

* The numbers of regions refer to the map in Figure 4.1 (on page 78).

Sources: *Suomen Lehdistö 6/2002*; National Readership Survey 2001.

Generally speaking, the political role of "the fourth estate" has moved gradually from debating politics and proclaiming policies toward setting the agenda for more general public discourse and providing a forum for a broader public debate. At the same time, the mass media's role as a critical "watchdog" of politics has become solidly established. Politicians feel uneasy because they cannot control the press, nor can they anticipate at any given time which issues or details will be brought to the fore by the newspapers, while the law on the freedom of expression and the accepted ethical norms of journalism do not protect the privacy of politicians to the same extent as they protect less known private citizens. It has even been claimed that the overly critical attitudes of the press have contributed to the negative mass attitude toward politicians and politics in general.

On the other hand, democracy needs the attention of its citizens, politicians need constant publicity, and the elections depend much on the amount of publicity that parties and politicians get in the newspaper's news pages and articles. The papers make a conscious attempt to analyze, for the benefit of their readers, the backgrounds of the events of current interest. Readers, in turn, send in many more letters to the editor than there is space available for publication.

Newspapers genuinely get attention from the people. The Finns are accustomed to getting their newspaper delivered to their homes before breakfast time. Only 15 percent of papers are bought from newsstands, and 88 percent of subscribed papers are delivered before 6 o'clock in the morning. Of all Finns aged at least 15 years, more than 90 percent read a newspaper every day in 1998, using an average of 42 minutes to do so.[25] The older the people, the more time they spent reading: persons between 15 and 24 years of age averaged 26 minutes, while the over 65 year-olds spent one hour and 20 minutes reading newspapers (Finnish Mass Media 2000, p. 215).

Naturally, the print media include books and magazines. The number of magazines and periodicals published in Finland was 4400 in 1990 and rose to 5100 in 1998 (these numbers include newspapers published fewer than three times a week). 43 magazines came out once a week and 381 once or twice a month. In 1999 Finland's mail service delivered to subscribers 361 million copies, while single-copy sales totaled only 25 million Finnish and 3 million foreign magazines. (Op. cit., pp. 223, 230.)

Most books published in Finland cannot hope for large audiences but the number of publications is quite substantial. In 1998, 12,900 different books were published. This number equaled 25 book titles per 10,000

---

25 According to a Gallup survey in 2000, 86 % of the population aged 12–69 years read a newspaper during a given day, while tv reached 84 %, magazines 80 %, and radio 66 %. The percentage of concentrated attention varied from 47 % to the newspapers and 37 % to tv, to only 4% to radio listening. The average total time consumed per day was 7 hours and 38 minutes, of which radio and tv combined took 142 minutes, magazines 42, newspapers 38, and the other media 94 minutes. (Virmasalo 2000, p. 18.)

population, which was the highest among the EU countries and much higher than 5 titles in Japan and 3 titles in the USA. Finland's 950 public libraries and 200 mobile libraries lend out about 100 million publications each year. (Op. cit., pp. 175, 187.) Some of the books and several periodicals may also be significant politically. For example, each year there are memoirs published by retiring politicians, and it is not unusual for politicians to reinforce their election campaigns by writing opinionated books that outline their goals and visions.

Radio and Television

As was indicated above, the electronic mass media take up more of people's time than newspapers and other reading materials. In measurements carried out by the "peoplemeter" system[26] and including people who were at least 10 years of age, 75 percent of people watched television and 79 percent listened to radio during an average day in 1999. They spent about 2 hours and 40 minutes watching, and more than three hours listening. In 2001 the times had grown to 2 hours 47 minutes watching and 3 hours 28 listening (Yle 1.7.2002). Again age made a difference: people over 65 years sat an average of four hours at their tv sets and added another four hours of radio listening to it, but an average young person between 15-24 years of age watched television only one hour 40 minutes and listened to the radio about two hours (op.cit., pp. 71, 104).

Nowadays there are plenty of programs to choose from. In Finland, three tv channels penetrated the whole country in 2000 and a fourth one covered most of it. Programs originating from Sweden were also relayed to southern and western Finland (see Table 6.3). Nationally distributed and local cable tv programs and some local tv broadcasts offered additional choices, and 14 percent of the people viewed satellite programs directly. National radio channels numbered about ten, and there were more than one hundred regional or local radio stations. In Helsinki, radio receivers could be tuned to 21 different FM stations.

Only recently has the supply of programs become this extensive. The history of the electronic mass media is naturally much shorter than the history of the printed press, and many of the advances date from the very end of the 20th century. There has been a stepwise development both in new technical possibilities and some keenly contested policy decisions.

Finland's first wireless signals were transmitted in 1900. Radio broadcasting started in early 1920s. Amateur radio broadcasts were first transmitted in 1923, and in 1926 radio associations formed the Finnish Broadcasting Company (Yleisradio, now generally known as YLE). All radio

---

26   This is a continuous audience survey by Finnpanel Oy, commissioned jointly by the Finnish Broadcasting Company, MTV3, TV4, and the Federation of Advertising Agencies.

stations around the country began to relay its national broadcasts. An enlarged audience and increased and more varied programming became possible in 1928, when the state constructed a powerful long-wave transmitter in Lahti. Later technical milestones have included the Pori short-wave station in 1948, the establishment of one of the world's first nationwide FM networks between 1953 and 1956, public tv transmission in 1955 and regular tv broadcasts by YLE in 1958, completion of the second FM network in 1963, regular stereophonic radio transmissions in 1967, regular color tv transmissions in 1969, broadcasted teletext transmissions in 1981, and digital radio in 1998. Digital television broadcasts started in August 2001.

Table 6.3

Availability and average daily viewing of Finland's national tv channels in 1999 (excluding text-tv)

	YLE TV1	YLE TV2	YLE Total	MTV3	Four	TV4/ STV	Total
Penetration (%)	100	100	100	100	79	32	100
Weekly program hours	112	80	192	105	83	–	>600
Daily reach (%)	58	53	66	64	35	5	75*
Daily viewing (minutes)	37	33	70	68	16	–	161*
Channel shares in %	23	20	43	42	10	1	100*

* Including satellites (14 % reach, 6 minutes and 4 % viewing).

Source: *Finnish Mass Media 2000*, pp. 55–74.

How the new possibilities were put into practice has depended much on the government. A complete reorganization in 1934 created a new stock holding company, and the new radio law stipulated that the state was the company's majority owner and that all program distribution was to be integrated with it. The government granted the single operating license, usually for five years at a time. This company enjoyed an actual monopoly of broadcasting for half a century, until the 1980s.

Originally, the question of permitting independent companies to broadcast advertising was much debated in European countries. For example, in the United Kingdom a fierce political controversy preceded the act of parliament in 1954 authorizing the Independent Television (ITV) network to compete with BBC as a consortium of private companies. Its broadcasts were subjected to much stricter regulation of advertising than in America's commercial television. Sweden and Norway allowed no commercials at all before the 1990s.

Finland's unique solution was to allow a commercially based company, MTV (later renamed MTV3) to broadcast its television programming using transmission facilities leased from YLE's two channels. MTV shared program time with YLE and paid enough for transmissions to provide 20 percent of YLE's total revenue. In legal terms YLE held the one and only operating license. Although MTV functioned independently, it was formally operating under YLE's license. The whole picture changed in 1993, when several licenses were granted for nationwide operations, and again in 2000, when the government allocated the thirteen digital channels to be launched in August 2001. The first local radio stations had been permitted in 1985.

It was apparent already in the 1970s that commercial MTV was not satisfied with its subordinate role. Its early goal was to become a fully independent "full-service channel." In order to move toward the goal, it lobbied in various ways for permission to start its own news broadcasts. YLE was irritated even by occasional MTV current affairs programs and opposed a competing daily news service. The matter became highly politicized until, after much preparation, the administrative council of YLE voted in 1980 in favor of a two-year trial period. The vote was 12 to 9, with the non-socialist majority in favor and the Social Democratic and Communist members against. The competing news service began in September 1981 and soon improved the evening news on both channels.

The monopoly position of YLE, the state-owned Finnish Broadcasting Company, did not mean that its programs were dictated by the government. It aimed from the beginning to be a neutral medium, providing education, information, and entertainment for the whole nation. The original model was comparable to the British Broadcasting Company (BBC), in which public service broadcasting was concentrated in 1922, or to the German system, where radio broadcasts to the general public began in 1923 in the hands of the country's postal authorities (Lyytinen 1996, pp. 14, 20). After the Second World War, YLE's programming twice slipped very far to the political left and both times a revised organizational structure helped to balance the situation. In 1948 the administration of the company was removed from the shareholders' (i.e., the government's) control and its administrative council became elected by parliament. In 1969 the director general's authority concerning programming policies was split among the heads of the various divisions.

Balanced or not, the 1970s were a decade of another kind of politicization. Party political "quotas" of personnel were the pattern. The party secretary of the Social Democrats was appointed director general in 1970, while the former secretary of the Center Party became program director and head of TV1. Even the journalists' partisan affiliation played a role in recruitment and assignments. More recently, professional ability has again been the foremost consideration.

Undoubtedly the electronic mass media have grown to be an important element in the country's political system, in Finland as elsewhere. There are times when they help to unify the nation; they inform the public; they provide a forum for political discourse; and they provide a direct link from the rulers to the citizenry. As early as in 1932, a rebellious extreme right-wing movement was stopped by a radio speech by the president of the republic. A comparison in 1999 of the audiences of various tv programs indicates that almost 50 percent of the whole nation gathered to watch the president's independence day reception on channel 1, and this was even more than the interest shown in Finland's performance in the ice hockey world championships (Finnish Mass Media 2000, p. 76). In its early years the radio distanced itself from politics, but nowadays ministers and other top politicians may face a reporter and a camera around any corner, press conferences are frequent, important debates in parliament are broadcast live, and tv and radio debates are a most central element of election campaigns.

Responsible for public service, the Finnish Broadcasting Company YLE cannot carry advertising. As elsewhere in Europe, its finances have been based on license fees. The number of radio licenses exceeded 100,000 in 1930 and 1,000,000 in 1955; when they were abolished in 1976 their number had risen to 2,200,000. In 1969, when the very first color tv licenses were sold, there were 1 million black-and-white television licenses, but in 1980 the number of color licenses (786,000) surpassed black-and-white ones (752,000). Only 51,000 of the latter remained in 1995, when the distinction was abolished. (Op. cit., p. 61). In 2000, there were 2 million tv licenses in Finland, in other words 386 licenses per 1000 population, and the average number of tv sets was 1.5 per household.

The annual television license fee was raised in July 2000 from FIM 882 to FIM 982 (€ 148 to € 165). It cost the same in 2002. Elsewhere in Europe the annual fees varied greatly, from 277 euros in Denmark and 226 euros in Norway to € 107 in Ireland and € 94 in Italy. According to YLE's audience research in 2001, 60 percent of the population considered the fee of 165 euros to be very or rather good value for the money, and 86 percent were very or rather satisfied with YLE's television and radio programming. Almost everybody appreciated having "programs available to all Finnish people regardless of where they live." (YLE annual report 2001, p. 29.) A survey in 1999 showed that many more valued "reliable news and current affairs programming" more highly than entertainment programs, and a large majority was satisfied with the news of both the YLE and the MTV3 channels. Only the new TV4 Finland had not grown to the same level of acceptance. Nevertheless, the newspapers were the main source of daily news for more people than any given tv or radio news program. (Kytömäki and Ruohomaa 1999.)

In December 1999, digital tv operators published their proposals for "The launch of digital terrestrial television broadcasting in Finland," which was approved by the ministry of transport and communications in March 2000. The "National Launch Day" was August 27, 2001. It introduced not four but thirteen tv channels in three groups. YLE's tv licenses will finance multiplex A: TV1-D, TV2-D, YLE 24 (non-stop news), Yle Plus (culture), and FST-D (in Swedish). Multiplex B is financed through advertising: MTV3-D, sports channel, Citytv (current affairs for three regions), and Wellnet (specialized topics, also pay-tv). Multiplex C includes the Channel 4 and three pay-tv channels: 24 hours movies, an education channel, and Canal+ (movies and sports). At the beginning of 2002, only three huge problems were looming:

how to find the necessary audiences, how to activate pay-tv subscribers, and how to provide the equipment for watching digi-tv?

And at least three additional questions needed to be answered: will the quality of the wider choice of programs be maintained, at a time when tv companies are cutting, not enlarging, their staff;[27] how many new tv channels will receive permits to start in 2003; and will people be ready to accept the planned termination of all analogue broadcasting in 2006? In spring 2002, there were no more than 25,000 digi-tv receivers tuned to the digital channels.

The New Media

The circulation of news on telset began in Finland in 1980. Telefax was also used to distribute newspapers that were specially laid out for this purpose. But technical development provided two additional, more convenient types of electronic mass communication, namely, text tv and the Internet. The former has been available on YLE's tv channels and on MTV3 and are updated with news throughout the night, too. The latter has made it possible for newspapers to publish an electronic version of the printed paper. By spring 2000, Finland already had 73 Internet newspapers and 138 internet magazines. In advertising the scope of the Internet has remained very small in Finland.[28]

The ministries and various authorities in public administration, as well as political parties and individual politicians, publish their own material on their web pages, which have become a natural element of election campaigns. In connection with the parliamentary election in 1995, YLE designed a web-based "election machine," and other media followed suit during the subsequent elections. Their idea is to record the responses of the candidates to some twenty or more multiple choice questions,[29] to let the web page reader answer the same questions, and then determine which candidates are closest to the voter's own thinking, and who deviate the most from it. This game became quite popular.

There has also been some discussion in Finland about whether the Internet could be used as a modern means of voting in general elections and referendums. Already the nationwide electric register of voters is of great convenience in the administration of elections in polling stations around the country. The apparent obstacle to proposed electronic voting at home, however, is the obvious possibility that such votes might not

27 MTV3 announced in January 2001 that it would dismiss one-quarter of its personnel, causing strong spontaneous resistance from its employees.
28 Worldwide, the internet's share of display advertising total is about 3%; *World Press Trends 2001,* p. 2.
29 For an analysis of the 18 answers that the Finnish candidates for the European Parliament gave in 1999 to the "election machine" of *Helsingin Sanomat,* see Paloheimo 2000.

remain as secret as the ballots cast in booths of public polling places.

It is getting increasingly difficult to draw the line between mass communication and personal communication. For example, mobile telephones are also becoming miniature-sized tv receivers, and tv channels are planning ways to combine digital television with internet applications. The first step will be a simplified two-way interaction between viewers and the program producers, not only for instant audience reactions, but also to get immediate responses to commercial offerings. But neither will it be easy to make a distinction between the printed press and the electronic mass media. The MTV3 is owned by a group that publishes ten daily newspapers, owns the one nationwide commercial radio channel, and is planning various ways to do business as a provider for electronic communications. The Channel 4 television station is owned by the company which became Finland's biggest publisher of both newspapers and books after a merger in 1999. As a consequence of such groupings and further plans, the same journalists may soon serve simultaneously quite different media, although so far the editorial contents of the media have not been influenced by the mergers.

In democratic societies, the authorities cannot control in advance the material that is communicated. How this is stipulated in the Finnish constitution was quoted in the beginnig of this chapter, and Article 12 continues: "More detailed provisions on the exercise of the freedom of expression are laid down by an act." Such an act was introduced in parliament in spring 2002; the government's bill aims to replace the separate acts on press freedom (1919), television (1971), and cable tv (1987). The new law will apply neutrally to all forms of mass communication, old and new media alike.

However, the principle of freedom is not applicable to all concrete situations. A familiar problem is how to protect children from programming that contains undesirable visual images.[30] Nor does free expression mean the freedom to violate another's legal rights. Sometimes the courts seem to find it difficult to draw the line between press freedom and the citizens' right to privacy. The government bill will continue to place legal responsibility for the contents of mass communication with the editor-in-chief or responsible program director, and with the publisher. However, it is not always easy to determine who is responsible in the new media, as it can be impossible to determine what information was disseminated or to identify the sender of anonymous messages via the web. The line between private and mass communication can also be unclear.

---

30 There is advance rating of motion pictures and videotapes and voluntary rating of tv programs.

7 People's Attachment to Politics

...the developments are the result of rising demands for political rights and influence.

Kaase and Newton 1995, p. 171

I feel as if I'm living in a house where all decisions about our lives are made on the top floor, beyond the reach of ordinary people.

A young voter in France in spring 2002

Political Involvement

People have a wide range of concerns. Among them, neither their attachment to organizations nor political activity rank very high. But although most people do not feel that politics belongs to the central areas of their lives, there are those who have a genuine interest in it. In Finnish survey studies almost all respondents say that the family is important for them, 80 percent calling it very important, and a large majority also value their friends, their work, and leisure time, whereas only 45 percent say that religion is an important area of their lives and no more than 20 percent find politics very or rather important. 25 percent think that politics has no importance at all. (World Values 2000.)

However, when people are asked "How interested are you in politics?" typically about one-half of the interviewees have said that they are very or rather interested. This share has not changed much over the years, nor do the Finnish findings differ much from the level of political interest that is found cross-nationally.[31] However, some decline may be occurring, because in one survey in 2000, only 28 percent of Finnish respondents answered that they were very or rather interested in politics and 22 percent claimed to be totally uninterested (World Values 2000).

---

31 See: Pesonen et al. 1993, p. 170; Bennulf et al. 1998, p. 105; *Political Action* 1979, VAR 0013.

One should keep in mind such differences in people's political involvement. Because of the variation, scholars like to group citizens according their political participation and interest in politics. The basic unidimensional picture has consisted of three levels, such as the nation's apathetics, spectators, and gladiators (Milbrath and Goel 1977, p. 21), or the levels of no, some, and active participation (Topf 1995, p. 68). Subjective interest and political activity, in turn, have been combined into four modes of political involvement, namely, into apathetic, detached, expressive, and instrumental involvement in politics (Kaase and Barnes 1979, p. 527).

The focus of people's attention to politics has changed in Finland, as in many other countries. It has moved to a large extent from mass meetings to private homes and from collective activity to individual attachment, as well as from ideologies to personalities. The expansion of television brought about a major change in political mass communication, and because the citizenry is more educated than before, voters can be mobilized more "cognitively" than before. Another development is the voters' gradual alienation from political parties and the trend toward personalized politics. Both of them have been observed in Finland and other western democracies alike, although increasing depoliticization appeared in Finland later than in the other Nordic countries (Allardt and Pesonen 1967, p. 364).

Elections, and especially participation as voters in elections, link most citizens to the political system. As mentioned in Chapter 2, Finland's level of voter turnout reached its highest levels during the 1960s and remained comparatively high for some time after. However, only 68 percent voted in the parliamentary elections in 1999 and 56 percent in the local elections in 2000. Participation in the Finnish elections will be discussed more in Chapter 8 below.

Naturally, in all political systems there is internal variation between citizens in how involved they are in the politics of their country, and the relative sizes of various groups or modes may differ between the countries. Voter turnout in elections declined quite generally in the 1990s.[32] Various other cross-national comparisons are by no means accurate, but it seems that there have been fewer "apathetic" people in Finland than in Belgium, Spain, or Italy, while fewer have been "instrumentally" involved in Finland than in Germany or the Netherlands (Topf 1995, pp. 84–85).

Many general patterns of mass political behavior tend to remain constant. But new patterns of behavior may also appear, and often they spread cross-nationally. For example, the wave of student radicalism, mentioned in Chapter 5, started in the United States, soon led to the "Paris revolution" in France in 1968 and spread unrest and unconventional political acts elsewhere. During the 1970s, new types of political actions became a common element in western political cultures, as also in Finland.

32 The median change from the 1950s to the 1990s in the OECD countries was a 10 percent decline in turnout. There was a decline in every country except Australia, Denmark, and Sweden. The most substantial drop-off happened during the 1990s. Finland's decline was somewhat smaller than the OECD average. (Wattenberg 2000, pp. 71–73.) – See also Dalton 2002, p. 36.

Table 7.1 summarizes five such political acts. They are called unconventional because their purpose is to influence political decisions directly rather than through the conventional route of elections and political parties. Nowadays there is nothing unusual about signing petitions; about one-half of the Finns have done it and most of the others would do so in order to advance some political goal. Such was not the case a quarter-century ago, because then only one out of five Finns had signed a petition, while one out of four considered such an act unthinkable. Participating in boycotts has also gained acceptance and more people have joined in demonstrations.[33] On the other hand, illegal political acts were resented by most Finns just as strongly in 2000 as in 1975.

Table 7.1

Participation and potential participation in five unconventional political acts, in 1975 and in 2000 (in %)

Political acts	Have done	Might do	Would never do	Don't know	Total
In 1975:					
Signing a petition	19	53	23	5	100
Joining in boycots	1	32	51	7	100
Lawful demonstrations	6	51	40	3	100
Wildcat strikes	4	25	66	5	100
Occupying buildings	–	16	78	6	100
In 2000:					
Signing a petition	47	35	13	5	100
Joining in boycots	14	50	30	6	100
Lawful demonstrations	14	41	39	6	100
Wildcat strikes	2	23	67	7	99
Occupying buildings	–	14	79	7	100

Source: Political Action Study 1979; The Finnish Gallup, October 2000.

New types of political action also gave rise to new ways of structuring people's political participation when analyzing it, such as the two-dimensional "typology of political action repertory" which gave the citizens five possible labels: either inactives, conformists, reformists, activists, or protesters (Kaase and Marsh 1979, p. 155). In the Finnish comparison, it seemed preferable to analyze nine different citizen-types, rang-

33 Participation in the same three acts increased also in Great Britain, West Germany, and the U.S.A. between the mid-1970s and 1995. Finland's general level of unconventional participation appeared relatively low in cross-national comparisons. Dalton 2002, pp. 62–65.

ing from inactives to "fully actives" (Pesonen and Sänkiaho 1979, p. 218). One finding about the Finns was that the citizens who felt they were politically efficacious were the most likely to rank high on both dimensions of political participation, on conventional participation and protest potential. In other words, they were "fully active" citizens who got involved in things like campaigning and party work, and were at the same time the most willing to resort to demonstrations, petitions, or even illegal protest acts (op. cit., p. 254).

During the 1990s there was a further decline in the minority of Finnish citizens who thought that politics occupies a very important or rather important place in their lives. It sank from 28 percent to the above-mentioned 20 percent, which is a very small share of the population when compared with Sweden where the corresponding figure was 47 percent in 1996.

Comparisons across nations and over time have also been made of people's value orientations, and the trends have appeared similar across many countries. Postmaterialist values are a case in point (Inglehart 1997, pp. 140, 157). The measure suggested by Ronald Inglehart shows that in Finland, as in many other countries, such values were assumed increasingly by each new generation. Among the total population, percent materialist subtracted from percent postmaterialist rose a great deal in two decades: It was –34 in 1975 but climbed to +18 in 1996. And different age cohorts have tended to think differently in Finland, too. In 1996 the figure measuring post-materialism was –7 for persons aged 65 years or more, but +35 for persons who were twenty-five to thirty-four years of age. On the other hand, Finnish studies have not confirmed that the youngest group, aged fifteen to twenty-four years, is the most post-materialist one (+23 in 1996). It seems that the temporary insecurity of the student generation counteracted to some extent the general trend toward increased postmaterialism. (Nurmela et al. 1997, pp. 262–263.)

Trust, Pride, and Resentment

Twice a year the European Commission conducts its general public opinion surveys, the Eurobarometers (already referred to in Chapter 3). Since 1994 many of them have contained the following question: "In the near future, do you see yourself as: nationality only/ nationality and European/ European and nationality/ European only?" The responses reveal that not only the Finns (cf. Chapter 3), but all EU citizens have a strong tendency to remain committed to their own nationality, without feeling themselves to be genuine Europeans. In autumn 2001, 44 percent described themselves as "nationality only," while no more than 3 percent said they are "European only" and a further 6 percent answered "European and nationality." The young tend to feel more European than the older age groups, but it is hardly possible to detect any process of "Europeanization" between 1995 and 2001. On the other hand, people who express a European identity have been constantly fewer in Finland than in all of the EU. The same is even more true of Britons, while the citizens of Luxembourg and Italy have felt the most European. (Eurobarometer 56, pp. 14, B.18.)

Another survey in Finland that offered a broader range of regional identities to choose from, did not find the Finns internationally oriented either. The most common choices were the home town and the country as a whole, while very few identified with either the whole world, western Europe, or the Nordic countries (Sänkiaho and Säynässalo 1994, p. 113). A more recent study confirmed this. Its respondents were invited to choose from five alternatives the two geographic areas to which they mainly belong; 74 percent chose the home town and 68 percent chose Finland as a whole. Many more Finns also identified with their region or province than with either Europe (10 percent) or the whole world (7 percent). (World Values 2000.)

National identity means a great deal to people everywhere, but it may be especially important for the citizens of small countries (cf. Chapter 3). And the Finns not only think of themselves foremost as Finns but are also proud of their country and many aspects of its political system. They recall how Finland pioneered female suffrage almost a century ago, and they learned to trust their political system during the war and through the central role played by the political-administrative establishment in crisis situations. During the postwar reconstruction period, the political-administrative system and the labor market organizations had central roles in building the foundations for Finland's growing material well-being.

One generation ago there were those who felt that life might be better elsewhere, but these views changed by the beginning of the 1980s. When asked in 1977, 1980, and 1983, "which country provides the best living conditions?" the proportion choosing Finland rose from less than one-half to more than two-thirds of the population (see Table 7.2). It even was fashionable to claim that "To be born in Finland is like winning the lottery." Either the Finns were becoming truly pleased with what their country provides for them, or they made the realistic observation that other nations, too, are pressed by unsolved problems. Then the overheated 1980s "boiled over," and the severe economic slump of the 1990s caused serious problems for Finland. Only slowly did the people begin to get back into a more optimistic mood.

Table 7.2

Public opinion in Finland on "Which country provides the best living conditions," from 1977 to 1983

Country	1977	1980	1983
Finland	47%	53%	68%
Sweden	25	21	10
USA	10	7	5
USSR	4	2	1
Others, Don't Know	14	17	16

Source: Pesonen 1985, p. 25.

Although the Finnish people are proud of their country, many have become alienated and skeptical about the role and performance of some political institutions. Most Finns feel that the political parties and even the government and the bureaucracy have too much power in society. In early 1990s people were very antagonistic towards banks and so-called market forces, both of which use power that is beyond the control of ordinary people. On the other hand, people have felt for a long time that families and individual citizens are much too powerless.

A comparison of the evaluations expressed in late 1992 with the opinions eight years previously shows that banks and big business really lost credibility when the economic depression hit the country. Criticism of the excessive power of political parties and the government had also intensified. Table 7.3 summarizes how the corresponding opinions were distributed again in 1999. By that year the extreme criticism of the banks had mellowed, although a majority of the Finns still considered banks and big corporations too powerful. During the late 1990s the mass media, the European Union, and market forces had risen to the top of the list of influences which people considered exceedingly powerful. The environmentalists had also lost a great deal of their popularity.

On the other hand, the desire for more power to the individual has remained strong and constant. Likewise, the Finns feel that both families and civil organizations are too powerless. Of the public influences, the police have become even more popular, and the balance of opinion favors giving more power to the courts as well. A large majority thought in 1999 that the president had the right amount of power. Also, opinions were rather balanced on the extent of influence of parliament, municipal decisionmakers, the church, and, especially, the defense forces.

Table 7.3

Public opinion in 1999 on the amount of power exercised by twenty-two different influences (in %)

Influence	Too much power	The right amount	Too little power	Balance*
The media	67	31	1	+66
The European Union, EU	65	33	3	+62
So-called market forces	63	33	2	+61
Big business	57	41	2	+55
The banks	54	45	2	+52
Political parties	50	45	2	+48
The bureaucracy	41	54	5	+36
The environmentalists	46	36	18	+28
Employers' organizations	30	62	7	+23
The government	28	66	7	+21
The trade union movement	33	53	15	+18
The church	21	65	13	+8
The president	21	64	16	+5
Municipal decision makers	21	57	22	−1
The defense forces	8	78	14	−6
Parliament	14	61	25	−11
The universities	4	71	25	−21
The judiciary	12	42	37	−25
Civil organizations	3	53	43	−40
The police	4	42	55	−51
The family	1	44	55	−54
The individual citizen	1	22	77	−76

* "Too little power" deducted from "too much power."

Source: Adopted from EVA 1999a, p. 20.

This picture of influential forces does not change much if one compares how much confidence the Finnish people have in the country's different institutions. In the early 1990s the undesirable social and economic consequences of the depression had an obvious impact on the evaluations. People did not trust the institutions that were mainly responsible for setting goals and implementing them, but they had faith in the things and institutions that felt permanent, especially in the institutions that protect internal and international security.

The police gained respect quite generally in the western countries during the "civic disobedience" protests in the 1970s (Pesonen and Sänkiaho 1979, p. 96). Now, according to the World Values Survey, the Finns are unusual not only in their willingness to give the police additional power, but also because they rank the police as their most trusted institution. Indeed hardly ever do letters to the editor contain criticism of the integrity of the police. Likewise, the defense forces enjoy the confidence of most people, and even more so in 2000 than two decades earlier. (Nurmela et al. 1997, pp. 165–172, World Values 2000).

Table 7.4.

Finnish people's confidence in thirteen institutions in 2000 by age, and change from 1981 (in %)

Influentials	Total	(Change)	Age groups in 2000				
			18–24	25–34	35–49	50–64	65–
The Police	89	(+1)	90	87	90	91	89
Defense forces	83	(+12)	76	83	80	87	86
The courts	65	(−19)	75	68	63	60	63
The church	57	(+8)	43	54	54	58	73
Trade unions	52	(−2)	59	53	50	49	49
Parliament	43	(−22)	42	35	37	46	54
Major companies	41	(+4)	48	42	42	35	40
The government	41	(+9)**	49	38	34	41	51
United Nations	41	(−10)**	55	49	45	37	33
Civil service	39	(−14)	41	35	35	42	46
Press	36	(+2)	36	39	36	36	35
European Union	24	(−14)*	30	24	22	27	19
Political parties	14	(+1)*	18	8	12	17	21

Note: Percentages of respondents who answered either "a geat deal" or "quite a lot." The other alternatives were "not very much," or "none at all."

* Change from 1990 to 2000.
** Change from 1996 to 2000.

Source: World Values 1981, 1990, 2000.

Table 7.4 lists thirteen influences, ordered according to the percentage of people who had confidence in them. Also, it shows what change has occurred in two decades or, in some cases, during a shorter period. In addition to the armed forces, only the church has gained some confidence. Most people continue to trust the court system, although fewer in 2000 than in 1981. Both parliament and the civil service have lost some confidence, and the European Union, not well trusted as the EC in 1990, has since sunk to near the bottom of the list. At the very bottom are political parties. While one-half of the citizenry would like to reduce the power of parties, only 14 percent has confidence in them. Even parliament and the government are under some suspicion, while the court system and the church enjoy the trust of the majority of Finns.

In spring 2001 the Eurobarometer also added to its surveys questions about people's trust in their country's media and political and other institutions. These results cannot be directly compared with the World Values Survey because the questions were worded differently. The responses given in the 15 EU countries were distributed more similarly than one might have expected: a majority of west Europeans trusted the police and the army, followed by the legal system and the Church, but few trusted the political parties. The Finns, however, appeared more trustful than most others. They trusted their government, parliament, and mass media more than Europeans in general, and, especially, they expressed the EU's highest trust in the police, the army, and also the trade unions. Only when expressing their trust in voluntary and non-governmental organizations did they express views that were average for Europe. (Eurobarometer 55, pp. 6–10, B.7–B.9.)[34] Interestingly, a majority of Finns expressed trust in the mass media when askede separately about *radio*, *television*, and *the press*, rather than about the media in general.

Finnish opinions within the different age groups are similar in some, but not in all respects (see Table 7.4). Similarities include the people's very high confidence in the police and relatively low confidence in the press. Age adds to confidence in *the church* but reduces confidence in the United Nations. In some cases, including the government, parliament, and the civil service, one finds a linear relationship: people are more confident the older they get, with the one exception that the very youngest show more confidence than the most 'suspicious' age group, those between 25 and 34 years of age. The youngest also differ from the others in their above-average confidence in the courts, the trade unions, big business, and the European Union. There were only small differences between persons with materialist and post-materialist value orientations, although the materialists has some tendency to doubt the civil service, and the post-materialists had below-average confidence in the defence forces, the church, and major companies (World Values Survey data 2000).

Generally speaking, the Finnish people trusted their institutions already in 1996 somewhat more than in 1993, although opinions had not yet returned to pre-slump levels. Thus the nadir of popular confidence in institutions seemed to be a thing of the recent past in 1996 but, as Table 7.4 indicates, the level of conficence that was typical of the mid-1980s does not return easily.

Clearly the mass attitudes illustrate that the legitimacy of the Finnish political system rests on a solid basis. Comparative survey studies also find relatively more people in Sweden, Norway, and Finland than elsewhere who feel that they can trust their fellow citizens. The sense of

34 The subsequent surveys in October-November 2001 again gave similar results, except that the Finns' trust in organizations had declined below the EU average (Eurobarometer 56, p. B.15).

subjective well-being of the Finnish people is as high as that of the Americans (Inglehart 1997, pp. 173–178) and slightly above the average European level (Eurobarometer 56, p. 2).

A Case Story: Suspected Favoritism

In October 1997, when the nation was struggling with serious political problems, a small incident grew into a major political issue that almost precipitated the government's resignation. Its background was the bank crisis of early 1990s. After the Bank of Finland liberalized foreign exchange controls in the 1980s, Finnish banks began offering cheap loans and opened an easy flow of money. Business was heated, GDP grew fast, but the worldwide economic showdown and a devaluation of the Finnish currency suddenly made it impossible for many businesses and individuals to service their loans, and the values of their collateral collapsed. A wave of bankruptcies followed, but the government rushed to the support of the banks, especially the savings banks. The credibility of the Finnish economic system was saved, and Finland's international credit rating is again very high but, as mentioned above, public attitudes toward the banks and bank directors were deeply altered.

The board members of some local savings banks were made to pay compensation for the harm they had caused their banks by granting loans against inadequate collateral. A special bank was established under government management to manage the real estate that fell in the hands of the banks as a result of bankruptcies.

One of the banks that was rescued and merged with its former competitors was the Workers' Savings Bank, a nationwide institution with about a 3 percent share of all banking business. Three of its directors were sued for damages. The chief executive officer of the bank had been appointed to that position in 1982, when he was the chairman of the Social Democratic Party. The court found him liable to pay 25 million markkas in damages but, after he appealed to the Supreme Court, the sum was reduced in September 1997 to 9 million (plus 6 million in interest). He then negotiated a deal with the government's supervising agency to pay only 1.2 million. The minister of taxation accepted the deal because she thought that it was better for the state to get 1.2 million than nothing.

The agreement was not illegal, and it may have been rational as a single case, but it was out of line. It was also a bigger political mistake than the minister and the prime minister, both Social Democrats, first realized. The case was brought to the attention of parliament during question time, the opposition initiated an interpellation – a formal challenge to the government – on the issue, and within a few days the minister had lost her support among the other parties in the government coalition and soon within the parliament group of her own party. Her only escape was

133

to resign quickly, before the interpellation was debated. It was the first time that a minister of the Finnish government had resigned because of criticism on moral grounds of a single decision or action. The party chose and announced the new minister at once.

This case illustrates many aspects of Finnish political culture in the latter part of the 1990s, such as the following:

- In all democracies, small and easily understood political issues may receive far more public attention than large and important ones.

- Finnish banks and bank directors have lost prestige and popularity, and the political parties are unpopular.

- Because of the red-white cleavage in Finnish society, separate "red capital" had been accumulated mostly as the result of two competing cooperative movements. The Workers' Savings Bank was one of the bastions of red capital, which disappeared almost completely in the 1990s.

- A broadly based majority government can steamroller parliament because of party discipline, but that may cause resentment and a "backbenchers' revolt."

- Typical of Finnish political culture is a very strong demand for fair and equal treatment of all citizens. It is also difficult to sweep any cases under the carpet because of the openness of society, including its very open public administration.

- Corruption is relatively rare in Finnish politics and administration. When, in 1997, the World Bank commissioned a study of the degree of corruption in fifty countries, Finland was found to be the second "cleanest." On a scale from 0 to 10 Finland scored 9.5 points behind only Denmark (9.9). Four years later their order was reversed: Finland scored 9.9 and Denmark 9.5 points. Comparable corruption rating for Sweden was 9.0, for Great Britain 8.3, for the United States 7.6, for Germany 7.4, for France 6.7, and for Italy 5.5; the lowest ratings in that comparison of ninety-one states were Nigeria's 1.0 and Bangladesh's .4 (Shively 2003, p. 14; Transparency International 2001).

Church and Religion

Secularization has been one characteristic of the 20th century. The links connecting churches and religiousness to political life weakened in Western Europe, where "the religious map... has not changed its basic structure since the end of the religious wars in the middle of the seventeenth century" (Lane and Ersson 1995, p. 66). Religious commitment had an impact on people's political outlooks despite ongoing secularization. A generation ago it still was strongly related to partisanship in many countries, including the Netherlands, Austria, and Italy, while it did not explain partisan choice at all in Finland or Sweden (Rose 1974, p. 17). Although religious awareness of the Finnish people tends to be weak, the church and religion have had a very important role in Finnish society (see pages 20, 23-24, 56, and 189), and their influence on the political culture remains significant.

Like the other Nordic countries, Finland became Lutheran as the result of the sixteenth century Reformation. The transfer from its Catholic heritage to Protestantism happened relatively smoothly. Bishop Henry, who in the 1150s was the first bishop of Finland, is thought of as the direct predecessor of the later bishops of the Turku diocese, the archbishops since 1817. The country was divided in two dioceses in 1554. Since 1959 the national church, the Evangelical Lutheran Church, has had eight dioceses. The number of parishes was 586 in 2001. The Church Law of 1686 requested all citizens to belong to the Lutheran Church. In the 1860s local government and church administration were separated, and so were the schools and the church, and the Church Law of 1869 separated in principle the church from the state.

Complete freedom of religion was legislated in 1922. In the Nordic countries, Sweden followed Finland's example in 2000 and separated church and state, whereas Denmark and Norway continue to have Lutheran state churches. Of the Finnish people, 85 percent belonged in 2000 to the Lutheran National Church, making it the world's third largest Lutheran church. The Orthodox Church, with about 56,000 members, is the second largest in Finland. Other significant religious groups in the country include the Pentecostal movement, Jehovah's Witnesses, Roman Catholics, Adventists, the Jewish community, Mormons, Baptists, Methodists, and the Islamic congregations.

By and large, Finnish society has a secular character, not least because of the strong element of individualism in Protestantism. In cross-national comparisons the Finns appear infrequent churchgoers, comparable to people in the other Nordic countries and Russia. Only 8 percent attend a Sunday service at least once a month, while 27 percent have not participated at any religious services during recent years (Salonen et al. 2000, p. 55). Church attendance is high only during the most important religious holidays. However, religious programs on radio and TV have large audiences. One obvious reason why Sunday services are not better attended is the geographic mobility of the population. It was more natural to go to church in traditional rural surroundings than in a confusing urban or suburban environment. A corresponding difference is apparent in the elections of parish councils. In 1998, 20 percent of church members turned out to vote in rural parishes, but only 10 percent voted in urban ones.

One century ago, the challenge of early socialism had an impact on the trend toward secularizing society, and during the first decades of independence the church and politically organized workers tended to drift far apart. Many ministers of the church were even elected to parliament as Conservative members. The distance became narrower during the war.

Once considered conservative, the church no longer has this political image.[35] In the 1990s its pronouncements may have received more support from leftist sympathizers than from conservative sympathizers. There has also been a religiously based party, the Christian Democrats, founded as a reaction to secularization in 1958 (Arter 1987, p. 32). It has been represented in parliament since 1970; in 1999 ten members of the party were elected. It speaks for Christian values in politics but does not cooperate with the Lutheran church.

In private lives, most weddings are church weddings, but divorce rates have increased and, moreover, the church has not been successful in safeguarding the marriage institution, because the lifestyle of unmarried cohabitation has gained social acceptance and legal recognition. About 88 percent of children born in Finland are baptized and 90 percent of fifteen-year-olds are confirmed; 28 percent pray to God every week and a majority of the people at least once a month.

Despite the secularization of society and freedom of religion, the Lutheran church continues to have an important position in Finnish life. Annual sessions of Parliament start with a religious service, the sermon of which may sometimes sharply criticize politicians.[36] The church is visible although not overtly present in the lives of many ordinary citizens, and its pronouncements are listened to. In 1999 the bishops jointly published a strong statement in support of the welfare state and launched a broad discussion on the topic itself and the political role of the church. Also, the new government program in 1999 contained anti-poverty goals drafted within the church. Furthermore, the church has tried to influence political decision-makers by setting an example in its own activity, for instance in development aid and through very concrete support to needy persons after the economic slump of the 1990s.

Some remaining links between church and state were discontinued during the 1990s. Until 1996, the state financed the bishops' councils, which are now paid for by the church itself. For traditional reasons, the president of the republic appointed bishops from three candidates who were elected within the church (customarily the one who ranked first was appointed), but this presidential prerogative was left out of the new Constitution of 1999. However, as the result of effective lobbying by the church, the cooperation of its synod with parliament when church law is amended, remains in the new Constitution (Article 76).

The church has also modernized itself, adjusting old traditions to social change. A tangible example of this was the amendment of the Church Law that has permitted women to become priests. The first women priests were ordained in 1988, and in 1999 25 percent of the parish pastors were

---

35 In its internal activity the church did not permit party labels before the 1990s. In the parish councils elected in 1998 more than ten percent were Social Democrats and Conservatives, about one third belonged to the Center Party, and 27 percent were elected without any party attachment.

36 As of 2000, these services have an ecumenical character.

women. This percentage will eventually rise above 50%, because 60 percent of theology students were women in 1999. Already during the three-year period 1996-1999 more women than men became priests of the Lutheran Church (Salonen et al. 2000, pp. 227, 248).

The Lutheran church has the right to levy taxes (but this is no longer mentioned on the level of the Constitution). Calculated on income taxable by municipal governments, parishes collect between 1.0 and 2.25 percent of their members' income. The actual collection is done in conjunction with state taxes, and the church pays a fee to the state for this convenience.

Government and Opposition

Finland has a multi-party system in which three large parties (the Social Democratic Party, Center Party, and Conservative Party) and a number of smaller ones are represented in parliament. Coalition governments used to be short-lived, averaging about one year, but during the 1980s and thereafter they have lasted the full four-year term of parliament. The periods that other parties are in opposition have grown correspondingly. (See Chapters 8 and 11).

Ordinarily it takes more than two political parties to form a majority government, but hardly ever has a government included all three of the largest parties. Because the large parties are not likely to reveal their preferred coalition partners in advance, the voters cannot base their choice on a clear distinction between two alternatives, one of which will run the next government. Neither do voters have a definite idea of the potential prime ministers fighting for the position. It often happens that the opposition party has a campaign advantage that helps it to an election victory, because it has been in a good position to freely criticize the government. On the other hand, the opposition's campaign can be muted by the desire to avoid burning bridges, as the only way to enter the government is to have a willing partner. Even an election success might not open the gates to the new government coalition if relations with other parties have been allowed to deteriorate badly or if "chemistries" are not compatible otherwise. Earlier, the president's likes and dislikes were also a significant factor in government formation.

Therefore, on the level of political elites there are tactical limits to the sharpness of the overt cleavage between the government and the opposition. One example is the situation in which the chairman of the Center Party, leader of opposition, found himself in 1997 and early 1998. It would have been tempting for him to approach the 1999 election with intense criticisms of relatively unpopular EMU membership, but he would have been unwise to disqualify himself as a potential prime minister in the likely situation that Finland would enter EMU despite the opposition's criticism. Such careful political strategies may confuse many voters.

To some extent the citizens really are divided into government and opposition supporters. An example of competing loyalties was the presidential election of 2000, in which conservative voters had to make their final choice between the bourgeois candidate of the Center Party, which was in opposition, and the female candidate of the ideologically more distant Social Democratic Party, which was in the coalition government with the Conservatives (see Chapter 10). As it turned out, more voters than expected preferred the government partner to the ideologically closer opposition candidate.

The need for government coalitions capable of united action is by no means the only reason why there prevails a certain willingness to reach consensus in the Finnish political system. For a long time, foreign policy was hardly debated at all. Differences in political ideology have largely diminished. As was described in Chapter 5, the system is also characterized by some neocorporate features. In case of a strike, state arbitration is an essential element of the negotiating procedures of Finnish labor market organizations. Also, the organizations may in fact decide national policies among themselves, outside parliament, thus leaving to parliament the mere role of 'rubber stamping' their decisions. They even request the government to take a seat at their negotiating table, because they do not want to settle comprehensive agreements before they know what the government plans to do about taxation (see page 109).

But the evidence shown in Tables 7.3 and 7.4 indicates that the Finnish people have some tendency to be in opposition not to a particular government, but to any government, and not because of the government's policies or its political composition, but simply because it consists of politicians and is formed by political parties. As was shown in Table 4.4, most Finns feel there is some conflict between the people and politicians. The people's desire to increase the power of the individual citizen was actually a driving force behind two constitutional amendments toward direct democracy, first when the possibility of consultative referendums was added to the constitution in 1987, and a second time when direct elections of the president replaced the electoral college in 1991. Similar popular pressure was not confined to Finland. The willingness to use more referendums and initiatives became rather general in democratic nations, where "strengthened commitments to the democratic ideal, and increased skills and resources on the part of contemporary publics, are leading to increased political participation beyond the present forms of representative democracy" (Dalton 1999, p. 76).

8 Elections and Political Parties

... the party systems of the 1960s were older than the majority of their national electorates. Thirty years on, these self-same parties still continue to dominate mass politics in western Europe.

Peter Mair 1997, p. 90

Politics needs sharper edges. The party must have a mission. It does not make sense that anything goes as long as one can sit in the government.

Erkki Pulliainen, Green MP, in 2002

The Electoral Systems

Finland's annual calendar does not name any one day as the year's election day. The national elections follow a full four different cycles, independent of each other. Only once, in October 1996, have two different elections been arranged simultaneously in Finland.

Parliament is elected every four years (1995, 1999, 2003, etc.). Its election day is the third Sunday in March. Early dissolutions would disrupt the predictable four-year circle but they have become quite unlikely; the last took place in 1975.

The president of the republic is elected for a six year term (1994, 2000, 2006, etc.). The presidential elections have two rounds, which take place in January and February with three weeks in between. There is no vice-president. If the president becomes incapacitated, a successor is elected for a full, new six-year term (the prime minister serves as interim president until the election).

The municipal elections, simultaneous in the whole country, take place every four years in October (always shortly before the American presidential elections): 1996, 2000, 2004, etc.

The European elections constitute the fourth cycle; the members of the European Parliament who were elected in June 1999 serve a five-year term from 1999 to 2004. The first election of Finnish MEPs in 1996 took place at the same time as municipal elections.

Consequently, the country's combined election calendar can include calm periods without any elections, such as the years 1997 and 1998, and again in 2001–2002, but some other times can be very crowded, as were 1999–2000, which were filled with five separate elections (Parliament, European Parliament, President in two rounds, and municipal councils).

For the purpose of parliamentary elections the country is divided into fifteen election districts (also known as constituencies). One of them is a single member constituency (Åland).The 199 other parliamentary seats are allocated among fourteen multi-member constituencies in direct proportion to their population.

Some changes in district boundaries may happen occasionally, but changes in the number of inhabitants are not dealt with by redistricting but by reallocating the 199 seats between districts. This is done before each election. In 1999 the representation of election districts varied between seven and thirty-two. This number of representatives was determined on the basis of quite fresh information, namely the head count obtained from the national population register less than six months before election day. The 1999 decision was rather typical: due to changes in population, two declining election districts lost one seat and the seats were added to two growing districts.

In the big parliamentary reform of 1906, Finland adopted the list system of proportional representation, which was very rare at the time. If maximum proportionality had been desired, the country would not have been divided at all into different constituencies, whereas if the aim had been close connection between representatives and voters, there should have been a large number of very small constituencies. The compromise was to divide the country into constituencies, but to make those large enough for a fair proportionality of representation.

The d'Hondt rule has been followed when determining how many seats each party wins in the constituency.[37] Although several details have been altered, the main principles of the electoral system have remained unchanged. There is no national threshold – a minimum number of votes needed to gain representation – such as the 5 percent requirement in Germany or the 4 percent requirement in Sweden. This enables nationally weak but locally popular parties to win seats. The larger the constituency, the smaller the percentage of votes needed for winning a seat. There is no pool of national seats for the purpose of evening out nationwide proportionality. Parliamentary seats are fought for, won, and certified separately in each election district.

In typical list systems of proportional representation, the voters make their choice between party lists in which the nominating parties have prear-

---

37 In order to determine how many seats the parties (or alliances) win in a constituency, the number of votes cast for each party (or alliance) are divided by 1, 2, 3, etc. For comparison, the Saint-Laguë rule uses the odd numbers 1, 3, 5, etc.; its modified method in Scandinavian countries uses the series 1.4, 3, 5, etc. as dividors for distributing seats.

ranged the preference order of their candidates. In some countries the voters are offered the option of changing the order in which the party placed its nominees, but in Finland individual candidates are emphasized even more. Uniquely, the Finnish system requires every voter to choose one single person from among the candidates on one of the party lists. Each candidate in the district has his or her individual number, and the act of voting consists of writing the number of just one candidate inside a circle printed on the small ballot paper. The voter then folds the ballot paper, has it stamped, and drops it in the ballot box. Secrecy of the ballot is guarded carefully and election fraud has been nonexistent.[38]

The choices of individual candidates serve two purposes. As in any list system of proportional representation, the ballots are first counted as votes cast for the parties. This count determines how many seats each party is entitled to have in the election district. But, second, personal votes also rank order the candidates within each respective party. This method does not grant the nominating parties any power to guarantee their favorite nominees' entry to parliament.

Originally Finnish election law made vote-counting somewhat more complicated. The party lists were called "electoral alliances" (primarily, because the word party was never used in formal legislation). Within each "alliance," voters had to choose between numbered lists of candidates containing up to three names (the weight of the second position being one-half, and of the third position one-third of the top place on the list). The maximum number of names on a list was reduced to two in 1936 and to one name since 1954. (See Törnudd 1968, pp. 35–40, 57.) It was formerly possible to nominate the same person in several election districts, but after 1962, when the leader of the Small Farmers' Party ran in every one of the fourteen multi-member constituencies, the law was changed to allow a person to be nominated in one election district only. The district does not need to be the one where he or she resides.

Until the party law was enacted in 1969, each individual candidate seeking nomination needed the supporting signatures of at least 30 eligible persons, who formed a so-called "voters' association." For all practical purposes such associations were only a formality, because the nominations and the signature-gathering were decided and managed by the parties' district organizations. The new law gave the right to nominate parliamentary candidates to registered political parties, and to nobody but the parties. In two elections, 1970 and 1972, the parties had such a monopoly, but since 1975 it has again been possible to nominate additional "wild" candidates. A group of 100 signatories can do it. This procedure opened the route to parliament for Finland's first Green MPs in 1983.

In 1995, the 199 MPs were elected from 2073 candidates (Åland included, there were 2083 candidates), and in the following election in 1999 there were 1981 candidates (including Åland, 1993 candidates).

---

38 Buying votes or or falsifying vote counts would be punishable crimes, but there has been no offences other than some isolated attemps to vote twice decades ago.

The maximum number of candidates one party can nominate in an election district equals the number of seats to be filled in it, except in small districts where the maximum number is fixed at fourteen. The relative share of votes necessary to win a seat in parliament depends on the size of the election district. In North Karelia with only seven seats, more than 14 percent of the ballots were needed but in Uusimaa with 32 representatives, 3.2 percent sufficed.

The parties, and especially the small ones, can improve their chances, albeit with obvious risks, if they join forces and form electoral alliances. If they do, the group of allied parties is treated like a single party within the constituency in question. The risk in joining an alliance is due to the difficulty of predicting which party's candidates will receive the highest numbers of personal votes within the alliance. A party's chances within an alliance are improved if it can persuade its voters to concentrate their votes.

For example, the Christian League (now Christian Democratic Party) has been a clever user of electoral alliances. With 4.2 percent of the national vote in 1999 the party won 10 seats, but it would have won only three seats if it had stood alone in every district. It gained three of the seats with the help of additional votes cast for various miniparties. In one district it gained its seat through an alliance with Conservatives and in three districts through an alliance with Center Party (and in one case, the Center Party lost to its Christian ally a seat that would have otherwise gone to itself).

An obvious consequence of the Finnish election system is that, in addition to typical competition between the parties, there is mutual competition between the individual candidates of the same party. Personal campaigns are a much more important element in Finnish parliamentary elections than in other list systems of proportional representation. As will be discussed later in this chapter, there has also been a growing tendency among the voters to pay more attention to the choice of individual MPs and, accordingly, to consider the choice of party relatively less important.

The elections of the president of the republic used to follow the pattern of parliamentary elections: an electoral college of 300 (later 301) members, which met to make the final choice, was elected like parliament. However, in 1994 this indirect system was replaced with elections in which the people vote for presidential candidates directly. Unless one candidate gets over 50 percent of the votes, the two top-ranking candidates face each other in a runoff three weeks later. France has used similar direct elections since 1965, but has only two weeks between the two rounds.

When elections are held to the European Parliament, the Finns elect their sixteen MEPs in the country at large. Originally political parties had the option of presenting their candidates in four separate districts, but no party chose to do so in the 1996 elections, and the option was eliminated in 1998. Among the fourteen other EU countries, there are only four (Belgium, Ireland, Italy, and the UK) that are divided into election districts in EP elections.

In Finland's municipal elections, even the largest city constitutes one single election district. This maximizes the proportionality of party representation in the city council, but invites the voters to make their one single choice from a very large number of individual candidates. For example, when the 85 members of the Helsinki city council are elected, a party can nominate 127 candidates. Consequently, the city council was elected in 2000 from the total of 906 candidates; in 1992 from even more: 1077 candidates.

Finland used to have two election days, a Sunday and the following Monday, until one-day elections were begun in 1991. A new Election Act became effective in 1998. It did not greatly change the manner in which the four kinds of elections are administered, but was intended mainly to simplify legislation by combining the four separate election laws into one comprehensive act.

Earlier changes in legislation also lowered the voting age step by step from 24 to 18 years, as was outlined above (on page 36). The age requirements for eligibility and suffrage have always been the same. And although it is normal in the world that foreign nationals cannot vote in the country where they live, since 1975 the Nordic countries have allowed the citizens of other Nordic countries to vote in local government elections. Later, this right was extended to all foreign citizens who are permanent residents of Finland. In the European elections of 1999, voting rights and eligibility were granted to all EU citizens resident in the country.

The Party System

A three-dimensional party system developed in the Diet of the Four Estates. The first political division arose from nationalist agitation about the language issue. "By the 1880s the language question had emerged as the most highly charged and salient question in Finnish politics" (McRae 1997, p. 191). The second cleavage concerned Finland's relations with Russia: a strict constitutionalist position was championed by the Swedish Party and the Young Finns (since 1904), while the Old Finns preferred the more careful tactic of compliance and compromise. The third political front resulted from bad social problems and it was linked with the new socialist ideologies. (Teljo 1949, pp. 10–13, 29–30.)

The Finnish Labor Party, founded in 1899 and since 1903 called the Social Democratic Party (SDP) of Finland, organized the country's first mass membership party among industrial workers, tenant farmers, and farm laborers. In the election of March 1907 the party took 80 of the 200 seats, with 37 percent of the vote. The Old Finns, which also had an extensive social reform program, ranked second with 59 seats and 27 percent. The Young Finns got only a disappointing 26 seats, the Swedish People's Party 24, and the Agrarians 9 seats.

In March 1919, in the first election in independent Finland, the SDP again won 80 seats. But it was not the only party of the political left.

143

During the 1920s and after the election of March 1945, it had a challenger on its own left side. As was described in Chapter 3, the Finnish Communist Party sought votes under various banners until it was outlawed in 1930. The Finnish People's Democratic League (FPDL, in Finnish SKDL) became the vehicle for communist electoral appeals after the war. It gained 49 seats with 23.5 percent of the vote in 1945, which made it relatively the third largest communist party in western Europe, smaller only than the communist parties in *Italy* and *France*. An internal opposition, called the Social Democratic League, also broke from the SDP in 1958, but it ran out of popular support in the 1970s.

On the nonsocialist side, the Swedish People's Party was organized in 1906 as a mass political party. The two Finnish parties, the Old and the Young, were restructured in 1918 as the National Coalition, or Conservative Party (the monarchists of 1918) and the National Progressive Party (republicans in 1918). The latter lost a splinter group when changing its name in 1951, until the two merged again in 1965. During the 1930s there was also a party of the far right, called the Patriotic People's Movement (IKL). It won 14 seats in 1933 and 1936.

One political division separated the producers and the consumers. Two agrarian parties were formed in 1906 and fused in 1908, and the Agrarian Union (since 1965, Center Party) grew to be Finland's strongest nonsocialist party in 1919. Only as late as 1979 did it finally – and even then temporarily – yield that rank to the Conservatives. The election of 1970 reduced Center Party representation by thirteen seats, primarily due to the success of its former splinter group, the Finnish Rural Party. The Finnish Christian League (founded in 1958, renamed Finland's Christian Democrats in May 2001) entered parliament in 1970. In 1983 Finland became the second country in Europe (two weeks after Germany) to elect Green representatives to its national parliament.

The party systems of Denmark, Finland, Sweden, and Norway have had a rather similar composition since the 1920s. They have consisted of five political parties, ranging from the far left to the social democrats, agrarians, liberals, and conservatives (see Berglund and Lindström 1978, pp. 16–20). Those elements continued to exist in Finland in the 1990s, although by then the Liberal People's Party had used up its popular support. In addition Finland has the language-based Swedish People's Party. The six parties are the following (the abbreviations refer to Table 8.1):

– The Left Alliance (LEFT) has continued the activity of the SKDL (1944–1990) since April 1990.

– The Social Democratic Party (SDP) has not quite achieved the dominant position of its Swedish counterpart, but it has been Finland's largest party most of the time since 1907.

– The Center party (CENT), having rested in opposition for one 4-year term, increased its number of MPs from forty to fifty-five in 1991 and, since 1995, has again been the second largest party.

- The Progressive Party was succeeded by the Finnish People's Party in 1951, which was succeeded by the Liberal People's Party (LPP) in 1965; in 1995 it lost its only seat in parliament.
- The Conservative Party (CONS), officially called the National Coalition, gained increasing support especially in the 1970s and has been in government since 1987, after twenty-one opposition years from 1966 to 1987.
- The Swedish People's Party (SPP) is the unique element in Finland's party system, and the one representative from Åland typically joins its parliament group.

Many other parties have gained representation over the years. They have included populist flash movements such as the Finnish Rural Party (FRP) in 1970 and in 1983, stable new elements like the Christian Democrats (CHR), and more recent new parties, notably the Greens (GR) who were formally organized as a party in 1988, and the Progressive who only survived from 1995 to 1999. Meanwhile, older political parties have left the scene. The Patriotic People's Movement of the right wing was in existence from 1932 to 1944, and the Finnish Communist Party, founded in Moscow in 1918, was discontinued in 1990; a very small new communist party has adopted its name.

Parliament was elected eight times between 1907 and 1917, and nine times between 1919 and 1939. Table 8.1 summarizes the results of the 16 parliamentary elections from 1945 to 1999. The parties of the left received the majority of the votes once, in 1966. In addition, they won a majority of the seats in 1958. Their poorest showing occurred in 1991, with only 32 percent of the votes and a minority of 67 seats, out of the total of 200.

Thus, Finland has a truly multiple-party system. It is obvious that so many parties reflect many more conflict dimensions than the three basic ones that were represented a century ago.[39] However, the basic ideological dimension from left to right still provides a fundamental base for the ordering of the parties, in parliament as well as within the mass electorate.

Consequently, the most obvious way to picture the entire party system, as it exists on the level of the mass electorate, is to study how the supporters of different political parties place themselves on the dimension which runs from the left to the right. Figure 8.1 illustrates where the supporters of the large parties placed themselves on a scale of left to right in 1975 and again in 1991 and in 2000. The figure gives the mean scores for each group of party supporters, and it shows how the supporters of each party were distributed along this basic dimension. For ex-

39 One analysis in the 1970s recognized among the electorate a party space of seven dimensions: left – right; producers and agriculture – consumers and urban industries; established parties – temporary small parties; recognized and noted centers – the "forgotten people;" Finnish – Swedish; communism – anti-communism; and victorious – losing. Pesonen 1973b, pp. 124–127.

ample, the very heavy line shows how supporters of the Center Party were distributed along the left-right dimension. The light dotted line shows how supporters of the SKDL (1975) or LEFT (1991 and 2000) were distributed, and so on.

Table 8.1

Parliamentary elections in Finland from 1945 to 1999.

	LEFT	SDL	SDP	FRP	CENT	LPP	CHR	CONS	SPP	GR	Other*
					Vote (in pecentages)						
1945	23.5	–	25.1	1.2	21.3	5.2	–	15.0	7.9	–	0.8
1948	20.0	–	26.3	0.3	24.2	3.9	–	17.1	7.7	–	0.5
1951	21.6	–	26.5	0.3	23.2	5.7	–	14.6	7.6	–	0.5
1954	21.6	–	26.2	–	24.1	7.9	–	12.8	7.0	–	0.4
1958	23.2	1.7	23.2	–	23.1	5.9	0.2	15.3	6.7	–	0.9
1962	22.0	4.4	19.5	2.2	23.0	6.3	–	15.0	6.4	–	1.2
1966	21.2	2.6	27.2	1.0	21.2	6.5	0.4	13.8	6.0	–	0.5
1970	16.6	1.4	23.4	10.5	17.1	6.0	1.1	18.0	5.7	–	1.3
1972	17.0	1.0	25.8	9.2	16.4	5.1	2.5	17.6	5.4	–	2.5
1975	18.9	0.3	24.9	3.6	17.6	4.3	3.3	18.4	5.0	–	3.7
1979	17.9	0.1	23.9	4.6	17.3	3.7	4.8	21.7	4.5	–	1.6
1983	14.0	–	26.7	9.7	16.6	1.0	3.0	22.2	4.9	1.4	0.6
1987	13.6	–	24.1	6.3	17.6	1.0	2.6	23.1	5.6	4.0	2.0
1991	10.1	–	22.1	4.8	24.8	0.8	3.1	19.3	5.5	6.8	2.7
1995	11.2	–	28.3	1.3	19.9	0.6	3.0	17.9	5.1	6.5	6.2
1999	10.9	–	22.9	1.0	22.4	0.2	4.2	21.0	5.1	7.3	5.0
					Elected members						
1945	49	–	50	–	49	9	–	28	14	–	1
1948	38	–	54	–	56	5	–	33	14	–	–
1951	43	–	53	–	51	10	–	28	15	–	–
1954	43	–	54	–	53	13	–	24	13	–	–
1958	50	3	48	–	48	8	–	29	14	–	–
1962	47	2	38	–	53	13	–	32	14	–	1
1966	41	7	55	1	49	9	–	26	12	–	–
1970	36	–	52	18	36	8	1	37	12	–	–
1972	37	–	55	18	35	7	4	34	10	–	–
1975	40	–	54	2	39	9	9	35	10	–	2
1979	35	–	52	7	36	4	9	47	10	–	–
1983	27	–	57	17	38	–	3	44	11	2	1
1987	20	–	56	9	40	–	5	53	13	4	–
1991	19	–	48	7	55	1	8	40	12	10	–
1995	22	–	63	1	44	–	7	39	12	9	3
1999	20	–	51	1	48	–	10	46	12	11	1

* Included in "Other" are the Swedish Left (one member in 1945), the Liberal Union (one in 1962), Constitutional party (one in 1975 and 1983), Unity party (one in 1975), the Progressive Finnish Party (two members in 1995), the Ecological party (one in 1995), and the Reform Group (one in 1999).

Figure 8.1

Self-placements on the left-right scale of the supporters of different parties, 1975, 1991, and 2000 (mean scores and distributions)

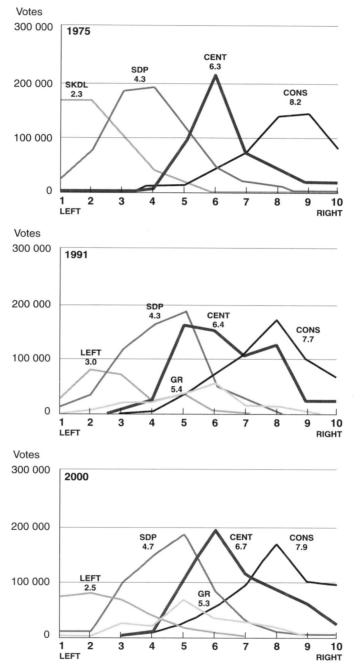

Source: Adopted from Pesonen, Sänkiaho, and Borg 1993, p. 131, and from World Values Survey 2000.

Even on the level of mass support the Finnish multiparty system differs greatly from any bipolar model. In 1975, the supporters of the four major parties clearly formed a quadrilateral system. Although there was some overlap, there were four distinct peaks, one for each party. The mean scores for the SKDL (FPDL) and the Conservative Party supporters were quite far apart, with about 6 scale points separating them (the maximum possible being 9 points).

Sixteen years later the profile of the party system was rather different. The party space had been shrinking among the electorate and it was getting more diffuse. Furthermore, there were only two peaks, because the supporters of the Left Alliance had become too few to stand out, and those of the Center Party were divided into two wings, one left-oriented and the other one overlapping with the Conservatives. The supporters of the Left Alliance were now avoiding the most extreme position and had moved, on average, one step toward the middle point. The Conservatives, in turn, had approached the center of the dimension from the other side. Consequently, the distance between the Left and the Conservatives had narrowed to 4.7 scale points. The Social Democrats had also moved slightly toward the center, although very few of them had crossed the middle point. The Greens entered the party system without any obvious place on the left-right dimension.

During the 1990s the picture returned somewhat to what was found in 1975. In 2000 the mean positions of the Left Alliance and the Conservative supporters are separated by 5.1 scale points; the minor widening being caused by a slightly increased readiness in both groups to again choose the extreme position. The voters of Center Party form only one peak, as they did in 1975, and now their typical self-placement is as close to the SDP as is possible without either one's peak crossing the left/right divide. The mean scale points of these two parties, however, are not closer than before, because the bulks of their supporters lean in the expected ideological direction.

The shrinking and the de-ideologizing of the Finnish party system have had unprecedented parallels on the elite level. First, in 1987, the Conservatives and the Social Democratic Party formed a coalition government without the mediating Center Party. Then, after the more "natural" Center-Conservative coalition, the government formed in 1995 again included the Social Democrats and the Conservatives, but left out the Center Party. And now the coalition also included the Left Alliance, heir to the Communists. Such cooperation between the far left and the political right would have been utterly impossible in the 1980s, not to mention the first twenty years of Finland's independence, when even the Social Democrats and the bourgeois parties were unable to govern together. But the five parties of the "rainbow" coalition formed in 1995 worked quite well with each other, and a similar government was again formed after the 1999 election (see Table 11.1 below).

In the real life of all European democracies, political parties had quite a central role long before their existence was acknowledged in formal legislation. In Finland, various roundabout expressions were used in order to regulate what was, in reality, done by the parties. This needed to be changed when the parties were granted state subsidies in 1967, and in 1969 the Party Act was legislated. At the same time a new Election Act gave registered parties the sole right to nominate candidates for national elections, until "wild" candidates were again permitted after two such restricted elections. In practice no wild candidate had ever won a seat in parliament before the election of 1983, when a party monopoly would have indeed prevented the election of the first Green MPs.

Party Organizations

The candidates for parliamentary elections are nominated by the district organizations of political parties, without much interference from the national leadership. The national boards or councils of the parties, in turn, choose candidates for the European elections, and party conventions are convened to decide who will be the party's candidate for president. The municipal-level party organizations nominate candidates for local elections. In addition, temporary citizen groups have the right to by-pass the parties and to put up their own candidates, if they collect the required number of supporting signatures (20,000 in presidential, 2000 in European, 100 in parliamentary, and 10 in municipal elections).

The three levels of candidate nomination illustrate the hierarchical structure of party organizations and, also, the different scopes of their political environments. In addition, there is a fourth level below the national, district, and municipal party organizations. It consists of the basic party units on the "grass roots" level.

In 1995, eight Finnish parties had a total of 7200 local units in their membership organizations, of which Center Party alone had 3600. The Social Democratic Party had 1200 and the Conservative Party 1100. The aggregate number of card-carrying members, according to the registers kept by the parties, was 448,000 (13 percent of the electorate), of whom Center Party had 257,000, the Social Democratic Party 70,000 and the Conservatives 47,000. In earlier years the party organizations had been larger: in 1979 there were about 9000 local party units and 600,000 individual members, and in the early 1970s the total may have exceeded 700,000 members. (Sundberg 1996, pp. 47, 89; Borg 1997, p. 40.) One review in early 2001 calculated that no more than 7 percent of the electorate belonged to a party organization.

Thus, the political parties have been losing members, and Finland is by no means the only country where this has happened. Examples of dramatic declines between 1960 and 1990 include Denmark, where the percentage of party members sank from 22 to 7 percent, and Great Britain, where total membership was reduced from 9 to 3 percent. The decline of party members is very much due to the parties' inability to recruit young persons; only 5 percent of Finns between eighteen and thirty years of age joined party organizations in the 1990s. The average age of the total electorate is forty-seven years in Finland, but in 1996 that of the members of Center Party was fifty years, and of the other parties, fifty-six years (Borg 1997, p. 45). Furthermore, political parties are losing the willingness of their members to participate actively: local organizations tend to meet seldom, and only one-third of the members say they take part.

Although political parties continue to perform very important functions in the society, they are handicapped by negative popular attitudes toward them and, especially, attitudes toward politicians in general (see Tables 4.5 and 7.4). Despite this, there are well motivated party members, too. In one survey among members of parties, where the respondents were offered a list of various possible reasons why they had joined the party, almost all said ideological reasons were important. More than one-half of members also thought that their general political interest, the desire to be better informed, the desire to influence political decisions, and the legacy from home were of importance (op.cit., p. 57).

It is possible that the regular public subsidies which fund party organizations have reduced both the need of the parties to recruit many more active members and the interest of people to volunteer their time for party work. Direct state subsidies for the parties amount to no more than .03 percent of the state budget, but especially at the beginning, they provoked much popular criticism (Pesonen 1973). Between 1968 and 1991 the total annual subsidy climbed from FIM 10 million to FIM 71.6 million, but due to the state's difficult financial position, the amount was reduced to FIM 60.4 million (from $14 to $12 million) in 1994. In 2002 the direct subsidy was 11.8 million euros.

Annual support from the state budget is divided between the parties' membership organizations in proportion to the size of the parliamentary groups, i.e. how many members each party has in parliament. In addition to regular party subsidies, party organizations receive direct support from the state for their foreign contacts and for the European, national, and local elections; the amount was 0.7 million euros in the non-election year 2002. Furthermore, they receive various kinds of covert state support, earmarked for their youth, women's, and pensioners' organizations, as well as for adult education, the party press, cultural organizations, adult activities, and temperance societies. (Wiberg 1997.)

According to the Party Act, an association can be registered as a political party if it meets four requirements: its primary purpose is political influence on the national level, it has at least 5000 eligible supporters, its rules guarantee democratic procedures in its internal decision-making and in its activities, and its political goals are stated formally in a party program. These requirements rule out parties with only narrow local interest, or without a declared party program. In the event that a registered party fails to win a seat in parliament in two consecutive elections, it is removed from the official party register (unless it can again show 5000 supporters, as the Liberal Party did in spring 2002).

To some extent these legal requirements combine three different aspects of the concept of a political party: they deal with the goals and the size of the parliamentary parties, with the popular support for electoral parties, and with the internal processes of membership parties. Indeed, while political parties are broadly defined actors in the political system, they can be analyzed and compared from any one of these three angles. The present description of Finland's party organizations has concerned the last-mentioned aspect, the membership parties.

The important roles of membership parties include recruiting people to political activity, discussing and defining political goals, and providing a link between people's desires and governmental decision-making. Electoral parties will be described in the next section, and parliamentary parties are primarily dealt with in Chapter 9 below.

On the national level, different political parties also have different rules and practices concerning the linkage between their membership organizations and their parliamentary or ministerial groups. The ministers and the parliament groups of the leftist parties have consulted the leading bodies of their membership organization more than the parties of the right which, in turn, have given more leeway to their parliamentary party groups. However, the chairman of the party's membership organization has become the focus of attention so that he or she is the most obvious link connecting all three elements: the chairman is the party's top candidate for a ministerial position while also personifying the entire party in the mass media and in the minds of the electorate.

Election Campaigns and Voting Behavior

The Election Act of 1998 stipulates that the deadline for nominating candidates is 40 days before election day in all four types of elections. In practice the parties act much earlier. For example, most candidates for the parliamentary election that took place in March 1999 were nominated by November 1998.

Primary elections, arranged by party organizations among their members, were widely used in the 1980s and early 1990s, but they have lost some of their appeal and usefulness. Even when the district organizations invite their members to vote for potential candidates, as for instance the Social Democrats must always do, some parliamentary candidates can be left to be named later by the district board.

It is in the tactical interest of the parties to present a balanced list of candidates, a list appealing to a variety of voter groups and to various areas of the district. This may include celebrities who have become well known outside politics, such as Olympic gold medalists, pop stars and tv personalities, even former beauty queens. Incumbents usually have the best chance of renewing their place on the party's list of parliamentary candidates. They also have the best chance of getting elected: of the 200 members elected in 1999, 122 were incumbents who returned from the outgoing parliament.

Election campaigns are costly, although many forums offer free exposure to the parties and candidates. In particular, tv and radio debates and other coverage, newspaper reporting and interviews, and so on, make the campaign visible. During the 1990s, it gradually became possible to buy political advertising on the electronic media. This was first permitted on local radio stations and cable tv, then on nationwide commercial radio and tv channels. Newspaper advertisements and outdoor posters have, naturally, very long traditions. Old-time campaign trails and meetings have been losing audiences and significance but they have not disappeared either.

The campaigns run by political parties are complemented and very much flavored by the personal campaigning of the candidates. The parties may determine general rules or guidelines, such as a request to make the party's name visible in each individual campaign advertisement, but the aim of the candidates is not only to draw support for their party at large. They want to attract attention to themselves in order to beat the candidates of the same party.

While individual candidates are essential for making campaigns lively and visible, they also carry a significant part of the total financing of Finland's election campaigns. In the European elections in June 1999, the elected Finnish MEPs used an average of 400,000 Finnish markkas (about 70,000 euros) to run their personal campaign, without receiving hardly any contribution from the party organization. In the parliamentary elections of 1999, with almost 2000 candidates, the elected representatives paid an average FIM 130,000 (€ 22,000) for their personal campaigns and the non-elected candidates about FIM 30,000 (€ 5000) but, of course, the actual amounts varied greatly (Venho 1999, pp. 12-18).

A new law on campaign finance was enacted in 2000 and became effective in connection with the municipal elections of that year. Its coverage is narrow: it does not concern the parties and it does not limit the amount of campaign spending, but it does require successful candidates to report their campaign expenditures and to make public any campaign contributions which exceed 1700 euros in parliamentary and local elections, or 4300 euros in European and presidential elections. In practice the candidates have long been rather open when interviewed by the media about their campaign costs.

An increasing number of voters have become more interested in the individual candidates than in the choice of a political party. In surveys in connection with the 1983 parliamentary elections and again in 1991, the voters were asked the following question: "What, ultimately, do you think mattered more in your voting, the party or the candidate?" The answers were distributed almost identically, with 51 percent in 1983 and 52 percent in 1991 replying "the party," while 42 and 43 percent said "the candidate" (Pesonen 1995, p. 118). Since then even more voters have claimed they focus on the individual candidate more than the party.

When asked, "Outside party affiliation, what was the most important reason you chose the candidate you voted for?" the respondents gave a large variety of explanations. The most common reasons concerned the personal qualifications of their chosen candidates: their reliability, talent, pleasantness, familiarity, and previous experience. Likewise, a factor analysis showed "experience" to be the strongest explanations of candidate choice, "issue orientation" and "womanhood" being additional but weaker ones. (Op. cit., pp. 125-126.) Consequently, it seems possible that when Finnish voters cast their ballot for one individual candidate, they add an element of confidence to the prevailing images of parliament and political parties. While politicians as a group are much criticized and distrusted (see Chapter 7), such negative feelings may be counteracted by the perceived trustworthiness of the voters' own representative.

There has been an increase in the volatility of voters, in Finland and elsewhere. More and more Finnish voters delay making their choice until close to election day, and party loyalty has been declining.[40] However, most voters continue to define themselves as supporters of some party and, by and large, the results of elections are not very unpredictable. In Finland the changes in voters' party preference seem more frequent fairly soon after the election than toward the end of the term or even during the next election campaign. Thus, the main function of the campaigns is to draw people's attention to the election, to strengthen party loyalties, and to increase interest in politics and to mobilize less motivated persons to vote.

The government, too, tries to add something to the mobilizing effect of campaigns. Not only is the registration of voters automatic, but a reminder of the approaching election is mailed to every person listed in the register. The letter details the location of the addressee's polling station and the time when votes can be cast in advance at a post office or in local government offices. The elections are held on a Sunday. The second election day, the following Monday, was eliminated in 1991, but, on the other hand, advance voting has become so common in Finland that about one-third of all ballots are cast before election day. Handicapped persons can even invite the election administrators to visit their home for voting.

Nevertheless, turnout has become a special problem. As was indicated in Chapter 2, the highest turnout percentages in Finland's parliamentary elections were reached in the 1960s and, since 1982, Finnish voters have

40 Majorities of roughly equal sizes voted in accordance with their pre-campaign intentions in the EU-referendum in 1994, as is found in elections; but very late decisions were more frequent in the referendum and opinion changes more frequent in elections. Pesonen 1998, p. 133.

153

been more activated by presidential elections than by parliamentary elections. Men used to be more active voters than women, until this was reversed in the 1980s. In all countries, young age groups tend to participate less than the middle-aged, and the very low involvement, or alienation, of some subgroups of young citizens has caused much concern in Finland. In the 1980s and 1990s the difference between age groups became even wider within a variety of social backgrounds, so that non-voting seems to be a permanent feature of young people's political behavior (Martikainen and Wass 2002).

9 Parliament

...we may say that the British members of parliament are there to talk, whereas the members of working parliaments are there to do legislative work.

Esaiasson and Heidar 2000, p. 5

I would like to have more influence, but in the Left Alliance it is not possible.

MP Marjatta Stenius-Kaukonen in 2002

Functions and Workload

According to Section 2 of the Finnish Constitution, "All sovereign power in Finland belongs to the people, who are represented by Parliament convened in session." Having said that, the Constitution Act of 1919 outlined the separation of powers as follows: "Legislative power shall be exercised by Parliament in conjunction with the President of the Republic;" "Supreme executive power shall be vested in the President of the Republic;" and "Judicial power shall be exercised by independent courts of law." Thus the Constitution Act put parliament above all other institutions. In the new Constitution of 1999 the corresponding Section 3 goes even further: it makes no reference at all to the president's role in legislation.

Indeed, the new constitution sought to make parliament's position distinctly more central than before, for example, by giving it the task of electing the prime minister. At the same time, the Constitution of 1999 added more efficiency to parliament's work. Some of its procedures were expedited and many stipulations were moved from the constitutional level of the old Parliament Act to the level of ordinary legislation, Parliament's Rules of Procedure, thus making them more easily changeable.

As mentioned above (on page 35), Finland's modern 200-member parliament (in Finnish: *Eduskunta*) was elected eight times between 1907 and 1917. Between the two world wars, from 1919 to 1939, there were nine parliamentary elections. The "long parliament" that was elected in

July 1939 served until March 1945. During the post-war period from 1945 to 1999 there have been sixteen parliamentary elections. Their results were summarized above in Table 8.1.

The parliamentary election term was originally three years, but it was extended to four years in 1954. Within the four years, the business of the Eduskunta is organized in annual sessions. According to the Parliament Act of 1906, the duration of the annual session was 90 days, extended in 1918 to 120 days. These became unrealistic time limits. The increased workload has gradually made membership of parliament a full time occupation; since the 1950s annual sessions have lasted more than 220 days, and during the 1991-1994 term the average number of annual sitting days was 265. However, MPs manage to take a leave during two months in the summer and more than one month around Christmas time.[41]

The wide spectrum of policy areas that the legislature deals with is well illustrated by the committee structure. There are fourteen permanent committees, namely, the Constitutional, Legal affairs, Foreign Affairs, Finance, Administration, Transport and Communications, Agriculture and Forestry, Defense, Eduction and Culture, Social Affairs and Health, Economic Affairs, Labor and Equality, Environment, and Future Committee. In addition, parliament appoints a Grand Committee, which used to resemble a second chamber because it reviewed all the bills. Since 1990 it has deliberated only those bills that the whole house refers to it. However, in 1995 it was given the new and laborious role of serving as parliament's European Affairs Committee.

Each year the government submits some 200 to 300 bills, and there are up to 200 private member's bills. For example, during the parliamentary term of 1983–1986 the total number of government motions was 989 (of which 952 were approved), and the number of private member's legislative initiatives was 608 (only 15 approved). But this was not all: the total number of items on the agenda was 17,884. They included 7975 private member's budgetary initiatives to amend the government's budget proposals (870 approved), 4331 petitions (12 approved), and almost 4000 written or oral questions to the ministers (Noponen 1989, p. 218). The total number of items on parliament's agenda was only 11, 837 in 1995-1998, due to fewer private members' budgetary initiatives, petitions, and legistlative initiatives.

Parliament's workload tends to increase toward the end of each election term. Comparisons between the first and the fourth annual session illustrate the pattern. Calculated for the five four-year terms between 1979 and 1998, the total duration of plenary sessions increased from 352 to 622 hours on average. The number of government bills grew from 218 to 303, and written questions more than doubled from 409 to 921. Only the members' petitions followed a reverse pattern: they averaged 1470 peti-

41 Occasionally the Eduskunta needs to break its break, as on 10 January 2002, when it met to authorize sending Finnish soldiers to Afghanistan. This was the first extra meeting of its kind since 1962.

tions following an election, but 665 in the last annual session. (Data source: http://fakta.eduskunta.fi.)

"Legislative power" defines parliament's central function. But, in addition, parliament decides the state's finances when approving the annual budget. In the area of foreign policy, the president and the ministers responsible for foreign affairs discuss the most important policy decisions with parliament's Foreign Affairs Committee, and parliament can also instruct ministers on matters that are on the agenda of the European Council. International treaties need to be ratified by it.

There are some administrative functions as well. The Eduskunta controls the Bank of Finland through the board of supervisors elected by parliament and, likewise, it has control over the Social Insurance Institution and the Finnish Broadcasting Company. More important, however, is the general control that parliament exercises over the entire administrative branch.

In short, the Eduskunta both determines the direction of national policies and controls how the country is governed. However, the source of "all sovereign power," the people of Finland, have somewhat ambivalent attitudes toward their Eduskunta. While they respect it they also tend to feel that it does not meet their expectations.

According to a study carried out in 1975, the Finns considered the government and parliament equally important institutions in their influence on people's lives, far more important than municipal councils, trade unions, state bureaucracy, etc. And fewer Finns than Americans, Austrians, or Germans thought that politicians occupy an unduly privileged position in society (Pesonen and Sänkiaho 1979, pp. 52–57, 94). Moreover, most Finns think that the Eduskunta has the right amount of power and those who do not are more likely to want to increase its power rather than to decrease it (see Table 7.3). Yet most Finns, not unlike the citizens of other western democracies, think that "Parties are only interested in people's votes, but not in their opinions," and "Those we elect to parliament lose touch with the people pretty quickly" (Pesonen et al. 1993, pp. 485–486; Political Action 1979, pp. 178–180). Even so, attitudes have changed: in 2000 fewer people had confidence in parliament than two decades earlier (Table 7.4).

Organization and Procedures

At the beginning of each annual session parliament elects its speaker and two vice speakers. These three are normally from different parties, and the first speaker cannot vote. It is also customary that the speaker and the prime minister come from different parties. Members of the fourteen permanent specialized committees are chosen for the duration of the entire legislative term. They must be appointed within seven days of the opening of the first session. Parliament may also appoint ad hoc committees. In practice, it selects the committee members unanimously and divides committee seats among different parties in proportion to the strength of the party groups. Likewise, all parties get their share when the committees elect their own chairpersons and deputy chairpersons.

The Grand Committee has 25 regular members and 13 alternate members. The Finance Committee has 21 and 19, and the other committees have 17 regular and 9 alternate members. The speaker of parliament and the deputy speakers do not belong to any committee; neither do government ministers. Because of the relatively large size of the committees, each member of parliament typically belongs to two of them.

The main task of the Eduskunta is to deliberate and approve new legislation. The scope of bills varies greatly: some government motions may concern minor amendments to existing laws, but others may involve important social reforms. The handling of a bill begins with a debate in a plenary sitting (a sitting of the whole parliament), after which the bill is assigned to a specialized committee. The plenary can also require other committees to issue a statement on the bill to the committee that is in charge of it. In its report the committee can propose that the bill be approved with or without changes or that it be rejected, and members of the committee who disagree with the report can have their dissenting opinion appended to it. After the committee stage, the bill returns to the plenary sitting, which may also refer it to the Grand Committee.

Until 2000, bills went through three readings but the reformed constitution combined the first and second reading and the procedure was condensed to two readings only. The first reading, after the general debate, examines the bill item by item, and at this time opposition members generally propose amendments. The second reading must wait at least three days. Its purpose is to either approve or reject the bill; the contents can no longer be changed. Bills lapse if they have not been dealt with before the next election.

If a bill involves amending, interpreting or repealing a constitutional norm, it must be reviewed by the Constitutional Committee and the approved bill is left pending until after the next parliamentary election. The newly elected Eduskunta must then approve the bill by a two-thirds majority. However, a practical shortcut is possible; a bill involving a constitutional law can be declared urgent by a five-sixth majority of votes, after which the same parliament can approve it by a two-thirds majority. This procedure has also allowed exceptions to be made to the constitution without a constitutional amendment. That is a unique feature of the Finnish constitution.

The annual budget of the state passes through one reading only. The preliminary debate, usually in mid-September, follows the Finance Minister's introduction of the budget proposal. After that the proposal is sent to the Finance Committee, which normally reports in December. Parliament deals with it in a single reading that typically lasts several days. Normally this scrutiny results in nothing more than minor changes in the government's budget proposal, because most private member's motions are rejected.

Other types of parliamentary business include annual reports required of the council of state (i.e. the government) and various state organs. They are also sent to a committee and subsequently handled by parliament in a single reading. In addition, the government can submit a report or statement to parliament on some matter concerning the nation's administration or relations with foreign states. These reports are dealt with in a plenary sitting with or without the committee stage. The relatively few interpellation debates take precedence over all other business (see Chapter 11).

The sittings are held on Tuesdays, Wednesdays, and Fridays. Parliament has attempted to make its plenaries the foremost venue for topical political discussion in Finland. Some debates are genuinely exciting and the most important ones also get live coverage on tv and radio, but other plenaries may degenerate into boring sequences of solo speeches read to an empty hall (or, at best, to monitors in the members' offices). All of them, including interjections, are published quickly in the official minutes.[42]

Actually the agenda for major political discourse in Finland is often set by the mass media. Parliament, in turn, has several opportunities to bring matters of current significance before a plenary session. As reviewed above, they include oral questions during the weekly question hour, interpellations (challenges to ministers signed by at least 20 members), topical discussions, and announcements by the prime minister. Which approach is chosen can be influenced by individual MPs and their party groups, by the Speaker's Council, and by the government. Individual MPs also submit written questions to the minister whose sphere of competence covers the matter, and the answers to these questions are also distributed in writing only.

Finland's constitution makes no reference to political parties, but obviously they form an essential element in the structures and work of parliament. In the plenary hall the members are seated as party groups from left to right (as viewed from the speaker's podium, see Figure 9.1). Five traditional party groups have seats extending to the front row, typically assigned to their senior members. Each party group (faction) decides jointly on its policies at least once a week, if not more frequently, in the permanent meeting room assigned to it. Party groups annually elect chairpersons who perform important functions in the Eduskunta, like their counterparts in other parliaments. The staffs of the party groups and the personal assistants of individual MPs are subsidized from public funds.

Legislative Behavior

Parliamentary parties occupy a truly central role in the work of parliament. They structure its votes to such an extent that it seems more realis-

---

42   During 2001, ten MPs (not counting government ministers) made between 110 and 200 speeches in the plenaries, while some spoke hardly at all.

Figure 9.1

Seating order of MP

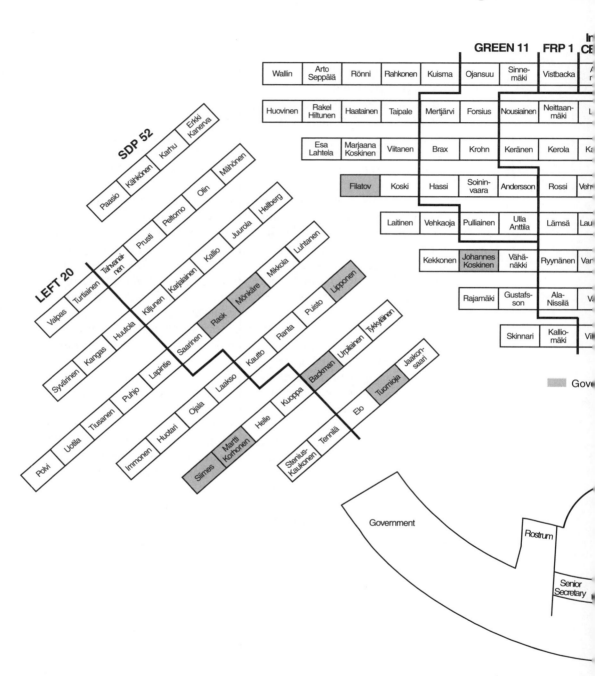

160

plenary hall in 2002

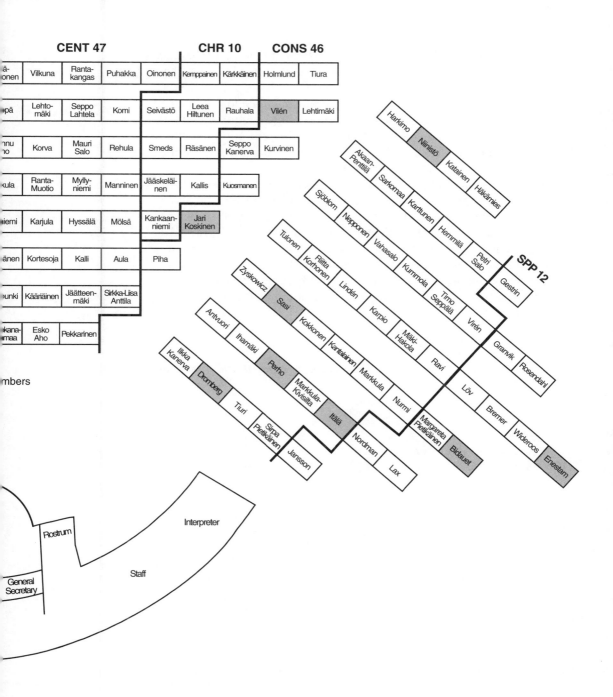

CENT 47 **CHR 10** **CONS 46**

| ä-
onen | Vilkuna | Ranta-
kangas | Puhakka | Oinonen | Kemppainen | Kärkkäinen | Holmlund | Tiura |

| pä | Lehto-
mäki | Seppo
Lahtela | Komi | Seivästö | Leea
Hiltunen | Rauhala | Vilén | Lehtimäki |

| nnu
no | Korva | Mauri
Salo | Rehula | Smeds | Räsänen | Seppo
Kanerva | Kurvinen |

| kula | Ranta-
Muotio | Mylly-
niemi | Manninen | Jääskeläi-
nen | Kallis | Kuosmanen |

| niemi | Karjula | Hyssälä | Mölsä | Kankaan-
niemi | Jari
Koskinen |

| änen | Kortesoja | Kalli | Aula | Piha |

| unki | Kääriäinen | Jäätteen-
mäki | Sirkka-Liisa
Anttila |

| kana-
maa | Esko
Aho | Pekkarinen |

mbers

SPP 12

Harkimo — Niinistö — Katainen — Häkämies

Akaan-Penttilä — Sarkomaa — Karttunen — Hemmilä — Petri Salo

Sjöblom — Nepponen — Vähäsalo — Kummola — Gestrin

Tulonen — Riitta Korhonen — Lindén — Karpio — Timo Seppälä — Virén

Zyskowicz — Sasi — Kokkonen — Kantalainen — Mäki-Hakola — Ravi — Granvik — Rosendahl

Antvuori — Ihamäki — Perho — Markkula — Nurmi — Löv — Bremer — Wideroos

Ilkka Kanerva — Dromberg — Tiuri — Markkula-Kivistö — Itälä — Margareta Pietikäinen — Bladauet — Enestam

Sipa Pietikäinen — Jansson — Nordman — Lax

Interpreter

Rostrum

General
Secretary

Staff

161

tic to view the Eduskunta as the sum total of its party groups than as an aggregate of its 200 individual members. In the event that the result of the vote will determine whether or not the government enjoys the confidence of parliament, party groups tend to be unanimous, whereas in politically less important decisions the parties may tolerate dissent, even though voting as a block is the normal state of affairs. Different parties may exercise different degrees of party discipline.

When the communist-dominated SKDL (FPDL) entered parliament in 1945, its party group was exceptionally well disciplined. This is seen in Table 9.1, which shows the values for Stuart Rice's index of cohesion, calculated for the party groups in open votes during three legislative periods, from 1945 to 1954. As the index values range from 0.0 to 100.0, the SKDL's score (95.1 in 1948-1951) came rather close to unanimity. However, even the lowest cohesion, that of the Swedish People's Party, indicated a fairly strong tendency to vote in unison.

The party system changed after the war, when a large new party of the left entered the scene. A comparison between all votes and those on SKDL proposals reveals that Social Democratic MPs were at first somewhat ambivalent in the new situation: their group tended to be divided on SKDL proposals, until it assumed the more general pattern of opposing communist proposals with above-average cohesion. However, the Agrarians and the SDP group were not as cohesive in those votes as were the right wing parties, possibly because the two parties competed for the same voters as the SKDL.

Table 9.1

Average cohesion of party groups in the Eduskunta during three legislative periods, 1945-1954*

Years	SKDL	SDP	AGR	PROGR	CONS	SPP
All Open Votes:						
1945–1948	92.1	76.6	81.9	83.3	85.7	75.5
1948–1951	95.1	86.6	87.3	82.0	84.0	74.5
1951–1954	94.9	81.7	82.6	86.2	85.5	81.3
SKDL Proposals Only:						
1945–1948	95.7	55.0	79.8	82.9	85.4	77.4
1948–1951	99.2	82.0	84.3	91.8	93.6	90.2
1951–1954	97.1	84.7	88.7	91.6	92.7	93.9

* Rice's index, the values of which range from 0.0 (a 50/50 division) to 100.0 (unanimous).

Source: Nyholm and Hagfors 1968.

Indeed, cohesive party groups have become the norm in parliamentary voting. According to a comparison of divisions in final third readings in 1995-1996, the index scores for cohesive voting appeared higher than those found four decades earlier. All bourgeois parties (Christian League, Swedish People's Party, Conservatives, and Center Party) scored about 90 on the scale of 0 to 100; the SDP group (84.9) scored also higher than previously. The only exception was the Left Alliance, whose score 85.3 indicated that its group was looser than the SKDL group had been. But although the party groups in the Finnish Eduskunta approach unanimity, they are not more but less cohesive than party groups in the four other Nordic parliaments. Such a difference may be caused by the emphasis which Finland's election system places on individual candidates. (Jensen 2000.)

One obvious reason why individual MPs do not deviate much from their party group's line is their increasingly heavy workload. They simply do not have enough time to stay abreast of all the issues. Also, party groups may overcome their internal differences before votes are taken. When the government's standing is at stake, it is natural for the government parties to come together to support the government, while the opposition parties oppose it. Moreover, the system of proportional elections emphasizes the members' belief in the party as the main focus of representation.

On the level of the prevailing principles of representative democracy there is a certain inconsistency in Finland. According to the Constitution (Section 29), "Each Member of Parliament is obliged to act in line with justice and truth in the exercise of his mandate. He should observe the Constitution and is not bound by any other instructions." Obviously this means that neither the political parties nor any outside interests should interfere with the independent legislative decisions of any individual MP. However, such a principle of uninstructed "trustee" legislators is hardly consistent with the purpose of proportional representation, which aims at a representative body that correctly mirrors the distribution of votes cast for each of the parties or, as they used to be called, each "direction of opinion."

During the early years of the unicameral parliament, the public really viewed the ideal representatives of the people as "trustees," in fact not unlike the earlier members of the Diet of the Four Estates: "He (or she) interrupted his regular activity annually and left his place of residence, where he was a respected, talented, and well-known citizen, in order to offer his experience and expertise temporarily to taking care of public affairs." Such was the ideal portrayed mainly by the bourgeois press of the time, although by 1907 the first professional politicians had risen to parliament from the political and trade organizations of the workers. Only gradually – since the 1940s or even later – has it become generally accepted that membership of parliament should be treated and rewarded as a main occupation. (Törnudd 1982, p. 738.)

Even the members of parliament do not think of themselves as elected only for the purpose of using their own, independent judgment. In their minds they manage to combine the "other instructions" with their "own" judgment. A comparison of role orientations illustrates this. Four decades ago John C. Wahlke and his colleagues distinguished three representa-

163

tional role orientations that were characteristic of how American state legislators relate to their decision-making behavior. Those were called trustee, delegate, and politico. Most state legislators had the trustee orientation (Wahlke et al. 1962, p. 281). However, about one-half of American congressmen were politicos, an orientation which combines the two others (Davidson 1969, p. 117). In the Finnish Eduskunta the combining politico-orientation was held by no fewer than 67 percent. Only 20 percent were trustees and 13 percent thought of themselves as delegates. (Oksanen 1972, p. 186.)

In the mid-1990s, many Finnish MPs still adhered to the "Burkean" idea and thought it important to "promote views one personally considers important." These MPs were more numerous than those who considered it important to represent either their own constituency, "private citizens seeking help," particular economic interests (businessmen, farmers, etc.), or some socio-economically disadvantaged group (youth, women, etc.). But the widely held independence principle could be regarded as a complement to the representation of specific interests, rather than an alternative to it, and this is true not only of Finland but in all Nordic parliaments. Characteristic of Finnish MPs was to consider their mandate less party-bound than their Nordic colleagues did. (Esaiasson 2000, pp. 58–62.)

The professionalization of the membership of parliament and the lessening role orientation of purely trustee-type legislators have also had an impact on how the mass public thinks about parliamentarians. It has become common among Finns to assume tough "employer attitudes" toward members of parliament, meaning an unwillingness to pay high salaries to them and a tendency to scrutinize their attendance, activity, and accomplishments.

One easy way of observing the working habits of MPs is to examine how regularly they attend meetings of the whole house and of the committees. Occasionally newspapers publish counts of attendance, commonly doing so at the end of the annual sessions and close to elections. Hardly ever is everybody present, and some members are absent more than others. Typically some 30 members do not push their roll call button, often due to increasing international obligations but also for other reasons. MPs are supposed to give advance notice of absences and state why they will not be attending a plenary.[43]

Although some members may be absent for an extended period, the

43 In order to illustrate such reasons, we might review the count of non-attendance for one single Friday (*Helsingin Sanomat* April 7, 2000). On that day, 37 of the 200 MPs were not present. Four women MPs had been granted maternity leave. Five other MPs were ill. Eight members were on their way home from the parliamentary assembly meeting of the Council of Europe in Strasbourg, and five ministers of the government were taking part in meetings or consultations abroad (China, USA, Portugal etc.). One minister simply entered the unusually short session too late. Other reasons, given by 14 absentees, included meetings of three European-level parties in Brussels, one tv interview, meetings of various non-political organizations, and private business.

Finnish parliament has not solved the problem of substitution in situations when an MP obtains a long leave of absence. Only those elected to the European Parliament were temporarily replaced in 1995 by their deputies (the candidates of the same party who were closest to being elected in the previous parliamentary election).

A much publicized case of long leaves occurred in 1970, when three young MPs vacated their seats temporarily in order to do their military service. Maternity leaves of one year's duration have not been uncommon either. Election to parliament is a serious commitment, and it requires parliament's approval and a very good reason to terminate membership before the end of the four-year term. Temporary leaves of long duration became a heated issue in March 2000, when Esko Aho, the defeated presidential candidate of the Center Party, was invited for one academic year to lecture and study at Harvard University. Parliament simplified its rules just enough to make the leave possible, but the basic problem of temporary duties remained unsolved.

The Members of Parliament

Once elected, members of parliament have a good chance of being re-elected at least twice. In 1999 there were 78 who had not been in the outgoing parliament, among them fifty-eight "freshman" legislators. Most of the others (127) had already served two or more four-year terms, although only eight had been in parliament for twenty years or more.[44]

The members of the Finnish parliament come from a wide spectrum of social backgrounds. Of the 200 MPs elected in 1999, more than 130 are university graduates, including 20 holding a law degree, 13 physicians, and 9 with a Ph.D. Thirty-five have master's degrees in the social sciences and seven in agriculture. There are nine other farmer MPs. The number of MPs with blue-collar jobs was down to five in 1999, and eight others had been working full time as trusted representatives of their co-workers.

Over the years, the social background of Finnish MPs has changed much, as has society in general. The number of farmers elected to parliament was 58 in 1958, but declined to 12 in 1987. During the same period the number of civil servants in parliament rose from 35 to 100, and the number of MPs with at least an masters-level university education rose from 67 to 106 (Noponen 1989, pp. 127, 131). What is unchanged is the general tendency of Finnish (and other) voters to select candidates whose social status is higher than their own.

Almost all Finnish MPs have participated actively in local government and about two-thirds have had active roles in their party organizations. Both forums have provided important training grounds for parliamentary candi-

---

44 Very long lasting memberships have gradually disappeared. Earlier, eleven MPs had served more than 40 years. (Noponen 1989, p. 160.)

dates. Trade unions have also been an important background for many MPs of the left, and a variety of producer's and businessmen's organizations have added to the background, especially of non-socialist members. In addition, a very important source of the accumulating qualifications of any MP's has been parliament itself. (Op.cit, pp. 134–138).

For many, although not all, election to parliament involves an elevation in social status. On the other hand, distinguished service in parliament may open gates to other careers. It is common during each election term for a few members to resign because they are appointed to high civil service positions, and there are others who do not seek re-election, because they have more attractive private positions waiting. Naturally, there are also some who remain in a political career and may rise to the government or become leading politicians of the opposition.

Retired MPs are paid a pension after they reach 65 years of age (full pension if they have served 15 years or more). The law also guarantees a leave of absence to government officials who are elected to parliament, and most municipal governments act accordingly. Consequently, about one-quater of the MPs have a "frozen" public post waiting; the longest leaves still effective in 2002 had been granted in 1983.

There have been women among Finnish legislators from the very beginning of the unicameral parliament; in the election of 1999 their number rose from sixty-seven to seventy-four. The election of 19 woman MPs back in 1907 was a unique aspect in the history of the Eduskunta, because at that time no other country in Europe had even given their women the right to vote. In 1908 the number of women in parliament rose to 25, then declined somewhat but began to rise again in 1951, reaching 45 in 1970 and 62 in 1983 and peaking at 77 in 1991. The first woman to be a government minister was the social democratic Miina Sillanpää, appointed in 1926, and the first female speaker of parliament was the conservative MP Riitta Uosukainen, elected for the first time in 1994. Once, in 1996, both of the two deputy speakers also happened to be women. Moreover, woman MPs of different parties began to pull together in 1991 and launched regular cooperation within the "Network of Women in Finland's Parliament."

10   The President of the Republic

... a qualitative change from ruler and policy-maker to mediator, opinion leader and interpreter of popular feelings.

Nousiainen 2000, p. 350

The presidency is a bloody awful post.

President J.K. Paasikivi in 1949

The Presidency

The president of the republic is Finland's head of state, but in the 21st century he or she can no longer be called the head of government. The role of parliamentary government has been strengthened consistently since the 1980s and the president's independent powers have weakened accordingly.

Two quotations from the constitution illustrate this change. The Constitution Act of 1919 (Section 2) stipulated the following: "Supreme executive power shall be vested in the President of the Republic. In addition thereto, for general government of the state there shall be a Council of State, consisting of a Prime Minister and a sufficient number of Ministers." But the new Constitution of 1999 (Section 3) no longer pictures such a supreme presidency. According to it, "Governmental powers are exercised by the President of the Republic and the Council of State, the members of which shall have the confidence of the Parliament."

Moreover, parliamentarians also wanted to remove the president's restraints on the approval of new legislation. Whereas the constitution of 1919 had given legislative power to " Parliament in conjunction with the President of the Republic," the new constitution prescribes merely that "legislative powers are exercised by the Parliament, which shall also decide on State finances."

The desire to emphasize parliament and parliamentary government was one of the main reasons why Finland's eighty-year-old constitution was replaced by the new one in 1999. During the first seventy years of the Constitution Act, Finland had applied the innovative principle of dual executive power. It combined the presidential system with parliamentary government, a concept that France has also applied since 1958. But eventually the phrase "normal parliamentarism" was taken more and more seriously, until it became the generally accepted norm.[45]

The notion that parliamentary government is somehow more democratic than presidential power may have been a reaction to the very strong position that President Urho Kekkonen acquired during his long term in office from 1956 to 1981. But obviously members of parliament also felt that the new direct mandate from the people (since 1994) would strengthen the president too much at the cost of parliament. His or her term of office is also rather long. As in Austria, the Finnish president is elected for six years. The term is one year shorter than in Italy (and in France until 2002), but it is two years longer than in the United States or Iceland. Only one consecutive re-election is now permitted in Finland.

For a long time the political left wanted to abolish the president's independent popular base completely and simply move his election to parliament. The Social Democrats changed their position on this issue in the 1980s, after their own candidate won the election for the first time. The parties were not eager to reverse their position completely, by replacing the electoral college with direct elections, but eventually they could not resist the growing pressure of public opinion urging more direct democracy.

The first direct elections in 1994 showed that the parties had had good reason to be reluctant. Certain obvious candidates of the party leadership were rejected in the party primaries, some dissident party members were nominated as independent candidates, and there were some unexpected opinion changes during the campaign. The Social Democratic candidate Martti Ahtisaari, who was elected president in 1994 (see below), had never held an elected office before. He had made his reputation as an accomplished diplomat. Six of the nine presidents that preceded him had been prime ministers at the time they were elected to the presidency.

After the election, the new president inaugurates his (or of course her) term on March 1st in parliament, facing "the representatives of the people of Finland" (the president of the supreme court having no role when the oath is taken). Otherwise he makes personal visits to parliament only to declare the annual parliamentary sessions open or to close the four-year term.

The president still continues to be involved in the passing of new legislation, because he signs government bills sent to parliament and confirms the laws passed by parliament. But only a trace remains of his

---

45 Max Jakobson made reference to the monarchical origins of the strong presidency prevailing in Finland since 1919 and to the Swedish constitution of 1809, when he wrote: "The whole legacy of King Gustav IV was at stake. In Finland the counteraction against the *coup d'état* by the Swedish king in 1772 did not start until more than two hundred years later."

earlier suspensive veto - that is, the right to slow down the enactment of a law. Earlier, the president's veto, which was used slightly more often than once a year (Jansson 1982, p. 153), could be overturned by a newly elected parliament and, since 1987, by next year's session of the same parliament, but under the new constitution, parliament can readopt, without delay, any bill that the president has returned for additional consideration.

The weakening and near abolition of the veto power is a concrete example of the strengthening of parliamentarism in the Finnish constitution. Another step in the same direction was the amendment, in 1991, that removed the president's right to dissolve parliament unless the prime minister requests him to. When the entire constitution was rewritten in 1999, the touchiest point was again the relative powers of the president and the prime minister, both in government formation and in certain policy decisions.

The government proposed the new Constitution Act in February 1998, seven years after a broadly based government commission had begun to work on the revision. Parliament needed one more year before the new constitution was passed in February 1999. The new parliament elected in March 1999 accepted the act expeditiously by the required two-thirds majority and it became effective on March 1, 2000, the day when the eleventh president took office. The new Constitution Act combined and replaced the four constitutional laws that Finland had had since 1922 (the Constitution Act, the Parliament Act, the Ministerial Liability Act, and the High Court of Impeachment Act).

Although the parties were in considerable agreement, one particular detail in the reform was very difficult to resolve: who would choose the prime minister and how? This is, of course, a critical decision. In two-party systems and even in the two-bloc multiparty system of Sweden, voters in a parliamentary election usually have a clear notion as to which two potential prime ministers are competing for the position. But in Finland there are more than two potential prime ministers. The composition of the coalition government and, consequently, the opposition, are determined in inter-party negotiations held after a parliamentary election.

The Constitution of 1999 minimizes the independent role of the president quite explicitly. It stipulates that "Parliament elects the Prime Minister, who is thereafter appointed to the office by the President of the Republic. The President appoints the other Ministers in accordance with a proposal made by the Prime Minister." (Section 61). The same section stipulates that the "groups represented in the parliament" negotiate about the government program and the composition of the government, and that the president is to consult the speaker of parliament and the parliamentary groups before he formally announces to parliament the nominee for prime minister.

Only the future will show how much political power the Finnish president actually can and will wield under the new constitution. Much will depend on the prestige and personality of President Tarja Halonen and her successors, and on her working relationship with the prime minister and other ministers. What the constitution really emphasizes is the need to maintain close communication between the president and the ministers. In her inauguration address on March 1st 2000, Ms Halonen also spoke of the president's direct contact with parliament.

The president continues to direct Finland's foreign policy, although now "in co-operation with the Council of State." However, matters related to the European Union are excluded from the president's sphere of influence. Obviously the distinction between EU-related matters and more general foreign policy decisions is not quite clear. Among the details that needed to be settled at the very outset in March 2000 was the question of who would chair the meetings of the ministerial committee on foreign and security policy: is it the president or the prime minister? The compromise agreed was that the committee would be chaired by the prime minister, but whenever the president attends the meeting she holds the gavel and summarizes the discussions.

The Finnish president also continues to have constitutional powers in domestic affairs, appointing high civil servants and judges, and acting as supreme commander of the armed forces. But, in addition, the president is expected to assume quite a meaningful informal role as a visionary, a voice of national conscience, and an initiator of new policies.

Two Direct Elections

Originally the election of the Finnish president was indirect, taking place in two stages. First the people elected an electoral college of 300 (later, 301) members, and then the college assembled to choose the president. This happened ten times: in 1925, 1931, 1937, and seven times between 1950 and 1988. The meeting of the electoral college was by no means a pure formality and there could be a great deal of partisan maneuvering behind the scenes. Both in 1931 and in 1956 the college, in its third and final ballot, chose between the two remaining candidates with the slimmest possible majority, 151–149. And in 1937 it ultimately rejected a candidate (who had been Finland's first president) who received 150 votes in the first ballot.

Direct elections of the president were held for the first time in January and February 1994. Table 10.1. shows what happened. There were eleven candidates, and public opinion polls showed the Social Democratic nominee, Martti Ahtisaari, to be the apparent frontrunner. The important question was who would win the second place and thus eliminate the nine others from the decisive run-off election. This appeared to be a contest between the candidates of the two other big parties, until the campaign of Elisabeth Rehn, the candidate of the Swedish People's Party, suddenly snowballed and eliminated both of them. During the second campaign she "ran out of steam", handing Martti Ahtisaari a victory in the decisive second ballot three weeks later.

Table 10.1

Presidential elections, January 16 and February 6, 1994

Candidates	Number of Votes Advanced*	Election Day	Total	Total %
1st Ballot				
Martti Ahtisaari (SDP)	369,400	458,600	828,000	25.9
Elisabeth Rehn (SPP)	210,400	491,800	702,200	22.0
Paavo Väyrynen (CENT)	295,100	328,300	623,400	19.5
Raimo Ilaskivi (CONS)	230,500	254,500	485,000	5.2
Keijo Korhonen (Center/Ind)	87,500	99,400	186,900	5.8
Claes Andersson (LEFT)	49,500	73,300	122,800	3.8
Pertti Virtanen (Ind.)	40,700	55,000	95,700	3.0
Eeva Kuuskoski (Center/Ind)	40,000	42,500	82,500	2.6
Toimi Kankaanniemi (CHR)	15,600	15,900	31,500	1.0
Sulo Aittoniemi (FRP)	13,600	17,000	30,600	1.0
Pekka Tiainen (Communist)	3,600	3,700	7,300	0.2
Total	1,355,900	1,840,100	3,196,000	100.0
2nd Ballot				
Martti Ahtisaari (SDP)	780,900	942,600	1,723,500	53.9
Elisabeth Rehn (SPP)	712,600	763,700	1,476,300	46.1
Total	1,493,500	1,706,300	3,199,800	100.0

* Mail-in votes cast on January 5–11, and on January 26 – February 1.

Table 10.2

Presidential elections, January 16 and February 6, 2000

Candidates	Number of Votes Advanced*	Election Day	Total	Total %
1st ballot				
Tarja Halonen (SDP)	511,300	713,100	1,224,400	40,0
Esko Aho (CENT)	522,600	528,600	1,051,200	34,4
Riitta Uosukainen (CONS)	185,300	207,000	392,300	12,8
Elisabeth Rehn (SPP)	96,700	145,100	241,900	7,9
Heidi Hautala (GR)	27,900	72,800	100,700	3,3
Ilkka Hakalehto (BASF)	12,800	18,600	31,400	1,0
Risto Kuisma (REF)	5,600	11,300	16,900	0,6
Total	1,362,200	1,696,600	3,058,900	100,0
2nd ballot				
Tarja Halonen (SDP)	772,700	871,800	1,644,500	51,6
Esko Aho (CENT)	737,300	803,500	1,540,800	48,4
Total	1,510,000	1 ,675,300	3,185,300	100,0

* Mail-in votes cast on January 5–11, and on January 26 – February 1.

BASF = Basic Finns; REF = Reform group.

Nevertheless, the success of Elisabeth Rehn was a breakthrough that encouraged other parties to nominate woman candidates in 1999. At that time four women and three men ran for the presidency. Table 10.2 shows the results of Finland's second direct presidential election in January and February, 2000.

The direct electoral system functioned differently in the two elections. Whereas in 1994 the two top-ranking candidates received only 48 percent of the votes on the first ballot, six years later the first round made it very clear which two candidates the voters wanted to move on to the second round. Together, Tarja Halonen of the Social Democratic Party and Esko Aho of the Center Party received three-quarters of the votes, leaving only one-quarter for the five other candidates.

The campaigns in Finland's presidential elections have changed much over the years. Between the two world wars it would have been considered quite improper to have the hopefuls openly seek the position. The candidates who ran for the electoral college campaigned on their behalf, and in some cases political parties did not even name their candidate for the presidency. It was not until 1956 that all presidential candidates made public campaign speeches.

The style changed much more. The direct elections were preceded by quite professionally organized campaign activity. Furthermore, they included highly personalized elements, publicizing candidates (and even their spouses) not only in political but in various other roles and appearances. The mass media provided much visibility for the candidates and their messages. After the election, it is the custom in Finland for the president to formally sever party ties and "turn in" his party membership card, because the presidency is thought of as being non-political, or "above politics."

As mentioned above, the Social Democratic candidate Martti Ahtisaari, who was elected president in 1994, had never held elected office. This was a time of strong anti-party feelings in many western countries, and in Finland the people also had a general desire to use their newly acquired direct power to the full. The mood was again different in the election of 2000. This time there was very little "interference" from the rank and file of party members during the nominations, and the two candidates with the most governmental experience were the voters' favorites for the second round; largely, because tv debates had revealed their experience and solid factual knowledge.

The multi-party system and the subsequent large number of candidates favors clean and carefully worded campaigning in Finland, because attacking rivals or taking extreme political positions during the first round could backfire during the second round, when the two most successful candidates are trying to attract new support from the voters of the eliminated candidates. Also, in their campaign appearances the candidates like to emphasize their personal qualities and to avoid narrow party labels.

Voters, in turn, are more volatile in presidential than in parliamentary elections. Before the elections, public opinion ratings of the candidates fluctuated a great deal, and the results of published opinion polls had an apparent influence on the voter's decisions. In January 1994, late polls showed growing support for Elisabeth Rehn and this snowballed rapidly. She ranked only fourth in the advance votes cast in post offices twelve to five days before the election, but she rose to be the most popular candidate on election day. Somewhat similar dynamics occurred during the first round in 2000. The male candidate of the Center Party ranked first in the advance ballots, but on election day he was overtaken by the female candidate of the Social Democrats.

Eleven Presidents

The following eleven people have been presidents of the republic:

- 1919–1925: K.J. Ståhlberg (1865–1952), doctor of laws, president of the Supreme Administrative Court, Progressive Party (elected by parliament)
- 1925–1931: Lauri Kr. Relander (1883–1947), PhD, district governor, Agrarian Union
- 1931–1937: Pehr Evind Svinhufvud (1861–1944), judge, prime minister, regent in 1918, Conservative Party
- 1937–1940: Kyösti Kallio (1873–1940), farmer, prime minister, Agrarian Union, resigned in 1940
- 1940–1944: Risto Ryti (1889–1956), master of laws, prime minister, director general of the Bank of Finland, Progressive Party (elected in 1940 and reelected in 1943 by the 1937 electors, resigned in 1944)
- 1944–1946: C.G. Mannerheim (1867–1951), Marshall, supreme commander of the armed forces, regent in 1918-1919 (elected by parliament, resigned in 1946)
- 1946–1956: J.K. Paasikivi (1870–1956), doctor of laws, prime minister, Conservative Party (elected by parliament to complete Mannerheim's term, reelected in 1950 by electoral college)
- 1956–1981: Urho Kekkonen (1900–1986), doctor of laws, prime minister, Agrarian Union (elected in 1956, 1962, 1968 and 1978, third term extended by parliament from six to ten years, resigned in 1981)
- 1982–1994: Mauno Koivisto (1923–), PhD, prime minister, director general of the Bank of Finland, Social Democratic Party (elected in 1982 and 1988)
- 1994–2000: Martti Ahtisaari (1937–), teacher, secretary of state at the ministry for foreign affairs, Social Democratic Party
- 2000– : Tarja Halonen (1943–), master of laws, minister for foreign affairs, Social Democratic Party

The ten presidents of the 20th century served, of course, during quite different circumstances. Posterity also tends to label them with different personal characteristics. Ståhlberg, who had been professor of administrative law, senator, and speaker of parliament, is remembered as the father of the Finnish constitution and as a symbol of political consensus. Relander, who was elected as a surprise candidate in 1925, kept a low profile in office but is thought of as the president who opened up personal contacts with the Nordic and Baltic countries. Svinhufvud, in turn, was known as the nationalist who, in the years before Finland's independence, had been exiled to Siberia and who had led the "Independence Senate" in 1917–1918. He is remembered for his strong personal charisma, which helped him to block authoritarian moves by the extreme right wing movement.

Kallio was a moderate and realistic farmer who built his entire career in politics: as party chairman, speaker of parliament, and prime minister. He helped to launch the "red-green" political co-operation between the Social Democrats and the Agrarian Union in 1937, thus bridging the nation's deep red-white cleavage. Ryti, a skillful banker, was a cool and rational thinker. He gained the people's grateful respect for having carried heavy war-time responsibilities. Mannerheim, who had had an exceptional military career in tsarist Russia and in Finland, guided the nation back to peace and became a respected symbol of Finnish independence.

Paasikivi, old enough to have been effective in politics before Finland's independence, had been a high civil servant, party chairman, and chairman of a private bank. He made foreign policy the president's important prerogative, and also remained a central actor in domestic politics. He laid the foundations for Finland's post-war foreign policy and helped to guard democracy against communist threats. Kekkonen, a five-time prime minister, served as president for the unprecedented period of one quarter-century. He skillfully continued Paasikivi's foreign policy which, in political rhetoric, was named the "Paasikivi-Kekkonen line." Its primary goal was protection of Finland's neutrality. At the same time he concentrated much domestic power in the president's own hands and, in using his constitutional power to appoint ministers, his personal likes and dislikes played an important role in government formation.

The actual role of the president was not strictly fixed in the written constitution: the powers he used depended on his personality and political power base, and on the country's external situation, or, more generally, on how the president's constitutional powers were interpreted and implemented at any given time. President Ståhlberg acted very independently as a regulator and arbiter, but did not initiate policies. President Kallio was an even weaker counterforce to the parliamentary government. After the war, the position of parliament and parliamentary government was again strong in domestic affairs, but President Paasikivi interpreted to the very letter the constitution's article which made the president responsible for Finland's relations with foreign powers. He clearly established that "foreign policy precedes domestic politics." President Kekkonen went even further: not only did he make himself indispensable in the area of foreign policy, but he acquired the upper hand in domestic politics as well, and made the prime minister and his cabinet dependent on the will of the president.

Koivisto, while maintaining the integrity of the office, launched a constitutional "counteraction" in the 1980s. He started a gradual move toward the new balance of executive power, in which the parliamentary type of government was emphasized. As an individual, he is remembered as the man who had fought the Russians with a light machine gun in the war and who earned his PhD as a longshoreman. Later he used broad popular support to circumvent the political elite of the Kekkonen era, and remained an independent thinker throughout his presidency and afterwards. Ahtisaari had a civil service career in the ministry for foreign affairs and also held high positions in the United Nations Organization. He spent much time abroad and was a skillful negotiator in international conflicts, while attempting to cultivate a direct touch with ordinary people.

The eleventh president of Finland, Tarja Halonen, is the third to come from the Social Democratic Party and the first born in the capital city. More importantly, she is Finland's first woman president. Only four other countries had female presidents in 2000, namely, Ireland, Latvia, Panama, and Sri Lanka. Is March 1st 2000 a more important landmark as the date when the new constitution took effect or when the first woman became president?' The latter seems to be the better answer. The reform of the constitution had become timely and it greatly reduced the powers of the president, but it also was regarded as a mere "maintenance check-up" whereas having a woman as president entails significant symbolic and practical consequences throughout Finnish society.

The eleven presidents were not "born" to their high position. To the contrary, many rose from rather humble backgrounds. However, attached to the presidency has been the traditional prestige that is to some extent the legacy of the old monarchies. Developments during the 1990s and the new constitution have made the presidency much more prosaic today. Presidents are expected to uphold their prestige and position constantly through their own actions and public appearances.

During the election campaign of 2000, all the candidates obviously understood that most voters desired an influential president rather than a weak one. Before the campaign, a large majority of Finns also were satisfied with the amount of power the president had and were unwilling to reduce it (see Table 7.3). Moreover, there is some evidence that a person's expectations regarding the president's role are related to how politically powerful he feels. A strong president is most important for citizens who are alienated and feel powerless in the political system, whereas the emphasis on parliamentary government seems to appeal most to politically efficacious citizens and, naturally, to the political elite (Pesonen and Sänkiaho 1979, pp. 441–443; Pesonen 1994, p. 181).

11 The Executive

As seen from the opposition's side, this government's greatest weakness is its great strength.

MP Risto Kuisma in 2001

Personnel savings have been slight. The... reason for this has been the implementation of reforms by simply dressing the old administration in new clothes.

Savolainen 1999, p. 144

The Council of State

In common usage the word "government" refers in Finland to the council of state or, as the governing body can also be called, the cabinet. It consists of the prime minister and the "appropriate number" (no more than seventeen) of other ministers. Most of them, and sometimes all, are also members of parliament, although this is not a formal requirement.

As was described above, the dualistic constitution enacted in 1919 placed the government in a tricky position between the president and parliament, because Finland was either "semi-presidential" or "semi-parliamentary," as it combined the presidential system of government with the parliamentary one. In other words, the president of the republic was elected independently and had strong powers of his own, but the cabinet must also enjoy the confidence of parliament. The Constitution of 1999 expresses the idea of parliamentarism in the following two phrases: "The Ministers are responsible before the Parliament for their actions in office" (Section 60), and "The President shall in any event dismiss the Government or a Minister, if either no longer enjoys the confidence of Parliament..." (Section 64).

Table 11.1

The presidents and governments of Finland from 1944 to 2003

The Presidents and Prime Ministers	Party affiliation of Cabinet Members								Seats
	LEFT	SDP	CENT	LPP	SPP	CONS	Other	Ind	
C.G. Mannerheim									
8/44: Antti Hackzell	–	5	4	1	2	**3**	–	1	190
9/44: U. J. Castrén	–	5	4	1	1	**2**	–	2	190
11/44: J. K. Paasikivi II	**4**	4	4	1	2	–	–	3	165
4/45: J. K. Paasikivi III	**5**	4	4	1	1	–	–	2	171
J.K. Paasikivi									
3/46: Mauno Pekkala	**6**	5	5	–	1	–	–	1	162
7/48: K. A. Fagerholm I	–	**15**	–	–	–	–	–	1	54
3/50: Urho Kekkonen I	–	–	**10**	2	3	–	–	–	75
1/51: Urho Kekkonen II	–	7	**7**	1	2	–	–	–	129
9/51: Urho Kekkonen III	–	7	**7**	–	2	–	–	1	119
7/53: Urho Kekkonen IV	–	–	**8**	–	3	–	–	3	66
11/53: Sakari Tuomioja	–	–	–	**3***	2*	4*	–	6	–
5/54: Ralf Törngren	–	6	6	–	**1**	–	–	1	120
10/54: Urho Kekkonen V	–	7	**6**	–	–	–	–	1	107
Urho Kekkonen									
3/56: K. A. Fagerholm II	–	**6**	6	1	1	–	–	1	133
5/57: V. J. Sukselainen I	–	–	**6**	3	3	–	–	1	79
7/57: - " -	–	–	**9**	4	–	–	–	1	66
9/57: - " -	–	5*	**6**	2	–	–	–	2	66
11/57: Rainer von Fieandt	–	–	**4***	–	–	–	–	10	–
4/58: Reino Kuuskoski	–	4*	**5***	1*	–	–	–	4	–
8/58: K. A. Fagerholm III	–	**5**	5	1	1	3	–	–	147
1/59: V. J. Sukselainen II	–	–	**14**	–	1*	–	–	–	48
7/61: Martti Miettunen I	–	–	**14**	–	–	–	–	–	48
4/62: Ahti Karjalainen I	–	–	**5**	2	2	3	–	3	112
12/63: Reino Lehto	–	**1***	–	–	–	–	–	14	–
9/64: J. Virolainen	–	–	**7**	2	2	3	–	–	112
5/66: Rafael Paasio I	3	**7**	5	–	–	–	–	–	145
3/68: Mauno Koivisto I	3	**7**	5	–	1	–	–	–	164
5/70: Teuvo Aura I	–	4*	3*	1*	1*	**1***	–	3	–
7/70: A. Karjalainen II	3	5	**5**	2	2	–	–	–	144
3/71: - " -	–	8	**5**	2	2	–	–	–	108
10/71: Teuvo Aura II	–	3*	4*	1*	1*	**1***	–	5	–
2/72: Rafael Paasio II	–	**17**	–	–	–	–	–	–	55
9/72: Kalevi Sorsa I	–	**7**	5	1	2	–	–	–	108
6/75: Keijo Liinamaa	–	5*	3*	1*	1*	**1***	–	6	–
11/75: M. Miettunen II	4	5	**4**	1	2	–	–	2	152
9/76: M. Miettunen III	–	–	**9**	3	3	–	–	1	58
5/77: Kalevi Sorsa II	3	**4**	5	1	1	–	–	1	142
3/78: - " -	3	**4**	5	2	–	–	–	1	132
5/79: M. Koivisto II	3	**5**	6	–	2	–	–	1	133
Mauno Koivisto									
2/82: Kalevi Sorsa III	3	**5**	6	–	2	–	–	1	133
12/82: - " -	–	**8**	6	1	2	–	–	1	98
5/83: Kalevi Sorsa IV	–	**8**	5	–	2	–	2	–	123
4/87: Harri Holkeri	–	8	–	–	2	**7**	1	–	130
4/91: Esko Aho	–	–	**8**	–	2	6	1	–	115
Martti Ahtisaari									
4/95: Paavo Lipponen I	2	**7**	–	–	2	5	1	1	145
4/99: Paavo Lipponen II	2	**6**	–	–	2	6	1	1	140
Tarja Halonen									
5/02: Paavo Lipponen II	2	**7**	–	–	2	7	–	–	129

* Without explicit backing of own party.
  Prime Minister's party in bold type.

The best guarantee for enjoying parliament's confidence is, naturally, to have a government coalition consisting of political parties that together have a majority in parliament. What has happened in practice is seen in Table 11.1, which summarizes the compositions of the cabinets of twenty-three prime ministers during six presidencies. There have been forty-one governments between 1944 and 2003, but the prime ministers have been fewer, because five persons have become prime minister more than once, as the table's roman numerals indicate. Earlier, between 1917 and 1944, Finland had twenty-seven different governments and eighteen prime ministers (see Vaarnas 1976, p. 8; Numminen 1999, p. 83).

For half a century, from 1937 to 1987, the basic pattern was known as the "red earth" coalitions, i.e. governments formed jointly by the Social Democrats and the Agrarian Union/Center Party, and possibly including smaller parties, most often the Swedish People's Party. During the war the model was expanded into grand coalitions of all or almost all the parties, and after the war it was broadened to the "popular front" model, which included the communists but excluded the conservatives (1944–1948, 1966–1971, and 1975–1982). In addition, there has been one large coalition without the communists (1958–1959), three one-party minority governments (1948–1950, 1959–1962, 1972), two minority coalitions of parties of the center (1950–1951, 1976–1977), and three majority coalitions of the bourgeois parties (1962–1963, 1964–1966, 1991–1995).

On occasion, when a political crisis kept the parties from working together, the temporary solution was to appoint caretaker, non-party cabinets of civil servants without a parliamentary base (1953, 1957, 1963, 1970, 1971, and 1975). They sometimes included politicians, but mainly as experts and without the explicit backing of their party. (See Pesonen and Thomas 1983.)

As was mentioned in Chapter 8, a completely new coalition type terminated the "red earth" era of 1937–1987, when the chairman of the Conservative Party formed a "blue-red" government. Now the Center Party became the outsider, first in 1987–1991, then again since 1995, when even the Left Alliance and the Greens were included in the five-party "rainbow coalition." The second such government of Paavo Lipponen, appointed in April 1999, had the backing of a broad 140–60 majority in parliament; the base of his first government in 1995–1999 was even broader (see Tables 11.1 and 8.1).

Although a broad political base may cause internal tensions within a government coalition, it is obvious that the broader its parliamentary support, the stronger the government vis-à-vis the opposition. In Finland majority governments have been much more common than in the other Nordic countries (cf. Arter 1999, p. 201) and have now become normal practice. Among the 37 new governments appointed between 1948 and 1999, there were 23 majority governments (plus 7 minority and 7 non-party as shown in Table 11.1). Of the 23 majority coalitions, eight faced an opposition smaller than 67 MPs. This is an important threshold because constitutional amendments need the backing of a two-thirds majority. A more frequently used advantage of the opposition was, until 1995, the right to delay a bill if one-third of MPs so voted. There is also the larger qualified majority, five-sixths, needed to declare urgent a decision to amend the constitution, another threshold that might occasionally obstruct the government's intended policy.[46]

The constitutionally defined procedure of government formation changed in 2000 when President Tarja Halonen took office (see Chapter 10 above), but, because governments no longer resign when the president changes, her first chance to participate in forming a new government was due to occur after the parliamentary election of March 2003. The Constitution of 1999 (Section 61, quoted in the preceeding chapter) does not leave her much to say about it: "The Parliament elects the Prime Minister." The election of the prime minister takes place in parliament, and it does not happen before the parliamentary parties have agreed on the composition of the government and on the government's political program. The president has the formal role of informing parliament about the nominee for prime minister, but it is parliament that then elects him or her.

There are twelve ministries in the Finnish government (the ministries for foreign affairs, justice, interior, defense, finance, education, agriculture and forestry, communications, trade and industry, social affairs and health, labor, and environmental affairs), and often the responsibility for some ministries is divided between two ministers (thus, the government appointed in 1999 also has ministers responsible for foreign trade, taxation, regional administration, culture, and basic services). The prime minister's office has significant duties of its own and could be counted as the thirteenth ministry. The maximum number of ministers is not determined by the constitution itself, but is limited by law to eighteen. The old constitution required that all ministers must be native-born Finnish citizens and two must have a law degree, but these qualifications were omitted from the Constitution of 1999.

The president exercises her or his constitutional powers in the weekly presidential sessions of the council of state which she chairs: bills to be sent to parliament and laws to be promulgated, the issuing of decrees, and the appointment of high civil servants. She is free of any formal political responsibility, whereas parliament holds the cabinet politically responsible for governmental policies and for the central administration. The cabinet (council of state) also makes decisions without the president in its weekly plenary meetings, normally on Thursdays, which are preceded by an unofficial "evening school" on Wednesday nights. The plenary meeting of the council of state is competent when a quorum of five ministers is present.

---

46 One noteworthy example was the extension of President Kekkonen's six-year term 1968–1974 to ten years, passed in January 1973. All major parties supported this proposal, but it also needed to receive a five-sixths majority over the opposing constitutionalist MPs from different parties. The bill was declared urgent by a 170–28 majority. Six more no-votes would have been enough to block it.

The Council of State Act of 1994 limited the scope of the cabinet's plenary sessions to important questions of principle, and the new constitution permits the council of state to issue decrees without the president's signature. Decision-making has also been decentralized, so that lower-level decrees can be issued on behalf of the government by individual ministers, and in each ministry by the civil servants to whom such authority has been delegated.

Of increased importance in the working of the government have been specialized cabinet committees. The four statutory ones deal with foreign and security policy, finance, economic policy, and European Union affairs. They are chaired by the prime minister and have from five to nine other ministers as members (the president chairs the meeting of the committee on foreign and security policy if she attends it). There is also the cabinet's "neighboring-areas" committee. In addition, there are ministerial working groups of five to ten ministers that are chaired by the relevant minister.[47]

Parliamentarism

As stated above, the council of state can govern only as long as it enjoys the confidence of parliament. Interpellations (challenges to ministers) are the most powerful method parliament can use to test whether the government enjoys its confidence. This tool has been used in Finland only about twice a year (but averaged 5.5 per year in 1990–1995), and less for "purely propaganda aspects" than might have been expected (Isaksson and Helander 2001, pp. 25, 122). Of the 36 government resignations between 1948 and 1999, only two were forced by a vote of no-confidence, and two others were due to a decision by parliament against the will of the government. The communist minister of the interior who was appointed in 1945 had to resign after a personal vote of no confidence in 1948.

The concrete issues of the two successful interpellations concerned the manner of changing the government's composition in 1957, and reduction of subsidies for agriculture in 1958. More often, in seven cases, the government resigned because of internal conflicts within the coalition. Fourteen resignations were the result of parliamentary and five of presidential elections. (Nousiainen 1998, p. 251; Jansson 1982, pp. 139–140, 149.)

Some governments have changed their political composition without actually resigning (1957, 1971, and 1978). The average lifespan of governments was approximately one year until President Koivisto made it the accepted norm that a government stays in power during parliament's

---

47 For example, in January 2001 there were seven ministerial working groups dealing with administration and regional development, social policy, communications policy, the Kyoto climate protocol, immigration policy and ethnic relations, education, and the Natura 2000 network.

entire four-year election term. A major political change occurred, as was mentioned above, when the long-lasting pattern of Social Democratic-Center cooperation was replaced in 1987 by broad majority governments without the Center Party (1987–1991 and 1995 onward). In 1987 the election victory of the Conservative Party was one reason for the political change, leading to the appointment of the party's chairman Harri Holkeri as prime minister. The subsequent premierships in 1991 and 1995 of the Center Party leader Esko Aho and the Social Democratic leader Paavo Lipponen, in turn, followed their parties' election victories.

Small parties, and possibly individual ministers of large ones, can also express their disproval of the government through stepping out of the government which, nevertheless, continues to govern as a majority coalition. Examples include the leader of the Christian League Toimi Kankaanniemi, the only minister from that party since 1991, who resigned in June 1994 because he did not approve prime minister Esko Aho's request for a unanimous decision in favor of Finland's EU membership; or Satu Hassi of the Green League, whose party was opposed to granting permission to build additional nuclear power facilities (see Chapter 4).

When stable four-year-long governments became the pattern in the 1980s, amendments to the constitution gradually strengthened parliament's power to control not only the performance, but also the first steps of governments. In 1987, it was stipulated that the president must listen to the parliamentary parties before appointing the government. An amendment in 1991 required the government to inform the Eduskunta about its program "without delay" and stated that significant changes in the government's composition can take place only when the Eduskunta is in session.

The Constitution of 1999, which reduced the president's role in government formation, also includes a formal reference to the negotiations which take place before the appointment of a new government: "Before the Prime Minister is elected, the groups represented in the Parliament negotiate on the political program and composition of the Government." (Section 61:2). The period of approximately four weeks that follows the election is of crucial importance for the whole term of the Eduskunta. This is when policy goals are outlined and when the cards are dealt for a period of four years, offering either influence or a weak role in the opposition.

Ministers are constantly in the limelight. They make political initiatives and they defend the government's policies both in parliament and in the mass media. They are criticized by the opposition and they are repeatedly interviewed and asked for their intentions and explanations by television and the daily press. They have also become increasingly vulnerable within their own parliamentary party groups.

When parliament started the 2001 legislative session, Prime Minister Lipponen selected "parliamentarism and the new constitution" as the theme of the opening discussion.[48] One could conclude from the debate that, in the opinion of MPs, the new constitution had been less successful in its aim of strengthening parliament's position than in making the prime minister and his government more powerful. Also, day-to-day cooperation of the five coalition parties received less attention than the relations of the parliamentary groups of the governing parties with their own ministers in the government. Members of the opposition parties even spoke of two different oppositions, the large "real opposition" that often publicly criticizes the government, and the smaller opposition that also opposes the government formally when actual votes of confidence are taken.

Central Administration

In the planning of new policies and new legislation, as well as in the execution of policies, the council of state is obviously very dependent on the civil servants who work in the ministries permanently. Their numbers have reflected the increased responsibilities of the executive branch of government. The numbers of civil servants working in the ministries grew more than tenfold during the course of seven decades. They were 480 in 1925 and 730 in 1939, but 1350 in 1956, 4540 in 1988, and 5240 in 1994 (Numminen 1999, p. 76).

However, the total number of state employees is much higher, more than 200,000. Many civil servants work in specialized offices and agencies of the state's central administration, operating in their own fields of expertise outside the ministries, although directed by the council of state. Since the 1970s the total number of such governmental units has been about seventy. In recent years the total number of civil servants has been reduced because functions traditionally run by the state have been reorganized so that they are now counted as part of the private sector.

It would be too broad a task to list here all the offices of central government. For illustration, however, let us review the general structures of four of the twelve ministries (without claiming that these are more interesting or important than the eight others: justice, interior, defense, education, agriculture and forestry, trade and industry, labor, and environment).

In the second government of Prime Minister Lipponen, the responsibilities of the ministry for foreign affairs were divided among four ministers. The Minister for Foreign Affairs, Erkki Tuomioja of the Social Democratic Party (since 2000), was in charge of the departments for po-

---

48   The opening discussion was added to parliamentary procedures in 2001. The theme of the first discussion was a surprise, because it was generally expected that the debate would deal with the government's plans for new legislation. The theme of the second such debate in February 2002 was, more predictably, the government's program for the fourth and final annual session of this legislature.

litical, administrative, judicial, protocol, and press and culture affairs. The second minister, Kimmo Sasi of the Conservative Party, handled matters covered by the department of foreign trade, while the department of development cooperation was assigned to the government's Minister of the Environment Satu Hassi, leader of the Green League. In addition, the Minister of Defense Jan-Erik Enestam, chairman of the Swedish People's Party, coordinated policy with regard to neighboring areas. The most important outside offices directed by this ministry are the 76 Finnish embassies and numerous consulates around the world.

Political responsibility for the ministry of finance, semi-enviously named "the superministry," has long been divided between two ministers. In 1999–2003 the budget was the responsibility of the Conservative Party chairman Sauli Niinistö, and taxation was under Suvi-Anne Siimes, chairperson of the Left Alliance. The six departments of the ministry deal with the national economy, the budget, taxation, personnel, the development of administration, and financial markets. The national level institutions under this ministry include the state treasury, customs board, office of inspections, the national board of taxes, the statistical office, and the center for economic research. On the regional and local level the custom offices and tax bureaux are visible representatives of this branch of public administration.

The ministry of communications was directed by one minister, who was, until 2002, Olli-Pekka Heinonen of the Conservative Party. Its four departments deal with traffic economy, road traffic, telecommunications, and general affairs. Two very significant government services under this ministry, services run by the post and telegraph board and the railroad board, have been transferred to corresponding stock holding companies owned by the state (see Chapter 15). What remains of them directly in the state's hands, are the centers for tele administration and rail administration. The biggest office under this ministry is the road office; the others include the navigation office, aviation office, center of motor vehicle administration, marine research institute, and meteorological institute.

Our fourth example is the ministry of social affairs and health. Its six departments are the departments of administration, insurance, social welfare and health services, preventive social welfare and health policy, economy and planning, and labor protection. State-wide offices outside the ministry include the center for social and health research and development (STAKES), the product control agency for welfare and health, the insurance supervision authority and the centers for radiation and nuclear safety, public health, medicines and medico-legal affairs. Again, a great deal of state administration takes place in regional offices, and it is of major political importance that much responsibility for the implementation of policies was transferred in the 1990s from the state to local self-government. Maija Perho of the Conservative Party directed the ministry, but some areas were hived off, to be dealt with by the minister of health and social services, whose portfolio was divided (two years each) between Eva Biaudet (Swedish People's Party) and Osmo Soininvaara (Green League).

In the early years of independence, each ministry had one of its senior civil servants appointed as the chief civil servant, or permanent secretary, responsible for the general supervision and coordination of the ministry's work. Only during the 1960s did ministries gradually introduce full-time permanent secretaries (who are called state secretaries in some ministries). They manage the operations of the ministry under the political leadership of the minister or ministers. The civil servants in the council of state "have adopted a loyal and professional attitude to serving successive governments irrespective of their political complexion" (Numminen 1999, p. 78). Nevertheless, many appointments to high civil service positions had been political and, in the 1970s, membership of either the Social Democratic or the Center Party became a de facto qualification for many civil service positions. This trend toward further "politicization" was reversed in the 1980s.

Over two centuries, Finland has weighed two different principles of decision-making in the central units of public administration. Within ministries the situation is clear: each minister has monocratic authority, whereas the plenary sessions of the council of state make their decisions collectively. But back in the 19th century all decisions in the senate were collegiate and the individual senators (later ministers) had no independent decision-making powers before 1917. Many national boards also adopted the collegiate principle, which was inherited from Sweden. It was practiced to some extent until November 1993, when the final session of the last remaining collegium in Finnish public administration, that of the national housing board, "marked the effective end of a tradition in Finnish administrative history dating back to 1643" (Savolainen 1999, p. 139).

The development of administrative decision-making has to be observed in connection with another contrast of organizational principles: should the specialized tasks of central government be performed by the administrative departments of the senate (later the ministries of the council of state), or should they be trusted to national boards and agencies that function outside the ministries? In the Nordic context, the ministerial system is applied in Denmark and Norway, whereas the central administrative boards are traditional in Sweden. In the grand duchy of Finland there were even some Russian plans to make the district governors into powerful administrators and to link them to the emperor, bypassing the Finnish senate.

Finland has not made a clear choice between the ministerial system and separate national boards and offices. In the early 19th century there was an attempt to avoid the incoherence and inefficiency of the Swedish system, but ultimately the increasing responsibilities of the state necessitated new departments in the senate and new administrative offices or boards that were closely subordinated to the senate. By 1881, there were 24 national boards or other separate offices, and "there had been an enforced retreat from the principle of concentrating all governmental affairs in the Senate" (op.cit., p. 123). More national boards and smaller offices were soon introduced. The restructuring of administration in the 1920s involved the merging of some national boards with the ministries, but new boards and offices were also established. After the Second World War, there was again a declared policy to strengthen the ministries, but at the same time it became the practice to entrust more expert preparation to national boards.

From 1986 onward, Finland has made a special effort to eliminate overlapping administration between the national boards and the ministries, and to improve the quality of public services. Also, a wave of central government reform swept widely over Europe in the 1980s, and several countries, including Finland, adopted performance budgeting and restructured parts of their central government as market-oriented state enterprises. By the end of 1995, around 60,000 people worked in such market-oriented units. Together with other reforms, this cut the head count of government employees from 208,000 in 1991 to some 122,000 in 1996. Only the latter remain in the state budget. The activities of the Finnish state as a business operator will be discussed below, in Chapter 15.

What had been a clear demarcation between the private and the public sector has become more diffuse since the 1990s, when public services became more market-based and customer-oriented. However, according to a government resolution of spring 1998, it is not important who produces public services, as long as the services match the wishes of the citizenry. The public do not suspect bureaucratic misconduct but they are not happy about all the public services they receive and also tend to be dissatisfied with how services are provided. In 1992 about half of the Finns thought that both the government and the bureaucracy had too much power in society; by 1998 critical opinions had mellowed, but differently, so that the role of the government was accepted more generally than the role of its bureaucracy (EVA 1999a, p. 27).

Naturally, the administrative functions of the state are not limited to the national level. They are also performed in the regional and local offices of state administration. The provincial governors have been traditional representatives of central government in the administrative provinces. Their number was six when Finland was annexed to Russia in 1809 and rose to eight in 1831; in 1960 the number of provinces became twelve. These multisector regional arms of central government also became an object of their inhabitants' regional identification, but this aspect was ended by the new Provincial Administration Act of 1997. Only Lapland, North Ostrobothnia (the province of Oulu) and Åland remained, while the nine other provinces were condensed into three artificially formed major provinces (different from the major regions shown in Figure 4.1).

The provincial state offices are under the Ministry of Interior, but they handle matters under the purview of many other ministries as well. The list of their regular functions is extensive: "social welfare and health administration, police administration, the rescue services, transport, consumers and competition, food administration, veterinary services and animal welfare, judicial administration, and sport and youth affairs" (Selovuori 1999, p. 154), and the central government sets demanding goals for all these functions (cf. the government's budget proposal for 2002, pp. 115–117). Many of these functions are practiced at the level of the state's 90 local districts, such as police departments, register offices, employment offices, and tax offices. In addition, the provincial state offices take part in some regional planning and they "supervise and evaluate" functions of the self-governing municipalities.

Simultaneous with the reform of provincial state offices in autumn 1997 was the establishment of 15 employment and economic development centers. They assumed tasks of a large number of separate district offices for the purpose of promoting business and regional development. Administratively these centers come under the Ministry of Trade and Industry, but they are also subordinated to the Ministry of Agriculture and Forestry, and the Ministry of Labor. The areas they cover are identical with those of the regional councils.[49] The Ministry of the Environment works through a separate network of regional environment centers, and there are many other district authorities working in their own fields of administration.

National Defense

The central aim of Finland's security policy is to expand cooperation and maintain a stable situation in northern Europe and the Baltic area. The official policy line from the end of the second world war into the 21st century has been that this aim is best promoted by maintaining a credible defense capability, remaining outside military alliances, and participating in international cooperation in order to strengthen security and stability. The country's security policy and international cooperation will be discussed below in Chapter 16. Military defense capability is the duty of the armed forces, but total defense also includes economic and civil defense, dependability of the society's technical systems, measures in social welfare and health care, public law and order, and national defense information.

According to the Constitution Act of 1919 and, again, the Constitution of 1999 (Section 127), "Every Finnish citizen is required to participate or assist in the defense of the fatherland, as provided by an Act." Finland has a conscription army; the conscription of the male population is stipulated in the Conscription Act and only the residents of Åland are exempted from it. On grounds of ethical conviction a conscript may be directed into unarmed service. The duration of the conscripts' military

---

49 The 19 regions of continental Finland, listed in Chapter 4 (Table 4.6 and Figure 4.1), were reduced to 15 by joining Uusimaa with Itä-Uusimaa, Häme with Kanta-Häme, Kymi with South Karelia, and Pohjanmaa with Keski-Pohjanmaa.

service is 6, 9, or 12 months depending on the type of training. Women can also volunteer for military service (some 400–500 do so annually).

The president of the republic issues military orders and appoints the officers of the defense forces in his or her capacity as the supreme commander (Section 128). He or she may relinquish this task to another Finnish citizen, as President Kyösti Kallio did in 1939 when he invited Marshall Mannerheim to take over the responsibilities of supreme commander. But according to the new constitution this can happen only if the government proposes it. In other ways, too, the Constitution of 1999 brought the government, and especially its minister of defense, into closer cooperation with the president in military decisions. The mobilization of the defense forces would require a proposal by the government, and the president now "makes decisions on matters relating to military orders in conjunction with a Minister" (Section 58).

The council of state is responsible for total defense, and its ministry of defense has a central role in coordinating the activities of different ministries in this area. The government's committee on foreign and security policy, which is chaired by the president or the prime minister, is the consultative and planning organ for total defense.[50]

Matters of military command are proposed for the president's decision by the commander-in-chief of the defense forces, who is directly subordinate to the president in these matters; military command also includes operational planning and training. The Finnish forces are organized into the defense staff, in which the army staff also functions, three supra-regional commands with 12 military districts, plus the air force and the navy. The administration of the defense forces is under the ministry of defense. However, the border guard is separate and its senior command and control are subordinated to the ministry of the interior.

About 27,000 conscripts, approximately 80 percent of the relevant age group, complete their military service each year. The total number of salaried staff is some 16,500. These are rather small numbers but, if necessary, Finland would be able to mobilize 22 wartime brigades, with 490,000 trained and adequately equipped men, because commissioned officers and NCOs remain in the reserve until aged 60, and other ranks do until 50. Conscripts must participate in refresher training if asked to do so.[51] The use of the traditional conscription system has the support of a very large majority (79 percent in October 2001) of the people, while 13 percent would prefer selective service and only 7 percent favor a professional army (MTS 2/2001).

People feel high confidence in the defense forces (see Table 7.4) and also are, in principle, very willing to defend the country. "If Finland is

---

50 In March 2000 this committee replaced the former defense council, which was the highest consultative planning organ and also advised the president in defense matters.

51 The government plans to reduce wartime manpower to 350,000 by the end of 2008 (VNS 2/2001, p. 9).

attacked, do you think the Finns should take up armed defense under all circumstances, even if the outcome seems uncertain?" has been an annually repeated survey question, to which respondents have reacted affirmatively. In the 1990s more than three-quarters said yes and less than 20 percent said no. An even bigger majority (85 percent) would be willing to participate personally in national defense to an extent their skills and ability permit, although a smaller majority (56 percent in October 2001) actually believe that Finland could emerge successful from a conventional war. (Kekäle 1999, pp. 11, 14, 27; MTS 2/2001.)

Despite such favorable public opinion it is quite demanding for a small nation to maintain a credible defense capability. Because of the large territory, Finland's strategy needs to include a readiness to organize separate regional defenses. Nowadays it is not always easy to get those summoned to participate in refresher training, one reason being tougher competition in the economy, which has made employers reluctant to release their skilled employees for weeks in the military. The defense forces must also operate, modernize, and plan for the future within narrow fiscal limits. Decisions to close up military bases due to rationalization have caused critical local reactions.

Finland's defense expenditures amounted to 1.3 percent of the GDP in 2000, the same as Spain' and more than Austria and Ireland (1.0%), but less than Germany (1.5%), Sweden (2.0%), Great Britain (2.4%), or France (2.7%) (VNS 2/2001, p. 91). However, when making cross-national comparisons one might add that a conscription army with trained reserves provides defense capability less expensively than a professional army.

Finland has also had a role in international peacekeeping operations. It can take part in operations if they are implemented by the UN, the OSCE, the EU, or NATO, and if they are under a UN or OSCE mandate and consistent with the Finnish Act on Peace Support Operations. Finland participated in the First United Nations Emergency Force in Sinai in 1956-1957, since when it has been one of the leading peacekeeping countries under the flag of the UN. In 2001, there were 1600 Finnish peacekeepers participating in ten operations. In total, Finland has placed more than 40,000 peacekeepers at the UN's disposal.[52] Finland also maintains a UN training center, and since 1996 volunteering conscripts have been selected for training for the special Finnish Rapid Deployment Force. This force went into the field for the first time in 1999' as part of Kosovo's KFOR operation.

52　The operations have included UNEF II in Sinai in 1973–1979, the UN Peacekeeping Force in Cyprus since 1964, the UN Disengagement Observer Force in Golan in 1979–1993, the UN Interim Force in Lebanon since 1978, the UN Transition Assistance Group in Namibia in 1989–1990, and several operations since 1991 in the Balkans (in Kroatia, Macedonia, Bosnia-Herzegovina, and Kosovo).

12 Local Self-Government

More and more matters which the municipalities had decided quite independently began to be regulated by legislation.

Halila 1965, p. 219

...this conception of local government as an autonomous local arm of the State.

Pulma 1999, p. 168

The Self-Governing Municipalities

As described in Chapter 11, the state's central offices are mostly located in the capital city and state administration also functions through various regional offices. But there is no self-government at the intermediate level. Finland is a unitary state without a federal arrangement like that of the states of the USA, Germany, or Austria. Neither are there any self-governing regional units between the central and the local level, as there are in Sweden and many other countries.[53]

On the other hand, self-government serves very important functions at the local level. The country is divided into 448 municipalities (in Finnish, "kunta"), which complement the central government. They make their own policy decisions and they have special responsibilities to implement national policies. Thus, it is local self-government that actually manages the services provided by the welfare state, while the functions of the municipalities also include the planning and maintenance of the people's living environments.

It seems fair to call Finland's local government modern and efficient. On the other hand, it can be viewed as the result of very old traditions.

---

53 The Constitution Act of 1919 (Section 51), as well as the Constitution of 1999 (Section 121), made intermediate-level self-governing units possible, but such have never been established, except in Åland.

To-day's local self-government has grown from distant, even prehistoric roots, although the standards of democratic government were not fully realized in the municipalities before the country became independent.

When the state government of Sweden-Finland was centralized from the 16th century onward, it "secured its legitimacy by guaranteeing the people at least some measure of participation and influence over the process of government" (Pulma 1999, p. 162). Thus the parishes of the Lutheran church, with their parish councils, became the cornerstone of local government autonomy. In practice it depended much on the attitudes taken at the local level whether or not various national policies, including the educational and poor relief legislation of the 18th century, were really implemented.

In the Grand Duchy of the 19th century, it became both necessary and possible to reform the system of local self-government. Again the main inspiration came largely from Sweden's local government reforms of 1842 and 1862, and not from Russia. The most significant step of the 19th century was the severing of institutional connections between local government and the parishes of the church. This was enacted in 1865. Village councils became the decision-making organs of local government. The Town Government Decree of 1873 obliged towns with a population of over 3000 to have an elected town council and allowed smaller towns to make a choice between having an elected council or holding town meetings. The franchise in local government remained property-based even beyond 1906, when universal and equal suffrage was introduced in parliamentary elections.

The next obvious step was due as soon as Finland became independent: local self-government was organized on an entirely representative basis and the inhabitants of municipalities were given the equal right to vote in local council elections.[54] On the other hand, the grip of the central government, which had already started in the 1880s, became tighter and tighter, adding nationally determined responsibilities and central supervision to local affairs. In the 1990s, local autonomy was again emphasized and the municipalities became more responsible for determining their own policy preferences, naturally within the limits set by the resources available.

There used to be a difference between the legal status of rural communes ("maalaiskunta") and towns ("kaupunki"), the towns having additional rights but also more responsibilities and being under closer central supervision. Industrialization created densely populated localities with a status somewhat in-between, and those were called townships ("kauppala"). The Municipal Administration Act of 1976 finally gave all local authorities the same legal status, although the name "kaupunki" (town, city) remains in use, now as a kind of 'status symbol' of an increasing number of municipalities.

54　Universal and equal suffrage was first stipulated in 1917 in the separate laws on rural communes and towns.

According to the Constitution of 1999 (Section 121), "Finland is divided into municipalities, the administration of which shall be based on self-government by their inhabitants." The same section also guarantees the right of municipalities to levy taxes, but all further preconditions concerning administration and the tasks of municipalities are stipulated at the level of ordinary legislation and not in the constitution.

Table 12.1

Finland's largest cities: Population in December 2000, growth (in %) in 2000, and location (region)

Cities	Population	Growth	Region
Helsinki	555,500	0.8	(11) Uusimaa
Espoo	213,300	1.7	(11) Uusimaa
Tampere	195,500	1.2	(24) Pirkanmaa
Vantaa	178,500	1.2	(11) Uusimaa
Turku	172,600	0.3	(21) Varsinais-Suomi
Oulu	120,800	2.6	(51) North Ostrobothnia
Lahti	97,000	0.3	(25) Päijät-Häme
Kuopio	86,700	0.1	(32) North Savo
Jyväskylä	79,000	1.4	(41) Central Finland
Pori	76,000	−0.3	(22) Satakunta
Lappeenranta	58,000	0.8	(27) South Karelia
Vaasa	56,700	0.1	(43) Ostrobothnia
Kotka	54,800	−0.7	(26) Kymenlaakso
Joensuu	51,800	0.5	(33) North Karelia
Mikkeli	46,700	0.1	(31) South Savo
Hämeenlinna	46,100	0.3	(23) Kanta-Häme
Porvoo	45,000	0.8	(12) East Uusimaa
Hyvinkää	42,500	0.5	(11) Uusimaa
Rauma	37,200	−0.6	(22) Satakunta
Kajaani	36,100	−0.8	(34) Kainuu
Järvenpää	35,900	1.3	(11) Uusimaa
Kokkola	35,500	0.1	(44) Central Ostrobothnia
Rovaniemi	35,400	−0.8	(52) Lapland

Note: For location of regions, see the map in Figure 4.1 (on page 78).

Source: *SYF 2001,* pp. 78–96, 118.

The number of Finland's self-governing municipalities was reduced gradually during the latter part of the 20th century. They numbered 549 in 1951, but 448 in 2001.[55] Each of them has its own scope of activities, its own administrative authorities, and its own taxation. The membership of a municipality comprises all who are domiciled in it according to the Census Register Act. The size of municipalities varies greatly: in 2000, six of them had more than 100,000 inhabitants while twenty-two had fewer than 1000 (nine of those in Åland). Their land areas and population densities are also quite different. For example, the city of Helsinki with 555,000 inhabitants covers 185 square kilometers (72 sq. mi), but only 7000 inhabitants populate the 15,173 square kilometers (5927 sq. mi) of the most spacious municipality, Inari in Lapland. Table 12.1 lists Finland's largest cities.

As was mentioned above, the autonomous municipalities both decide policies of their own choosing and carry out the duties which national legislation prescribes for them, but the Municipal Administration Act of 1995 (Section 2) does not list any more specific municipal tasks. It only states very generally that "the municipality strives to advance the well-being of its inhabitants and sustainable development within its area" (Section 1). Other state legislation makes local government responsible for the schools, the hospitals, the health centers, and social welfare, and gives it responsibility for technical infrastructure and local planning. As in other countries, the various other functions of Finland's towns and most other municipalities include the maintenance of streets and parks, water and sewage, and protection against fire. Several cities also operate their public transportation systems and provide electric power, district heating, and a variety of cultural services.

Many responsibilities of local self-government exceed the capacity of single municipalities. Intermunicipal cooperation is necessary. About 250 joint municipal authorities have been established by two or more municipalities. Some were founded voluntarily to advance mutual interests, but the most important joint functions are statutory. They include district general hospitals and central hospitals that take care of the municipalities' responsibility for public health work and specialized medical care. There is care for the mentally disabled as well as districts for special care services. Other joint authorities operate emergency services, vocational schools, and so on. The Helsinki Metropolitan Area Council was set up by special legislation.[56]

Already in the 1930s there were ten regional councils and others were founded in the 1950s to develop common cultural and economic activities within their area. In 1994 the Regional Development Act connected

---

55 Sweden proceeded quite differently: there the number of municipalities was reduced from 2498 in 1950 to only 278 in 1974. Denmark now has 272, having had 1388 in early 1960s.

56 This council represents Helsinki, Espoo, Vantaa, and Kauniainen with a total of 956,000 inhabitants.

them to the regional planning associations, which had previously functioned separately, and also transferred to them the planning functions of the state's provincial governments. Their borders were fixed by the national government (see Table 4.6 and Figure 4.1). The statutory task of the 20 regional councils is to plan and promote their region's development and general policy. Their delegates also represent Finland in the EU's Committee of the Regions. They act according to the principles of local self-government; their members are elected by the municipal councils and, consequently, the regional councils substitute to some extent for the intermediate level self-government that Finland does not have.

The primary sources of revenue are local income tax and the fees the municipalities charge for services, and they collect some tax on real estate. Municipal taxes have amounted to about 22 percent of all taxes collected in Finland. The central government also contributes to municipal budgets. This has happened in two ways: via state subsidies for local activities, and by income transfers that level out differences in local government revenue. During the 1990s there were two significant changes. Annual state grants were reduced dramatically and they were paid in lump sums, no more earmarked for specific purposes.

These changes were characteristic of the overall transition from traditional bureaucracy to New Public Management and self-management, which was first introduced into Finland's public administration in the program of the "red-blue" coalition government in 1987. It is reminiscent of this aspect of "Thatcherism" in the UK, or "Reaganism" in the USA. (Haveri 2000, pp. 7–14.) As far as local government is concerned, the cornerstones of the reform were the comprehensive change in the system of central government grants, effective in 1993, and the Municipal Administration Act, in force since 1995. This new legislation has loosened state regulation on the administration, finances, and activities of municipalities, while emphasizing the responsibility that the municipalities have for their own affairs.

Local decision-making power is vested in municipal councils, which are elected for four-year terms at the same time throughout the country. Councils vary in size between seventeen and eighty-five members, depending on the number of inhabitants in the municipality.[57] The council elects its chairmen and the municipal board for two-year terms, and also appoints standing committees, which exercise considerable delegated power of their own. Administration is of the city-manager type. The municipal manager and possible assistant managers are appointments made by the council and they work subordinate to the municipal board. Typically these are tenured positions, although some recent appointments have been made for a fixed term of five or seven years.

57 Very small municipalities may be granted the right to elect a council of fifteen or thirteen members.

Local elections are proportional and, in other respects too, they are comparable to parliamentary elections. The biggest difference lies in the fact that municipalities are not divided into election districts. The number of candidates each party can nominate is one and a half times the number of members to be elected. As mentioned in Chapter 8, in Helsinki this amounts to the maximum of 127 candidates per party. For the elections of 2000, no fewer than 906 candidates were actually nominated in the capital city. Altogether the country's 432 municipal councils have 12,300 members, and in 2000 the members were elected from 39,700 nominated candidates. These councils are serving a four-year term from January 2001 to December 2004.[58] A majority of their members (56%) had also served during the preceding term from 1997 to 2000.

Because the size of councils is not proportional to the number of inhabitants, the nationwide count of council seats shows an 'overrepresentation' of the Center Party, which is strong in small rural municipalities. In the 2000 election it received 23.8 percent of votes in the country, but won 37.7 percent of council seats and became the largest party in 301 municipalities (70 percent of all). Counted this way, the Social Democrats were slightly underrepresented while the Conservatives, with 20,8 percent of the national vote, won 16,5 percent of seats and became the largest party group in only 22 municipal councils.

Local Government in Action

Many Finnish municipalities faced serious financial difficulties as a consequence of the recession of the early 1990s and because the state reduced its financial support. The grants that the state allocated to municipalities in 1999 were less than 20 percent of their gross expenditure. More than eighty municipalities had budget deficits in that year. In 2000, the financial status of 252 municipalities deteriorated and it improved in only 111. As many as 192 were operating with a budget deficit. However, there were also many municipalities in which the situation was quite satisfactory and, taken as a whole, municipal finances were becoming stronger.

Municipalities constitute a major factor in the national economy. In 2000, local government expenditure totalled 140 billion markkas (23.5 billion €), amounting to about 18 percent of Finland's gross domestic product. Together with the joint municipal authorities the municipalities employ about 400,000 people, or approximately 20 percent of the total workforce. Altogether, tax revenue of the municipalities amounted to 13,900 markkas (2340 euros) per inhabitant in 1999, and they received,

---

58 In the province of Åland the timing is different, as will be described later in this chapter.

in addition, FIM 3700 (€ 620) per inhabitant as state subsidies. The rates of local income tax averaged 17.5 percent. Two years later, in 2001, the average rate was 17.7 percent. It varied between 15 percent in Kauniainen (with taxable income of FIM 166,900 or € 28,000 per inhabitant) and 19.75 in Karkkila (with FIM 65,900 or € 11,080 per inhabitant), both of which are located rather close to the capital. Helsinki itself collected 16.5 percent (from an average taxable income of FIM 129,900 or € 21,850). The rates in Lapland's municipalities varied between 17.5 and 19.25 percent, the mean being 18.6 percent (on FIM 64,200 or € 10,800). Gross taxable income in Finland's municipalities in 1999 was FIM 414 billion or € 70 billion, which consisted of primary income (FIM 332 billion or € 55 bn.) and the municipalities' share of taxable corporate income (FIM 82 billion or € 14 bn.). The general tax rate imposed on real estate averaged 0.7 percent, and the rate on permanent residential buildings averaged 0.26 percent. (*SYF 2001,* pp. 327, 346–356.)

Of their net operating costs, which totaled € 2875 per inhabitant in 1999,[59] the municipalities spent 61 percent on social welfare and health care services (12% for primary health care, 19% for special medical care, 11% for child day care, and 8% for care for the elderly and handicapped). Education and culture was the other large area of local expenditure. Its net share was 29 percent of total operating costs (including 16% for comprehensive schooling, 3% for upper secondary general schooling, 3% for vocational schools, and 3% for libraries and recreation). Various other municipal services cost 6 percent, and general administration 4 percent. (Op. cit., p. 357.)

Thus, the municipalities provide a wide range of services for their inhabitants. In addition to the obligatory and most costly operations and services, their cultural activities deserve special mention. They maintain libraries and museums; several cities have permanent symphony orchestras on their payroll; and many support permanent theaters. Almost all municipalities provide sport facilities and other opportunities for recreation. Business premises and leasing services, water supply and sewage services, and energy supply have actually yielded some revenue above their operating costs.

Citizens have become accustomed to the availability of such local services and they expect high standards. Any cuts and reductions in services make people very critical. Unsatisfactory care for the aged became the most salient nationwide issue in the local elections of October 2000, and during the campaign every party promised to pay more attention to this problem.

---

59 Gross operating costs were FIM 119.4 billion or € 20.1 bn., which was FIM 23,100 or € 3885 per inhabitant.

By and large, the people in Finland are satisfied with their local government. According to an opinion survey conducted in 2000, almost all agreed that a Finnish municipality "is the central provider and guarantee of the citizens' wellbeing," and a very large majority agreed with statements such as the following: "Local government provides social justice and equality; ..has been subjected in recent years to excessively severe cuts; ..is ruled too heavily by the central government." Furthermore, a sixty percent majority disagreed with the statements that local government "overprotects its inhabitants and makes them too passive" and that "many of its services ought to be privatized." (*Kansalaismielipide ja kunnat 2000*, p. 39.)

In a parallel survey the members of municipal councils reacted to the statements even more favorably than did citizens at large, while a majority of both groups thought that local taxes were too high. What really pleased local decisionmakers in the summer of 2000 was the public's response to the following statement: "If necessary, it would be better to increase local tax than to cut municipal services." As many as 69 percent of respondents agreed, a figure 14 percentage points higher in 2000 than in 1996 (op.cit., pp. 40, 43). Also, 91 percent of the people agreed, to some extent at least, with the statement that local services were good enough to satisfy existing needs (see Table 12.2).

When more focused opinions were invited on the quality of listed local services, some ninety percent said that municipal libraries, sports facilities, and schools were good enough. The greatest dissatisfaction concerned the care that their municipality was giving to the aged. The decisionmakers looked at the services somewhat differently. Members of the municipal councils were more satisfied than the public with children's day care and the care provided for the old, as well as with poor relief and local health care centers, whereas they were more anxious than their voters to improve streets and to increase cultural offerings.

As was mentioned above, many municipalities are too small to produce all the necessary services by themselves. Therefore, they cooperate through joint municipal boards and they purchase services from each other. All participating municipalities are represented on the governing boards of cooperative organizations, but in a sense they lose some of their independent power when they function through joint municipal authorities. The strengthening and formalization of Finland's nineteen regions in 1994 was motivated, among other things, by attempts to improve their ability to draw and lobby for benefits from the regional policies of the European Union.

Table 12.2

"How sufficiently are needs satisfied by the municipal services that your home town provides?" Responses by the people and the members of municipal councils (in %)

	+2	+1	0	−1	−2	Score*
Local services as a whole						
The people	19	72	1	8	1	+100
The council members	18	77	1	4	0	+109
Library services						
The people	58	34	2	4	1	+144
The council members	60	32	1	5	1	+145
Sport and Exercise possibilities						
The people	54	37	1	7	1	+136
The council members	41	49	1	7	1	+122
The schools						
The people	49	39	1	7	1	+128
The council members	53	38	1	6	1	+136
Cultural services, e.g. theater						
The people	44	37	3	13	3	+104
The council members	29	36	3	23	9	+53
Children's day care						
The people	30	45	9	13	2	+88
The council members	55	39	1	4	0	+145
Health care centers						
The people	29	42	1	23	6	+65
The council members	29	55	1	13	2	+98
Streets and street lights						
The people	26	45	0	21	7	+62
The council members	17	51	1	26	5	+49
Social support, poor relief						
The people	14	40	20	21	5	+37
The council members	36	50	4	9	1	+111
Care of the aged						
The people	11	37	9	33	10	+6
The council members	20	55	1	20	4	+67

*) +2 = fully sufficiently; +1 = fairly sufficiently; 0 = can't say; −1 = fairly insufficiently; −2 = completely insufficiently.
The satisfaction score is the sum total of positive and negative percentages, the values +2 and −2 being dublicated.

Data source: *Kansalaismielipide ja kunnat 2000*, pp. 81–83.

In order to further their own nationwide interests, the municipalities act through their own interest organization, the Municipal League. It was formed in 1993 by combining the three existing central organizations, namely the League of Rural Communes, the League of Finnish Cities, and the League of Swedish Rural Communes in Finland. However, the most direct political link between local government interests and the national legislature is the fact that a majority of the members of parliament are themselves members of a municipal council.

Local politics are important in their own sphere, and in various ways they also prepare the ground for national politics. Visible political careers typically originate in local politics and, later, nationally significant politicians continue to need and nourish their local strongholds. In the membership activity that takes place in party organizations, the municipal level is quite essential. And although it is not easy for the political parties to declare national programs which are relevant in all local situations, the results of local elections often suggest important conclusions on the national level.

Despite the fact that Finns are rather satisfied with the functions and accomplishments of their own municipality, local democracy has its problems. One has been declining voter turnout in local elections, down from 78 percent in 1980 to only 56 percent in 2000. Another is the growing role of local bureaucracy in political decisionmaking and the seemingly declining impact of elected members of municipal councils. However, the majority of citizens do not consider that their trustees or local political parties should be given more power. Rather, the people would like to exert more direct influence: to attend more issue-related meetings with local authorities and to have local opinion surveys and referendums (Borg 1998, p. 127).

Åland's Regional Autonomy

Åland is an offshore province and has 25,000 inhabitants. It consists of 6500 islands, more than 100 of which are inhabited. It was separated in 1918 from the administrative district of Turku-Pori and obtained the status of an autonomous province, with a special language status. The extra conditions were defined in the Autonomy Act of 1920 and the act's supplement of 1922.

A second Autonomy Act was passed in 1951 and the present Åland self-government law has been in effect since 1991. Within the Nordic context, Åland could be compared with the position of the Faeroe islands and Greenland in Denmark. These three self-governing island regions also have had independent representation in the Nordic Council since 1971 and one of them, Greenland, even left the European Community in 1985 although Denmark was a member.

In 1917 a movement, supported by Sweden, was launched in Åland demanding that the area become part of Sweden. A movement for independence also developed. In more recent years symbolic benefits have generated various kinds of compensating psychological satisfaction for the Ålanders: the province has had its own flag since 1954, postage stamps since 1984, and passports additionally designated "Åland" since 1991 (McRae 1997, p. 328).

Since 1951 it has been possible to speak of a specifically defined Åland citizenship, the so-called resident's rights. Åland's citizens have a privileged right to own land in the region. Residential rights run in the family or can be granted by the provincial government to Finnish citizens who have moved to Åland permanently, have lived there at least five years, and have a "satisfactory" ability to speak Swedish.

Because of their location, the Åland islands have been of obvious military interest. In the early 1800s Russia began to fortify them, but this was stopped by an international agreement in 1856. Later, Åland's demilitarization was again recognized by international treaties in 1921, 1940, and 1947. The male inhabitants of Åland have been exempted from the compulsory military service required of other male citizens of Finland; they are trained instead in pilotage and the lighthouse service.

The Autonomy Law of 1920 reserved a long list of enumerated powers to the central government and left other matters to Åland's new regional parliament. It is obvious that regional powers were circumscribed and not very important, but the element of self-government was increasingly underscored. The second Autonomy Act of 1951 included a specified list of regional powers and narrowed the president's power to veto Åland legislation. In 1991 the regional authorities were also assigned responsibility for administration of some fields over which legislative competence remained with the Finnish parliament. Moreover, intergovernmental consultation with the regional authorities – the right to be heard, joint negotiation, or even approval by the Åland executive – was specified for 23 listed topics before decisions could be taken (McRae 1997, pp. 322–327).

Finnish political parties are not active in Åland's regional politics. The province has developed its own party system, which is most visible in elections to the provincial parliament. This parliament has 30 members who are elected, together with Åland's 16 municipal councils, one year ahead of the mainland's local elections. The regional parliament elects, in turn, a seven-member regional government to implement the parliament's decisions and, increasingly, to administer a range of national legislation. The courts in Åland are national only.

12,045 votes were cast in the election of October 17, 1999. This meant a 65.9 percent turnout, up from the 62.5 percent recorded in 1995. Six regional parties gained representation, none of them getting as many as one-third of the 30-member parliament. The two biggest ones, with 9 elected members each, were the victorious Liberals (28.2% of the vote) and Åland's center (27.3%). Two parties got 4 seats: the declining League for Tolerance (14.5%) and the winning Independent Åland coalition (12.7%). The Social Democrats (11.9%) went down from four to three, and a new progressive group (4.8%) won one seat. Parliamentarism functioned in government formation; the center was, for the first time, pushed into opposition and the Liberals took over. Together with the independents and the Social Democrats, the Liberals formed a majority coalition backed by 17 members in the regional parliament.

When the Ålanders gained their special citizen status in 1951, they did not lose their right to participate fully in Finnish politics. Åland's main Swedish political organization, designated as the Åland Coalition, has presented its own separate list in every parliamentary election since Åland was established in 1948 as a single member constituency. This party has always won the one seat in the Finnish parliament. Åland's turnout in the parliamentary elections has been about 20 percentage points lower than in all of Finland and 10 percentage points lower than turnout in the elections of Åland's own parliament.

Because Finland is not divided into constituencies in the presidential and European elections, Ålanders then need to take a stand on national politics just like other Finnish citizens. Most voters in Åland favor the Swedish People's Party. In the European elections in October 1996, 80 percent of those who voted in Åland cast their ballot for the SPP and 10 percent for the Center Party; in the 1994 presidential elections the favorite of the region was the SPP candidate Elisabeth Rehn. She received 79 percent of Åland votes in the first round and 82 percent in the second round of the election, with 70 and 74 percent of Åland's electorate participating. Thus the turnout of voters in the province was only about ten percentage points lower than the 82 percent recorded for the whole country.

In 1994 the voters in Åland were consulted twice on the issue of membership of the European Union. In the national referendum on October 16, the yes-votes from Åland were a narrow 52 percent, with 61 percent of the region's electorate participating. Five weeks later, when Åland's own membership was the issue, the proportion of yes-voters was much larger, 74 percent, but only 49 percent turned out in the regional referendum.

In membership negotiations with the EU, completed in June 1994, Finland obtained full recognition of Åland's special constitutional status, including a special accession procedure and a special protocol concerning Åland in the accession treaty itself. The protocol also provided customs exemptions for ferry traffic to and from Åland. (McRae 1997, pp. 356–357). Consequently, as long as the ships make a brief stop in Åland, the closing of Europe's tax free stores in 1999 for all inter-EU travel did not inconvenience the two million passengers who sail annually between Finland and Sweden and desire some inexpensive alcoholic beverage.

13 Law and Order and Public Control

The Law, born long before me, will remain firmly after me.
Governor Wibelius in 1808, in a poem by J.L. Runeberg 1804–1877

A new ideology of the law is also about to emerge, an ideology with a welfare state as its central aim.
Yrjö Blomstedt 1985, p. 38

The Legal System

The Finnish legal system is a part of the continental European system and also has developed as part of it. Back in the Middle Ages, the legal traditions and customs of the Finns were gradually superseded by Swedish common law, and in the 14th century the great reforms that began to replace the provincial laws of their time were influenced by the direct contacts that Scandinavia in those days had with the French and Italian law schools and canonical law. The emerging Scandinavian conception of the law had three solid cornerstones, namely, the powers of the ruler, the rights of the people, and the sanctity of the law. (Blomstedt 1985, pp. 29–30.)

King Magnus Ericson's National Code of Laws of the 1350s and the National Code of 1442 are past history now, whereas some aspects of the General Code of 1734 – the oldest common codification for a whole country in Europe – still remain effective in today's Finland. The early decades of the Russian era did not change the laws much; one change in criminal law was the manifest of Emperor Nicholas I in 1826, which meant that capital punishments were no longer carried out.

"The Golden Age of Finnish Legislation" began when the Diet of the Four Estates was summoned in 1863, and it continued until the 1890s. During those decades liberalism had an impact on extensive reforms in almost all fields of law. The modernized penal code was passed and confirmed in 1888 in line with the new German theories of criminal law; in the area of family and probate law men and women were made equal in

1878 with regard to the right of inheritance; and reforms in the area of trade law and economic law portrayed the gradual transition to freedom of trade (op. cit., pp. 32–34). As free enterprise and the freedom of contract became the leading principles in Finland's civil and commercial law, "the legal framework for a market economy was established at this time" (Kekkonen 1999, p. 177). Social legislation, however, lagged behind the other Nordic countries.

The first steps to protect labor against some unwanted consequences of economic liberalism were also taken during that period. In 1879 the use of child and female labor was limited and an act on laborers' industrial injuries insurance was passed in 1895. More extensive new social legislation became effective in 1917 and between the two World Wars, when the values and legal traditions were still typical of an agrarian culture (Aarnio 1993, p. 7). As was described in Chapter 2, the birth of the Finnish welfare state really took place after World War II, generally following the Nordic approach and also influenced by Nordic cooperation.

In the 1970s there emerged a new type of goal-oriented legislation in Finland as a consequence of the then-prevailing strong faith in planning and in the power of legislation as a means of directing social change. The set of principles that characterized the 1980s included internationalization, deregulation, competition, cost cutting, and efficiency (Kekkonen 1999, p. 181). Because Finland joined the European Union in 1995, a great deal of national legislation has been and will be adjusted to the EU's union-wide requirements[60] but this does not imply major changes in the principles of law in Finland.

Unlike the Common Law tradition of Great Britain, the German-Roman system of pandect law emphasizes the primacy of written laws and general legal concepts. Finland has a statutory law system. In theory, citizens are presumed to know the contents of all laws as soon as they are published in the Statutes of Finland. However, there is no comprehensive law code. For practical purposes, existing legislation and relevant references to earlier decisions are compiled in the massive two-volume book *Suomen laki* (The Law of Finland), which the Association of Finnish Jurists updates and publishes every second year for the benefit of the legal profession. Public law is compiled in the book's volume I[61] and civil law is covered in volume II[62]. Tax laws and customs regulations are published in a separate volume.

---

60 The applicant countries that negotiated EU membership in 2001 needed to change their domestic legislation to satisfy some 80,000 requirements of the EU.

61 The volume is outlined to cover the following ten fields: constitutional law; general administrative law; administrative districts and self-government; international relations and foreigners; security and general order; education and culture; environment and housing; agriculture; social and health care; pensions and accident insurance.

62 Including the following eight fields: basic and human rights; civil law; business enterprises; financing and insurance; communication and transport; labor relations and service; criminal law; legal procedure.

It is not possible here to point out many detailed characteristics of the Finnish approach to law. Guarantees of freedoms and rights of the citizens will be discussed below, in Chapter 14. For instance, capital punishment is not permitted in Finland, nor in most other established democracies. Finland's most significant trend has been from formalistic jurisdiction to "signs indicating the changing role of the rule of law in the Welfare State" (Aarnio 1993, p. 20). This implies a move toward material justice, toward more goal-oriented and flexible legal norms. The process of internationalization and European integration has also strengthened the role of the courts as the final arbiter in solving social conflicts (Kekkonen 1999, p. 181). The rising importance of precedents by the European court strengthens the position of the courts, as the difference between legislation and the application of law becomes less clear. The exact content of laws is also becoming less predictable than it has been in the formalistic Finnish approach (cf. Ojanen 2000).

The hierarchy of legislation consists of several levels. At the top in Finland is the Constitution of 1999, which cannot be contravened by the very large body of ordinary acts, passed by parliament and signed by the president. Next, "The President of the Republic, the Government, and a Ministry may issue decrees on the basis of authorization given to them in this Constitution or in another Act... Moreover, other authorities may be authorized by an Act to lay down legal rules on given matters... The scope of such an authorization shall be precisely circumscribed." (Constitution, Section 80.) The last-mentioned level of legislation also includes municipal by-laws.

The Judiciary

Two principles are fundamental to the functioning of Finnish courts of law: the judiciary is independent and the courts are permanent. There cannot be temporary courts, and Finland has career judges who cannot be removed from office and whose decisions are not influenced by outsiders.

Finland, like many other countries, has three levels of courts of law for civil and criminal cases. First, there are sixty-eight general courts of first instance. They vary in size: the smallest courts have only three judges and the largest in Helsinki has seventy-three. The second level consists of six courts of appeal, and the supreme court is the highest level. What is more unusual, however, is Finland's parallel court system for administrative cases. All cases that concern administrative matters, such as taxation, social welfare, health care, and local government, were tried by the county courts until they were replaced by the eleven provincial administrative courts in November 1999. From them appeal is to the supreme administrative court.

Until 1993 the first level consisted of two different kinds of courts: city courts in most towns, and district courts mainly in rural areas. The latter were chaired by a judicially trained chairman and had a lay board of at least seven laymen. The members of the city courts were generally judicially trained judges who functioned mostly in divisions of three members. The reform of 1993 made all lower general courts uniform in structure and named them district courts. They also continue to have lay members, so-called lay assessors, who participate in deciding criminal cases and civil suits under family law.

In 1999 Finland's district courts handled a total of 138,000 civil cases and 57,300 criminal cases, plus 605,000 petitions and registrations. In the same year the courts of appeal handled 4600 cases and the supreme court, 3000 cases. The county courts, meanwhile, made 18,200 decisions, and the supreme administrative court handled 4700 cases (*SYF 2001*, p. 527).

Most decisions made by the courts of appeal are final, because a reform of the system of appeal in 1980 limited the right of appeal to the supreme court to only the cases that the supreme court agrees to hear. No more than about one case in ten passes this threshold. According to the law, appeals may be granted for cases that are important for similar cases or are in pursuit of uniformity in legal practice, or seek to correct a procedural error. The supreme court can also grant leave to appeal if it sees other important grounds. The purpose of this reform was to gain more efficiency and, especially, to strengthen the role of the supreme court in guiding legal practice and due process. However, precedents are not legally binding in Finland so lower court judges have the right to decide ambiguous cases against a precedent.

In addition, Finland has established various special courts. They include the labor court that hears disputes concerning collective agreements on employment relationships, the market court that can prohibit misleading advertising and unreasonable contract terms, the insurance court, the four land courts, and the prison court. The three water courts were discontinued in 1999 and their cases transferred to the environmental permit authorities. There is also the High Court of Impeachment, which has been convened only four times (in 1933, 1953, 1961, and 1993).[63]

The president of the republic appoints the presidents and the members of the two supreme courts and the six courts of appeal, as well as all the judges for the courts of first instance. Normally this is done according to nominations made by the supreme court. The judges cannot be removed from office before they reach the compulsory retirement age, 67 years. On the other hand, it is quite possible for career judges to take an active part in political life; some may become members of parliament and even government ministers.

An occasionally debated aspect of the Finnish constitution is the lack of a separate constitutional court. Legislation's constitutionality is ex-

---

63 The cases of "unlawful conduct in office" have not been so serious as to ruin the convicted minister's political career: the former minister of finance who was convicted in 1961 became minister of justice in 1966, and the former minister of trade and industry who was convicted in 1993 was re-elected to parliament in 1995.

amined in parliament by the Constitutional Committee, and parliament is required to refrain from enacting laws that violate the constitution. Alternatively, if the Constitutional Committee finds that a law would make an exception to the constitution, it can be enacted if supported by a majority of two-thirds. One example is a one-year tax law that is found to be in conflict with the strict property rights guaranteed by the constitution. But neither the supreme court not the supreme administrative court has the right to interpret the constitutionality of acts of parliament.

The duties of the ministry of justice include the drafting of new legislation, the administration of the courts, and carrying out the prison sentences. In 2000 the daily average number of prisoners in Finland was 2855 (including 144 women). This equals 55 prisoners per 100,000 inhabitants, a rather low number when compared with some 460 prisoners per 100,000 people in the United States (see page 209 below). The powers of the president of the republic include the right to grant pardons, having first consulted the supreme court.[64]

The Supervisors of Legality

"Attached to the Government, there is a Chancellor of Justice and a Deputy Chancellor of Justice, who are appointed by the President of the Republic, and who shall have outstanding knowledge of law" (Constitution of 1999, Section 69). The chancellor of justice attends the meetings of the council of state and ensures that the authorities, including the president and the ministers, observe the laws and fulfill their duties. He is the highest law officer in the country and because he is a permanent official, his position is not dependent on the government of the day. He also was the highest public prosecutor of the country until a state prosecutor's office was established in 1997.

Parliament, in turn, appoints for four-year periods the counterpart of the chancellor of justice, the parliamentary ombudsman and the two deputy ombudsmen. They, too, ensure that the courts and civil servants observe the law. Individual citizens have the right to complain to either the chancellor of justice or to the ombudsman if they feel that they have suffered injustice at the hands of public authorities. There is therefore an obvious overlap in the roles of the two high supervisors of legality.

However, the roles are not identical. In particular, the chancellor of justice supervises the legality of the work of the president of the republic and the council of state, also participating in their meetings, and must advise them and the ministries on legal questions when asked to do so. On the other hand, only the ombudsman deals with the defense forces and prisons.

---

64 Approximately every eighth application has led to a pardon.

The chancellor of justice receives some 1000 to 1300 complaints from the public each year and the ombudsman about twice as many; in 1999 the numbers were 1240 and 2640. Both of them can also handle cases at their own initiative, and they perform inspections of public offices. Only about ten percent of the initiated cases have actually led to action. In 1999 there were no prosecutions and only a very few admonitions were given; the most common outcomes were pronouncements of opinion and guidance. (Härmälä and Tala 2000, pp. 132–147.)

The parliamentary ombudsman is a typically Scandinavian office; Sweden established it back in 1809 and the Finnish one was started in 1920. Denmark followed suit later, adapting a somewhat different model. In recent years the office has become well known internationally and also the European Parliament established such an office in 1995. The roles of the ombudsmen are not identical in different countries: in some, such as the French médiateur, the ombudsman attempts to mediate between the citizen and the public administration, in Latin American countries he emphasizes the protection of human rights, whereas in Sweden and Finland the ombudsman watches over the legality of all public administration and is required to prosecute in cases of serious wrongdoing.

In addition to the two general supervisors of legality, Finland has sectional ombudsmen whose function it is to provide specialized safeguards for individual citizens, and to protect them not only against public authorities but also within the private sector. Such offices have been established since the late 1970s in the central state administration, under four different ministries.

The consumer ombudsman has protected consumers since 1978 against poor quality and unfair business practices, and he also directs the state's consumer agency. The agency comes under the purview of the ministry of trade and industry which cannot, however, direct its decisions. The number of cases referred to it has been increasing (from 1430 in 1994, to 2180 in 1998). Most of them have been about marketing, and many also about contract terms and advice. There has been an emphasis on the advance prevention of unfair practices, and negotiations have been the most common type of action of the consumer ombudsman's office. (Op. cit., pp. 148–158.) For example, in 2001 the office warned businesses against rounding up their prices too much when Finnish markkas were due to be converted to euros.

The data protection ombudsman, since 1987 connected to the ministry of justice, watches and guides the various registers of individuals so that personal information remains confidential and different registers are not combined. In 1987 the equality ombudsman was connected to the ministry of social affairs and health to oversee the implementation of anti-discrimination laws, both in public administration and in businesses. The ombudsman for aliens, in turn, took over the job of the curator of aliens in 1991 and works in connection with the ministry of labor. His duties have included statements of opinion on asylum seekers (619 cases in 1998) and deportations of aliens (176 cases); giving advice has been the most time-consuming task of this office. (Op.cit., pp. 158–178.) There is also the national center for medical care, which protects the rights of patients.

In the control of public offices the trend has been toward increased internationalization. A variety of controlling bodies can already be used for the protection of human rights: never before have citizens had so many channels available for their complaints as today. The growth of the control machinery seems quite justified, because public functions have increased and the people have become in many ways more dependent on public administration. Finland's sectional ombudsmen for their part are also internationally oriented, maintaining close contacts with their foreign counterparts.

Like all public administration, the legality of the work of the sectional ombudsmen is supervised by the chancellor of justice and the parliamentary ombudsman. Moreover, their term of office is fixed and not permanent, and they (except the consumer ombudsman) are appointed by the council of state and not by the president of the republic. They, too, serve as supervisors of legality, but they also function as specialists regarding the material substance of their field of legislation. Thus, they advise the government both in the implementation of laws and in the planning of new legislation, and their advice to citizens and businesses helps to interpret new laws and to prevent breaches of law. Actually, the roles of the high-ranking supervisors of legality seem to be changing in the same direction as those of the sectional ombudsmen (Lehtimaja 1999, p. 900).

The People and Law and Order

The citizens of any democracy can expect that "Everyone has the right to have his or her case dealt with appropriately and without undue delay by a legally competent court of law or other authority, as well as to have a decision pertaining to his or her rights or obligations reviewed by a court of law or other independent organ for the administration of justice" (Constitution, Section 21). In other words, the purpose of the courts is to provide legal security for the people.

"Everyone" and "without undue delay" are important statements, but such words may not always describe accurately what happens in reality. Court cases take time. In the district courts the simplest civil processes in writing last an average of two months but the more complicated processes almost 15 months; the appeal courts average 6.6 months, and the supreme court, 16 months (Ervasti and Teittinen 2000, pp. 84–89). The provincial adminisrative courts decide tax complaints in about 11 months, and the average time for decisions by the supreme administrative court is nine months (Härmälä 2000, pp. 113, 125). The time span is expanded significantly whenever the supreme administrative court invites the European Court of Justice to decide a precedence, because the average time taken to get a reaction from Luxembourg is over 20 months (Ojanen 2000, p. 179). Besides, in criminal cases the suspect may have had to wait a long time before the prosecution was ready to go to court.

About 30 percent of respondents who were interviewed in a survey in 1999 recalled some legal problem during the 1990s. The most common problem areas had been the family, loans, crime, and work. Two-thirds of these people had solved the problem by themselves, although in most cases after having asked for guidance, and one-third had relied on a lawyer. Only a few dropped their problem unsolved because of the cost, typically being unaware of the availability of legal aid. (Litmala 2000, pp. 13–25.)

Naturally, most people have never attended a court session in person; only 27 percent of the Finns have had any contact with a court of law as parties, witnesses, etc. (14 percent in a criminal case, 8 percent in a civil case, and 5 percent in both types of cases) (Lappi-Seppälä et al. 1999, p. 45). One might even say that the procedures of Finnish courts are less familiar to the Finns than those of American courts, due to the constant flow of American tv shows staged in a courtroom setting. But the opinions people have about their legal security are not necessarily linked to any concrete personal experiences, nor to the persons' own need to rely on the courts. More important for the feeling of security is the belief that the courts are trustworthy.

Courts belong to society's most trusted institutions in western Europe, although more so in the northern than in the southern countries of Europe (op. cit., p. 73). During the 1980s there was a decline in many countries in the percentage of people who said they had confidence in the courts; in Finland the drop was bigger than in most other countries, from 80 to 65 percent. Nonetheless, the latter percentage still is relatively high and it has not changed during the 1990s. Even more Finns say that they trust two other institutions which provide security, namely, the police and the defense forces, while fewer people trust the country's political institutions: parliament, the government, and, especially, the political parties (see Table 7.4).

The police became popular in other western countries, too, particularly during the 1970s, which was a decade of many protest actions. One experience that Finland had in 1976 was a police strike of two weeks' duration. In such a situation it was feared widely that the lack of police protection would cause serious disorder. There was an increase in petty theft and traffic violations, but in general life continued as orderly as usual (Takala 1979). Apparently social pressures served as effective constraints, and many felt it would have been unfair to break the law when there was no risk of getting caught.

But it is obvious that crime exists in every society. Table 13.1 summarizes the incidence of various offences in Finland in 1980, 1990, and 2000. It indicates some increase in violence and theft in the 1990s, and it shows an alarming increase in offences involving narcotics. If one makes a comparison with the United Sates, the Finnish rate of robbery appears very low. Also, the rate of manslaughter and murder in Finland is only about one-half, and rape about one-third the American one. On the other hand, recorded cases of assault and theft are no less frequent in Finland than in the USA.

What mainly explains the big difference in the rates of prison populations, is the length of punishments. In general American statistics, it is not customary to summarize sentences of under one year at all, but of the 11,560 unconditional prison sentences in Finland in 2000, only 689 were for one year and only another 626 for two or more years (including 7 for life). 1520 sentences were between 6 and 11 months and the large majority, 8720 sentences, were even briefer imprisonment ranging from a few weeks to 5 months (*SYF 2001*, p. 525). As one might expect, the general public in Finland would often like to see stricter punishments than the legislators are first willing to stipulate and the courts are then willing to impose.

Table 13.1

Selected offences in 1980, 1990, and 2000 (the numbers and rates per 100,000 inhabitants)

	Numbers			Rates per 100,000		
	1980	1990	2000	1980	1990	2000
Manslaughter, murder	111	145	146	2	3	3
Attempted manslaughter, murder	140	244	333	3	5	6
Assault	13,964	20,654	27,820	292	413	537
Rape	367	381	579	8	8	11
Robber	1,869	2,627	2,600	39	52	50
Theft, petty theft	97,793	158,839	189,112	2,042	3,178	3,650
Aggravated theft	3,362	4,800	4,297	70	96	83
Motor vehicle theft	7,808	18,233	26,391	163	365	509
Drunken driving	20,436	29,759	22,783	427	595	439
Offences involving narcotics	955	2,546	13,445	20	51	260

Data source: *SYF 2001,* p. 518.

Order also concerns public behavior. Finland has not experienced the kind of large and violent demonstrations that have taken place in some countries during important international meetings, even forcing summits of world leaders into remote, non-accessible locations. On the level of individual public behavior there have been some unsatisfactory trends and excessive festivities, possibly due to too lax policing and weakened parental authority. In the 1990s a few cities issued local ordinances that regulate behavior in public areas, for example, prohibit drinking in public. This was standardized in 2002 with a government bill that attempted to set natiowide guidelines for public behavior, limiting the use of alcohol on the streets, although not necessarily in public parks. Sale of alcohol to persons under 18 years is prohibited, but somewhat unsuccessfully. Fortunately, the use of drugs is not spread in Finland as widely as in many other countries, but the seriousness of the problem is increasing.

14 Materialization of Values and Goals

Everyone has the right to a standard of living adequate for the health and well-being of himself and his family, including food, clothing, housing and medical care and necessary social services, and the right to security in the event of unemployment, sickness, disability, widowhood, old age or other lack of livelihood in circumstances beyond his control.

Universal Declaration of Human Rights, December 10, 1948. Article 25

Freedoms and Rights of Finnish Citizens

The Parliament Act of 1906 granted to Finnish men and women alike the right to vote and the right to participate as a candidate in general elections. Naturally, both universal and equal suffrage and universal eligibility are essential rights in a democratic political system. Likewise, any democracy must guarantee for its citizens various additional rights to participate freely in its political life. Such political rights include both the freedom of speech and the freedom of the press, and the freedom of assembly and association. They were stipulated in the Constitution Act of 1919 (Section 10) but, like several other fundamental rights, they had in fact been observed in Finland before national independence was reached.

The original Chapter 2 of the Constitution Act listed the fundamental rights of Finnish citizens. Only much later, in 1995, was a comprehensive list of social and cultural rights added to it. Chapter 2, as it was adopted in 1919, was not very innovative. It contained a brief, fairly self-evident list of fundamental rights, including the following protections of the individual citizens (Sections 5-13, 60; see Uotila 1985, pp. 64–66):

- equality before the law;
- protection of life, honor, personal freedom, and property;
- unhindered right to be in the country, and freedom of residence and movement there;

- freedom of religion;
- freedom of speech, assembly, and association;
- the privacy of the home;
- the privacy of postal, telegraphic, and telephone communications; and
- prohibition of any temporary courts of law.

In addition, the Constitution Act of 1919 guaranteed some fundamental social and cultural rights: the right to use the citizen's native language, either Finnish or Swedish, in an administrative agency or in a court of law (Section 14), and the right to have free basic education (Section 80). The protection of labor was added to it in 1972.

Certain other civil rights, which the Constitution Act itself did not mention, ought to be added to the above list. They included the following:

- access to public documents;
- freedom of trade (a separate act in 1919); and
- the right to strike (Finnish labor law).

The new comprehensive list of fundamental economic, social, and cultural rights was added to the Constitution Act when its Chapter 2 was expanded in July 1995. Furthermore, now these rights covered not only "Finnish citizens" in particular, but "persons" more generally. In other words, the protection of fundamental rights was extended to cover all persons within the jurisdiction of Finland. All the sections of the revised Chapter 2 were, in turn, moved unchanged to the new constitution that was enacted in 1999. The added rights included the following:

- prohibition of discrimination on the basis of gender, age, origin, language, religion, conviction, opinion, health, or disability;
- prohibition of torture and capital punishment;
- the right to more than basic education, without restraints caused by a lack of financial resources;
- the government's responsibility for a healthy environment;
- the right of any minority group to maintain and develop its own language and culture;
- the government's responsibility to try to guarantee full employment;
- the right to a decent standard of living and to receive personal care, and the right to receive social security, health care, and child care.

Many of these principles had actually guided Finnish legislation for a long time. Therefore, the amended list of citizens' rights did not add much to the contents of existing legislation or to parliament's policies, nor did the formal expression of additional social rights actually change the life situation of individual Finnish citizens. The reform was significant, first of all, because it outlined clearly the individuals' social and educational rights and raised them to the level of constitutional law. Therefore, it illustrated the ongoing change from the paradigms of the law society to those of the welfare state. Also, the rights now covered aliens as well as Finnish citizens. The reform had its particular Finnish aspects but it was by no means unique. Comparable clauses had been written into other constitutions since the Second World War, for example in Italy already in 1947.

Finland, for its part, had ratified about 60 international conventions that can be characterized as human rights conventions. The International Covenant on Economic, Social and Cultural Rights and the International Covenant on Civil and Political Rights, which were adopted within the United Nations in 1966, entered into force for Finland in 1976. The European Convention for the Protection of Human Rights and Fundamental Freedoms was ratified by Finland in 1990. It was incorporated by an act of parliament and motivated several amendments to existing Finnish legislation.

On the other hand, a new approach was added to the constitution itself in 1995, particularly because people's social rights were now included in the list of fundamental rights. Now, next to strictly binding stipulations, there are policy declarations in the constitution that either can or cannot become fully implemented in reality, depending on the will and the available resources of future parliaments.

What makes such fundamental rights even less concrete, is the fact that Finland does not have a constitutional court that could interpret the constitution in individual cases, in order to rule whether or not a citizen's constitutional rights have been violated. The unique idea of the Finnish constitution and Finnish practice is that court cases are decided only on the basis of ordinary legislation, because parliament is presumed not to pass any legislation that would contravene the constitution. For that purpose the Finnish parliament has its Constitutional Committee to which bills are referred whenever there are fears that the law might contravene the constitution, including the fundamental rights guaranteed by it (see pp. 158, 205 above).

Nevertheless, the International Covenant on Civil and Political Rights was placed at the same level as other acts of parliament when it was incorporated by parliament already in 1976, and there have been several examples of direct application of the Covenant before Finnish courts. And the signatories, including Finland, have agreed to observe many other international declarations that concern human rights. Their contents might not have brought anything particularly new to existing Finnish rights and practices, but they have offered Finnish citizens the possibility of taking their individual grievances to international courts. The rulings of these courts, in turn, are binding in Finnish courts of law.

In any political culture the individual citizen also has rights that are not formalized in the constitution or in ordinary law, and much depends on how the formal norms are implemented in actual practice. In reality the implementation of civil rights may differ greatly between countries that have signed the same international declarations, and in any one country there may be contradictions between the formal norms and the reality of actual practice.

Furthermore, the citizens have learned to assume some basic values and expectations so firmly that political decision-makers need to convince their followers of their best efforts to pursue whatever expectations the people perceive as their legitimate rights. And vice versa: political decision-makers need to communicate to the people not only their political promises, but also what they think is and what is not realistically achievable.

Chapter 2 (Sections 6 to 23) of Finland's new constitution covers a very wide range of "Basic rights and liberties," both fundamental and social. The following text will not review how all of them are implemented. This chapter will focus primarily on the area that is the topic of the constitution's Section 19: "The right to social security." The materialization of "Educational rights" (Section 16) will also be reviewed. *[PP]*

Goals of the Welfare State

The concept of welfare state surfaced during the Second World War, as noted in Chapter 2. Lord Beveridge's advice was to fight the five giants of want, disease, ignorance, squalor, and idleness (unemployment), and gradually such aims were accepted, particularly in West European countries. The motives of social policy have included solidarity and humanity towards underprivileged people, and it is not possible to separate the goals of a welfare state from more general policies and popular demands.

Another aim has been to strengthen the legitimacy of the social system. The legitimation motive was strong especially during the Cold War, when Western democracies wanted to make the foundation of their social system stronger against the threat of communism (Riihinen 1992). Political parties have had different emphases in their policies, the Left stressing solidarity, the Right national unity. The aims of welfare states were gradually considered on a more abstract level, because achieved aims lead to new problems. The new themes included universalism and decommodification.

In a *universal system* all citizens have an equal right to certain benefits. The equal right entitles all persons to receive benefits as far as they meet the prescribed conditions and it means that the benefit is the same for all beneficiaries. Finland, as well as the other Nordic countries, emphasizes the idea of universalism.

There are only a few areas that are completely universal. The most common ones are comprehensive schooling and child allowance. In Finland, as in many other countries, every child is entitled (and required) to receive education for a certain number of years, and child allowance is the same for all families regardless of their incomes. In several countries health care is also universal to a large extent: the services are financed by public funds and the users pay part of the costs only. Some of these costs are compensated through health insurance that covers all citizens.

However, national health insurance does not cover all health care services. For example, dental health care in Finland is only beginning to cover people of all ages. The forms of social insurance that cover all citizens, such as the national pension systems in the Nordic countries, also mainly meet the criteria of universalism. Health care and national pension systems are, however, not as universal as comprehensive schooling and child allowance. It is for experts, mostly doctors, to decide whether a citizen is ill or incapable for work, so the realization of universalism depends on experts' opinions.

It has been claimed that one of the aims of welfare states is *decommodification*, that is, citizens' liberation from market dependency. Decommodification weakens the absolute power of the market and employers, and increases the power of employees. Different types of models of a welfare state can be distinguished on the basis of decommodification although there are no countries purely representing any single model.

The least developed welfare states in terms of decommodification are those in which the core of social policy is typically based on needs tests and social assistance. Employees are dependent on the market and the aims of the state are mostly the same as those of the market. The Anglo-Saxon countries are closest to this model. Another model, pioneered in Bismarck's Germany, typically has compulsory social insurance with considerable entitlements. In such a system the benefits are almost entirely dependent on contributions and, therefore, work, employment, and ultimately the market determine the fates of beneficiaries. The realization of decommodification is very limited in a welfare state of this type. In the third model equal benefits are available for all, regardless of earlier earnings, contributions, and performance. This Beveridge-type social policy is characterized by solidarity but not necessarily by decommodification since the level of benefits does not usually offer a true option for earnings from work.

In a perfect decommodification system the citizens would be given the option between working and other means of livelihood. Thus, for example, sickness insurance should fully compensate citizens' earnings and medical expenses. So far such benefits have been available only for some academics, officials, and professionals in high positions of the private sector (Esping-Andersen 1990, pp. 21–23). In practice, perfect social decommodification is not possible.

The Nordic welfare states, which have adopted the ideal of universal social policy, have taken the realization of decommodification the furthest. These states emphasize not only general civil liberties but also the opportunity of all individuals to obtain extensive freedom: it is not sufficient that the legal system guarantees the right to freedom of speech and similar freedoms; every citizen has to be able to acquire the tools with which these rights are realized. For example, they need to be able to subscribe to newspapers. Thus, being free from something, such as oppression or discrimination, is not enough; one has to have access to something, that is, freedom of pursuing those opportunities important in one's culture.

In the political life and policies of the Nordic welfare states, *equality of opportunity* and *equality of result* are emphasized simultaneously. Equality of opportunity is best seen in the education system, which is practically free of charge all the way to higher learning. Equality of result represents egalitarianism. Finland's unusually equal distribution of income represents a high degree of egalitarianism (see Chapter 17). Still, equality of result is always relative and it remains unattainable in an absolute sense.

The concept of decommodification introduces some problems that have been widely discussed in Finland, too. It has been argued that significant income transfers have a negative effect on the incentives of working life and that they weaken productivity. This argument, favored by neo-liberals, conflicts with the historical goals of social policy, which have always included rehabilitation and activation of people in general, as well as normalization of living conditions of those whose circumstances are poor. The neo-liberal claim is especially difficult to justify in Finland, since the country's productivity is at one of the highest international levels. Still, Finnish social policy experts worry constantly about the working motivation of long-term unemployed people.

Certain changes in economic and social structures have influenced the broader criticism of the welfare state. An important change is that society is becoming more and more middle-class as a result of the rising education level and of the change in the industrial structure, illustrated by the growing proportion of service industries and, especially, intellectual work (see Table 2.1). The disintegration of the old working class can be seen in both national and local politics and in the structure of the trade union movement. The middle class calculates matters of its own interest and of common interest differently from the working class (Riihinen 1984, pp. 2–6).

Globalization has increased doubts about the welfare state. In the opinion of the critics, tougher international competition puts the competitiveness of businesses to an increasingly hard test, which makes it impossible for them to endure the high costs of the welfare state. These critics ignore the welfare state's emphasis on the essential precondition of competitiveness, namely, human capital, which requires investments in education and health care. The current high competitiveness of Finland's national economy makes the critics' arguments seem ideological rather than fact-based.

When Finnish politicians have justified cuts in social expenditures or their reluctance to expand them in recent years, they have generally pleaded that they wish to maintain the sustainability of the Nordic welfare state. Finland's low national debt increased significantly in the severe slump in the early 1990s. Now the big issue concerns the allocation of government revenue: should the debt be reduced or should social conditions be improved. Those in favor of social income transfers argue that Finland's national debt in proportion to national income is one of the lowest in the European Union, whereas the other side argues that the change in age structure will cause pension costs to increase substantially in the near future, which will pose a threat of another recession. There hardly is an objective solution to the dispute.

A large majority of Finns are in favor of maintaining the welfare state. In four surveys since 1992, Finnish respondents have been presented with the following statement: "Although maintenance of good social security and other public services is very costly, the Finnish welfare state is worth the cost." Judging from the increasing size of the middle-class, from globalization, and from certain ideological changes, one would have expected the responses to become more and more negative. However, the trend has been the opposite: in 1992, 61 percent agreed with the claim fully or to some extent, in the autumn of 2000 the percentage was 84 (EVA 2001a, pp. 48–49). The Finns value the security of the system, being aware of the fact that, among other things, health care is significantly cheaper as a public than as a private service. They value the welfare state although a majority votes for non-socialist parties. *[OR]*

Social Welfare and Social Insurance

Social policies have been built on the foundation of *social welfare*. As welfare states have developed, social policies have, however, expanded beyond the limits of social welfare. The growth of social policy is mainly due to the expansion of social insurance and its transformation into an important factor that enhances social security and makes a large economic contribution to society.

Although all members of the Finnish society have a statutory right to *social welfare,* the universality of social policy is restricted: it is provided and paid for according to the principle of need, especially as the means are tested individually. While municipal day care for children is part of the most universal part of social policy, the main methods of social welfare are preventive social welfare, social services, and last-resort income support (also called living allowance, supplementary benefit, or means-tested income support). With the help of different social services the public sector supports individuals and families in need of help, such as the elderly, children, families with children, intoxicant abusers and persons with disabilities. In some cases the services are directed at communities and called community work. The help offered may or may not be purely financial.

The main goal of social welfare is to prevent social problems, to increase social security, and to encourage independence and initiative. The aim is to offer the services in as "normal" a way as possible in order to make it easier to use them and to avoid stigmatization. The law also requires confidentiality: social welfare personnel have an obligation to maintain the confidentiality of any and all information concerning their customers.

The responsibility for organizing social services lies with the municipalities. The central government tries to respect the autonomy of the municipalities and the law does not regulate in detail the scope, content, or method of organizing the services. There are several ways possible: most services are organized independently by the municipalities as their own functions; some services are offered in cooperation with other municipalities or by inter-municipal unions; and others are taken care of by private companies and non-governmental organizations. The municipalities' varying abilities to meet their responsibilities are a problem that might be eased by merging neighboring municipalities, but the idea has been resisted by the inhabitants of almost all municipalities.

A new social and health care planning system came into effect in 2000; the government's four-year program (for 2000–2003) is called the Social Welfare and Health Care Target and Operating Plan. Each new government will prepare such a plan[65] and the government will report to parliament every two years what progress has been made (Järvelin 2001, p. 81).

The role of civil society in organizing social welfare should be emphasized: voluntary organizations supplement municipal services in a humane way. Activities they organize for unemployed people and afternoon clubs for schoolchildren are important because of the large number of single-parent families and families where both parents are working. The organizations are partly funded by public funds and by Finland's Slot Machine Association (cf. Chapter 5). Lutheran congregations, which in the early 19th century were responsible for most of the charity work, carry on the social work of the church, and other churches have also assumed an active role.

Social work is an essential part of the realization of social welfare. Finnish social workers are required to have a masters-level degree, with five to six years of university studies. The range of their work has expanded from services for individuals and families and traditional community work to cooperation with health care authorities and even to societal planning. Important partners also include authorities in education, town planning, building, housing, employment, culture and leisure, and public transport.

---

65 The Ministry of Socil Affairs and Health prepares the plan with representatives of municipalities, nongovernmental organizations, and health care employees and professionals. The municipalities are not bound to follow it.

One expensive form of social welfare is municipal day care for children. In Finland, all children of pre-school age have an absolute right to municipal day care after the mother's or father's period of entitlement to a parental allowance has ended. This right does not depend on the parents' assets or working status. Parents pay for the day care according to their income and family size. In 2002, the maximum monthly payment was 200 euros per child and the minimum was 18 euros. In autumn 1999, there were 190,000 children below school age in municipal day care, equaling 46 percent of the total number of pre-school children.

Other major forms of social welfare are child welfare, welfare and support services for older people, welfare and services for persons with disabilities, welfare for intoxicant abusers, and income support. Income support, the second largest expense of social welfare, has awakened particularly lively debate concerning which families and persons truly need it and on what grounds it should be granted. Also, it has been debated whether the social expenditures system could be simplified and the work incentives for low-income people strengthened by creating a new kind of basic income system concerning all working-age people below a certain income limit.

Services for older people have become a major challenge, not the least because the age structure of the population will change faster in Finland than in any other European country. There is a wide variety of services available for the elderly (see Table 14.1). The most pressing need for such services concerns very old people. Of all Finns aged 75 and over, three-quarters still manage by themselves or with the support of their families, while relatively few make use of even the drop-in services, such as home care. The elderly and their relatives are generally satisfied with the municipal services; complaints have referred mostly to insufficient home care, the quality of institutional care, and the exhaustion of the personnel (Vaarama et al. 2002, pp. 3, 13).

Table 14.1

Coverage of services for the elderly in Finland in 1999

Services	Clients, % of population aged 65–74	Clients, % of population aged 75 and over
Regular home care services	6.7	12.4
Service house for the elderly	2.7	4.7
Old people's homes	2.8	5.5
Health centers, long-term inpatients	1.8	3.5
Psychiatric wards, long-term inpatients	0.1	0.1
Other heath care, long-term inpatients	0.1	0.1

Source: Statistical Yearbook on Social Welfare and Health Care 2000, p. 62.

An extensive *social insurance* system provides aid and security in case of an accident, illness, work incapacity or unemployment, and upon retirement. The principles of the insurance systems are not identical. Some systems are based on the principle of joint national responsibility, the aim of which is a universal and equal basic level of compensations. This principle is most clearly represented by the idea of a national insurance. An example from Finland is the national pension scheme. The earnings-related systems represent another kind of principle, namely, the equivalence between premiums and benefits.

In Finland the national pension scheme was created first (1937). The wage earners did not consider it fair enough, noting, among other things, that they also had to pay for farmers' pensions. This speeded up the statutory earnings-related pension scheme (1962). Applying different principles of justice the systems complement one another. The *need principle* is followed by the national insurance, which also covers those not participating in the labor market and guarantees income support for everyone living in Finland with an emphasis on human dignity. The *desert (merit) principle* is followed by the earnings-related insurance, which takes into account people's own efforts.

By the late 1980s the creation of the national social insurance system accomplished a transfer from weak to stabilized basic security in Finland, and the work pension system provided income security (Jäntti et al. 1996). It seems that the concurrent application and balance of the two principles increases the societal system's legitimacy (Hellsten and Riihinen 1985, pp. 38–39).

National insurance and the earnings-related pension scheme have different organizations and different relationships to the state administration. *The Social Insurance Institution* (KELA) operates under the supervision of parliament, independent of the government. Its board (director general and five directors) are appointed by the president of the republic and its administration and operations are supervised by a supervisory council of twelve members elected by parliament.

The *Central Pension Security Institute* is the statutory central body of the earnings-related pension scheme. Its managing director has not represented any political party as visibly as the director general of KELA, although political views do sometimes play a role when electing the managing director. The operations are supervised by a body of representatives of 27 members, the majority of whom come from labor market organizations so that employers and employees have an equal number of representatives. The representatives also include members of trade associations and pension insurance companies and an insurance medicine specialist. The central government has only two representatives.

The operations of KELA are based on a pay-as-you-go system: most of the funds distributed as benefits are received as regular payments from various sources. In contrast, the earnings-related pension scheme is a funding system: it aims at long-term investment of its funds in order to be able to fulfill its obligations in the future.

220

The programs administered by KELA include minimum pension security, general health insurance, rehabilitation, basic unemployment security, basic income security for families with children, general housing allowance, financial aid for students, school transportation subsidies and conscript's allowance.[66] KELA has a nation wide network of 341 local offices. In 2000, its total expenditure was 55.3 billion markkas (€ 9.3bn.), of which the benefit costs were 53.6 billion markkas (€ 9 bn.), that is 6.8 percent of GDP. The highest proportion (30%) of the expenditure was spent on national pension, the second highest (23%) on health insurance and the third highest (15%) on child allowances. Unemployment benefits also formed a large part (11%) of the total expenditure. KELA had 1,061,000 pension beneficiaries, of whom 773,000 were on old age pension.[67]

The operations of the Central Pension Security Institute are covered by several acts on the earnings-related pension. The most important acts involving the private sector are the Employees' Pensions Act, the Temporary Employees' Pensions Act and the Self-Employed Persons' Pensions Act. Civil servants have a long tradition of both tenured positions and secure pensions. Since 1964 and 1966 there are two acts in the public sector governing employees' pension benefits: the Local Government Employees' Pensions Act and the State Employees' Pensions Act.

The legal age for old-age pension is 65. However, only a minority of employees continue to work up to this age. Many retire years earlier and may receive disability pension or partial disability pension. Cash rehabilitation benefit is payable to employees who have an injury or illness from which they are expected to recover, and individual early retirement pension has been available for persons with a long work history. Unemployment pension can be granted to a long-term unemployed person who has reached the age of 60. The death of a family provider can entitle the widow or widower and children to survivor's pension. Early old-age pension is available for persons aged 60, but in comparison with the ordinary early-age pension its amount is reduced.[68]

---

66 For example, under national health insurance, some medical expenses are refunded regardless of the length of the illness. 60% of the doctors' fees and 75% of the cost of examinations and treatments ordered by a doctor exceeding 13.45 euros are refunded. For costs over € 8.40 a 50% refund is granted for prescribed medicine. Sickness allowance represents a compensation for lost earnings. The maximum daily amount is € 50.45, which is paid for up to one year. The employer pays a full wage for the first day of work incapacity and the following seven weekdays.

67 Statistical Yearbook of the Social Insurance Institution 2000, p. 24. – The other pensions included unemployment pension, spouse pension, orphan's pension, change-of-generation pension, and front-veteran's pension.

68 In the private sector the statutory earnings-related pension is provided by private pension institutes. Earnings-related pensions are always protected against possible insolvency of a pension institute: in such a case the institutes are jointly liable. In the public sector, the State Treasury and the Local Government Pensions Institute are responsible for implementing pension insurance.

The number of non-retired persons covered under statutory earnings-related pensions was 1,485,000 in the private sector and 635,000 in the public sector at the end of 1998. At the same time private sector pension funds totaled FIM 222.6 billion (€ 37.4 bn.) and public sector funds FIM 70.9 billion (€ 11.9 bn.). The coming decades give rise to great concern: the number of pensioners will increase considerably faster than the people who will pay for future pensions. The question is whether the funds will increase fast enough so that future pensions can be paid without unreasonable effort.

The pension system has greatly reduced poverty. In 1980 the poverty rate was clearly higher in Finland than in the other Nordic countries, the Netherlands, or Germany, but by the mid-1990s Finland was, with Sweden and Norway, one of the countries with the least poverty (under 5 percent). The rate was about 7.5 percent in central Europe and considerably higher in the English-speaking countries (Canada about 10%, UK slightly over 12 %, and the United States 17.5%). (Ritakallio 2001, pp. 13–14.) *[OR]*

Health Care

In a welfare state, health care is one of the essential sectors of social security. Accordingly, when the chapter on "Basic rights and liberties" was added to Finland's constitution in 1995, the following promises were included: "The public authorities shall guarantee for everyone, as provided in more detail by an Act, adequate social, health and medical services and promote the health of the population."

The organization and financing of health care have long been considered a public responsibility in Finland. The Mannerheim League for Child Welfare, founded in 1920, deserves the credit for initiating the internationally first-rate health care for mothers and children from the 1920s onwards. In the 1940s, the authorities joined in developing this sector of health care. Pregnant women and children of pre-school and school age began to have regular health check-ups. One of the world's lowest infant mortality rates has been a good illustration of how this action has benefited Finland in the long term; the figure was 3.6 per thousand in 1999. Systematic health care for all adults did not start until the 1960s, but the development has been fast since then (cf. Chapter 2). The burgeoning development of a network of district and central hospitals was started in the 1950s, and 1963 saw the creation of a general health insurance, an integral part of a welfare state.

The Primary Health Care Act from 1972 has been the basis of the primary health care system. The act obliges municipalities, alone or jointly, to provide primary health care services and preventive health care. There are usually several general practitioners along with public health nurses and clerical staff working at the health centers. Patients in need of secondary care are referred to specialized care in a hospital. The country's

270 health centers usually implement the municipalities' responsibilities described by the Primary Health Care Act: medical care, ambulance service, home nursing, health promotion and prevention of illnesses, work in schools and other educational institutions, family planning services, occupational health care, rehabilitation services, and dental health care. They participate in prevention of drug and alcohol abuse, smoking, and obesity, and take part in community planning and environmental health care together with other authorities.

Specialized care is also the responsibility of the municipalities (the Secondary Level Care Act, 1989). Each municipality must belong to an inter-municipal union, which owns and governs district hospitals with specialist doctors and equipment; the number of such hospital districts is 21. All the medical services under the Public Health Acts were produced publicly until 1992, but since then the municipalities have also been able to opt to purchase the necessary medical services from the private sector.

There are some 11,000 doctors employed in health care services provided by the public sector. The costs of using the private health care services are partially refunded under the national health insurance. Approximately 4000 doctors are actively working in the private sector and, in addition, many employed in the public sector have private patients. The number of dentists is about 5000.

Health policy pays special attention to the economically active population. Under the Occupational Health Care Act (1979), employers are obliged to provide occupational (but not other than occupational) health care services for their employees. The services can be purchased from either municipal health centers or the private sector. Occupational health care covers over ninety percent of employees and is provided for them free of charge. Half of the expenses incurred by the employer are covered under the national health insurance.

Health insurance covers the whole population, and health insurance payments are made by everyone paying municipal tax; recipients of other than pension income pay 1.5 percent and pension recipients have paid 3.2 percent of their taxable income (both age groups 1.5 percent in 2003). Daily sickness allowance is paid on account of an illness for a period of no longer than 300 working days. As with health insurance payments, the allowance is also determined on the basis of the recipient's earnings. As a consequence of the recession in the 1990s, cost-containment was applied and earnings-related benefits were also cut. For the same reason the waiting period for sickness allowance was changed from seven to nine days in 1993. Thus, the total expenditure on the allowance dropped from FIM 3.5 billion in 1991 to 2.4 billion in 1997. To the wage earners this has little significance, because the collective labor agreements guarantee to almost everyone full pay for the first nine days of work incapacity, too.

After prolonged incapacity for work, that is after the first 300 days, all working-age people are entitled to disability pension and those between

58-64 years of age also to individual early retirement pension. In 1996, the latter was revised so that pensions are replaced by rehabilitation allowance for a specified time. Thus, decision-makers hope that work incapacity is only temporary.

Health services organized by local authorities have become more and more expensive in recent years. However, the prices paid by the patients are still low. In 2001, customers paid FIM 100 to 150 (€ 16.80–25.25) per year for their health center visits and approximately FIM 100 for each visit to a hospital out-patient clinic and FIM 125 per each day of admission. Many services, most typically preventive ones such as well-mother clinics and school health care, are free of charge and the same applies to the dental services of under-18-year-olds.

The recession of the 1990s increased the citizens' responsibility for their health care. Cost-containment had to be taken into account in developing and applying the health insurance, which had an impact especially on the refunding of private health services and medical drugs. At the same time, heavy cost cuts were made. In 1991, the government decided that tax deductions on medical costs would no longer be approved. As the prices have risen, compensation levels been lowered, and tax deduction rights removed, the share paid by the patients of the total costs of health care stands now at 21.5 percent, after approximately 13 percent in the late 1980s. This change adds to social inequality because those with the biggest financial difficulties are forced to compromise the most in terms of necessary health services and medicines.

In 1993 the central government's subsidies to the municipalities were changed. Earlier, state support was earmarked for specific purposes, including health care, but since 1993 state support for the social sector has been undifferentiated. The central government lacks the authority to interfere with local priorities and, when given a free choice, many local governments tend to rank other needs higher than developing their health care. A very notorious problem has been the increasingly long waiting time for specialized care.

The total cost of health care in Finland in 1999 was 49 billion markkas (€ 8.2 bn.) and distributed in the following way: municipalities 43 percent, private households 20 percent, the central government 18 percent, the Social Insurance Institution 15 percent, and other private funding 4 percent. These costs formed 6.9 percent of GDP in 1998. (Statistical Yearbook of the Social Insurance Institution 2000, p. 55; *SYF 2001*, p. 467.)

Despite the cost-containment of the 1990s, the positive long-term results of improved health care in the second half of the 20th century can be seen in longer life expectancies. However, this development is largely due to overall improvements in living conditions, and there has been no success in the reduction of health differences among various socio-economic groups. But determined efforts to reduce major public health problems, above all cardiovascular diseases, have yielded many good results. *[OR]*

224

Financing Social Policy

In welfare states, government expenditure tends to be high and the financing of social protection clearly forms the largest part of it. The Finnish state alone paid FIM 44 billion (€ 7.4 bn.) for social security and health care in 1998. This amounted to 23.4 percent of all state expenditures (see Table 15.3 on page 253).

However, the main responsibility for financing Finland's social welfare belongs to the municipalities. A major part of the financing comes from local taxes, and these proceeds vary greatly in different municipalities. The local needs are also different because of, for example, differences in age structures. Therefore, a government grants system was developed to reduce the strain of operational costs. At the end of the 1990s, the share of municipal taxation in total financing was on average 64 percent, while state subsidies represented 24 percent and client fees 12 percent.

The share of public expenditures in GDP rose in nearly all EU countries between 1980 and 1995. In Finland, the rise was as high as 20 percentage points (from 39% to 59%). Yet in 1995, public expenditure in Sweden and Denmark was higher than in Finland (67% and 61% respectively). The 1995 figures in Belgium (55%) and the Netherlands (54%) came close to those of the Nordic countries although they were among the few countries where the proportion of public expenditure of GDP had decreased in 1980-1995. Norway stood out from the other Nordic countries with its public expenditure at only 48% of GDP, although its public expenditure had risen strongly in the 1980s. While government expenditures in relation to GDP increased in most European countries studied, they nevertheless converged in terms of standard deviation (Kautto 1999, p. 74).

The proportion of welfare services (education, health, rehabilitation, housing and social services) in GDP was distinctly higher in the Nordic countries than elsewhere in western Europe (except for Norway) in 1995. The percentages were 15.4 in Finland, 18.7 in Denmark, 18.5 in Sweden, and 13.2 in Norway. In Belgium and the Netherlands they were only 7.8 and in 6.7 respectively.[69]

The social policies in the European countries show certain consistency when income transfers received by households, consisting of social security benefits such as pensions and sickness benefits, are compared with welfare services. In Figure 14.1, fourteen countries are divided into two groups on the basis of the medians of both variables. Three Nordic countries (Denmark, Finland, and Sweden) and also Austria are in the quadrant that lies above both medians. In contrast, the Mediterranean coun-

69 Social services as part of these welfare services include social work, municipal day care for children and families, family counseling, etc. The cost of welfare services, however excluding education, is one part of the total social expenditure which uses public funds to finance social and health policy (see Table 14.2).

tries (Greece, Italy and Spain) plus Portugal lie below both medians. In Belgium, France, and the Netherlands income transfers rank above, but welfare services below the median, while Germany, Norway, and the United Kingdom are placed in the opposite quadrant.

Figure 14.1

Welfare services and income transfers to households in 1994–1995 in fourteen European countries.

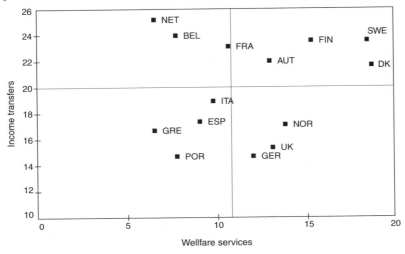

Source: Kautto 1999, p. 78.

Social policies are financed by three sources: the government (including the state and the municipalities), employers, and insured. The Nordic countries follow the principle of universalism in their social policies, more so than welfare states in general, and this increases further the public sector's contribution to the financing of social policy. Characteristic features of Finland, typical in the other Nordic countries too, are an equal income distribution, a low poverty rate, and women's high participation in working life, which has increased income transfers for family policy. The Nordic countries do not have as uniform a system of financing their social policies as is often assumed, nor do they differ from other welfare states as much as might be expected (Kautto 1999, p. 76).

In the European Union, social expenditure in relation to GDP remained at approximately 26 percent through almost the entire 1980s. The proportion increased slightly more in the Nordic countries than in the EU countries on average. During 1991–1993, the increase was strongest in Finland (from 30% to 35%) due to both the decrease in GDP and an increase in social expenditure, particularly for unemployment (cf. Chapters 15 and 16). However, in Sweden the proportion of social expenditure in GDP remained higher than in Finland (see Table 14.2). In the late

1990s, Finland's economic growth was exceptionally fast and cost-containment was applied in social policy. This reduced the proportion of social expenditure in GDP to 27 percent already by 1998. There was a clear convergence of the GDP proportions of social expenditure in the EU countries in the 1990s, although the countries did not harmonize their social policies.

Table 14.2

Social expenditure as percentage of GDP in the EU countries from 1980 to 1996

Countries	1980	1985	1990	1991	1993	1996
Finland	20	24	25	30	35	32
Austria	–	–	27	28	30	30
Belgium	28	29	27	27	29	30
Denmark	29	28	29	30	32	32
France	25	29	28	28	31	31
Germany	29	28	25	27	29	30
Greece	–	–	23	22	22	23
Ireland	21	24	19	20	21	20
Italy	19	23	24	25	26	25
Luxembourg	27	23	24	25	25	25
Netherlands	30	32	33	33	34	32
Portugal	13	14	16	17	21	21
Spain	18	20	20	22	24	23
Sweden	33	33	31	34	39	36
United Kingdom	22	24	23	25	29	28
EU (15)	–	–	27	28	29	28

Source: Eurostat and NOSOSCO.

The financing sources of social policies can be divided into four categories: central and local authorities, employers, insured, and others including property income and social security funds. The proportions of these categories vary significantly in the EU countries, giving a good characterization of the financing policies that different countries pursue over a longer period of time.

As is shown in Table 14.3, the share of the central government and local authorities in 1996 was large in Denmark and Ireland and small in the Netherlands and Greece. The employers paid a large share in Spain and Italy, and very little in Denmark. Other EU countries with a relatively small employer share included the Netherlands, Great Britain, and Luxembourg, while the share of the insured was clearly the largest in the Netherlands and smallest in Sweden. The Netherlands also reported the largest share of other financing sources, with Portugal closest behind. In

227

Ireland such other sources cover very little. This comparison places Finland among the Nordic welfare states and those other EU countries, where the share of public funding is large.

Table 14.3

Financing of social expenditure in the EU countries in 1996 (in %)

Countries	State and local authorities	Employers	Insured	Other	Total
Finland	45	35	13	7	100
Austria	36	37	26	1	100
Belgium	20	45	26	9	100
Denmark	69	10	15	6	100
France	20	50	28	2	100
Germany	30	39	29	2	100
Greece	20	38	23	8	99
Ireland	63	22	14	1	100
Italy	30	49	18	3	100
Luxembourg	47	26	23	5	101
Netherlands	16	23	44	16	99
Portugal	42	26	17	15	100
Spain	28	52	18	3	101
Sweden	45	40	7	8	100
United Kingdom	48	25	15	12	100
EU (15)	31	39	24	5	99

Source: Eurostat

A statistical analysis of the EU countries from 1980–1995 resulted in three different financing clubs: the Nordic oriented (Ireland and the United Kingdom in addition to Denmark, Finland, and Sweden), the corporative oriented (Austria, Belgium, France, Germany, Italy, Luxembourg, Portugal, and Spain), and the single-member club of the insured oriented, consisting of the Netherlands (Hagfors 1999, pp. 49–52).

Thus, the financing of social protection can be organized very differently, even in countries of about the same level of welfare. The differences are probably due to at least two factors. Firstly, the final costs of social policies may be relatively similar from the point of view of the payers, although the employers' costs would be divided differently into taxes and direct employer contributions. Secondly, the financing systems reflect to some extent the different distribution of power between the state and civil society. In Finland and Sweden, the financing of social protection is distributed very similarly, but in Finland the earnings-related pension scheme is mainly controlled by employer and worker organizations, which is illustrated by the larger relative share of the insured. It should also be emphasized that conclusions drawn from the financing shares are somewhat uncertain, primarily because the definitions of tax and contribution may vary across countries.

Different countries not only finance their social policies in different ways but also allocate their resources differently. Table 14.4 shows that the proportions, for example, of health care and illness of total social expenditure vary substantially. In 1996, Denmark used for this purpose about one-half of what was used by Ireland and Portugal. Italy spent on old age almost twice as much as Luxembourg. Finland's most significant deviations from the EU averages were its relatively low share (30%) on old age and relatively high (14%) on unemployment. The proportion spent on health care and illness in Finland was also below the EU average.

Table 14.4

Social expenditure by functions in the EU countries in 1996 (in %)

Countries	Sickness and health	Dis- ability	Old age	Sur- vivors	Family and children	Un- employ- ment	Hous- ing	Other
Finland	21	15	30	4	13	14	1	2
Austria	25	8	38	11	11	6	0.3	1
Belgium	26	6	32	11	8	15	0	2
Denmark	18	11	39	0.1	12	14	2	4
France	29	6	37	7	9	8	3	2
Germany	30	7	39	2	9	10	1	2
Greece	26	9	41	8	8	4	2	1
Ireland	34	5	20	6	13	17	3	2
Italy	22	7	54	12	4	2	0	0
Luxembourg	26	13	30	14	13	4	0.2	0.3
Netherlands	28	15	33	6	4	12	1	0.4
Portugal	33	12	36	7	6	6	0	1
Spain	29	8	41	4	2	15	1	1
Sweden	22	12	36	3	11	10	3	3
UK	25	12	35	5	9	6	7	1
EU (15)	27	9	39	5	8	8	2	2

Sources: Eurostat and Ministry of Social Affairs and Health.

The different ways of resource allocation are the result of not only different kinds of needs – for example, differences in age structures - but also, and possibly even more so, of the different values emphasized in each nation. It is likely that within an institution such as the European Union, the values will converge in the long run, but so far the differences have seemed clear.

Finland, for example, places strong emphasis on families and children. Recently there has appeared growing criticism of the scarce resources directed to health care, while at the same time the efficiency of the country's health policy has been emphasized. The welfare effects of the distribution of social policy costs have not been studied, which makes it impossible to estimate the "right" distribution. In addition, the right distribution is difficult to find and define because of the wide influence of the various contributions. *[OR]*

Regional Policy and Development

The welfare state cherishes equality and is expected to help citizens by leveling their inequalities. This concerns individuals, but a similar principle can be applied to inequalities between regions. That is the purpose of regional policy. Expressed in EU phraseology, "every effort is made to reduce disparities between the levels of development of the various regions." Equality of regions is a valuable goal, but it can be in conflict with another important policy goal, namely, allocative efficiency. The leveling of regional inequalities needs to be adjusted to whatever benefits the national economy.

Chapter 4 pointed out some differences between Finland's regions. Geography explains why different parts of the country have different characteristics. There are areas where industry developed because of forest resources, waterpower, or mining, but the most important causes for regional variation are the country's northern location and its great dimension from north to south. The growing season lasts only 60–90 days in the north, but 180 days in the south (in central Europe 260 days, in southern Europe over 300 days). Distances to foreign markets can be illustrated by a circle using Helsinki as the focus and Finland's length as the radius. It would encompass Sweden, Denmark, and the Baltic States, as well as St. Petersburg, Moscow, Warsaw, Oslo, and Germany's northern harbors. Even Berlin and Hamburg would be close to it. Moreover, Finland's southern and western coastal towns have direct access to the sea, while other parts of the country depend on more expensive land and air transportation.

Regional disparities are amplified by the character of markets and people's attraction to centers. In late 1950s Gunnar Myrdahl presented the theory of cumulative growth in which he outlined the spectrum and interrelationships of economic and social factors that cause regional differentiation. The system is not approaching equilibrium; on the contrary, its internal mechanisms favor disequilibrium. A positive thrust starts spiral growth. An enterprise attracts movers to the region, or at least improves employment, thereby encouraging services that in turn attract more people and again make the region more appealing to industry and services. Furthermore, migration is selective: fast developing regions receive well educated, healthy, and young inhabitants. This strengthens the financial base of public services and reduces public expenditures.

In the Nordic countries where local taxes are very important, public resources depend greatly on the inhabitants' income level. If a region is losing people, the structure of its population and its public finances develop unfavorably. Myrdal called such a development the backwash effect. Widening differences in infrastructure and cultural services make the declining regions less attractive (Myrdal 1957). This kind of inevitable trend was already apparent in Finland half a century ago (Riihinen 1965). Understandably, positive thrusts occur more frequently and more effectively in the south than in the north.

Urbanization economies facilitate effective division of labor. Industrial enterprises create demand for specialized service and repair businesses. A competitive economy also needs swift cooperation, another advantage of urban regions (Riihinen 1973, pp. 151–156). The concept of networking economies refers largely to the same economic factors as the advantages of urbanization. Concentration enables even small firms to utilize external economies and benefits of scale. The advantages of networking economies include monitoring and disseminating information and opportunities for effective training. Firms and their personnel may also have influence in local government and help to improve infrastructure.

While Finland is seeking to develop an increasingly efficient post-industrial society, it also finds large inequalities of regions unacceptable. The premises of regional development reflect traditional values both in culture and in attitudes to security. A sustainable rural environment and a fully inhabited land area have been considered necessary for self-sufficient food production, availability of timber resources, national defense, and even the maintenance of rural culture (Eskelinen 2001, p. 17). Such premises can be debated, but they have an influence on policy decisions.

Finland's modern regional policy developed in three stages: first, the industrialization of developing areas until the mid-1970s; second, a regional planning stage until the late-1980s; and third, regional development based on programs (Vartiainen 1998). It is not possible to distinguish these stages clearly, but they outline the general trend.

Finland, Sweden, and Norway, where geographic differences are comparable, all started proactive regional policy in the mid-1960s. Capital subventions were used. Labor force subventions were added in Finland in the 1970s. The central government began to complement investment support with subsidies for employment, training, and transportation, as well as offering tax exemptions and advice. Support was directed not merely at industrial activity but also to tourism, fur farming, fish farming, horticulture, and turf production. The first support areas were defined in 1966, then enlarged twice in the 1970s. Industrial employment in the developing regions improved greatly at the beginning of the 1970s, but it is difficult to estimate to what extent this was the result of public subsidies. In 1975 a scheme was introduced to assist the launching of new businesses in slowly developing areas. It was an era of planning optimism when designers of the policy believed strongly in their methods. (Nordiska arbetsgruppen för regionalpolitisk forskning 1978, pp. 101–125.)

The planning stage from the mid 1970s onward involved attempts to diversify economy and to strengthen industrial enterprises in slowly developing regions. Loans and tax exemptions were still used, regional policy contributions were launched. Other forms included regional development programs and assistance in the search for sites. The term rural policy was also introduced. Differences became smaller, but the policy was not being targeted accurately at the most problematic areas. Thus, Lapland and north-eastern regions became so-called project areas. The Regional Policy Act for 1982–1989 added a "special areas" policy to deal with declining industry and mining, and the most problematic rural areas. (Komiteanmietintö 1986:6, pp. 31–39.)

Nevertheless, nothing could halt the cumulative process: central areas grew and backwash effects continued. Between 1970 and 1980 Finland's urban population increased from 51 to 60 percent. Without successful regional policy the differences would have become even larger.

The latest stage reflects the economy's changing premises: more open competition, unification of commodity markets, expansion of markets, increasing importance of information and skills, and pressures to form larger enterprises, while networking and requirements for flexibility open up opportunities for small and mid-sized firms. Globalization and the internationalization of companies set the framework for domestic regional policy.

Now large companies can select new locations from an almost-global range of possibilities, the home country being but one alternative. Consequently, regional development necessitates increased concern for the preferences of enterprises. Despite all the changes, the strategies of regional development remain based, to some extent, on the principles followed 30 to 50 years earlier, when decisions were made on the location of state-owned companies, universities, and investments in infrastructure. (Talousneuvosto 2000, pp. 26–27, 138–139.) One apparent change in attitudes deserves mentioning. During the two earlier stages the aim was to overcome results of urbanization, whereas the latest stage involves some conscious utilization of them.

The new orientation in regional policy transferred responsibility for regional development from the central government to the level of regions (see the map in Figure 4.1). This is served by two overlapping organizations. One consists of the 20 regional councils mentioned in Chapter 12 that were established by the municipalities as regional development authorities. In 1994 they were restructured, with the aim of making them participants in the EU's "union of regions." The other organization, set up in 1997, consists of the 15 employment and economic development centers mentioned in Chapter 11. They function under the Ministry of Trade and Industry, but combine administrative tasks of several ministries for business services and technological development, local employment offices, and agricultural districts.

The backgrounds of the regional authorities have slightly different party flavors: the regional councils are closer to the Center Party which is relatively strong in municipal government, while the employment and economic development centers became a tool of the central government run by the Social Democrats and the Conservatives (Sandberg 2000, p.187). The regional councils make plans but lack resources. The state offices are the primary distributors of public subsidies.

The EU's structural funds finance a part of EU regional policy. From 2000 to 2006 Finland is receiving 2.1 billion euros to help finance the Objective Programs; in 2002 Finland's annual budget authorized commitments to new programs worth 139 million euros. The same year's "matching funds" from the Finnish government amounted to 151 million. The map in Figure 14.2 shows how Finland is divided into two support areas; they concern the EU's Objective 1 "promoting the development and structural adjustment of regions whose development is lagging behind" and Objective 2 "supporting the economic and social conversion of areas facing structural difficulties." The additional transitional areas are also entitled to modest support. Objective 3, implemented in the whole country, supports "policies and systems of education, training and employment" initiated and planned in Finland and screened and approved by the EU.

The central government determines national goals for regional policy. They include the regional center development program that was launched in autumn 2001; 34 functional regions around the country were selected to receive support for their planned strengthening of the urban center through cooperation between municipalities, educational institutions, and civil organizations. Another idea is the centers of expertise program. Eleven such centers were named in 1993, and from 1999 to 2006 their number is fourteen.[70] There are also two national centers for networking expertise, one for wood products the other for food sector. (www.intermin.fi.) Regional policy emphasizing center programs is reminiscent of the growth pole policy that was quietly abandoned in the 1970s because of the fear of unequal impacts.

---

70 Jyväskylä (in Central Finland) and Tampere (in Pirkanmaa) are examples of expertise centers. The former specializes in information technology, management of paper production, and energy and environment techniques, the latter in machine construction and automation, information and communication techniques, health technology, and communication.

Figure 14.2

EU objective areas in Finland, from 2000 to 2006. (Objective 1 areas cover 21% of Finland's population).

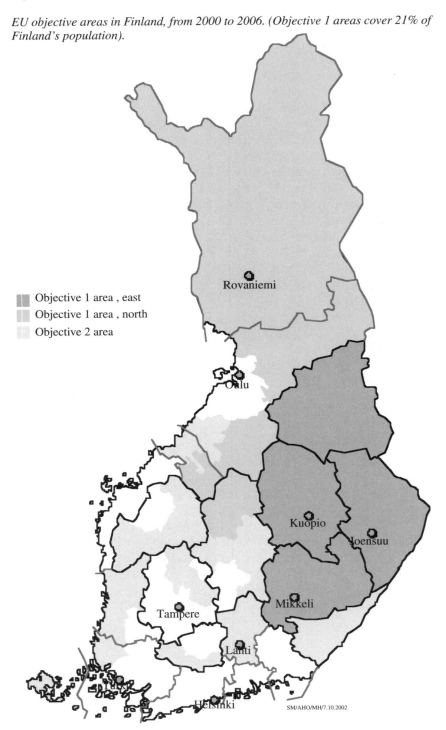

The Act on Regional Development concerns the planning and implementation of nationally funded regional development. The law requires the ministries to pay adequate attention to regional development in their own plans, underscores the role of the regional councils, and emphasizes interaction between regions and the central government. The state will continue to fund regional development by subsidizing programs of fixed duration.

Regional policy covers only a part of all regional leveling that takes place in the welfare state. More leveling is motivated by the uneven resources available to the municipalities to implement basic services. Realization of the citizens' social and educational rights necessitates equalization of local government funds. The central government's transfer of resources for the purpose of fulfilling municipal responsibilities is not an actual part of regional policy, but it equalizes differences in regional welfare and regional development.

Thus, one can distinguish between actual and major regional policy. The latter covers all government measures having a regional impact. Such measures include promoting entrepreneurship, improving labor relations, and developing communication and other infrastructure. Employment policy has a considerable regional impact because unemployment afflicts regions very differently (see Table 4.6). Naturally, major regional policy had its greatest impact when the welfare state was enlarged from the 1960s to late 1980s. That is when the growth of employment in the public sector benefited peripheral regions the most.

The allocation of state subsidies since the late 1980s has been named the system of state grants to local authorities. Earmarked grants were converted into lump sums to each municipality and joint municipal authority. In 1999 the central government paid FIM 19 billion (3.7 billion euros) in state subsidies. The regional impact is clearly revealed by differences in support paid to different groups of municipalities: 400 euros per person to urban municipalities, 740 euros per person to semi-urban, and 1070 euros per person to rural municipalities (*SYF 2001*, pp. 68, 358).

According to the central government's own summary, appropriations worth 2.3 billion euros (FIM 13.7 billion) were used to influence regional development in 2001. Table 14.5 summarizes the impact of major regional policy in 1998: how regional distribution of taxes collected by the central government compared with the distribution of central government expenditure. The small East Uusimaa region in the south paid the most, while North Karelia and Kainuu in the north-east received the most. The overall picture is obvious: two major regions, Uusimaa and Southern Finland, paid relatively more in taxes, while government expenditures were directed relatively more to Eastern, Mid-, and Northern Finland.

Table 14.5

Taxes and expenditure of the central government by region in 1998 (in %)

Major Regions and Regions	Taxes	Expenditure	Ratio
Uusimaa	33.4	27.6	1.2
11. Uusimaa	31.6	26.4	1.19
12. East Uusimaa	1.8	1.2	1.51
Southern Finland	34.2	32.2	1.1
21. Varsinais-Suomi	8.6	8.1	1.06
22. Satakunta	4.3	4.1	1.06
23. Kanta-Häme	3.1	3.6	0.84
24. Pirkanmaa	8.5	7.9	1.07
25. Päijät-Häme	3.5	2.9	1.22
26. Kymenlaakso	3.6	3.3	1.07
27. South Karelia	2.6	2.5	1.04
Eastern Finland	11.0	14.8	0.7
31. South Savo	2.7	3.5	0.77
32. North Savo	4.2	5.2	0.80
33. North Karelia	2.6	3.9	0.68
34. Kainuu	1.5	2.2	0.69
Mid-Finland	11.3	13.5	0.8
41. Central Finland	4.6	5.3	0.87
42. South Ostrobothnia	3.1	3.7	0.85
43. Ostrobothnia	3.1	3.2	0.97
44. Central Ostrobothnia	1.1	1.3	0.85
Northern Finland	9.7	11.7	0.8
51. North Ostrobothnia	6.2	6.9	0.89
52. Lapland	3.4	4.8	0.71

Source: Statistics Finland; cf. Talousneuvosto 2000, p. 141.

A comparison with Table 4.6 (on page 79) reveals that the two 'fiscally supporting' major regions were the country's most urbanized and economically best performing part, and the government paid relatively the most to Eastern Finland, the least urbanized major region with the smallest economic growth and quite high unemployment. A comparison made separately of the 19 regions shows only a few exceptions to the general picture: obviously the central government aimed for equalization when allocating its expenditure.

Despite all regional policies the power of cumulative growth has had a decisive influence on Finland's regional development. Even during the economic slump of early 1990s the concentration of population continued, and it became stronger again during the recent years of rapid growth.

Figure 14.3 compares the growth of population in four groups of sub-regions.[71] The cumulative process reflects the important role information has in the new economy, as the fastest growth has taken place in university towns. A similarly differentiated development happened in employment after the slump years of the early 1990s: employment grew the most in those sub-regions where universities are located (Talousneuvosto 2000, p. 74).

Figure 14.3

Population growth in different sub-regions 1988–1999 (ind. 1988=100)

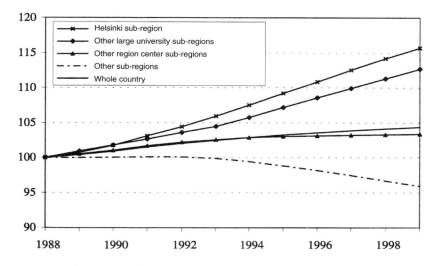

Source: Talousneuvosto 2000.

Recent economic growth also intensified the familiar exodus from peripheral areas. In regions that depend on agriculture and forestry there was continuous erosion of the workforce from primary production, and employment opportunities in the public sector deteriorated simultaneously. Reduced population led to the closure of primary schools, and basic health services became more problematic because of the unwillingness of health personnel to move to declining regions.

Nevertheless, a comparative study of the Nordic countries published in 2002 called Finland the model country of regional policy. This was justified by Finland's active attempts to develop means of reflecting nation-wide the success of large urban areas. Regional support reaches 41 percent of the population in Finland, more than in the other Nordic countries (38% in Iceland, 25% in Norway, 18% in Denmark, and 16% in Sweden). Expenditure on actual regional policy is 335 euros per capita in Finland, while the comparable expenditure is 259 euros in Sweden and 83 euros in Denmark. The biggest challenge to Finland's regional

71   The 19 regions of continental Finland are divided into 79 subregions (in EU terms, NUTS IV regions).

development is the modest growth of job opportunities in the peripheries. (Hanell et al. 2002.)

The pessimists predict that some peripheral areas of Finland will actually become empty during the decades ahead. Such a development might be a meager problem for the national economy, but it would breed many social and individual problems and it conflicts with values of many Finns.*[OR]*

Education

The right and the duty of everybody to receive basic education is stated in Section 16 of Finland's Constitution Act, and basic education is promised free of charge. In addition, "the public authorities shall, as provided in more detail by an Act, guarantee for everyone equal opportunity to receive other educational services in accordance with their ability and special needs, as well as the opportunity to develop themselves without being prevented by economic hardship." The freedom of science, the arts, and higher education is also guaranteed.

Emphasizing the importance of education is nothing new. In Finland, the philosopher J.V. Snellman stated already in the mid-nineteenth century that the power of a small nation lies in education. He did not refer solely, hardly even primarily, to technological knowledge. But since the late 20th century, globalization has put all education systems under a great deal of expectations and pressure. Different nations wish to maintain the best possible economic competitiveness (cf. Webster 2000, pp. 312–315), while the pace of scientific development has accelerated as a result of research and global communication. In order to secure their competitiveness, nations need to direct more and more funds to maintain the up-to-the-minute skills and knowledge of their citizens and their national research capacity. Technological know-how has proved itself especially important.

Concerned about the continent's competitiveness, the European Commission presented a White Paper by the name of "Teaching and Learning: towards a Cognitive Society" in the Madrid summit in 1995 and declared 1996 to be the year of European Life-long Education and Training. In the Lisbon summit in 2000, the Union set the goal of making Europe the most competitive and dynamic knowledge-based economy by 2010. As a countermove, president George W. Bush proposed a bill on extensive school reforms three days after his inauguration in 2001. And three weeks from Bush's proposal the British Prime Minister, Tony Blair, announced that the Labour Party would change its education policy in a way that, unlike the old comprehensive school system, would emphasize the needs of the most talented children. Instead of real capital, human capital has become the central resource of the new economy (cf. EVA 2001b, pp. 1–3).

Together with globalization, changes in ideologies can explain the emphasis on competitiveness and the primacy of markets. Neoliberalism is of particular importance. The resulting emphasis on deregulation and decentralization was applied to the school system, too. As described in Chapter 12, Finnish municipalities decide for themselves what portion of their available resources are used for schools, and since 1993 they have drawn up the curricula of the schools. The central government retains only the power to determine general national goals for education and to regulate the basic structure of the curricula. The decentralized system concerns comprehensive and upper secondary schools (grade schools and high schools), as well as vocational schools and polytechnics.[72]

The school reforms coincided with the slump of the 1990s and the necessary budget cuts. In 1990–1994 the operating costs of the school system were reduced by about FIM 2.3 billion (11 percent). Because of the growing number of students, the available expenditure per student was actually cut more, by 17 percent. Larger classes, fewer electives, and various other means were used to save money. The workload of teachers also became heavier. In higher learning the operating cost of universities were reduced by some 10 percent. Although the pre-slump level was regained by 1998, available resources have not covered the costs of expanded teaching and the many more degrees awarded; severe savings have limited, in particular, library acquisitions and purchases of new equipment. (Cf. Poropudas and Mäkinen 2001, pp. 13–26.)

Nevertheless, Finland seems to have been successful in international competition: according to a technology achievement index, Finland was the most developed country in the world at the turn of the millennium, with the United States, Sweden, and Japan in the following places. Finland also allocates a substantial proportion (7.5 percent) of its national income for education: Of the developed industrialized countries, only the contribution of the Nordic countries (Sweden 8.3, Denmark 8.1, and Norway 7.7 percent) was greater than that of Finland in 1995–1997 (Human Development Report 2001, pp. 48, 170).

The indicators describing technological development do not reveal how successful the countries have been in developing and distributing humanistic knowledge. Especially when outlining the content of university education, it has been debated in Finland how the resources ought to be allocated between vocational education serving practical objectives and education promoting knowledge as such in the spirit of Humboldtian university ideals. The creation of a net of polytechnics must be seen as a partial answer to this debate (see Figure 14.4) as it launched vocational education above secondary level, yet outside universities. In this way

---

72 The new concept of schooling was certified in five new laws in 1998: the acts on comprehensive school, upper secondary school, vocational schools, vocational adult education centers, and free education.

vocational and humanistic education were partially separated in the post-secondary level. However, the education of doctors, teachers, and MBAs, for example, still belongs to the universities' territory. Disagreements between the two trends are still continuing, which is illustrated in its name alone by a 2001 publication *Mestareita vai maistereita* ("Masters of Skills or Masters of Arts") (EVA 2001b).

The school system as a whole reflects the values and objectives a nation sets for itself. The Finnish education system follows the familiar three levels: (1) primary and lower secondary (compulsory schooling), (2) upper secondary, and (3) tertiary education. The following three complete the picture: pre-primary education, post-graduate education, and adult education.

The age of compulsory education in Finland is from seven to sixteen years. After these nine years it is possible to voluntarily continue in comprehensive school for one more year. Pre-school education for six-year-olds was started in 2001 and is voluntary. The extensive day-care system, which all children are entitled to, has for its part replaced pre-school.

The comprehensive school carries out the task of compulsory education. Its costs are mainly covered by the municipalities with the state also participating. Some schools are financed chiefly by various organizations and private persons, for example, schools in which the tuition is given in a foreign language (English, German, French, or Russian). In the common comprehensive school system, tuition and school supplies are free of charge for the pupils and there is a free hot meal once a day. In addition, the pupils are entitled to free school transport when the distance between their home and school is more than five kilometers.[73] Special tuition is arranged for children with learning difficulties. The school year has two semesters and lasts 190 school days.

The general educational objectives of comprehensive schooling are defined by the government. One distinguishing feature of the Finnish school system is the large number of languages taught. This is partially due to the fact that the country has two official languages: Finnish speakers study Swedish although the percentage of Swedish speakers in the country is less than 6 percent, and the Swedish speakers study Finnish. The very small Sami minority is given the chance to receive comprehensive school education in their own language. English is the most popular non-domestic language. In most cases, its popularity surpasses that of the second domestic language in schools in which it is possible to choose foreign languages before the second domestic language. German and French follow, Russian is studied by very few due to historical prejudices, and several other languages can be offered.

---

73   In practice, most municipalities apply shorter maximum distances.

Figure 14.4

The education system of Finland

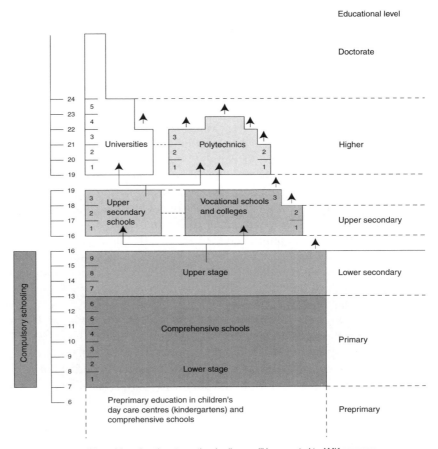

*Most of the education at vocational colleges will be upgraded to AMK programs.

Almost all comprehensive school pupils - in 1999, 99.7 percent of the age group – finish their compulsory education successfully. When compared internationally, the Finnish school system succeeds very well in teaching the basic knowledge and skills (cf. Linnakylä et al. 2000, pp 21–25). One of the most interesting issues debated in Finland concerns the emphasis of different subjects in the curriculum: mathematics, natural sciences, the native language and other languages, history and social studies, music and arts, and physical education. In addition, the dispute on the necessity of compulsory Swedish is never-ending: would it be appropriate to direct some of its resources to other subjects, for example, the major languages of the world? The dispute over the curriculum content applies rather similarly to the upper secondary level, too.

After the compulsory comprehensive school the pupils have a chance to choose upper secondary education: either the upper secondary general school or vocational schools and colleges. The upper secondary school normally lasts three years. It ends with a national matriculation examination, which includes tests in the native language, the other domestic language (Swedish or Finnish), the first foreign language (in most cases English), humanities, mathematics, and natural sciences. In addition, it is possible to take a test in an optional foreign language. The final evaluation of every test paper is made by the Matriculation Examination Board appointed by the Ministry of Education, so the grades of secondary school graduates are nationally comparable. Over 50 percent of pupils choose the upper secondary school after comprehensive school. In 2000, the number of students passing the matriculation examination was 35,700; of them 59 percent girls and 41 percent boys.

The Finnish matriculation examination corresponds roughly to junior college level in the US education system. After matriculation a student has the possibility to apply for university or polytechnic. Admission requires, almost invariably, good grades in the certificate of matriculation.

Another option after comprehensive school is the three-year vocational school. Secondary school graduates can also enter these schools; their training period is shorter than that of comprehensive school graduates. Almost one-fifth of the studies of those from comprehensive school are subjects similar to those in the upper secondary school, such as mathematics and languages. Approximately three-fifths of the studies deal with the chosen occupation and the rest, just under one-fifth of the studies, is on-the-job-learning. There were approximately 55,000 places for new students in vocational schools in 2000, and about 45 percent of comprehensive school graduates continue their studies in these schools. Thus, there are places left for secondary school graduates and more mature students as well.

The polytechnics offer courses similar to the vocational schools, but on a deeper theoretical level. They are either municipal or private institutions and financed by both the state and local authorities. Alongside education they carry on research and development that supports working life, but not basic research. Neither do they offer postgraduate education or corresponding degrees. At the beginning of the new millennium there were 29 polytechnics in Finland. Approximately 70 percent of the entrants were secondary school graduates and 30 percent came from vocational schools.

Originally the universities were prejudiced against the polytechnics, fearing that these would lead to the kind of easy degrees that would weaken the traditional respect and salaries connected with academic learning. This seems not to have happened and the polytechnics have apparently facilitated Finland's recent technological success. They offer places for 38 percent of the relevant age group, while the universities offer for 29 percent and, accordingly, all of higher education for 67 percent.

The University of Helsinki was originally the Royal Academy of Turku, founded in 1640. It was transferred as a university to Helsinki in 1828 and was the only university until 1920. At the beginning of the 21st century the country has twenty universities: ten multi-faculty universities, three universities of technology, three schools of economics and business administration, and four art academies. University-level education is also given in the National Defense College, which operates under the Ministry of Defense. Higher education has expanded very rapidly: in the academic year 1950–1951, there were under 15,000 students in the Finnish universities, in 1985–1986 over 92,000, and in 1999–2000 approximately 152,500. The last-mentioned figure includes some 20,000 postgraduates but not the 33,000 students in the polytechnics. The quantitative aim of higher education, about 65 percent of the age group, is nearing.

It was intended that completing a graduate degree should last four years, but in reality the time taken ranges on average from five to seven years. When the degree system was reformed in the 1990s, one aim being to make it more suitable for international comparison, ideal norms were set for the degree completion times. A bachelor's degree was estimated to require about three years (120 credits) and a master's degree about five years (160 credits) of studies. In fact, the average study times in Finland are still significantly longer due to the requirements, the fact that many students also hold other jobs, and so on. The number of academic degrees has, however, increased rapidly; for example, the annual number of degrees increased from 9300 to 14,400 in the 1990s.

The increase in degrees on postgraduate level was even faster. There are two different degree levels in the Finnish postgraduate system: licentiate and doctorate. The Finnish doctorate degree is demanding in international comparison, which is symbolized by the time taken but also by the fact that doctoral dissertations are almost invariably published as printed books.[74] Postgraduate education has been significantly expanded since the beginning of the 1990s, and in some fields universities cooperate in maintaining national graduate schools. The state sponsors those admitted to graduate schools by paying their salaries. Outside these schools postgraduate degrees are often financed with grants and income from work.

The state takes care of about 70 percent of the funding of universities. The universities negotiate their target outcomes with the Ministry of Education. The general lines of university budgets are also defined on the basis of these agreements. The universities choose their students; if the number of students needs to be restricted, as almost always is the case, consistent grounds must be applied. Admissions are normally based on the entrance exam scores and matriculation examination grades. Those who make their way into a university study without tuition fees. Ap-

---

74   A published book (a monograph) has been the requirement, but since the 1970s a collection of reprinted articles can also be accepted.

proximately 75 percent of all students over the age of sixteen years receive student financial aid. Despite the emphasis on equality of opportunity, the education level of the students' parents is visible in the student selection and study success.

Values and aims of universities are stated in the law: they are to promote free research and scientific and artistic education, offer the highest education based on research, and educate the youth to serve their country and mankind. In recent decades it has been feared that freedom of research would narrow, as the aims of economy and technology push aside free research and the educational ideals related to it. The most worrying scenario is that selfish aspirations without regard for common interests will strengthen in the thinking of young academics.

Due to global economic and technological competition, free research and scientific and artistic education are under threat of sliding into the shadow of values that emphasize international competitiveness. The change has been described by researchers of intellectuals such as Alan Bloom and Carl Boggs: "Nowhere has the impact of modernization been more deeply felt than in the higher education, where the traditional intellectuals (classical scholars, philosophers, clerics, literary figures, etc.) have been increasingly replaced by a technocratic intelligentsia organically tied to the knowledge industry, the corporate economy and the State. While conventional (liberal, conservative) wisdom views the university as an autonomous sphere where truth and knowledge can be dispassionately sought, in modern society higher education has become fully integrated into a matrix of institutionalized power relations." (Boggs 2000, pp. 299–300; cf. also Bloom 1987.) It is hard to determine to what extent the ties of the Finnish university institution to the state protect it from the extreme effects of globalization. The state must also conform to market forces if it is to look after its citizens' material well-being.

The administration of universities was, for centuries, the responsibility of collegial bodies formed by professors. In the 1960s and 1970s, demands for a system of "one man, one vote" were turned down (as noted in Chapter 5) but since the 1970s the university law has made not only professors but also other members of the university community active participants of the administration. The University Board is chaired by the rector and includes representatives elected by three categories of the university community: (1) professors and associate professors, (2) other teachers, researchers, and staff and (3) students. A corresponding tri-partite pattern is followed in the faculties and departments. The students are no longer ideologically similar to those who demanded radical changes. During the past twenty years or so, there has been a transfer of power to the rector and other administrators such as faculty deans; universities have changed towards a more authoritarian model.

In a world where intellectual requirements are continually and rapidly changing, the capacities of the population must be advanced also by means of adult education. The 1980s were a time of especially strong growth for adult education and the request for and necessity of life-long learning was more and more widely accepted. At the beginning of the new millennium, Finland has over 1000 institutions that provide adult education. They are organized by universities applying the idea of an open university, by polytechnics, public and private vocational schools, municipal adult education centers, summer universities, upper secondary schools, study centers, sports institutes, music institutes, the traditional folk high schools, and even the Finnish Broadcasting Company. Much of this activity is based on the tradition of the folk high schools, which also continue their educational functions. The Ministry of Education has annually allocated about 3.5 billion markkas (€ 588 m.) to adult education. According to a recent study, Finland leads the OECD countries in organizing life-long learning possibilities (OECD: Education Policy Analysis 2001).

The goals set for the Finnish education system at the end of the 1990s reflect the search for a compromise between competitiveness and values emphasizing civilization. The goals were far from being modest. They included the principle of life-long education, internationalization of education, responding to changes in the workplace and creating jobs, introducing a more varied language syllabus at all levels of education, implementing the information strategy for research and education, improving mathematics and science skills, emphasizing the cultural mission of universities and schools, providing basic educational security, rewarding centers of excellence and upgrading the training of researchers, and strengthening the status of evaluation as an integral part of steering and development (Higher Education Policy in Finland 1996, p. 33).

There is no free market within the school system itself. Private schools are very few and tuition fees are not charged. Most costs of education are paid from public funds and the goals are centrally determined and nationally evaluated. It is also possible that municipalities have been able to direct resources to the most important aspects in the local school systems. However, reduced resources have obviously limited the decisionmakers' freedom of action while responsibility has been transferred to the local level. There may be differences in the quality of education offered in different areas, and even neighboring schools may not always be of the same quality.*[OR]*

15 The State and the Economy

So-called market forces will always pull development in their own direction, disregarding the wishes of states and citizens' organizations.

Pihkala 2001, p. 284

A temporary increase in revenue should not be used as a justification for a further increase in spending.

Bank of Finland, 2001

Performance of the National Economy

As was described in Chapter 2, Finland became industrialized rather late. Only around 1960 could it be called an industrial society. But its further transition to a post-industrial economy proceeded swiftly. The economy entered the post-industrial stage and the society late modernism during the last two decades of the 20th century.

There were times after the Second World War when the growth of Finland's economy was called a "Cinderella story," and the country itself the "Japan of Europe." Indeed, according to the World Bank, only seven countries in the world had a gross national product per capita that was higher than Finland's in 1988; in 1990 Finland's GDP per capita was the third highest in Europe, below only Luxembourg and Switzerland. However, this ranking may have been exaggerated, because in those years the Finnish markka was overvalued. And soon an unforeseen slump disrupted the positive trends of the economy. In January-October 1991, industrial output sank 8.9 percent below that of 1990. Growth of the country's total output halted in 1990, and a steep decline (–7.1 percent) followed in 1991. Negative growth continued for two more years. Despite the rapid upturn that then followed, it took three more years until the country's economic performance was back at the level of 1990.

Figure 15.1

Gross domestic product in Finland, EU, USA, and Japan:
Annual changes fom 1988 to 2001 (in %)

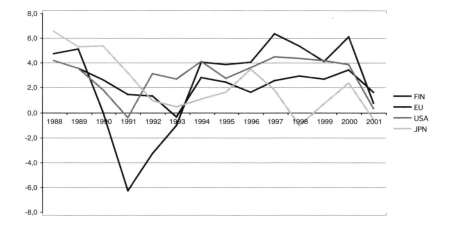

Source: ETLA.

Figure 15.1 outlines the story and also suggests some comparisons. Among the member countries of the EC/EU, GDP grew faster than in Finland only in Luxembourg and Ireland. In 1991 the economic growth of the EU members, taken as a whole, also began to slow down and in 1993 it became slightly negative (–0.4 percent); GDP had already been falling in Sweden and Great Britain in 1991 and 1992. However, the fate of these two countries was nothing like Finland's: –10.7 percent in the same two years.

The oil crisis of 1973, which caused an international recession, had not hurt the Finnish economy very much: Finland's economic growth was halted for one year but it did not become negative. On the other hand, between 1991 and 1993 total output fell 12 percent and unemployment rose from 3 to almost 20 percent. The obvious question is: What went wrong in Finland? Figure 15.1 offers one partial answer: the economy did not fare well in the outside world either, and the Finnish economy is very dependent on foreign trade. Another reason was likewise beyond Finland's control. More than ten percent of exports were sold to the Soviet Union, and that market was lost at a time that was the worst possible one for Finland's economy.

But such external reasons offer only partial explanations for the magnitude of the recession of 1991–1993. The Finnish economic policies may also have contributed to it. The public sector had expanded greatly during the 1970s and 1980s. The Bank of Finland made two liberalizing decisions in 1986–1987 that did not fit well with the economic situation: both interest rates and the movement of foreign capital were deregulated. This caused uncontrolled expansion in borrowing, doubled the prices of

247

houses and securities, and motivated excessive rises in salaries. The Bank of Finland reacted to the overheated economy by pushing up interest rates, which handicapped businesses by adding to their costs and lowering their earnings. Monetary policies became even tighter, more and more bankruptcies took place, and record unemployment followed. A devaluation of the Finnish currency helped exporters but burdened others who had borrowed money from abroad. (Ahtiala 1997.)

On the other hand, something must have gone right after the slump, because Finland's economy was revitalized rapidly. In 1997, for example, aggregate output increased by 5 percent. To quote the governor of the Bank of Finland: "The Finnish economy performed well in 1997, as growth continued at a robust pace and unemployment declined markedly... The central government budget deficit was reduced substantially but was still large in light of present cyclical conditions" (Hämäläinen 1998, p. 3). The people became more optimistic, too, and so did their predictions for the future performance of the economy.[75] Starting from 1994, GDP grew each year faster in Finland than in the EU as a whole, although not as fast as in Ireland.

In 1997 Finland's gross domestic product equaled USD 23,309 per capita. It was higher than EU average, but did not rank higher than eighth among the 15 EU members. Rapid growth continued during the years that followed. "Finland's faster economic growth than in the euro area on average has been driven by strong export demand since the middle of 1999, when the export markets started to recover from the effects of the Asian and Russian economic crises," explained the Bank of Finland (*Bank of Finland Bulletin* 1/2001, p. 8). In 2000 the growth of the economy reached the "robust" level of 5.7 percent while growth in the whole EU was 2.5 percent, but soon it became slower again.

The economies of small countries depend greatly on foreign trade, and that is very true for Finland too. In 1999, when the country's GDP was FIM 724 billion (122 billion euros), the export of goods amounted to FIM 233 billion (€ 39 bn.). The balance of trade became positive back in 1992, and it has remained favorable since then; in 1999 imports totaled FIM 212 billion, which was FIM 57 billion less than the exports. And "the year 2000 crowned the outstanding export success that started in the 1990s," declared the ministry of finance (Taloudellinen katsaus 2001, p. 22): exports reached FIM 294 billion (€ 49 bn.), imports FIM 219 billion (€ 37 bn.), and the trade surplus was FIM 75 billion (€ 13 billion).

More than one-half of Finland's trade is with other EU countries (58 percent of both exports and imports in 2000), the biggest single partners being Germany, Sweden, and the United Kingdom. After the collapse of the Soviet Union, the relative importance of Russia in exports declined,

---

75 The "consumer barometer" indicated unusually big changes in people's perceptions and expectations: Recent improvement in the economy of the country was perceived by only 9 percent in 1993 but 40 percent in 1994; a better coming year was predicted by 31 percent in 1993 but 55 percent in 1994 (*Trends* 2001, p. 57).

Table 15.1

Finland's top ten export partners in 1990, 1995, and 2000
(countries and percent of total exports)

1990		1995		2000	
Sweden	14	Germany	13	Germany	13
USSR	13	UK	10	Sweden	9
W.Germany	12	Sweden	10	UK	9
UK	11	USA	7	USA	7
France	6	Russia	5	France	5
USA	6	France	5	Italy	4
Netherlands	4	Netherlands	4	Russia	4
Denmark	4	Denmark	3	Netherlands	4
Italy	3	Norway	3	Estonia	3
Norway	3	Belgium	3	China	3
All others	34	All others	34	All others	38
FIM million: 101,327		174,660		294,221	

Data source: *SYF 1991*, p. 178; *SYF 1996*, p.226; *SYF 2001*, p.239.

but it remains one of Finland's three big import markets (next to Germany and Sweden). Of non-European countries, the USA has been an increasingly important export and import partner for Finland (see Table 15.1).

In 2000 exports were 26 percent higher than in 1999 and amounted to almost 43 percent of GDP. However, the growth of exports was rather one-sided: during the fourth quarter of that year output of the electronics sector was almost 50 percent higher than it had been the previous year, while other Finnish exporters grew by 5 percent. Such a comparison illustrates the general trend of the 1990s. Between 1995 and 1999, when Finland's total industrial production increased by 30 percent, the manufacture of electrical equipment increased by 220 percent and communication equipment by 363 percent, but paper products by only 17 percent. Naturally wood and paper production has remained important and been strengthened through foreign investments, but within Finland it has become secondary to the metals and engineering sector. This, in turn, has been caused by the strength of the electronics sector. Figure 15.2 illustrates the rapid expansion of engineering.

More specifically, the strength of the electronics sector was due to the growth of a single company called Nokia. Having been a conglomerate of a number of unrelated activities, in 1992 it sold off most of its businesses and concentrated on mobile communications. Soon it outranked its competitors and became the world leader in mobile telephones.

Figure 15.2

*Trends in Finland's industrial output from 1970 to 2000
(volume indexes, 1995=100)*

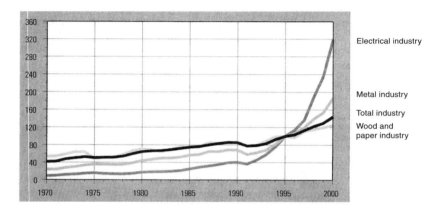

Source: *SYF 2001*, p. 205.

Its share of all Finnish exports was 6 percent in 1995, rising to 26 percent in 2000. It accounted for 70 percent of Finland's information technology exports. The entire Finnish IT cluster contained more than 3000 companies, 300 of which were Nokia's suppliers. (Pihkala 2001, p. 291; Castells and Himanen 2001, pp. 11–18.)

Despite its good performance since the recession, Finland's national economy is vulnerable for two reasons. First, domestic markets are not big enough, so the economies of the countries that buy Finnish products have a strong influence on Finland. For the same reason Finnish companies need to expand abroad. Secondly, international competitiveness in an increasingly globalizing economy requires specialization which may be risky.

The industrial companies listed in Table 15.2 illustrate the internationalization and specialization of Finnish industry.[76] About 60 percent of the production of key Finnish industrial companies is performed outside the country. In 1980 Finnish companies employed only some 20,000 persons abroad, but by 2000 the number had grown to about 200,000. This was countered by the activity of some 1500 foreign companies in Finland, employing about ten percent of the private sector's labor force. Until 1993, but not afterwards, foreign subjects needed the government's permission to own companies and real estate in Finland. (Cf. Pihkala 2001, pp. 328–342; Väyrynen 1999, pp. 71-85.)

---

76 Examples of concentrated production, in addition to Nokia, include Ahlström (wood processing and engineering in the 1980s, now fiber solutions) and Huhtamäki (food products, medinine, and plastic in the 1980s, now packaging).

Table 15.2

Largest Finnish industrial enterprises in 2001: sector, personnel (total and % abroad), and turnover (in € million)

Name	Sector	Personnel Total	Abroad	Turnover € mill.
Nokia	Mobile phones and networks	53,800	59	31,190
Stora Enso	Forest products	42,900	66	13,510
UPM-Kymmene	Forest products	36,000	44	9,920
Metso	Process industry machinery, systems, and services	30,200	63	4,340
Kone	Elevators and related services	22,900	95	2,820
Metsä-Serla	Pulp and paper	21,500	72	6,920
Outokumpu	Metals and related technology	19,400	66	5,320
Huhtamäki	Packaging	16,400	96	2,380
Fortum	Energy	14,800	47	10,410
Rautaruukki	Steel	13,000	42	2,910
Partek	Engineering	12,400	63	2,740
Wärtsilä	Metal industry	11,000	71	2,360
Kemira	Chemicals	10,200	52	2,500
Ahlström	Fiber solutions	7,700	83	2,050

Source: The companies' annual reports.

Finland's growth in 1999–2000 was possible because of the strength of the American economy and also the improving performance of the big EMU countries, whereas in the summer of 2001 when the government was finalizing its budget proposal for 2002, it was already apparent that slower economic growth in the United States, Germany, and others, had made the prospects for the coming year less promising than the Finns had believed only a few months earlier. Consequently, growth predictions were lowered. That helped the government rebuff many demands for higher state spending.[77]

Even during the years of rapid growth, high unemployment remained a persistent legacy of the recession. Finland's rate has been lower than Spain's, but consistently higher than that of the whole EU. In 1993 the ILO definition of unemployment, used by EUROSTAT, showed 11 percent for the EU, and 19 percent for Finland. Since that year Finland has been gradually approaching but not quite reaching the EU average. In 1999 the rates of unemployment were 9 percent in the EU and 10 percent in Finland; in 2000 Finland's rate was 9.6 percent. (*Eurobarometer 54*, p. 8.)

When eleven countries started Europe's Economic and Monetary Union in 1999, the value of the Finnish markka was irrecovably bound to the euro. Its rate was fixed at 0.1682 euros or, in other words, one euro be-

---

77 In the spring of 2001 the government predicted a 4 percent growth for 2001, but in September, when the budget proposal was presented, its prediction was lowered to 1.5 percent. The final fact was 0.7 percent.

came worth 5.946 markkas. Subsequently, when the euro became weaker against the dollar, the Finnish currency was also automatically devaluated. One euro cost 1.18 US dollars in January 1999, but the all-time low was $0.84 in October 2000. During a good part of 2001 the exchange rate was $0.88, and in July 2002 the weakening of the dollar pushed the euro to $1.00. The final set in EMU was taken in 2002 when the national currencies of twelve EU countries were lost and gone forever.

The Public Purse

Obviously, the slump of 1991–93 strained the finances of the Finnish state. Tax revenue declined, bailing out banks was very expensive, and high unemployment was a burden on the budget. Despite these problems, both the government and the Bank of Finland tried hard to ensure Finland would qualify for the common European currency, due to be launched in 1999. A comparison of the 15 EU countries in 1997 showed that, at that time, Finland, France, and Luxembourg were the only ones that met all the convergence criteria set for participation in economic and monetary union. The criteria were the following:

(1) Inflation must not exceed by more than 1.5 percentage points the average calculated for the three lowest inflation rates in the EU. Finland's 1.2% was the 2nd lowest.

(2) The public sector's budget deficit must not be more than 3% relative to GDP. In Finland it was 1.6% (ranked 4th lowest).

(3) The gross public debt must not exceed 60% relative to GDP. In Finland it was 58.5% (ranked 4th lowest).

(4) Long-term interest rates must not exceed by more than 2 percentage points the average level prevailing in the three countries with the lowest inflation (6.2%). Finland's rate was 6% (6th lowest).

The fifth EMU criterion was to keep the currency within the "normal" fluctuation band of the Exchange Rate Mechanism during two years. (*The Finnish Economy* 4/1997, pp. 7–8).

The economy's later performance would have met the EMU criteria even better. This was especially true in 1999, when there was a surplus in central government and substantial debt payments reduced the central government's debt to 48 percent of the GDP. That was the second lowest in the EU after Luxembourg. Long-term interest rates have fallen quite widely across the EU. Inflation has been higher in Finland than the EU average, once reaching 4 percent for a short while in 2000, but the difference has not been as high as the 1.5 percentage points that was the original EMU limit.

Attempts to meet the EMU criteria after the recession were one reason why Finland's fiscal policy became tight and taxes remained high. Although the economy began to perform well again, unemployment remained a sore point, but unemployment was not one of the EMU convergence criteria. The government appointed in April 1995 promised to cut unemployment by one-half in four years, but the target was too optimistic. Unemployment came down to 14.5 percent in 1997 and reached the 10 percent level in 1999. Because of the accepted principles of the welfare state, the unemployed persons are supported financially, which, in turn, has necessitated cuts in other expenditures. Table 15.3 summarizes how the state allocated its expenditures in 1990, 1995, and, according to the budget, in 1998 (because of a different budget structure, a similar comparison cannot be made with more recent years).

Table 15.3

State expenditure by function in 1990, 1995 and 1998 (FIM billion), and change in percent from 1995 to 1998

State functions	1990	1995	1998	% Change 1995–1998
General Administration, etc.	9.9	10.6	11.2	6
European Union	–	4.8	5.9	23
Public Order and Safety	4.8	6.1	6.7	9
Defense	6.4	8.3	10.0	21
Education, Research, and Culture	23.1	27.1	25.9	–4
Social Security and Health Care	34.7	49.1	43.8	–11
Housing and Environment	6.4	5.1	3.9	–23
Labor Force, Employment	3.7	12.2	12.9	5
Agriculture and Forestry	9.9	15.1	12.0	–21
Transport and Communications	10.9	8.1	7.0	–13
Manufacturing and Other Industries	4.3	8.3	5.7	–31
State Debt	9.4	24.6	25.6	4
Pensions Paid by the State	5.5	12.1	13.6	12
General Contrib. to Municipalities	1.4	6.8	2.7	–60
Total	129.5	198.3	186.9	–6

Source: Adapted from *SYF 1992*, pp. 265-266; and *SYF 1998*, pp. 298-299 (1990 and 1995 according to balance sheet, 1998 according to budget proposal).

Within the three-year period 1995-1998, the state's total expenditures were reduced by FIM 11.5 billion (1.9 bn. euros), although expenditure on public debt servicing and labor market measures was more than before. The most dramatic cuts concerned the central government's general contributions to the municipalities. Other substantial savings hurt social security and health care, agriculture, and education. There was much criticism and frustration among the people but, on the other hand, there was also a general consensus, especially among the elite, about the need to balance the budget and to keep the inflation low. For that reason, trade union leaders agreed in December 1997 to relatively modest, although real, rises during 1998 and 1999, when a comprehensive wage settlement was negotiated. Equally realistic rises were again accepted in the comprehensive agreement signed in December 2000 for the two-year period ending in February 2003. The government helped with its promise to lower taxes.

The last budget ever to be decided in Finnish markkas was that of 2001; the budget for 2002 was prepared in the new euro currency. The government's proposed expenditures for 2001 amounted to FIM 196.6 billion (€ 33.1 bn.) and an unusual extraordinary proposal added FIM 0.5 billion; parliament boosted expenditures by only another 0.5 billion markkas. In addition, the 2001 budget showed a surplus of FIM 14.6 billion (€ 2.5 bn.), to be used for repaying state debt. The highest annual expenditures so far had been FIM 211 billion in 1995 (then 37 percent of the GNP). In 1999, when state spending was 191 billion (€ 32 bn., 28 percent), the government was also able to pay down debt more than anticipated, namely, by 22 billion markkas. In the following year central government income and expenditure ultimately showed a record surplus of FIM 27 billion (€ 4.5 bn.).

Table 15.4

Taxes in Finland in 1991, 1995, and 2000

Type of tax	In FIM billion			In %		
	1990	1995	2000	1990	1995	2000
State taxes and levies:						
Income and property tax	43	40	85	21.7	15.8	23.2
Taxes on turnover	47	44	66	24.2	17.4	18.1
Excise duties	17	22	26	8.8	8.6	7.2
Taxes on imports	2	-	-	1.1	-	-
Other taxes and levies	11	10	17	5.9	3.3	4.6
Total state taxes	121	117	194	61.1	46.2	53.1
Municipal taxes	51	56	77	25.4	21.9	21.1
Social security contrib. to the Social Insurance Institution	24	22	20	11.7	8.6	5.6
Employment pension insurance contributions	-	45	64	-	17.8	17.4
Other social security contributions	-	13	9	-	5.1	2.6
Taxes, levies to the EU	-	1	1	-	0.4	0.2
Total all taxes	196	253	365	100	100	100
As % of GNP	37.3	44.1	46.6			

Source: *SYF 1992*, p. 294; *SYF 1997*, p. 294; *SYF 2001*, p. 324.

Naturally the central government covers most of its expenditure through tax revenue. In 2000 it collected FIM 194 billion (€ 32.6 bn.) in taxes. This was more than one-half of the country's entire tax burden, which amounted to FIM 365 billion (€ 61.4 bn.), or 46.6 percent of the GDP (see Table 15.4). More than one-fifth of the total consisted of municipal taxes, and the rest included various compulsory social payments that are comparable to taxes.

The income tax payable to the central government is graduated. The rate for earnings beyond 315,000 markkas (€ 53,000) was 37.5 percent in 2000. Taxes were reduced both in 2001 and 2002.[78] Interest earnings and capital gains are taxed a flat rate, 29 percent. The government lowered income taxes a little in the 'good years' in order to respond to political pressures and to make wage negotiations easier. Thus, in 2000 the government offered a total income tax reduction of FIM 9 billion, but also an additional FIM 4 billion conditional on the outcome of the central wage agreement. Turnover tax is the other major source of state revenue. The general rate of Finland's value added tax is 22 percent, which is the EU's second highest after Denmark. For food purchases the Finns pay 17 percent VAT, and for medicine, hotels, bus and taxi rides, and books, 12 percent.

Thus, Finland's tax burden appears high in cross-national comparisons. At its peak total taxation reached 50 percent of the GDP; in 2000 it was almost 47 percent, and the estimate for 2002 was 43 percent.

The State as Economic Policy-Maker

Voters in democracies tend to hold their government responsible for the performance of the country's economy, much beyond the government's actual possibility to influence it. Naturally, the voters are not entirely wrong. The state sets the stage for economic activity through its fiscal and economic policies, the infrastructure, and, especially, through the large body of legislation which regulates and sometimes aids economic activity. The international environment, in turn, increasingly restrains the state's possibilities to act freely.

In many countries the central bank occupies a rather independent position. Also the Bank of Finland makes policy decisions without being formally linked to the government. The bank was founded in 1811 and came under parliamentary scrutiny in 1867. According to Finland's Con-

---

78   In 2001 the lowest central government tax on income was 50 markkas for earnings of 66,000 markkas (€ 11,000) plus a marginal rate of 14 percent on income above it; for earnings of 325,000 markkas (€ 55,000) the tax payable was FIM 66,850 (€ 11,243) plus a marginal rate of 37 percent. In 2002 all tax rates were lowered by one percentage point. These rates understate the full marginal rate of tax on income, because of the extra flat rate of local government income tax – about 17% (see Chapter 12).

stitution of 1999 (Section 91), the bank "operates under the guarantee and supervision of Parliament," and "For the purpose of supervising the operations of the Bank of Finland, Parliament elects its supervisors." The central bank is thus separated from the government in order to safeguard its independence and, indeed, there have been situations in which the government and the Bank of Finland have disagreed, although most of the time they tend to liaise and attempt to coordinate their policies. The nine supervisors (the parliamentary supervisory council), who are elected by parliament for four years, both supervise the bank and make some monetary decisions, whereas the governor and the other members of the board of the Bank of Finland are appointed by the president of the republic.

When the European Central Bank was launched in Frankfurt, Germany, in January 1999, the Bank of Finland and its counterparts in the other EMU countries lost a great deal of their traditional independence, becoming dependent on the ECB's policy decisions. In some situations this may involve big risks for a small and specialized economy such as Finland.

In all economic activity, a vast amount of the legislation of the country regulates working conditions and competition practices, and numerous sharp-eyed public controllers from different offices monitor companies. For example, Finland's first law on labor protection was passed in 1889, the work day was reduced to eight hours in 1917, and the 40-hour week became the law in the early 1970s. Children have been increasingly protected: persons under 16 years of age cannot be offered employment, and full working days cannot start before 18. Competition between businesses must be genuine. The list of requirements and controls imposed on all kinds of economic activity has grown vastly, and the European Union adds more.

As was described in Chapter 14, responsibility for social welfare of the citizens requires public spending on health, pensions, family allowances, other social transfer payments, services, and unemployment benefits. Before the recession, such expenditures in Finland amounted to 26 percent of the GDP. Within two years, rapidly growing needs pushed those expenditures up to 36 percent in 1992, and they have remained around 32 percent of the GDP. The distribution of spending, not counting unemployment benefit, has been rather similar in all Nordic countries: 25% going on health, 54% for pensions and disablity, 15% for family allowances, and 6 % for the rest (Piekkola 1996). Table 14.3 (on page 228) shows that 35 percent of public social welfare expenditures is paid by the employers, and a smaller portion by the insured themselves.

The normal pensionable age in Finland, for both men and women, is 65 years, although in many occupations the age is lower. Because of various arrangements, most people retire so much earlier that the average age of retirement has been 58 years. Extensive education also reduces the number of years spent actively working. Furthermore, Finnish legislation requires plenty of leisure in each year worked. In 1995, the average length of vacations in manufacturing was 37.5 workdays in Finland, but only 25 days in Sweden and 12 days in the United States. There was a corresponding difference in regular annual working time. It was 1716 hours in Finland, 1808 hours in Sweden, and 1896 hours in the United States.

Naturally, the government does not only regulate and tax economic activity. In some sense, most legislation and budget decisions affect the economy, and many political decisions are motivated by economic interests. Not only the infrastructures, but also regional policies and a large variety of more direct political decisions aim at improving the environment for enterpreneurship. Also, economy is guided through international agreements, both multilateral and bilateral. Some of them will be discussed elsewhere in this book (see page 277).

The State as Entrepreneur

All states have a very direct presence in the economy, because they function as entrepreneurs and investors. Some of their economic activities are thought of as common elements of the country's infrastructure: these have included postal services and airport operations, and in Europe they have ordinarily extended to the railroads, broadcasting and telecommunications, and energy supplies. Local governments, in turn, take care of businesses of their own, for instance local transit systems.

Many advances in the Finnish economy required such heavy investments or such a complex organization, that,in a country short of capital, only the government had the necessary resources. For example, the state has run Finland's postal services since 1638, telecommunications since 1855, the railroads since 1862, a copper mine since 1910, an airline since 1923, national wheat storage since 1928, an electric power company since 1932, broadcasting since 1934, oil refinery and distributor since 1948, a computing center since 1964, and a nuclear power plant since 1977.

There were several possible ways to organize such enterprises. The government agencies running the state railways and postal and telecommunications services were part of the ordinary state administration. Another arrangement was to establish state-owned companies to function like any private company. Some, like the state liquor company, had a monopoly, but many functioned in the competitive market like any other businesses, the only difference being that they had no or very few private owners. In most European market economies, the state became a large owner of businesses; in Finland its share of industry rose to about one-fifth, which was below the level of state ownership in France and Germany.

Frequently public ownership has been viewed purely from the economic point of view. However, state-owned industries have also served regional policy goals and, in particular, nationalized industries have been an ideological issue. In Britain, for example, Labour nationalized and Conservative governments then denationalized coal mines after World War II. In Finland, state ownership was one of the ideological goals of the Social Democratic Party and it remained an element of the leftist party programs until the 1970s. In the 1980s the mood began to change world wide. Privatization became the neo-liberalist policy goal. Even the leftist parties in Finland have dropped the idea of socialization, assuming instead a pragmatic approach to ownership: state-owned companies or parts of them have been offered for sale to private shareholders, and the state has benefited from such new revenue. But the mass public has not quite forgotten the ideological approach: the supporters of the Left Alliance and the Conservative Party still have quite different opinions on privatization (see Table 15.5).

Table 15.5

"Our country ought to privatize a great deal of public services, in order to provide the services more efficiently:" Responses related to party preference in December 1994 (in %)

	LEFT	SDP	FRP	CENT	CHR	CONS	SPP	GR	Total
Agree	16	33	30	55	58	73	54	39	47
Disagree	74	50	42	21	21	15	24	37	32
Can't say	10	17	28	24	21	12	22	24	19

Source: Adapted from EVA 1995, p. 20

In 1997, the Finnish government controlled 36 large companies through majority ownership. They employed 149,000 persons, had a total turnover of FIM 169 billion, and earned a profit of 7 billion. In some of them the state was interested purely as an investor (e.g., a paper mill and a steel plant), others involved both an economic and a public policy interest (e.g., an oil company, railways, airline, power plant, and motor vehicle inspection), and, in addition, there were four state-owned companies that had been established to serve a significant public interest (liquor, gambling, broadcasting, and army supplies).

Many state-owned companies have been created in the 1990s. For example, the railroads were governed by the central administration until 1989, and in the manner of a corporation since 1990, but since 1995 have been operated by a state-owned company. The general public hardly notices the difference. The Post and Telegraph Office was reorganized in 1994 and to a large extent privatized after that (see following section). In addition, the state was a minority owner in nine companies, and indirectly in many others. In 1996 the state earned FIM 0.4 billion in dividends from minority shareholdings, and dividends from state-controlled companies brought in 1.1 billion. More substantial income, however, came from the sale of shares, the limits for which have been set by parliament for each company.

In 2002 the government's dividends rose to 911 million euros, about 3.5 times higher than in 1996, and 475 million euros were budgeted for 2002. In the meantime, the state had sold more of its shares had been sold to private owners. There was some political debate concerning further privatization, and in spring 2002 parliament turned against the Ministry of Trade and Commerce refusing the government's request to sell Kemira to its Swedish competitor. Three ministers also debated on the virtues of having all state ownership concentrated under one ministry and, if so, under which one.

No fewer than eight ministries were in charge of the state's interests in 2002. The government controlled 32 companies, being the sole owner of 21 and a majority owner of 11. In addition, it had a minority share in 17 companies. Seven industrial enterprises listed in Table 15.2 belonged to the sphere of the ministry of Trade and Commerce - the government had a 61 percent majority in Fortum (a combination of the electric power company and the oil company since 1998), and 56 percent in Kemira; also, 40 percent remained of ownership of the metal companies Outokumpu and Rautaruukki, and a smaller share was held in Kone and the two large paper companies. Seven smaller companies were also controlled by this ministry. But eight companies were under the Ministry of Communications, including the Finnish Broadcasting Company (100%), Finnair (58%), motor vehicle inspection (100%), the two large descendants of the Post and Telegram Office (100% and 53%), and the state railways (100%). In addition, 13 state-owned companies were under the Ministry of Finance, including the former Government Printing Center, since 1993 Edita Ltd. Five other ministries had a company or two under their control. (Cf. *Helsingin Sanomat* 11.8.2002.)

Another pragmatic process has been that of introducing the principles of corporate governance to the traditional areas of state administration, thus adding more flexibility, better public relations, and also new charges for services. The necessary legislation became effective in 1988, and corporate governance started in 1989. However, many reformed state agencies, such as the Railway Board, were further transferred into state-owned companies. The most important administrative agencies that remain governed as corporations are the former Forestry Board, the Aviation Board, and the National Road Administration. A real estate office was established to charge rents to the state from the state.

State-owned companies participate in the employers' interest organizations, like any other companies. Civil servants who work in traditional public administration are unionized as well: in addition to government-owned enterprises, the state itself and the municipal governments even more so, are the employer side in labor contracts, facing the employee side consisting of workers who, once upon the time, were supposed to be the government's devoted and obedient servants. In fact, many labor conflicts occur between public employees and their governmental employer. At the beginning of 1998, firemen and the drivers of the Helsinki city transit system were on strike and judges also threatened industrial action; in 2001 doctors working in the public health care system organized a partial strike that lasted five months; and in all such cases the strikes were directed against democratically controlled state or local government and not against any "capitalist exploiter and class enemy."

A Case Story: Telecommunications

In Finland, as in many European countries, telecommunications well illustrates the development of government enterprises from a public service or a monopoly, run by state bureaucracy, to a business corporation that operates in an open and competitive market.

In the 19th century, all European countries declared telegraph operations the exclusive right of the state and many applied the same principle to the newer innovation, the telephone. In Finland the senate's proclamation in 1886 concerning "Those terms by which telephone lines can be placed in the earth and used," separated the two activities: telegraph traffic remained with the Finnish branch of the Russian Empire's Telegraph Office, but telephones were operated by private companies subject to Finnish administrative control.

In 1927 Finland's Telegraph Office was attached to the Post Office. The Post and Telegraph Office started its telephone networking in thinly populated Lapland, while numerous private companies and cooperatives were building telephone networks in densely populated areas. Gradually it acquired both long-distance telephone operations and the equipment of hundreds of small local telephone companies; in 1980 there were 61 telephone companies left in the country. Demands to nationalize the entire telephone network never received sufficient support.

The Post and Telegraph Office was at odds with the private companies, because it was not only an operator, but also the supervisory authority since 1949. There were disputes in connection with purchases and with the regulation of data transmission. The state office viewed data transmission as an advanced version of the telegraph and demanded that data transmission be subject to telegraph legislation, while private telephone companies considered data transmission to be a part of telephony. A compromise solution in 1970 granted both camps the right to transmit data.

The rapidly developing telecommunications field remained subject to the Telephone Statute of 1886, until the Telecommunications Act of 1987 finally consigned the 100-year old statute to history. Supervisory functions were transferred from Posts and Telecommunications (this name adopted in 1981) to the new telecommunications administration center in the Ministry of Transport and Communications.

The 1980s were characterized by efforts to foster competition. One example of such "Thatcherism" was the deregulation of Britain's telecommunications industry. Competition also started in Finnish network services. Data networks and GSM were opened to competition in 1990, and competitive licenses were granted to both long-distance and local telecommunications in 1992. The Telecommunications Market Act of 1997 replaced the act of 1987. It abolished license requirements, except for the construction of mobile communications networks; required telecommunications companies to separate their network and service operations; and also subjected the companies to more stringent obligations.

In 1990 the Post and Telegraph Office had begun to function as a state enterprise, free from the commitment to annual state budgets. In 1994 it was structured as a limited company called PT Finland Ltd. Within this corporation, postal services and telecommunications became two separate companies, one of which was named Telecom Finland. (Cf. Turpeinen 1997; and www.telegalleria.fi.) The next step was taken in 1997, when parliament approved the partial privatization of Telecom Finland, which was artificially renamed "Sonera."

The parent company Sonera Group was listed on the Helsinki Stock Exchange in November 1998, when the government sold 22 percent of the company's shares to domestic and international investors. Trading in the Nasdaq National Market started in October 1999. In June 2000, the government obtained parliament's permission to sell all of it, "when necessary." At that time the state owned a 53 percent majority of the company, having sold 47 percent. The best-timed sale had taken place in March 2000, when the state sold a 3 percent slice for the price of FIM 12 billion (€ 2 bn.). In theory a full privatization at that price would have produced enough revenue to pay all central government expenditure for one year. But within three months the shares had lost 50 percent of their market value, and by 2001, 97 percent had vanished.

Optimistic expectations concerning telecommunications and information technology lead to frustrations around the world. Among others, the British Telecom, Deutsche Telecom, France Telecom, and Spain's Telefónica faced severe difficulties. Sonera had also overextended itself when paying FIM 20 billion to Germany for the right to be one of the six "third generation" operators within that country (in March 1999 the Finnish government had distributed four corresponding UMTS[79]-licenses quite free of charge; in 2000 Great Britain, Germany and Italy auctioned off their licenses for the total of € 93 billion).

Sonera considered internationalization the only road to success. "A leading provider of fixed-line, mobile, data and media telecommunications services," it acted in 14 countries and had equity stakes in compa-

---

79 UMTS = Universal Mobile Telecommunications System, enabling the "third generation" mobile communication.

nies that have UMTS licenses in Spain and Italy, in addition to Germany. Although burdened by heavy debt and public criticism, Sonera was efficient in the competitive market[80] but there were problems with the company's management. Between 1997 and 2001, Sonera had four different CEOs. Criticism of the first of them even led to the resignation of the government's minister of communications.

The surprise finale in March 2002 was the announcement, soon approved by the Eduskunta and the EU, that Sonera had decided to merge with its Swedish competitor Telia, which had made a rather unsuccessful attempt to gain a slice of the Finnish market. Of the new company, the Finnish government owns 14 percent and the Swedish government 36 percent. The new CEO is a Swede. In July 2002 Sonera wrote off its German and Italian UMTS investments and acknowledged that it had paid 4.3 billion euros for nothing, thus acknowledging the largest investment failure in Finland's economic history.

Various general conclusions might be drawn from the telecommunications experience:

- In European countries in general, and in small countries in particular, only the state has been in strong enough position to invest in big economic activities that have been essential for the development of the national economy.
- The concept of public interest has changed. Serving the people and building the necessary infrastructure was the unquestioned responsibility of the state, until "market forces" took over and productivity and competitiveness became overarching values.
- Traditional bureaucratic procedures do not allow for the kind of flexibility and quick action that is required in the business world, and the politicians do not always understand all aspects of business culture, including the greed of some business executives.
- Public opinion does not easily grasp the difference between the state's own functions and the functions of state-owned corporations. At least as long as the state remains a majority owner, the government or its individual ministers may be held politically responsible for decisions taken by managers, where the shareholders in fact have no direct say.
- If a state-owned company makes wrong business decisions, it is virtually impossible to determine who is responsible for violating the taxpayers' interests. Business secrets can cover state-owned companies while public administration is transparent.
- In today's globalized world, a business-like approach involves not only activity abroad, but also foreign owners, international mergers, and joint ventures.

---

80 For example, in the fall of 2000 the World Communication Awards event in Cannes named Sonera the best wireless/mobile telephone operator, and the ISP Forum in Rome, the best European provider of internet services.

16 The International Environment

Finland continues to have its own goals and does its best to present them, but most major matters are handled through Brussels according to an EU script.

Lappalainen 2000, p. 32

Deeper practical cooperation with NATO has not placed the issue of NATO membership on the acute decision-making agenda.

Sivonen 2001, p. 92

The European Union

No country can change its geopolitical location in the world, but the surrounding social, political, and economic environments are constantly changing. At the end of the 20th century changes were exceptionally dramatic: the Cold War ended and the Soviet Union collapsed, globalization accelerated, and Finland took its place in the core of West Europe's deepening integration.

In November 1994 the Finnish parliament followed the advice given by the consultative referendum and approved the country's accession to the European Union, effective since January 1st, 1995. This was Finland's most important political decision in the 1990s. The most important single decision of the next parliament, elected in March 1995, again concerned the EU. The Eduskunta accepted the government's report on Economic and Monetary Union in April 1998, thereby sealing Finland's participation in EMU since January 1, 1999. This replaced Finland's national currency with euros from the beginning of 2002. The parliamentary opposition voted against the report but was not strong enough to challenge the majority government. Earlier, the government had rejected any requests to hold a referendum on the EMU issue.

Thus Finland first became one of the 15 members of the EU, and then the only Nordic country to belong to the EU's "inner circle." Obviously this implied some change in the customary marching order, because hitherto Finland had typically been the slowest rather than the quickest Nordic country to approach any structures of West European integration, such as EFTA, the Council of Europe, or the EC/EU itself. The new urge to take a recognized place at the core of the EU seems to correspond to Finland's attempt to emphasize its western identity and strengthen its national security in the international environment of the post-Cold War era (see Chapter 2, pages 52-53).

The coalition government headed by Prime Minister Paavo Lipponen aimed at EMU membership from the day the government was formed in 1995. In that it was still doubtful whether the third stage of EMU would be launched at all according to the established schedule; the most likely prediction was that EMU would begin in 1999 with very few key states. What was obvious in Finland at the time was the fact that the country's public finances were not in good enough shape to fulfill the strict convergence criteria laid down for participation in the single currency, unless drastic measures were taken to meet the criteria (see Chapter 15 above). By 1997 these problems were solved, and in March 1998 the European Commission announced that altogether eleven countries met the EMU criteria.

The European Union of 12 states, which was in 1995 enlarged to 15 when Finland, Austria, and Sweden joined it, was quite different from the original European Economic Community of "the Six." There had been enlargements as well as plenty of "deepening" in 35 years. In its own accession treaty Finland agreed to accept the pre-existing norms and the future decisions and policies of the EU. The latter included full participation in the EU's foreign and security policy. The forthcoming EMU was also implied in the accession treaty, albeit not very overtly. The bulk of EU legislation thereby imposed upon Finland was enormous. Even a very condensed version of EU laws, and one which does not cover the norms concerning agriculture, is a book of some 2700 pages.

One problem with the EU laws is their somewhat uneven character: they are massive and they cover a wide variety of topics, but they do not constitute a balanced legal system, nor are they always free of internal inconsistencies. Fortunately, by and large they fit well with Finland's own legislation. But there is always the potential of a "jack-in-a-box," as Thomas Wilhelmsson has called it: When applying existing national legislation a court may face a strange EU creature that suddenly springs out of the box when the court opens the lid (Letto-Vanamo 2000, p. 68).

A great deal of EU rules and procedures would have concerned Finland even without membership of the EU. As a member of the European Economic Area since January 1994 Finland had already committed itself to the norms of the single European market. Even as an outsider Finland would have needed to adjust its policies to developments in the EU. One of the advantages of membership is the right to take part in the EU's decision-making. This has been emphasized constantly in Finnish discourse, although Finland's numerical weight in the EU institutions is small: it got 3 out of 87 votes in the Council of Ministers, one member in the Commission and one in the Court of Justice, 9 out of 222 members in both the Economic and Social Committee and the Committee of the Regions, and 16 seats in the 626-member European Parliament.

It has been difficult to convince the voters that they exert real influence on the EU's or even on the European Parliament's decisions when they fill Finland's meager 2.6 percent of EP seats.[81] This explains to some extent why interest in the European elections has declined. In Finland's first EP elections in 1996, 60.3 percent of the electorate turned out to vote, but in the European elections of 1999 turnout dropped to 31.4 percent (only Great Britain and the Netherlands having lower scores). The drop was dramatic in comparison with the entire EU's decline from 58 percent in 1994 to 53 percent in 1999.

In Finland's EP election in 1999 the Conservative Party was the winner, with 25 percent of the votes (having had 21 percent in the parliamentary election of March 1999); yet a loss of 44 percent of its voters can hardly be called a victory. But the SDP lost 64 percent, Left Alliance 61 percent, and Center Party 56 percent of the votes they had received three months earlier. The Greens lost only 11 percent.

Finland's 16 MEPs joined five different party groups in the European Parliament. The Conservatives (who belong to the European People's Party) and Center Party (the EP's Liberal, Democratic, and Reformist Party) each had four members elected, the Social Democrats (Party of European Socialists) three, and the Left Alliance (European United Left/ Nordic Green Left) one. The other Finnish winner, the Greens, now received two seats, the Swedish People's Party (ELDR) one, and the Christian League (now Christian Democrats, EPP), also one. Individual distinctions in the parliament included Ms Heidi Hautala's election to the co-chair of the Green group and Ilkka Suominen's vice-chairmanship of the Conservative EPP group.

The EU employs altogether more than 25,000 people, of whom 16,500 work for the Commission and 4100 for the Parliament. In 1997, the EU's employees included 626 Finns.[82] The most visible one was Jacob Söderman, Finland's former parliamentary ombudsman, whom the European Parliament elected in 1995 to serve as EU's first ombudsman. His duty is to handle EU-citizens' complaints and to monitor administrative behavior by bureaucrats. His office has enabled him to request more open or 'transparent' administrative procedures, something the Finnish government and Finnish MEPs also constantly demand of the EU. In a few

---

81 In December 2000 the European Council decided in Nice that Finland will elect only 13 out of 535 MEPs (the treaty's ratification was delayed by a referendum in Ireland); when 12 new member states enter the EU, the size of the European Parliament will rise to 732 and Finland's share will be 1.8 percent.

82 The Commission targeted in 1995, that by 1999 it would employ 250–350 Finns and 400–500 Swedes. In 2000, its employees (grade A1 to grade D) included 396 from Finland and 447 from Sweden.

cases Söderman's criticism has brought him into open conflict with the commission, for instance in 1999 with its new Italian chairman Romano Prodi. The performance of the Finnish member of the Commission since 1995, Erkki Liikanen, has been reviewed sometimes very favorably.[83]

The EU's 15 member states finance the Union in three ways. They collect customs duties for the EU, and they pay from their own tax revenue both a portion of their value added tax and a resource based on their GNP. However, the EU's "own resources" are not allowed to exceed 1.27 percent of the entire Union's GNP. Finland's payments to the EU budget increased from FIM 5.8 billion in 1995 to FIM 7.5 billion (€ 1.3 bn.) in 2000 (see Table 16.1). Of the revenue that Finland receives from the EU, more than one-half supports agriculture. In total, Finland does not get back as much as it contributes (with the exception of 1995); in 1998 and 1999 net payments to the EU were unusually large. The amounts summarized in Table 16.1 do not account for the EU's additional contributions to various Finnish projects, an estimated 0.4 or 0.5 billion markkas (€ 65–85 million) each year.

Table 16.1

Payments to and revenue from the EU in 1995–2000
(in FIM million, according to balance sheet)

Payments to the EU:	1995	1996	1997	1998	1999	2000
Collected customs and agricultural levies	953	976	951	910	847	940
Value Added Tax	3,027	2,948	3,085	2,945	3,128	3,243
Resource based on GNP	1,272	1,791	2,292	3,041	3,341	3,304
Capital payments	484	506	249	70	32	32
Other	44	45	12	–	–	–
Total	5,779	6,266	6,519	6,966	7,348	7,519
Received from the EU:						
Transitional support	2,701	859	380	198	–	–
Customs administration	87	99	94	93	85	94
Agriculture	2,135	2,939	3,349	2,802	3,044	4,868
Regional fund	174	212	450	661	966	507
Social fund	379	285	945	142	442	649
Other to state budget	25	49	90	109	178	175
Outside state budget	407	728	877	795	809	815
Total	5,907	5,171	6,185	4,800	5,528	7,108
Net Payments	−128	1,085	334	2,166	1,820	411

Source: Ministry of Finance.

83 See, for example, evaluations in *The Economist*, August 30th 1997, p. 24.

Naturally, membership in the EU influences Finnish economy far beyond the mutual exchange of public money shown in Table 16.1, but there has been no comprehensive analysis of the total impact of the EU on Finland's national economy. One estimate, made before joining the EU, concluded that membership of the EC/EU would add about 4 percent to GDP, due to more efficient allocation of resources in agriculture and other industries, various positive impacts of EMU membership, and, to a lesser extent, the elimination of some practices that inconvenienced exports and direct investments (Alho et al., 1992). In their campaigns supporting EU membership both the business organizations and most trade unions used economic arguments, and the people discovered during the first year of EU membership that food prices really came down some 10 percent.

Finland's approach to the Inter-Governmental Conference in 1996–1997 can be traced to two identities: first, a country with Nordic political and cultural traditions, and second, a small country on the border of the EU (Kivimäki and Tiilikainen 1998, p. 112). The former explains why Finland has aimed at more efficient and transparent administration in the EU, and the latter why Finland consistently emphasizes equality between small and large member states and attempts to gain recognition of the concept of Europe's northern dimension. The Amsterdam treaty in 1997 already adopted such Finnish goals as the emphasis on employment, the environment, and the social dimension, all of which can be counted as aspects of Nordic cultural identity. The nothern dimension was acknowledged formally in 1997,[84] but so far it has not been widely implemented.

The Finnish people do not identify themselves as Europeans,[85] but they have learned during a short period of time to take their country's EU membership for granted, and they want to get the most out of it. In addition, they desire an increasingly global orientation in foreign trade, because they do not think that the EU can be sufficient by itself. And they want to protect Finland's national sovereignty.

In one survey at the end of 1996, Finnish respondents were asked to express their opinions on 31 national decisions concerning the country's international position (EVA 1997b, p. 39). Typically, they viewed the EU from the domestic point of view and rejected a stronger union. Of the list of different policy orientations, the following five were supported by the largest majorities:

– Take an active part in developing the EU and thereby benefit the country (supported by 85%, opposed by 4%);

84 In December 1997 the European Parliament accepted Finland's suggestion to add a statement on the northern dimension to its pronouncement on the results of the summit meeting held in Luxembourg.

85 In late 2001, 59% of the Finns identified "with nationality only" and 36% were "Finnish and European;" only 4% placed European before Finnish identity. The corresponding EU averages were 44%, 44%, and 9%. (*Eurobarometer 56,* p. 14.)

- Carefully protect Finland's national sovereignty (85/5%);
- Increase cooperation with the Nordic countries, for instance with Sweden (83/4%);
- Strongly champion Finland's own interests in the EU, get all possible benefits out of it (77/9%); and
- Be more active at the United Nations (68/9%).

As an example of opinions that were almost evenly divided, one could mention responses to the suggested need to "slow down rather than speed up the major development projects of the EU" (30/35%). On the other hand, federal developments in the EU were clearly opposed (12/57%).

Important international goals that the Finnish people want their government to pursue in the EU include the fight against international crime, environment policies, employment policies, and relations with Russia. In these respects public opinion reflects the government's policy goals. Concerning the EU itself, the people, like their government, want more transparency and less bureaucratic procedures. On the other hand, the people are not keen on enlargement, which is supported by the government. Many have even found it difficult to formulate an opinion on EU membership by neighboring Estonia, and those who did express an opinion tended to be against it. The "northern dimension" is also very unclear to most Finnish people. (EVA 1999b, p. 31.)

There is big variation in how different people estimate Finland's influence on the decisions of the EU: those who view membership positively tend to think that Finland has been influential, whereas EU opponents think that Finland has not been heard in EU decision-making. The government has made it clear that many Finnish goals have advanced in the EU, but there have also been some disappointments. An unexpected one was in December 2001 when the European Council meeting in Laeken, Belgium was unable to decide on the location of the new European Food Safety Authority (EFSA), which Finland was prepared to host when it was started in January 2002.[86]

The distribution of Finnish opinion on the country's EU membership has remained almost constant over the years. In the referendum in October 1994, 42 percent voted "yes," 32 percent voted "no," and 26 percent did not vote. Table 16.2 shows the corresponding distributions of opinion on EU membership one month before the referendum, and seven years thereafter. Only a very small shift toward negative opinion can be detected and differences between the supporters of different political parties have also remained. Of the big party groups, the Conservatives have

---

86 None of the EU-offices was located in Finland and the country was ready to house the EFSA in the "biocity" of the University of Helsinki. Finland's first disappointment was the postponement of the decision during Sweden's presidency, the second occured in Belgium when an otherwise unanimous decision in favor was vetoed by Italian Prime Minister Silvio Berlusconi, who wanted the new office placed in Parma.

positive feelings and the Center Party supporters negative ones. The supporters of both leftist parties had become more positive toward EU membership, while only the Christian Democrats and Swedish People's Party supporters had become more critical. Consequently, it seems that the slight move toward negative opinion in Finland has largely occurred among people with no party preference.

Table 16.2

Opinions on EU membership related to party preference in September 1994 and in November – December 2001 (in %)

	Party preference							
	LEFT	SDP	CENT	CHR	CONS	SPP	GR	ALL
In 1994:								
Yes	20	42	20	10	68	71	35	39
No	50	18	52	60	12	12	39	29
Undecided	30	40	28	30	20	17	26	32
Total	100	100	100	100	100	100	100	100
In 2001:								
Positive	28	52	25	9	62	49	42	37
Negative	48	16	44	69	14	31	34	31
Neutral	22	30	31	22	24	20	34	30
Don't know	2	2	0	–	–	–	1	2
Total	100	100	100	100	100	100	100	100

Source: Pesonen 1994, pp. 57, 60; EVA 2002, p. 13.

When Finnish people are compared with the citizenry of the entire EU, the Finns show two distinct characteristics: they tend to be more critical of the EU than average EU citizens, and they are better informed about it. According to the Eurobarometer surveys in October–November 2001, only 37 percent of the Finns thought that EU membership was a "good thing" (while the EU average was 54%), and 39 percent said Finland had "benefited" from its EU membership (EU average was 52%). On the other hand, the Finns paid relatively great attention to EU news, showed the second highest awareness of the EU institutions, felt the most informed about enlargement, and were, together with the Dutch, the best informed about the single currency. (*Eurobarometer 56*, pp. 88, 98–99.)

In fact the people in all three new EU members have relatively negative feelings about the Union, although not as negative as the British. Among the three, the Swedes generally appear to be the most and the Austrians the least critical, but opinions are in all three countries more critical than EU average. The three peoples do not tend to support EU membership or to find it useful. They are proud of their own nationality and want relatively many decisions made on the national level. They tend to dislike the policy matters of the EU and do not want the EU to interfere with their daily lives. Among them only the Finns have a tendency to trust various EU institutions, notably the Ombudsman and the Court of Justice, more than EU citizens do on the average. On the question of enlargement, public opinions deviate; the Swedes, contrary to the Austrians, tend to support the inclusion of new members while the distribution of Finnish opinion is in the middle. (Cf. op. cit. and *Eurobarometer 54.*)

It is also tempting to compare how Finland and Sweden have performed in the EU. Both countries have held the council presidency, Finland in 1999 and Sweden in 2001. At the beginning it was customary to say that "Sweden entered the EU to teach, Finland to learn," and many concluded that Finland's style has produced better results. The Swedish observer Karl Magnus Johansson wrote in 1999 that the Finns "were praised for everything," while "the Swedes were thought of as squabblers... The Finns can play the game. They can give and take. They do not have opinions on everything, but rather, they aim at getting attention whenever they open their mouth" (quoted in Raunio and Wiberg 2000, p. 287). In fact, Finland and Sweden have shared many goals and often cooperate. The Finnish people are frequently reminded by political leaders that their country has gained genuine influence in the EU and that EU membership and policies have benefited Finland. This, however, does not seem to bridge the gap between the Union's institutions and the people's perceptions. *[PP]*

Globalization

The coverage of globalization extends, by definition, far beyond the gradually deepening integration of Europe. Although there has been worldwide economic activity, foreign trade, and other kinds of international contacts for a very long period of time, current globalization illustrates quite a recent expansion of contacts and an unforeseen time-space compression. It is most visible in how improvements in communication have eliminated delays in data transmission. Communication is becoming nonstop, and an up-to-the-minute information flow affects lives almost everywhere. Internet enables worldwide personal communication and an unprecedented acquisition of information.

The rapid strengthening of international dependencies is most apparent in the economy. Companies and capital lose their national connotations and there is growing financial interchange and dependency between countries. Networking of companies is part of this change, not only domestically but also internationally. The risks caused by technological development, such as environment changes, are not altogether a new phenomenon either, but they too become more international and have worldwide consequences.

Finns have had some contacts with distant peoples since ancient times; in modern times the small size of the country and its specialized economy make international contacts especially important. Due to Finland's late industrial development, remote location, and distinctive language its international relations diversified at a later stage than those of many other European countries. On the other hand, the change in Finnish society became very rapid in the second half of the 20th century. At least since the 1990s Finland's industrial structure has been one of the most modern in the world (cf. Table 2.5); technologically Finland has been classified as the world's most developed country (see Chapter 14).

Therefore, one might well ask to what extent postmodern Finland is a globalized country and what does globalization mean for Finland. To be able to say that globalization touches a country as a comprehensive phenomenon, it must concern not only the economy but also the government and civil society.

From a small northern state's point of view, the prehistory of globalization contains various bilateral trade agreements and, especially, agreements made with international organizations (see page 276 below). Finland has built much of its economy on the tradition of foreign trade from the 18th and 19th centuries, and the liberation of international trade was one of the basic preconditions that allowed small countries to turn increasingly to world markets. Now states are forced to release some of their power to the markets run by large international corporations. It seems that small states, the very states that are most dependent of international markets, are losing power more than the large states (cf. Held and McGrew, 2000).

The changes that have taken place, communication especially, broaden the range of people's thinking from a local frame of reference to more global perception, in the direction of 'world citizenship.' However, people in welfare states are also well aware of the potential disadvantages of globalization: intense competition may lead to the exclusion of those with low education and to heightened social differences. The threats also bring together citizens of different countries and give rise to global citizens' organizations such as Greenpeace and Attac.

During the post-war decades, Finnish civil society has also, through central organizations, joined international non-governmental organizations. There are hundreds of examples of this. One worth mentioning here is the International Council on Social Welfare (ICSW), which has had a national committee actively operating in Finland since 1948. Through this council hundreds of Finnish social and health organizations communicate with international and foreign organizations while many of them are also members of the international organizations directly, in their special fields. The global nature of ICSW is illustrated by the fact that its member organizations represent 75 different countries.

The number of annual congresses held by various international organizations has increased and Finns have been eager participants. The biggest citizen organizations also have continuing contacts with the European Union through their representatives and lobbyists. The global connections of citizen organizations bring international contacts increasingly to the grass-root level, as Finland is among the top countries in the world in association memberships.

Reacting to the internationalization of business corporations, the large interest organizations have established their own permanent international connections. Finland's central labor organizations belong to the International Confederation of Free Trade Unions (ICFTY), the European Trade Union Confederation (ETUC), and the Council of Nordic Trade Unions (NFS). They also participate in the work of the OECD's Trade Union Advisory Committee, the Finnish ILO Committee, and the European Economic and Social Committee. They even have plans to launch a joint forum for international issues. Similarly, the Union of Industrial Employers' Confederations of Europe (UNICE) has its own office in Brussels and it, too, has permanent ties to the OECD, ETUC, and ILO. Obviously, Finnish interest organizations will strengthen their international activity still further.

The other types of international organizations in which the Finns participate work in the areas of economic activity and professions, research and culture, social and charity work, athletics, etc, and they really are too numerous to be listed here. The European-level organizations of political parties include the Socialist International (SI), founded in 1951, and the European Democratic Union (EDU), founded in 1978. Individual citizens have frequent foreign contacts: tourism is popular, and more and more tours are sold to very distant places. In 2000, eight million passengers departed (and equally many arrived) on ships, however, sailing mostly only between Finland and neighboring Sweden and Estonia. At Finnish airports the total number of embarked and disembarked international passengers reached seven million. (*SYF 2001*, pp. 296–297.)

Index numbers can provide concrete illustrations of the decades of internationalization. Table 16.3 shows how rapidly international traffic through Finnish ports and airports increased in four decades. In 2000 passenger traffic through airports was almost 26 times the number of passengers in 1960, international goods traffic through airports was 35 times higher than in 1960. International goods traffic through Finnish ports quadrupled. Furthermore, Table 16.3 indicates that the take-off phase of Finland's internationalization occurred already in the 1960s. This coincided with the period of Finland's fast economic growth: if the gross domestic product in 1950 is given the value 100, the corresponding index number rose to 162 in 1960 and was no less that 259 in 1970 (Vartia and Ylä-Anttila 1996, p. 65).

Table 16.3

Index numbers of exchange between Finland and foreign countries from 1960 to 2000 (1980 = 100)

Year	Net tonnage by sea	Air passengers	Air freight (weight)	Air mail (weight)
1960	39	13	9	15
1965	49	22	22	28
1970	66	43	49	49
1975	64	84	60	61
1980	100	100	100	100
1985	105	147	148	134
1990	119	261	228	158
1995	144	246	305	194
2000	163	335	320	239

Data source: *SYF 2001*, pp. 294–298.

The different speed of development in shipping and air transportation describes the change in Finland's foreign trade: the transition from heavy raw material cargo to lighter end products. At the same time, globalization required ever faster delivery times. For example, there is a very different price-weight ratio for lumber, important historically, and mobile phones, important today. In moving from material products to information technology products such as computer software, the value may be transferred without mass. International data transmission is to certain extent, if in a very imperfect way, described by passenger and postal traffic between countries. By 2000 passenger traffic had increased to almost 26 times and postal traffic to 16 times that of 1960; between 1980 and 2000 the volume of air freight more than tripled and air mail more than doubled.

The Internet represents the latest and fastest-expanding stage in the history of globalization. In 1998, there were 88 Internet connections per 1000 inhabitants in Finland; by summer 2000, this number was 135. In 1998, approximately 24 percent of Finns, including children and the elderly, used the Internet at least once; in 2001 the percentage was 47. The development illustrates an astonishing change in terms of globalization, too, although not all Internet users are internationally connected.

Because globalization is essential in international competition, but because it also poses certain dangers, Finland faces a basic dilemma: how can it be successful in the essential arenas of globalization while managing to reject its negative aspects?

One of the important manifestations of globalization is the new economy, based on information technology and intensive utilization of know-how. To a significant degree, the new economy has adopted the principles of market economy and free trade, something that favors the internationalization and networking of companies. There is a big gap between the old and new economies. While the old economy invests in the manufacture of goods, the new economy primarily invests in increasing the productivity of information.

As stated in Chapter 14, Finland's emphasis on education is at a high international level, which is also reflected on how the country ranks in productivity comparisons and competitiveness. Know-how and competitiveness are buffers that a small nation can use to acquire operating possibilities in a globalizing world. In the new economy, making use of know-how is not restricted to domestic circles alone. One of the most successful new economy companies in the world, Nokia, is an example of worldwide utilization of know-how and networking: at the beginning of 2001, Nokia had 55 cooperating research and development laboratories in 15 countries. However, the emphasis of research and development is still in Finland: less than 3 percent of Nokia's sales revenue comes from Finland but 45 percent of its basic research units and 65 percent of its total research and development operations are located in Finland (Castells and Himanen 2001, p. 21).

In the 1990s, especially after joining the EU, Finland has continued removing restrictions on foreign investments and free competition. The growth of investment by foreign companies is, however, best explained by increasing emphasis on technology and know-how and by a high standard of infrastructure. According to comparative studies, Finland also has high quality social capital: in comparisons concerning trust between citizens Finland belongs to the world leaders. The results show that as parties to agreement, Finns tend to be more trustworthy than other nationalities in average (Inglehart 1997, p. 174), which may somehow compensate the disadvantages of the country's remote geographic location and climate.

Figure 16.1

Direct Investments between 1980 and 1999 (FIM billion)

1 = To Finland
2 = From Finland

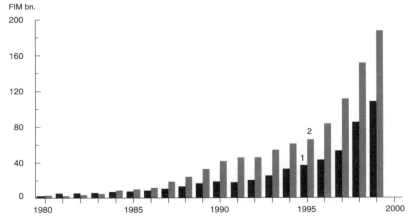

Source: Pajarinen and Ylä-Anttila 2001.

Know-how and competitiveness are reflected both in Finnish companies' investments abroad and foreign companies' investments to Finland. Since the end of the 1980s, with the exception of the slump years in the early 1990s, direct investments to and from Finland have increased very rapidly, as seen in Figure 16.1 (Pajarinen and Ylä-Anttila 2001, p. 12).

A typical aspect of the globalization of Finnish economy is the growing use of foreign labor. In 2001 Finnish companies employed 212,000 persons abroad. Between 1997 and 2001, their personnel grew by 3 percent in the home country, but persons working abroad increased by 28 percent, in other words from 26 to 33 percent of all employees of industrial enterprises. The growth of R&D personnel working abroad was slower, from 19 to to 22 percent. This indicates a willingness of Finnish industry to retain experts in the home country. (www.tt.fi/arkisto/getoriginal.pl)

In its industrial policy, Finland has aimed at making the country an appealing location especially for high technology companies, both from Finland and abroad. A look at the growth of foreign investments by sectors on industry may give an idea on the success of that policy. When a distinction is made between the traditional (i.e., resource-intensive, labor-intensive, and scale-intensive) sector on the one hand and the new specialized-suppliers and science-based sector on the other, certain bases of Finland's rapid globalization become clear. From 1980 to 2000, the employment of the science-based sector increased by almost 60 percent whereas employment in the labor-intensive sector decreased by approximately 40 percent. Correspondingly, employment in high technology increased by 80 percent while low technology lost 40 percent of its employment. This development illustrates on a general level the qualitative change of Finland's employment. The rapidly rising level of know-how has attracted increasing numbers of foreign companies to Finland, which shows in their investments' emphasis on high technology (Pajarinen and Ylä-Anttila 2001, pp. 2–4, 15–20).

Traditionally, the location of industrial production has been determined by three key factors: the search for raw material, markets, and labor force. However, this situation has changed as a consequence of the lighter weight of raw material and products, and improved transportation techniques. Also, the closeness of markets has lost some importance. On the other hand, it seems that both the skills and the costs of labor have become more important. An additional consideration may be the cultural environment and other infrastructure available to the personnel.

The problems faced by the welfare state are often mentioned as the downside of globalization (Cf. e.g. Esping-Andersen 1996; Julkunen 2001b, pp. 48–56). Multinational corporations can transfer their production wherever the production costs – above all labor costs – are the lowest. This creates unemployment and brings down wage levels in the developed countries which are no longer able to execute independent social policies but must listen to the demands of multinational corporations. These corporations demand a competitive level of capital taxation and, frequently, less progressive personal taxes. For example, Nokia CEO Jorma Ollila's remark on Finland's high taxation levels and the possibility of moving the company headquarters out of Finland caused a stir in November 2001.

A relatively even income distribution is, however, one of the characteristics of welfare states and they cannot function without fairly progressive tax rates. They may also offer many advantages. The education system in Finland, free of charge, tax-funded and of a high standard, and the efficient yet inexpensive health care system are examples of the advantages not within reach of the developing countries. In addition, developed infrastructure, stable political climate and a high level of social capital (trust) speak in favor of welfare state. However, welfare states, too, have begun competing in taxation and this may well lead into some social dumping. The extent to which the Finnish welfare state took the pressures of globalization into account is discussed in the following Chapter 17.

Finland is a globalized country, dependent on world markets. Its business fluctuations promptly follow whatever changes occur in larger economies, especially in the USA and Germany. So far the internationalization of Finnish companies has not advanced as far as the internationalization of companies in many other industrial countries, but the process has been very rapid at the turn of the millennium. Finland has also become globalized in another sense: in cross-national comparisons it ranks among the most developed countries in the world, and there are abundant tools for communication, such as Internet connections. Contacts on the level of civil society are numerous as well. It would be tempting but is not yet possible to conclude what impact globalization has had on the welfare state. Only the coming years will prove whether or not Finns need to sacrifice some of their earnings and social security in order to meet pressures from the outside. *[OR]*

Foreign Policy

"Finland participates in international co-operation for the protection of peace and human rights and for the development of society."

The sentence may sound like a quotation from a government program, but it is actually another example of the new approach to constitutional law (see Chapter 14). It belongs to Section 1 of the Constitution of 1999 which, first of all, defines Finland as a sovereign republic. Perhaps one might interpret the final words "development of society" to imply that Finland also attempts to act in the world for its own benefit, in order to protect and further its national interests, which is the most obvious goal of any country's foreign policy.

Transnational organizations are essential for the role that governments have assumed in globalization. Forty years ago the *Yearbook of International Organizations* already listed over 1200 such organizations, of which 150 were intergovernmental. In Chapter 2 (page 53) references were made to Finland joining such organizations. Between the two world wars the League of Nations was considered very important, and since the Second World War Finland, too, has been active in several world wide and regional organizations. Their emergence and activity have reflected globalization and, on the other hand, they have played an important role in facilitating the process of globilization. Indeed, and perhaps for the first time in history, they have proved that nations have become aware of common interests and that their shared problems can only be solved through some solidarity and cooperation.

The international institution with the broadest global coverage is the United Nations Organization, founded in 1945 and joined by Finland in 1955. Already in 1956 Finland participated in the First UN Emergency Force in Sinai, and an active role in UN peace keeping operations has continued ever since (see Chapter 11, page 188) Twice, in 1970–1972 and 1989–1990, Finland was member of the United Nations Security Council, and in 2000–2001 former prime minister Harri Holkeri chaired the 55th General Assembly. In its own UN policy Finland has stressed consistently "the protection of peace and human rights" which are central goals also in the UN Charter and in the Universal Declaration of Human Rights. Finland has attempted to strengthen the United Nations Organization in many ways because of its goals and because it is considered particularly valuable for small countries.

The liberation of international trade was one of the basic preconditions permitting even small countries to turn increasingly to world markets. As described in Chapter 2, Finland became an associate member of the European Free Trade Association (EFTA) in 1961 and a full member in 1986. Before that, Finland had strengthened its intergovernmental relations in several functional organizations joining the International Bank for Reconstruction and Development (IBED, the World Bank) and the International Monetary Fund (IMF) in 1948 and the General Agreement of Tariffs and Trade, GATT (since 1994 the World Trade Organization WTO) in 1949. It has belonged to the Organization for Economic Co-operation and Development (OECD) since 1969, and a free trade agreement with the EEC was made in 1973.

A regional multinational forum of great significance for Finland has been the Conference on Security and Cooperation in Europe (CSCE), which became the Organization for Security and Co-operation in Europe (OSCE) in 1995. Finland also took part in the activities of the Council of Europe long before joining it as a member in 1989.

The Nordic Council, which Finland joined in 1955, supplemented by the Nordic Council of Ministers in 1971, represents close cooperation within a smaller region. It continues to act as permanent reminder and initiator of cooperation, and it can be thought of as a pioneer of many practical achievements in integration: abolishing passports within the Nordic area (1952), agreeing on an open labor market (1954), social security (1955), and non-citizens' right to participate in another Nordic country's local elections (1973).

However, from Finland's point of view, one multinational organization is more important than any of the others. "The European Union is the most central field of action of our foreign policy," declared Dr. Erkki Tuomioja, the minister for foreign affairs, and the ministry's annual report certified that "the European Union is the cornerstone of Finland's international activity. The EU is an umbrella, under which most European political and economic cooperation takes place. Finland wants to develop the Union to be a safer anchor of Europe" (Ulkoasiainministeriö 2001, pp. 4, 8).

In other words, Finland no longer acts alone on the international scene. Brussels has become the venue of many contacts that would have been dealt with directly in earlier years and that would have been discussed bilaterally rather than as a part of the EU's policy.

When the Cold War ended, Finland's neutrality lost its most essential content. The original purpose of NATO, the North Atlantic Treaty Organization, was also lost and soon it began to invent for itself new tasks in the less divided world. An innovative new idea was the launch of the Partnership for Peace program (PfP) in 1994. Finland joined the program already in May 1994. In 2000, NATO's 19 members could count 27 other countries as their "peace partners," extending from Ireland and Albania to Russia and Kyrgyzstan (Heikkilä 2000, pp. 154–157). Finland's bilateral cooperation with NATO has been deepened not only in practical military cooperation for crisis management purposes (see Chapter 11), but also in participation in the Intensified Dialogue with NATO and the Euro-Atlantic Partnership Council (EAPC) since it was established in 1997. An ambassador was also accredited to NATO in 1997. (See Sivonen 2001.)

None of this cooperation, however, is supposed to lead Finland to NATO membership. Non-alignment has remained the government's official policy line, while applying for NATO membership has been reserved, at most, as one policy alternative, applicable in that event that circumstances change and make membership justifiable. Sweden's policy has been similar, or even more cautious than Finland, and NATO membership has remained a non-issue in Austria, Switzerand, and Ireland. If the governments opt for membership in NATO, one difficulty they will face is the need to convince the very resistant public opinion. The Finnish people have ruled out NATO membership constantly. Opinions turned even more negative as a consequence of the war in Kosovo in 1999 and, again, during the 2001 war in Afghanistan. In late October 2001, military alignment had the support of no more than 16 percent of the Finns, while non-alignment was supported by 79 percent (MTS 2/2001).[87]

It is somewhat tricky to belong to the core of the EU while remaining outside NATO and being only an observer in the Western European Union. However, this did not prevent the election of Finland's commander-in-chief Gustav Hägglund to the chair of the EU's Military Committee, which began to function in April 2001.

---

87 One month later, another survey found that 11 percent favored and 65 percent opposed NATO membership "under the present circumstances" (EVA 2002, p. 65).

Generally speaking, the Finnish people have been accustomed to accepting the country's official foreign policy: a national consensus has been typical of both the elites and the people. During the Cold War, communists were the only important opposition to the country's security policy (Törnudd 2001, p. 259). Also membership of the EU and EMU are accepted by the opponents as unavoidable facts of life. Opinion surveys have indicated that a very large, albeit flexible, majority of the people (87 percent in 2001) have been satisfied with how Finland's foreign policy has been conducted (MTS 2/2001).

Foreign and security policy covers a broad range of tasks; on the one hand the stregthening of human rights, democracy, development, and legal order, and on the other crisis management, arms control, and preventive diplomacy. Furthermore, the tasks include the prevention of environmental hazards and the fight against terrorism, crime, and drug trade. Trade policy takes care of the preconditions of the nation's wellbeing. It thus furthers internationalization through agreements and cooperation, and it helps Finnish exports, opening doors for businesses.

The broad range of foreign policy is also evident in the fact that within the government appointed in 1999, political responsibilities of the ministry for foreign affairs are divided among four ministers. In addition to the minister for foreign affairs and the minister for foreign trade, the minister of defense handles Nordic cooperation, and development aid was the task of the minister of environmental protection (since 2002 of the minister of taxation). Because European Union affairs concern all ministries, their coordination was transferred in 2000 from the ministry for foreign affairs to the office of the prime minister. The personal role of the prime minister in foreign policy making has also become quite central.

In 2001 Finland maintained diplomatic relations with 170 countries. There were 950 persons working in the ministry for foreign affairs and 1590 persons in the 98 missions on five continents. About 400 honorary consulates complete the picture. There has been some pressure, for fiscal rasons, to reduce some missions, while the ministry for foreign affairs has wanted to strengthen the network of Finnish missions abroad.

The developing countries have been supported by Finland politically and financially in UN policies, through other organizations, through the EU, and directly. However, development aid has also met fiscal limitations. In 1990 Finland spent 0.7 percent of its GDP on aid to developing countries. That was the share agreed among the Nordic countries. However, due to the economic crisis it was lowered to 0.35 percent by 1994 and has remained on that level since then, only slightly higher than the average aid paid by other EU countries. Since 1994 development aid has increased only as the result of Finland's growing GDP, but not as a percentage. In 2002 it amounted to 479 million euros. The government's aim in 2002 was to raise it in five years to 0.4 percent of the GDP.

Globalization and the enlargening EU area also leave room for regional emphasis, such as the "northern dimension," which the EU acknowledged in 1997. Finland's neighborhood strategy focuses on north-eastern Russia, Estonia, Latvia, Lithuania, and Kaliningrad. This is the area that Finland has supported financially, concentrating mainly on environmental protection, nuclear safety, energy, and forestry. Also, Finland has supported the efforts of the three Baltic countries toward EU membership and cultivates close bilateral relations with Estonia and the two others.

Naturally one should not forget the great regional importance to Finland of well established Nordic cooperation. The five Nordic countries have been traditionally an important reference group in Finland's intergovernmental relations and they remain important even though the EU has replaced them as Finland's primary refence group. The prime ministers of the three Nordic EU members also meet to discuss how to coordinate their EU policies. Cooperation with Sweden has been especially close and practical. *[PP]*

A Case Story: Boycotting Another EU Member

On Sunday evening, 30 January 2000, Prime Minister Paavo Lipponen received a telephone call from his Portuguese counterpart Antonio Guterres inviting Finland to join the boycott that 14 EU countries would declare against Austria, a fellow EU member, if the Freedom Party were included in that country's new government. Lipponen agreed, and on the following Monday he approved the final text which was communicated on the same day to Austria's president Thomas Klestil. Austria would be punished if it adjusted its government formation to the result of the parliamentary election of October 1999, where the voters had strongly endorsed Jörg Heider and his anti-immigrant Freedom Party, which did not "share joint Europan values." Formally the boycott was not decided by the EU, but it contained 14 separate but coordinated governmental decisions.

The action did not have the intended effect: on February 4th, Austria formed a government with Freedom party as a coalition partner. Prime Minister Lipponen then advised the Finnish administration on how to avoid contacts with Austrians, as was done in the 13 other EU countries. Austrian diplomats were to be ignored in international meetings, hands were not to be shaken with them. Perhaps the hasty decision of the 14 governments was unwise but there was no easy way to call off the boycott either. Finally, a group of "wise men" chaired by Finnish ex-president Martti Ahtisaari was sent to Vienna and reported that there was nothing wrong with Austria's European attitudes. They reached their conclusion in one day, although normally their findings would have required quite extensive social science research. In the autumn the boycott was ended.

A comparable, even clearer case of a breach of "joint European values" took place when a new Italian government was formed in 2001. The conservative Silvio Berlusconi became prime minister and he included in his government Umberto Bossi, leader of the anti-immigrant Lega Nordia. This time the other EU states did not react, although Bossi continued to demand policies contrary to "joint European values," including his proposal to build a wall along the border between Slovenia and Italy. The Belgian foreign minister Louis Michel called Bossi "an anti-immigrant fascist." Ahtisaari's report had concluded that the ministers of the Austrian government had not used unacceptable racist and anti-immigrant language, whereas it would not have been possible to draw such a conclusion a year later from the speeches of all Italian ministers.

In Finland the opposition reacted to the Austria boycott as follows: "In taking its position Finland has interfered with the formation of another country's government... Such an important decision should be made with the participation of the central government members and the government's Committee on Foreign Affairs." And further: "It has not been revealed how the guidelines of sanctions against Austria were decided." To this the prime minister answered that the procedures were "decided on the basis of an informal discussion within the government."

Later, Prime Minister Lipponen was reprimented by Finland's chancellor of justice for overstepping his powers, because an agreement to Portugal's proposal, according to the Constitution Act, required President Ahtisaari's decision; only later was Ahtisaari asked his opinion and gave his approval to Lipponen's decision. It is possible that Lipponen already had in mind the new Constitution of 1999, although it became effective one month later.

This incidence warrants a few general observations:

- Situations may arise that call for instant foreign policy decisions at any time.

- A small country can hardly stand alone against the unanimous opinion of its reference group. Foreign policy decisions depend not only on their actual content, but also on the image they create outside the country.

- The members of the European Union do not treat each other equally; the small ones are more vulnerable to pressure from others than the big ones.

- European policies can be motivated by domestic policy considerations; in this case the socialist governments of most EU countries may have been motivated by their worry about conservative trends in Europe or by alarming right wing populism in their own country.

- Legally correct procedures are important; great care must be taken about exactly when new legislation enters in force and changes decision-making procedures.

- Finland's chancellor of justice makes his decisions independently of the country's political leadership. *[PP]*

17 Finnish Vitality

The new liberal stance in economics and economic policies has assessed the role and scope of the public sector much more critically than was the case with the dominant Keynesian economic policies during the era of the welfare state expansion.

Harrinvirta 2000, p. 187

Finland shows that a fully fledged welfare state is not incompatible with technological innovation, with the development of the information society, and with a dynamic, competitive new economy.

Castells and Himanen 2001, p. 114

New Features in Democracy

Many governmental institutions in to-day's Finland have their roots in the period 1809–1917 when Finland was an autonomous state within the Russian empire, and the Finnish political system has shown considerable continuity throughout its 85 years of independence. There are only twelve other countries that have had an uninterrupted democratic government during this period. The new constitution, passed by the Eduskunta in 1999 and effective since March 1, 2000, did not introduce deep changes either, although it revised Finland's Constitution Act of 1919 and Parliament Act of 1906/1928 far beyond a simple "maintenance check-up."

In the 1980s, popular pressure began to demand more direct democracy. At the same time, political pressure was pushing toward a more consistently parliamentary system of government. As a consequence, direct presidential elections replaced the electoral college in 1994 and a consultative referendum was arranged in the same year on the important issue of joining the European Union. Other amendments to the constitution had already reduced presidential power: in 1987 the power of veto was weakened and in 1991 the president's power to dissolve parliament was made conditional upon the prime minister's initiative. Such changes were justified as a counterbalance to the additional strength that the head of state gained when his/her mandate was drawn directly from the people.

It became customary to argue that parliamentarism is more democratic than presidential power, despite the fact that the president, too, obtains a mandate from the people. Obviously such an argument well suited the political elite, who want efficient and centralized procedures in national decision-making and a firm role for the political parties. It also suited the politically active citizens who feel efficacious and capable of acting through conventional party channels, whereas stronger parliamentary power at the cost of a less powerful president did not appeal so well to alienated and non-efficacious citizens. The government justified its proposal with an increase in democracy; parliament's own constitution committee went further than the government bill toward reducing presidential powers; and the mood continued in parliament's plenary debates. At this stage the president's independent powers were weakened in the areas of government formation and foreign policy.

Much of the actual content of the new constitution will be formulated when it is implemented in concrete situations in the future. Therefore, the actions of the first president under the new constitution and her relations with other governmental institutions are going to leave an especially strong mark. President Halonen seems to have stretched her powers in the direction of keeping the president an important political actor; perhaps she has also been helped in this by mutual trust strenghened during her previous political cooperation as an SDP minister in the governments of Prime Minister Lipponen, who has wanted to avoid the impression of challenging her.

Membership of the European Union since 1995 has had very important consequences in Finnish politics. According to the new constitution, "The Government is responsible for national preparation of the decisions to be made in the European Union and decides on the concomitant Finnish measures, unless the decision requires the approval of the Parliament" (Section 93). The EU connection has influenced Finnish legislation and it has multiplied the foreign contacts of almost every ministry of the government, also forcing ministers and high civil servants to travel frequently to various meetings of the EU. Parliament's grand committee was converted to a new role when it became the committee on European affairs. In other ways, too, the Finnish parliament monitors approaching EU decisions more closely than the parliaments of other EU states. The members and entire committees of the Finnish parliament also maintain foreign contacts by traveling to other countries (and willingly to very distant ones).

Parliamentary procedures have been streamlined in various ways. Until 1995 Finland's Parliament Act was exceptional in granting a suspensive veto to minorities of one-third: the agreement of at least 67 members could send a bill pending until a new parliament was elected. This right added much to the negotiating power of the opposition and, accordingly, its termination weakened the parliamentary opposition. As was described in Chapter 9, the Constitution of 1999 expedited the handling of bills by combining the first and the second reading and making the grand committee's review optional. The efficiency of individual MPs was increased, among other things when parliament began to pay for their assistants.

Despite the procedural reforms and the aim of the reformers of the Finnish constitution, it seems that parliament's role in decision-making is not as central as was intended, while both the government and the bureaucracy have gained in power. The real winner is the prime minister. His position is quite comparable to the other heads of government in the EU.[88] The era of short-lived and often unstable Finnish governments ended after the 1970s; once formed, the government has occupied an increasingly firm leadership position throughout the entire four-year election term. The new constitution and Finland's EU membership have strengthened the government and its prime minister, and very seldom has the government been frustrated by the will of parliament.

The development of the entire public sector has been characterized by the principle of more efficient public management. And because the scope for expanding public expenditures is politically very limited, it has been necessary, in Finland as in other OECD countries, to attempt to improve public services through results-oriented budgeting systems. Demands for efficiency have lead to privatization of public businesses, fees for the use of public services, and less government intervention in the market economy (cf. Harrinvirta 2000, pp. 186–190). While strengthening its position in political decision-making, public administration has become more transparent and service-oriented.

Democratic governance presupposes not only well functioning and well interacting political institutions, but also an active civil society, legitimacy of the political system, and channels for citizen participation in it. These prerequisits exist in Finland, and they too changed a great deal during the last decade of the 20th century. Information communicated in the mass media reaches more people in Finland than in many other nations, and international comparisons indicate that the Finnish people are relatively well aware of public affairs.

The linkages, even overlaps, between the state and civil society have made the Finnish system "a governmental civil society and a civil societal government." A majority of the Finnish people has felt that popular movements transmit citizens' opinions to decision-makers better than political parties do (EVA 2001a, pp. 42–43). As far as the large old movements are concerned, three of them have become especially strong, namely, the trade unions, the sports movement, and the cooperatives.

Labor market organizations in particular have acquired much power in Finland's political decision-making. The influence of the trade union movement has left its mark in labor legislation and economic legislation,

---

88 During his second government Paavo Lipponen also became the longest serving EU prime minister.

and its representatives are continuously present when economic policy decisions are made. An unusually high proportion of the Finnish labor force belongs to trade unions, and large numbers obviously add to the movement's power. The ordinary members are hardly active at all inside the unions, but they trust the leadership to take care of their interests. In their attachment to their union the rank and file members are becoming less communitarian; the young tend to be pragmatic and approach their union membership more instrumentally. (See Chapter 5, page 95).

The sports movement has a broad base among the population and it can also count on influence through political friends, because one-fifth of the members of parliament are themselves active leaders within the movement. They belong to the sports network of MPs. Being on good terms with sports obviously improves their chances in elections. The expansion of the cooperative movement, in turn, could be interpreted as a reaction to the victorious rise of capitalism and market economy since the 1980s, in Finland as well as abroad. The cooperative movement has a solid national base. It is easy for Finnish consumers to believe that cooperatives further people's interests better than large international companies that are entering Finnish markets.

Finland has its political tensions and conflicts. Nevertheless, consensus and corporatism are typical features of the political system. Nationalism and democratic values are deeply rooted, but declining voter participation has become a serious problem in Finland, as it has in many other western democracies.

A trend away from communitarian solidarity, comparable to what is happening in the trade unions, can be seen in people's class identification: fewer and fewer people identify with any social class. This makes the traditional description of the leftist parties as workers' parties seem rather obsolete, and it has made the old time "class struggle" a less and less realistic description of the social situation. The disappearing class identity is naturally related to a more general social change. The class differences have been diminishing in objective terms as well, while it is possible that new class structures are emerging, such as a tripartite division into "the successful, the persevering, and the ignored" (Silvasti 2002).

The citizens' political participation has become more individualistic and the mobilization of the electorate is more cognitive than before, in Finland and in other countries. New single cause movements appear, but such movements seldom organize large mass demonstrations any more. They have learned to make use of the publicity which the mass media provide for them. While the rising level of education has broadened cognitive mobilization within the electorate, emphasis on education has also been an essential precondition for Finland's new economy and economic growth.

In elections the Finns want to vote for individual candidates whom they trust, but politicians as a group are subject to much criticism and the people's trust in government is low in Finland. This may be a result of stable times with no particular external threats. The country feels more secure and also more influential than ever before; survival is no longer at stake, although national defense is strongly endorsed by the citizens. On the other hand, many feel that sovereignty is threatened by the increasing power of the EU and by the Union's gradual deepening toward federalism.

After more than seven years of membership the people of Finland really do not embrace the European Union, but it has had a deep influence on their legislation and political institutions. Globalization has been another essential aspect of the economy and it has influenced the political system and its various institutions. On the other hand, popular support for political and governmental institutions is very much directed toward those domestic institutions that provide order and security, while people are cool toward politics in general and politicians in particular. The same tendency is largely true of most other EU countries.

In its chapter on the basic rights of citizens, the new constitution lists general values and political goals that are similar to prestigious international declarations but which, therefore, differ from the more strictly legal-formal approach of the old constitution. In reality some of the basic social rights of the citizens may not be fully met and some are not even achievable. There also exists a built-in structural tension in the implementation of social services, although this is not the case in social insurance, which is handled on the national level. Namely, the state has given primary responsibility for implementing the people's social welfare and basic education to the self-governing municipalities, but local governments often lack the resources to comply to the extent the state and the citizens expect.

Changes in the Finnish political system have been caused both by internal and external reasons. Many developments, such as lower electoral participation, declining party activity, the personalization of politics, and the country's new approach to public sector management, are shared with other western countries, although some changes may have been faster in Finland than in many other countries. The party system represents fair stability in the country: although it has not remained "frozen," it has not changed as fast as the society around it. *[PP]*

Testing the Finnish Welfare State

In the end of the 1980s, Finland climbed to the welfare state level already reached in Sweden and Denmark. This achievement was a result of decades of development; social policy had been systematically improved especially since the beginning of the 1960s (see Chapter 2). The expansion of social policy was made possible by the country's economic progress: in the period from the early 1950s to the end of the 1980s the annual growth of gross domestic product averaged well over 3 percent.

However, at the beginning of the 1990s, the Finnish welfare state was harshly tested. It had to justify its existence in the hardship of a difficult economic recession by attempting to secure its citizens' welfare. "How did the welfare state survive the consequences of the serious recession?" was a crucial question asked in the early part of this book (page 51).

The threats lay mainly in the unexpected downward turn of the economy (see Chapter 15), although ideological reform pressures directed at the welfare state have also been mentioned. Its consequences included accelerated inflation, currency overvaluation, and major indebtedness of both households and firms. The situation became acute in the years 1989 to 1992 as the central bank continued to maintain a fixed exchange rate by raising interest rates. The rates fluctuated between 12 and 18 percent while inflation was reduced from 6 to 2 percent. This made the real interest rate rise radically in a short time, and many firms and households ended up in great difficulties. Seemingly insuperable problems accumulated for thousands of citizens of the welfare state. Many faced unemployment, bankruptcy, or long-term debt burden, some even two or all three of these personal disasters.

It has been said that "Finland fell from the heavens." Demand for export products decreased, the country's competitiveness weakened, and asset prices collapsed. In four years, from 1990 to 1993, the economy's output fell by over 10 percent (cf. Figure 15.2) while unemployment increased from 3.1 percent in 1989 to 17 percent in 1993. The depth of Finland's crises can be readily seen in the comparisons with other countries shown in Figure 15.1 and in Table 17.1. Furthermore, the exceptionally high unemployment was linked to numerous other social policy problems that the welfare state had to assume responsibility for. The consequences of bankruptcies and over-indebtedness were not as clearly designated the responsibilities of the welfare state as those of unemployment. A widespread banking crisis forced the government, in other words the tax payers, to rescue a significant part of the banking system (cf. Kalela et al. 2001, pp. 3–4; *SYF 2001,* p. 362). All these factors contributed to problems faced by the welfare state at the same time as rapidly growing public debt threatened the financing of social policy.

Due to budget deficits the fiscal balance worsened alarmingly. Some observers began to doubt the sustainability of the welfare state. They saw that the problems were results of excessively generous social benefits, labor market rigidities and high taxes, factors that, in their opinion, discouraged investments and job creation (Kalela et al. 2001, p. 7).

The entity of factors leading to the severe slump has been called "bad banking, bad luck, and bad policy" (op. cit., p. 4). The state did facilitate the solution of the banking crisis, and while not much could be done about bad luck, that is the international recession and the timing of the collapse of the Soviet Union, Finland alone was responsible for its own policy. One of the most important reasons for the depression, the overvaluation of the Finnish markka and the consequent lack of competitiveness, was removed when the markka, together with many other currencies in the European Monetary System (EMS), was first floated and, in autumn 1992, significantly devalued.

Table 17.1

The economic crises of the late 1980s and early 1990s in Finland, other Nordic countries, EU, and USA

Countries	Years of recession	Increase of unemployment (%-points)	Relative employment change (%)	Largest output gap* (% of GDP)	Change of inflation (%-points)
Finland	1990–93	14.9	−18.8	−11.3	−6.0
Sweden	1991–93	6.5	−14.7	−5.3	−9.5
Norway	1988–90	3.9	−8.7	−4.3	−7.3
Denmark	1987–93	4.5	−6.5	−5.5	−3.5
EU	1992–93	3.7	−4.0	−2.9	−3.1
USA	1990–91	2.2	−1.0	−2.5	−2.8

*OECD estimate

Source: OECD Economic Outlook (2000); cf. Kalela et al. 2001, p. 5.

The recovery, which began in 1993–94, had made Finland one of the most competitive countries in the world by the end of the 1990s. Lower interest rates, a rise and stabilization in asset prices, and the solution to the banking crisis were important ingredients in the recovery (op. cit., p. 8). Budget deficits were turned into surpluses which ended the emergency in fiscal balances (see Table 17.2). In any case, even at its worst, Finland's public debt had ranked second lowest in the EU, and its growth slowed down in 1997 and 1988. These factors eased economic concern for the welfare state.

Table 17.2

Fiscal balance in the crisis (percent of GDP)

Countries	Surplus in boom 1987–90	Surplus in bust 1991–95	Surplus in year 2000	Change from boom to bust	Change from bust to 2000
Finland	6.3	−7.9	4.0	−14.2	+11.9
Sweden	5.4	−12.3	3.4	−17.7	+15.7
EU	−2.5	−6.5	0.3	−4.0	+6.8
USA	−4.1	−4.7	1.7	−0.6	+6.4

Source: OECD Economic Outlook (2000); cf. Kalela et al.2001, p.7.

The quick recovery of the economy was apparently facilitated, not only by political corrections and improved economic trends, but also by two factors connected to the welfare state that have not yet been mentioned. Firstly, education, having become more efficient in the last decades of the twentieth century and now recruiting talent reserves effectively from all social classes and groups, provided high-level human capital (see Chapter 14). This made it possible to quickly adopt and create new technology, something that was illustrated by the very rapid growth in the IT sector (cf. Castells and Himanen 2001). Secondly, firms were offered a favorable environment thanks to high-level social capital. The level of Finnish social capital is visible in studies comparing trust between citizens and occurrence of corruption around the world. When the shift to the new economy required the creation of networking economy, rather than hierarchic corporate structures, social capital was of great significance.

The survival of social capital and social moral, and of legitimacy, through the slump years was backed by the welfare state structures that had been set up in the second half of the twentieth century. These structures were intended to help all citizens and especially those who face difficulties as a result of recession or similar misfortune. But did the structures also endure the pressure of attacks directed at the welfare of citizens and especially the least well-to-do? Despite the quick recovery of the economy, there has been much discussion in Finland about whether or not the recession left its mark on welfare state. Many think that Finland has still been unable to rid itself of certain problems that emerged then, despite the country's extraordinary economic rise; problems mainly concerning unemployment, the distribution of wealth, poverty, and exclusion. Although they are not independent of the economy, improving the economic parameters alone will hardly solve them.

Unemployment figures illustrate the extremity of the change caused by the recession. In October 1990, there were 90,000 unemployed; exactly three years later the number was 460,000 (*Bulletin of Statistics 1990–1994;* cf. Ritakallio 2001, pp. 426–427). Such a drastic development was thought to deeply influence the distribution of wealth and the nation's well-being. Studies on disposable income show that the inequality of the population had decreased remarkably between 1966 and 1976, the early stage of the development of welfare state, but then remained almost constant until the 1990s.

Despite the manifold growth of unemployment, inequality measured by disposable income increased only slightly during the slump and shortly after it (1990 to 1994). However, the distribution of wealth has changed very rapidly since 1994. Measuring by factor income, the distribution of wealth started to become less equal already in the second half of the 1970s and the trend accelerated distinctly at the beginning of the 1990s. Until the mid-1980s, building the welfare state and the related income transfers (see Chapter 14) were enough to flatten down the difference between population groups in gross income (factor income + transfers) and disposable income. A steady stage followed, lasting until the end of the recession, when the differences between gross incomes and disposable incomes started to increase rapidly (Riihelä et al. 2001, p. 386).

The social policy safety net managed quite well in taking care of households where the breadwinner had become unemployed. The most direct and severe impact was experienced by small entrepreneurs who had gone bankrupt, and by over-indebted households (cf. Ritakallio 2001, p. 426). The welfare state had largely been built on the assumption of full employment and it included the idea of a work society, the utopian nature of which has been emphasized critically (cf. Rahkonen 1990, 650–653; Riihinen 1985). A deep, long-term depression may be a problem endured better in welfare states than in other types of states, but one which nevertheless leaves its scars.

The reasons for unemployment have, understandably, been widely discussed in Finland. One theory is that technological development has increased unemployment; after all, it is precisely this factor that has been especially significant in Finland. However, scholars do not generally accept such an interpretation (Pohjola 1998, p. 8; Riihinen 1998, p. 31) and the increase in unemployment especially in the 1990s is mainly attributed to rising real interest rates and tougher taxation - that is, mistakes made in financial policy (Kiander and Pehkonen 1998, pp.172–175).

The recession seems to have expedited certain social changes. For one, the proportion of household income from work in relation to capital income started to decrease, although the majority of Finnish households (85.8 percent) still received more income from earnings in 1998, that is, from labor income plus entrepreneurial income. However, the proportion of capital income had increased from 6.6 percent in 1990 to 15.1 percent in 1998. Researchers have not been able to show any single reason for the distributional changes, but it has been argued that the redistributive role of the state budget has weakened (Riihelä et al. 2001, pp. 386–387). The new role has been justified by the aim of reducing public debt as quickly as possible. The importance of this aim is reinforced by the rapid change in the age structure and the consequent rise in pension expenditure from about 2010. Those who disagree cite the fact that Finland's public debt in proportion to its national income is one of the lowest in the EU.

The fact that unemployment is still at a high level is problematic, especially as the proportion of long-term unemployed has also increased. The government's goal of halving unemployment between 1995 and 1999 was not reached: the unemployment rate remained as high as 10.2 percent in 1999 (*SYF 2001*, p. 362). When unemployment was beginning to increase in 1991, the proportion of the long term unemployed (people out of work for more than a year) was only 2.5 percent of the total number. But this share grew rapidly, peaking at 30.5 percent in 1997. Since then, the proportion has not declined much; in 2001 it was 27.4 percent (www.mol.fi/tiedotus). Finland has started to resemble the majority of OECD countries and especially the EU countries in which, since the mid-1980s, almost 50 percent of the unemployed have been out of work for more than a year (Pehkonen 1998, p. 241).

The slump's effects were dampened by the fact that a significant part of the unemployed were entitled to earnings-related unemployment benefit at the beginning of the recession. Thus, low-income poverty, surprisingly, did not start increasing during the recession but remained at a low international level. In this respect, the fortifications of the welfare state endured very well. The extent of unemployment of course meant impoverishment, but due to the unemployment benefit system only a few fell below the poverty line. Poverty, however, is a multi-dimensional phenomenon: there are several other criteria besides low-income poverty (Ritakallio 2001, p. 427).

The content and development of poverty has been studied exceptionally closely in Finland by using five different measuring methods: (1) relative income – income less than 50 percent of the median; (2) consensual deprivation – the proportion who involuntarily forgo items ranked necessary by the majority of the people; (3) the subjective feeling of meager subsistence; (4) the subjective feeling of over-indebtedness; and (5) receipt of social assistance. Comparative studies made in 1995 and 2000 yielded interesting results: poverty increased using the relative income method but decreased using the other methods. Between 1995 and 2000, the proportion of those who were poor according to at least one indicator decreased from 28 to 21 percent and the proportion of those who were poor according to at least two indicators decreased from 13 to 8 percent.

In this light poverty seems to have decreased in the second half of the 1990s. When the data were divided according to various background factors, the same trend was visible quite consistently. There was one exception, however: the unemployed. In the 1995 study, the unemployed already formed the worst-off group, according to all the indicators. But by 2000, the gap between the unemployed and the others had widened. In 1995, a large proportion of the unemployed received earnings-related unemployment benefit but since this form of benefit is temporary in nature, an increasing number have been left with the minimum assistance (op. cit., pp. 420–422). Thus, long-term unemployment becomes a poverty problem for a group of people in a society that grows wealthier around them.

Long-term unemployment and poverty as its consequence do not affect all age groups similarly. They are clearly more common in the older age groups. Age itself does have some influence on employability, but what probably has more weight is the strong negative correlation of age and level of education. In 1995, 14 percent of the population aged 25 to 34 lacked post-primary level education while the percentage among people aged 55 or more was as high as 53. In Finland, the education level disparity between the youngest and the oldest age groups is one of the widest among the OECD countries (Rajavaara and Viitanen 1997, p. 55). This special feature is due to the strong education policy, a policy that has also led to international success (see Chapter 14.6). It has, however, also widened the gap between age groups. As stated before, the changes in the structure of the Finnish economy have been exceptionally dramatic. In a society like this, aging people with a low level of education are easily excluded.

Consequently, it would seem that Finnish society now tolerates phenomena such as poverty and exclusion better than before the recession. Did the recession really bring a new approach towards welfare state?

Years earlier it had already been predicted that a part of the middle-class population might change their attitude towards the welfare state when it calculated that its own interests would be better served and its own welfare better realized if social policy income transfers were reduced (Riihinen 1983). Since then the growth of the middle class and the collapse of the neighboring communist superpower have laid the way for possible welfare state reductions without fear of weakening the legitimacy of state and society (Riihinen 1992). This way of thinking has spread in the organs of both state and local government: they wish to limit the costs of the welfare state. The majority still disagrees with this although the population is becoming more middle-class. In the 1990s, support for the welfare state has steadily and significantly increased (see Chapter 14, page 217). The recession, having concerned not only the disadvantaged but a part of the middle class as well, has apparently taught citizens to value safety mechanisms more than before.

The post-recession attitude change, characterizing the thinking of the ruling elite rather than the majority of the people, has been interpreted in the light of certain international ideological and economic changes. The objectives set in the EU include an active welfare state, investment in human capital, productive social policy, employment-friendly social policy and taxation, inclusion (e.g., preventing and decreasing marginalization), efficiency of services, cost awareness, and quality. This program does not have deregulative features although it aims at limiting costs. It is, however, more market friendly than the building stage of the welfare state (Saari 1999; cf. Julkunen 2001a, p. 285).

It has been argued that blocking cost increases has become the central political goal. Reductions have begun in both the level of benefits and what they cover, and the availability and level of the services, while the citizens' own responsibility has been emphasized. This involves the aim to re-build incentive structures and control systems. Whereas the concept of decommodification was attached to the expansion of welfare state (see Chapter 14), the term now is recommodification, strengthening social security's dependency on labor and finance markets. In other words, the aim is to prune the part of social security that clashes with working.

In pension policy, the new approach is being realized by strengthening the benefits' dependency on working history and insurance contributions. More means-testing, activity, compensation, and sanctions will be applied (Mestrovic 1997; Rodger 2000, pp. 143–163; Myles and Pierson 2001; cf. Julkunen 2001a, pp. 287–288). This development as a whole can also be studied from the viewpoint of globalization and its competitiveness requirement (see Chapter 16), and it is often claimed that neoliberal ideology has spread even to the left-wing parties.

"Can the welfare society maintain its goals under the pressure of globalization and increased international competition?" was another question asked at the beginning of this book (page 48). The Finnish experience suggests a positive answer. Although inequality seems to have increased in Finnish society after the recession, the equity index, a comparison based on numerous indicators and covering practically all the countries of the world, ranks Finland the second most equal country after Sweden. Furthermore, the Human Wellbeing Index, also based on numerous indicators, ranks Denmark, Finland, and Norway as the three countries with the greatest wellbeing (Prescott-Allen 2001, pp. 150–153, 177–180). *[OR]*

Unsolved Political Issues

While the Finnish people consider the existing safety mechanisms of the welfare state an essential element of their governance, political decision-makers are under great pressure to find solutions for many crucial problems: what are the sustainable standards and the eventual preferences of social policy goals in the changing society; how can the policies agreed be most efficiently implemented; and how will the necessary resources be provided? As was implied above, there is a particular need to find new, innovative solutions to the country's problems of unemployment, wealth distribution, poverty, and exclusion, and to attempt to define the desirable distribution of wealth.

Unemployment and the changing age structure deeply touch the basic values of the welfare state as well as the economy of the country. The future wellbeing of the Finns depends much on how well these problems can be solved. Politicians and other citizens have conflicting opinions on the allocation of resources between the alleviation and elimination of unemployment, age-related services, and the reduction of government debt. Naturally, much will depend on the speed of economic growth. The government's predictions of future growth have been cautious since the 1990s rather than optimistic.

In this context, taxation requires decisions that concern both its level and its structures. The time has come to make serious plans for a comprehensive tax reform. As mentioned above, the CEOs of certain large Finnish companies that operate inrternationally have begun to warn about the dangers of excessively high taxation. Pressures to lower taxes have been appearing from various directions, while the minister of finance has warned about reducing state revenues too rapidly.

It is now generally accepted in Finland that the changing age structure will soon cause increasingly heavy financial burdens on the working population. Higher retirement ages are being planned and they will ease the situation somewhat, but the changing age structure would be tackled more comprehensively by looking at the question of population renewal. This problem is shared by all EU countries. Families are small and the present renewal rate is far below 2.1 which would at least keep the population constant. Therefore, there is need to scrutinize family policies, although this will not suffice unless social attitudes also change. It is already too late to raise the birth rate soon enough. Problems connected with immigration will need to be solved in Finland, a country that has received relatively few foreigners so far.

In the international context Finland belongs to the countries of Western Europe. The one issue that became salient at the beginning of the 21st century concerns Finland's membership of the North Atlantic Treaty Organization. During the Cold War Finland, together with Sweden, Austria, Switzerland, and Ireland, abstained from cooperation with either NATO or the Warsaw Pact. Neutrality was the basic foreign policy line. In the 1990s, the Warsaw Pact was discontinued and NATO broadened its functions. Finland, like numerous other non-members, began to cooperate with NATO as a peace partner and as a participant in joint peacekeeping missions (see Chapters 11 and 16).

However, membership of the organization remained out of the question and non-alignment was the accepted policy line. In the new millennium the president of the republic and the government's ministers began to treat NATO membership as one possible option for the future, although by no means a timely question. Public discourse on this issue intensified. Some opponents even feared that the political elite intended to "smuggle" Finland into NATO despite the strong opposition of mass opinion.

The government has not taken any stand beyond nonalignment. It is reviewing what is happening in the international environment and how NATO itself is changing, and will wait at least until NATO makes its decision on the membership of the Baltic countries. As of spring 2002 Finnish political leaders seemed to be aiming at a tactic that sounds inconsistent but could potentially help to bypass the unwilling electorate: they agreed that after the parliamentary election in March 2003 the new government program will only confirm the traditional policy of nonalignment, which might keep this issue out of the election campaign, whereas the new government will take a stand, possibly in favor of membership in 2004, when it is due to present to parliament its long-term plans in the second review of the government report "European Security Development and Finnish Defence."[89] The report was submitted to parliament in 1997 and covers Finland's defense development up to 2008. The first review, approved by parliament in 2001, dealt largely with the structures and the equipment of the defense forces, but the debate in parliament tended to concentrate on two separate problems, namely, NATO membership and the closing of local garrisons.

---

89   In 2002, as the parliamentary election of 2003 was approaching, two cabinet members raised their profiles, requesting a popular referendum on NATO membership. So did the national convention of the Center Party.

Even inside the Lipponen government there appeared some disagreement on this issue, or at least different tendencies. In the opinion of the minister of defence Jan-Erik Enestam, membership of NATO is no longer a big deal; in practice it would only mean a change in Finland's status. He also thought that in the future the core of the EU would include only countries that belong to both NATO and EMU (*Suomen Kuvalehti* 4/2002, pp. 20–21). But obviously the political decision-makers need to respect Finnish public opinion which opposes membership quite strongly.

Finland's relation to the future development of the European Union is not unproblematic either. The most central debate concerns federalist tendencies in the EU and the role of small member states when the biggest members are increasing mutual cooperation and, at the same time, apparently paying meager attention to the interests of smaller EU countries. The discussion about writing a constitution for the EU has been interpreted as an attempt to bring about federalism. Even without such a debate, the political elite in Finland, as elsewhere, has to meet much public criticism about the benefits derived from EU membership, about unwelcome directives, and of the functions and procedures of EU institutions.

The differences between regions (see Chapter 4) cause political tensions, and internal migration makes the regional problems very serious. While a modern economy attracts active population toward the centers, the age structure of the peripheral areas gets older relatively fast. There is no longer high rural fertility to compensate for the loss of inhabitants. The situation is becoming critical; many rural areas may soon be empty. Such a trend has been obvious for a long time, and the vicious circle involves even more: it is an interaction between population, the economy, culture, and politics (Riihinen 1965). Neither farming subsidies nor domestic and European regional policies seem to solve the problem; the few token transfers of government offices out of the Helsinki metropolitan region have offered symbolic rather than effective remedies.

In their analysis that focuses on the Finnish information society, Manuel Castells and Pekka Himanen name seven challenges that, in their opinion, are the most fundamental ones for Finland to address (Castells and Himanen 2001, p. 103). Three of them concern the economy, namely, the divide between the old and the new economy, the vulnerability of Finland to the volatility of the global economy, and the conflict which exists between the current needs of the new economy and the lack of business-oriented entrepreneurialism among young people. Two of the seven problems are social or value-related, namely, the rise of new inequalities and the cleavage between the old Protestant ethic and the new ethic[90] of the information creators. These contradictions are dicussed elsewhere in this chapter.

Finally, two of the seven contradictions on the list concern the political system more directly. One is found between the information society

---

90   The authors write about "hacker ethic," but they do not mean hackering as criminal activity.

and the governmental structures of the industrial age, and the other one is between strong national identity and integration in a multicultural world. To these observations one might add that at least many procedures within the Finnish bureaucracy have been modernized. For instance, e-mail is used to such an extent that paper has been largely eliminated from inter-administrative correspondence. Also, the present strong national identity and a global orientation of the people may often be complementary rather than opposing attitudes.

Finnish democracy would seem more vital if the citizenry were more active politically but the fact is that party organizations have become smaller and weaker, often unable to attract adequate numbers of young members, and the prestige of the parties among the mass electorate is low. More and more people abstained from voting in elections in the 1990s. Individualized political interest and single-issue movements do not compensate for the obvious need to introduce some new activism and new idealism into party organizations and more excitement into election campaigns. Even the election system is being reviewed with additional voter appeal in mind. *[PP]*

The Neomodern Country

Chapters 2 and 3 of this book described how Finland developed into a modern society greadually between 1860 to 1950: how a new kind of industry was born, legislation on civil liberty and economic freedoms was implemented, a Finnish identity and national ideology emerged, the Finnish language rose to a leading position, civil society was activated, the legislature was vitalized and democratically reformed, the nation state was built before the country gained its independence, and national defense and foreign policy safeguarded the final steps to modern Finland.

The Finnish welfare state emerged before the Second World War, but its actual breakthrough occured in the 1960s. When it matured enough to meet Nordic criteria, the society had already developed to a stage described as 'post-industrial.' At this stage, for example, the employment in the processing sector began to decrease while the service sector gained a stronger foothold. Soon the 'modern' society became old-fashioned, a development illustrated above by the changing trade structure (Table 2.1).

Modernization and modernism are two different concepts, but they have had somewhat similar effects on the history of Finland. One of the key triggers of Finland's modernization in the latter half of the 19th century was the national romantic ideology. It idealized the past and promoted the idea of Finnishness and the position of the Finnish language. This ideology advanced modernization by renewing political thinking and class consciousness and by furthering the creation of a nation state.

Modernism, on the other hand, represented a new way of thinking and a new ideology. It aimed at new, international ways of expression, most of all in the arts and architecture, and it caused a revolution in traditional

Finnish culture. Sibelius's music was not modernistic but it advanced the society's modernization by supporting national objectives. Eliel Saarinen's world-famous architecture was modernistic while also national romantic, as his work represented *art nouveau* (in Finland known by the German term *Jugend*), a style fitting the spirit of modernism. The architect Alvar Aalto who represented modernistic functionalism, no longer illustrated national emphasis, although he left a permanent mark in Finnish culture. Eric Hobsbawm has described modernism in the following manner: "...in the first half of the century 'modernism' worked, the feebleness of its theoretical foundations unnoticed, the short distance to the limits of development permitted by its formulas (e.g. twelve-tone music or abstract art) not yet quite traversed, its fabric uncracked as yet by inner contradictions or potential fissures" (Hobsbawm 1995, p. 515).

What succeeded modern society has been characterized with many terms, such as 'postmodern' and 'late modern.' On the other hand, society seems to have shifted into a global stage where international and global influences mark people's lifestyle. Therefore, the stage in the development of Finnish society from the end of 1980s is here called 'neomodern.' This concept refers to both postmodern and global characteristics. In addition, it refers to a society that aims at combining economic efficiency, sustainable development, and social justice. If modernization and modernism made Finnish society more international, then the neomodern stage will continue on the same path inestimably further.

A comparison of Figure 2.1 and Table 2.1 (in Chapter 2) makes it obvious that changes within the production structure of an industrialized society can no longer be described by means of the changing primary, secondary, and tertiary production. Society's transition from an industrial to a post-industrial one could be comprehended as rapid expansion of its service sector, at the cost of the two other sectors, but since the 1970s the expansion of the service sector has not continued much. What characterises society's new, still strengthening development is the central importance of education and information for occupations that support production. This change has brought about a new type of society, generally called the 'information society.'

Some changes have built foundations for the birth of a neomodern society. One of them is the expansion and improvement of education. It has been argued that a significant quantitative change also results in qualitative changes. This argument seems to apply excellently to the consequences of education in Finland. The expansion in education began at the end of the 1950s, and in 1972–1982 a comprehensive school reform laid the foundation for large-scale higher education. From 1950 to 2000, higher education expanded tenfold in Finland, as it did in a number of countries.

The efficiency of the Finnish school system, described in Chapter 14, is illustrated by a study by the OECD in 2000 on reading literacy, mathematical literacy and scientific literacy of the youth. It covered the OECD plus certain other countries. Finnish youth were clearly better than the rest in reading literacy and only Finland placed among the top four in all three categories. Both boys and girls were ranked best in reading literacy, and Finnish girls did extraordinarily well.

Finland's university education, too, has received very positive international evaluations. When the University of Helsinki celebrated its 362nd anniversary on March 26th, 2002, it noted its fifth place among the European universities carrying out basic research (after Cambridge, Oxford, Edinburgh, and Leiden). Furthermore, according to an OECD evaluation, adult education is organized best in Finland. Quite generally the people both understand and support efforts to continue improving education. In the fall of 2000, 79 percent of Finns agreed with the statement "Finland's success abroad is based on high-level and equal education" while only 9 percent disagreed (EVA 2001a, p. 62).

Finland's character as a neomodern rather than postmodern country involves the aim to develop as an information society. In addition to high-level education, the objectives of an information society also emphasize the creation of an innovation system. Government representatives see – justifiably or not – Finland as a forerunner in building an entity known as the national innovation system. This system consists of the producers and utilizers of new information and expertise, and their mutual interaction. Finland's national science, technology, and innovation policy is centrally shaped by the Science and Technology Policy Council, an expert body chaired by the prime minister. The share of research and development investments in GDP was 1.6 percent in 1985, but rose to 3.6 percent in 2001. Business has shown a growing interest in innovations: between 1991 and 2001 companies' share of R&D increased from 57 to 73 percent. (www.tekes.fi/eng/rd/policy; www. research.fi/k tk-menot fi.)

Since the state is responsible for funding Finnish universities, it provides industry and other business life with the basic knowledge exploited in technological and other innovations. Finland's actual research and development work is mainly carried out in four kinds of institutions: the National Technology Agency, the universities, state research institutes, and the Academy of Finland. In 2001, their respective funding shares in the state budget were 30, 26, 16 and 14 percent of total R&D funds, while 14 percent was used by others (www.research.fi/k tk-valtio.fi). Some scholars have criticized the state for exceedingly generous funding of the technological fields, while many liberal arts are struggling with quite unpleasant budget problems.

However, the institutions working with research and development do not have a clear division of labor and the work is not concentrated on technology alone but is multidisciplinary. For example, the research programs of the National Technology Agency in the 1990s included Genome Research Program and Cell Biology Research Program. Because more and more R&D funding comes from companies it is likely that business interests will weigh more in the future. Although the state emphasizes innovation, the educational programs of Finnish schools and universities cannot be considered one-sided or purely science-weighted.

Largely due to successful education and innovation policy, Finland has been able to rapidly increase its productivity and especially its research and development productivity. According to a comparison of 16 OECD countries in 1980 to 1998, the productivity of research and development increased faster only in Ireland (cf. Guellec and van Pottelsberge de la Potterie 2001). The Finnish level of R&D is illustrated by the fact that the Human Development Report 2001 (p. 48) ranked Finland the most technologically developed country in the world.

After 1970, Finland's economic development has been successful despite the slump in early 1990s. Both labor productivity and overall productivity increased from the beginning of the 1970s to the turn of the millennium at a pace approximately double the European average. In addition to the emphasis on research and development the pace is explained by a change in the industrial structure: the share of high technology products of all exports increased approximately fourfold from the beginning of the 1980s to the mid-1990s. The ability of the economy is illustrated by the fact that in 2001 Finland placed third in an international competitiveness comparison after the United States and Singapore (*The World Competitiveness Yearbook 2001*).

In cross-national comparisons of wealth Finland does not rank as high as might be suggested by its levels of education, technological development, and competitiveness. Finland's GDP per capita ranked eleventh of the OECD countries in 1999, with Luxembourg, Switzerland and Japan occupying the leading positions (OECD 2001, p. 23). The impacts of late economic development and the recession have not diminished entirely. Nevertheless, Finland has ranked high in international comparisons of wellbeing. Finland's strengths, despite its high unemployment, include its even distribution of wealth and small percentage of the poor. Also, the two genders and the different population groups have quite equal opportunities for influence within the society. Wellbeing in Finland ranked the second in the worldwide comparison by Robert Prescott-Allen and the tenth in UNDP's Human Development Report 2001. These studies emphasize differerent aspects, but both of them indicate a successful development. (Cf. OECD 2001, pp. 62–67; Prescott-Allen 2001, pp. 49–57; Human Development Report 2001, p. 141.)

As an information society, Finland was discussed above from the point of view of education and innovation policy. But the most practical feature of an information society consists of everyday communication. In this respect Finland is highly developed in three areas: the number of mobile phones per capita is greater than in any other country; Internet penetration is at high international level (*SYF 2001*, p. 635); and so is the people's exposure to mass communication (see Chapter 6). Such factors influence the entire society and its values. In daily routines they manifest themselves, among other things, in the fact that bank transactions are managed via the Internet far more frequently in Finland than anywhere else (Castells and Himanen 2001, p. 12).

Already before Finland reached its present level as an information society, Finnish values were typical of a prosperous nation. Postmaterialist values were replacing materialist ones from the 1970s onwards (see Chapter 7). A materialist orientation, as defined by Ronald Inglehart, emphasizes security, whereas postmaterialist values reflect a high regard for a humane society characterized by a say in working life and politics, freedom of opinion, a beautiful environment, and a society in which the ideas of individual citizens have significance. Finns have become clearly postmaterialist in their value orientation (Inglehart 1997, pp. 108–159).

The high regard for humane society is, above all, seen in ever-increasing support for the welfare state in the 1990s (see Chapter 14). Humane values are also reflected in the concern about inequality: 78 percent were troubled by the decrease in economic and social equality and 88 percent showed concern for regional inequality. The high percentages indicate that concern was also widespread among well-to-do Finns. Other causes for concern were the concentration of property and the dominant position of the market forces. Concern about the abuse of drugs and drug-related crime has rapidly increased in spite of the fact that, on the cross-national scale, drug abuse remains at a low level in Finland (EVA 2001a, p. 13).

Environmental issues have started to worry the Finns increasingly, although the state of the environment in the sparsely populated country may still be considered good. A majority of the people are ready to give up some of their commodities for the benefit of the environment (op. cit., p. 13). Finns seem to be worried about the global environment, too. A comparative study on environmental sustainability, carried out by Columbia University for the World Economic Forum, ranked Finland first among 142 countries. The environmental sustainability index used in the study consisted of 20 core indicators and 68 related indicators (www.ciesin.columbia.edu/indicators/ESI).

There are scholars in Finland who are not at all satisfied with the development of the country's environment (cf. Kuronen 2002) and the Finns carry on a constant debate on the functionality of the country's education policy (see Chapter 14). Good news about the international success of their policy does not curtail the will to argue. Critical attitudes toward both education and environment policies are typical of the Finns – as is their criticism of several other policies and the decision-makers. This is very apparent in the media, especially in letters to the editor. However, active criticism by citizens does not prove poor performance in any absolute sense. Interpreted in a positive way, critical attitudes can be seen as an indicator of a functioning democratic system and the citizens' willingness to participate in improving their society.

Despite globalization and the intense growth of international communication the Finnish identity has remained strong. In 2000, 72 percent of the people thought it was worthwhile to protect Finland's own distinctive cultural features against internationalization. Most people consider it a privilege to be a Finn, whereas traces of a European identity are creeping in very slowly (EVA 2001a, pp. 73–76). One might even interpret the expansion of the domestically based cooperative movement as one reaction to increasing internationalization, in this case to the entry of large international companies into the Finnish market. This would indicate a new cleavage between a civil society that stresses national interests, and a more and more international business life. It does not contradict the increase of international contacts of civil organizations, but civil society may be reacting to the threats of globalization as it reacted to the threat of Russification in the 19th and early 20th century.

The most visible changes in Finnish society at the turn of the century have concerned the welfare state and information society. As a welfare state, Finland reached one kind of a peak in the end of the 1980s. Since then the country, as a welfare state, has to some extent moved on to a post-expansive stage, impelled and motivated by the recession experience and frightened by the changing age structure. Education and research and innovation policies, however, still continue to expand.

Consequently, at the beginning of the new millennium, the post-expansive problems of the welfare state and the expansive problems of an information society are perhaps the most striking characteristics of Finnish societal policies. These policies consist of many important issues. Unemployment is largely a problem of the aging work force. Many workers within the older group have a significantly weaker education level than the young generation, and their potential poorly answers the demands of an information society. They are far more likely to become long-term unemployed and they face the risk of exclusion in a changing society. Not even efficient adult education has been able to eliminate the problem. The demands of an information society also exceed the capabilities of many young persons whose education level is low.

Most Finns consider unemployment of over nine percent to be a major problem, one reason being limitations set by the costs of unemployment on the other functions of the welfare state. For many, unemployment also poses a moral problem that should not exist in a welfare state. One approach in the constant quest for an answer to unemployment is to create more jobs in low-income sectors and support these sectors with tax relief.

What also seems typical of today's information society is that while thousands are unemployed, others suffer from stress caused by excessive work load. In the information sector people often work very long hours. It is claimed that too much work increases the risk of sickness and interferes with family life, also having a negative effect on children. In early 2002, the government, parliament, and the citizens have widely discussed family policies that would allow parents to spend more time with their children. The divorce rate is also high: of the OECD countries, only Belgium and Sweden had higher rates than Finland in 1995 (OECD 2001, p. 33). As was mentioned above, there is great concern about the declining birth rate, but the most essential topic in recent discourse is concern about claims that children are increasingly disturbed.

Indeed, it would be a severe mistake to see the present or the future as problem-free, either politically or socially. It is to the credit of neomodern Finland that the country seems to be avoiding the risk of this delusion. It acknowledges openly its difficult social problems. And a typical welfare state has the capability of reacting quickly to problems.

On the other hand, if the desired goals include the citizens' wealth, level of knowledge, and interest in the functions of the international community, the success of Finns has reached an unprecedented level. Finland's economy lagged far behind the most developed countries long into the 20th century and the country was handicapped by its peripheral location and geopolitical difficulties, but closed the gap by making use of catch-up benefits and the emphasis on education and research.

In the European context, the relative speed of this development merits the word success. A comparison of the Nordic countries with the economic development of Latin America adds another perspective. Uruguay and Chile are countries that had a GDP per capita quite similar to Finland in 1950, but thirty-five years later Finland's was almost three times as high. A primary explanation of the difference was the very fast population growth in Latin America. In addition, scholars who have analyzed the differences added to their list of explanations land reforms, education, the utilization of natural resources, industrial and trade policies, and consensus among organized labor, capital, and government. (Blomström and Meller 1991.)

At least two additional explanations are in order. First of all, political stability is one of the basic preconditions for economic and social development. Even during extreme circumstances, Finland was able to maintain and develop its firmly established democratic system. Secondly, social and political stability are connected to the high level of social capital in Finland. The people trust each other, corruption is rare, and cross-national comparisons tell of high social morals. In the 19th century the philosopher Johan Vilhelm Snellman emphasized that the strength of a small nation is in education. In neomodern Finland of the 21st century one might add: and in dynamic innovativeness. *[OR]*

References

Aarnio, Aulis. 1993. "Introduction," in Juha Pöyhönen, ed., *An Introduction to Finnish Law.* Helsinki: Finnish Lawyers Publishing Company.

Ahtiala, Pekka. 1997. "Talouspolitiikka ja lama." *Kansantaloudellinen aikakauskirja* 1/ 1997:61–85.

Ala-Kapee, Pirjo, and Marjaana Valkonen. 1982. *Yhdessä elämä turvalliseksi. SAK:laisen ammattiyhdistysliikkeen kehitys vuoteen 1930.* Helsinki: KK laakapaino.

Alapuro, Risto. 1973. *Akateeminen Karjala-Seura. Ylioppilasliike ja kansa 1929 ja 1930-luvulla.* Porvoo: Werner Söderström Oy.

Alapuro, Risto, and Henrik Stenius. 1987. "Kansanliikkeet loivat kansakunnan," in Alapuro, Ilkka Liikanen, Kerstin Smeds, and Stenius, eds., *Kansa liikkeessä.* Helsinki: Kirjayhtymä.

Alapuro, Risto, ed. 1998. *Raja railona. Näkökohtia suojeluskuntiin.* Porvoo: Werner Söderström Oy.

Alho, Kari, Markku Kotilainen, and Mika Widgrén. 1992. *Suomi Euroopan yhteisössä – arvio taloudellisista vaikutuksista.* Helsinki: Elinkeinoelämän Tutkimuslaitos B 81.

Allardt, Erik. 1997. "Tvåspråkigheten, finnarnas attityder samt svenskans och finlandssvenskarnas framtid i Finland," in *Vårt land, vårt språk,* Finlandssvensk rapport nr 35. Helsingfors: Svenska Finlands folkting.

Allardt, Erik, and Karl Johan Miemois. 1982. *Roots Both in the Centre and the Periphery: The Swedish Speaking Population in Finland.* Helsinki: RGCS. Research Reports 24.

Allardt, Erik, and Pertti Pesonen. 1967. "Cleavages in Finnish Politics," in Seymour M. Lipset and Stein Rokkan, eds., *Party Systems and Voter Alignments.* New York: The Free Press.

Anttila, Jorma. 1993. "Käsitykset suomalaisuudesta – traditionaalisuus ja modernisuus," in Teppo Korhonen, ed., *Mitä on suomalaisuus.* Jyväskylä: Gummerus.

Aromaa, Arpo, and Seppo Koskinen, (eds.). 2002. *Terveys ja toimintakyky Suomessa.* Helsinki: Kansanterveyslaitoksen julkaisuja B3/2002.

Arter, David. 1987. *Politics and Policy-Making in Finland.* Sussex: Wheatsheaf Books; New York: St. Martin's Press.

Arter, David. 1999. *Scandinavian Politics Today.* Manchester and New York: Manchester University Press.

Auer, Jaakko. 1956. *Suomen sotakorvaustoimitukset Neuvostoliitolle: tutkimus tavaroiden luovutusohjelmista, niiden toteuttamisesta ja hyvityshinnoista.* Porvoo: Werner Söderström Oy.

Bank of Finland Bulletin 1/2001.

Bennulf, Martin, Per Hedberg, Per Arnt Pettersen, and Pertti Pesonen. 1998. "Political Participation," in Anders Todal Jenssen, Pesonen, and Mikael Gilljam, eds., *To Join or Not to Join.* Oslo: Scandinavian University Press.

Berglund, Sten, and Ulf Lindström. 1978. *The Scandinavian Party System(s).* Lund: Studentlitteratur.

Bergman, Solveig. 1998. "Naiskehän moninaisuus. 'Uusi' suomalainen naislikke yhteiskunnallisena liikkeenä," in Kaj Ilmonen and Martti Siisiäinen, eds., *Uudet ja vanhat liikkeet.* Tampere: Vastapaino.

Blom, Raimo, and Harri Melin. 2002. "Luokat ja työmarkkinat 2000-luvun alussa," in Timo Piirainen and Juho Saari, eds., *Yhteiskunnalliset jaot. 1990-luvun perintö?* Helsinki: Gaudeamus.

Blomstedt, Yrjö. 1985. "A Historical Background of the Finnish Legal System," in Jaakko Uotila, ed., *The Finnish Legal System*. Helsinki: Finnish Lawyers Publishing Company.

Blomström, Magnus, and Patricio Meller. 1991. "Issues for Development: Lessons from Scandinavian-Latin American Comparisons," in Blomström and Meller, eds., *Diverging Paths*. Washington: Inter-American Development Bank.

Bloom, Allan. 1987. *The Closing of the American Mind*. New York: Simon and Schuster.

Boggs, Carl. 2000. " Intellectuals," in Gary Browning, Abigail Halcli, and Frank Webster, eds., *Understanding Contemporary Society: Theories of the Present*. London. Sage.

Borg, Olavi. 1990. "Työmarkkinajärjestöt jälkiteollisessa yhteiskunnassa," in Olavi Riihinen, ed., *Suomi 2017*. Jyväskylä: Gummerus.

Borg, Sami. 1997. "Kiinnostus puoluejäsenyyteen ja aktiivisuus puolueissa," in Borg, ed., *Puolueet 1990-luvulla*. Turku: Turun yliopisto, Valtio-oppi.

Borg, Sami. 1998. *Puolueet ja edustuksellinen kunnallisdemokratia*. Tampereen yliopisto, Kunnallistieteen laitos 1/1998.

Braybrooke, David, and Charles E. Lindblom. 1963. *A Strategy of Decision, Policy Evaluation as a Social Process*. New York: The Free Press of Glencoe.

Bulletin of Statistics. *Statistics Finland 1991–1994*. Helsinki: Edita.

Burner, David. 1996. *Making Peace with the 60s*. Princeton: Princeton University Press.

Castells, Manuel, and Pekka Himanen. 2001. *The Finnish Model of the Information Society*. Vantaa: Sitra Reports series 17.

Chuev, Feliks I. 1993. *Molotov Remembers: Inside Kremlin Politics; Conversations with Feliks Chuev*. Chicago: Ivan R. Ree.

Dalton, Russell J. 1999. "Political Support in Advanced Industrial Democracies," in Norris, Pippa, ed., *Critical Citizens*. Oxford: Oxford University Press.

Dalton, Russell J. 2002. *Citizens Politics,* 3rd edition, New York: Chatham House.

Davidson, R. 1969. *The Role of the Congressman*. New York: Pegasus.

Dyson, Kenneth. 1980. *The State Tradition in Western Europe. A Study of an Idea and Institution*. Oxford: Martin Robertson.

Ervasti, Kaijus, and Sampo Teittinen. 2000. "Yleiset tuomioistuimet," in Marjukka Litmala, ed., *Oikeusolot 2000*. Helsinki: Oikeuspoliittinen tutimuslaitos.

Esaiasson, Peter. 2000. "How Members of Parliament Define Their Task," in Esaiasson and Knut Heidar, eds., *Beyond Westminster and Congress*. Columbus: Ohio State University Press.

Esaiasson, Peter, and Knut Heidar. 2000. "The Age of Representative Democracy," in Esaiasson and Heidar, eds., *Beyond Westminster and Congress*. Columbus: Ohio State University Press.

Eskelinen, Heikki. 2001. *Aluepolitiikka rautahäkissä*. Kunnallisalan kehittämissäätiön Polemia-sarajan julkaisu nro 41. Vammala: Vammalan Kirjapaino.

Esping-Andersen, Gosta. 1990. *The Three Worlds of Welfare Capitalism*. Oxford: Polity Press.

Esping-Andersen, Gosta. 1996. "Positive-Sum Solutions in a World of Trade-Offs?," in Esping-Andersen, ed., *Welfare States in Transition. National Adaptions in Global Economies*. London: Sage.

Eurobarometer 54 (Autumn 2000). Brussel: European Commission.

Eurobarometer 55 (Spring 2001). Brussel: European Commission.

Eurobarometer 56 (Autumn 2001). Brussel: European Commission.

EVA 1995. *Epävarmuuden aika*. Helsinki: Centre for Finnish Business and Policy Studies.

EVA 1997a. *Indicators of the Finnish Society 1996/97*. Helsinki: Centre for Finnish Business and Policy Studies.

EVA 1997b. *Menestyksen eväät. Raportti suomalaisten asenteista 1997*. Helsinki: Centre for Finnish Business and Policy Studies.

EVA 1999a. *Mielipiteiden sateenkaari*. Helsinki: Centre for Finnish Business and Policy Studies.

EVA 1999b. *Suomalaisten EU-kannanotot. Syksy 1999*. Helsinki: Centre for Finnish Business and Policy Studies.

EVA 2001a. *Erilaisuuksien Suomi*. Helsinki: Centre for Finnish Business and Policy Studies.

EVA 2001b. *Mestareita vai maistereita? Raportti Suomen koulutusjärjestelmästä*. Helsinki: Centre for Finnish Business and Policy Studies.

EVA 2002. *Suomi, EU ja maailma*. Helsinki: Centre for Finnish Business and Policy Studies.

The Finnish Economy 4/1997. Helsinki: The Research Institute of the Finnish Economy.

Finnish Mass Media 2000. Helsinki: Statistics Finland..

Gross, Bertram M. 1966. "Preface: A Historical Note on Social Indicators," in Raymond A. Bauer, ed., *Social Indicators*. Cambridge, MA: The M.I.T. Press.

Guellec, Dominique, and Bruno van Pottelsberge de la Potterie. 2001. *R&D and Productivity Growth: Panel Data Analysis of 16 OECD Countries*. STI Working Papers 2001/3.

Haatanen, Pekka. 1992. "Elämän varjopuolelle joutuneiden parissa. Sosiaaliministeriö 1917–1939," in Haatanen and Kyösti Suonoja, *Suuriruhtinaskunnasta hyvinvointivaltioon. Sosiaali- ja terveysministeriö 75 vuotta*. Helsinki:VAPK

Haatanen, Pekka. 1998. *Työsuhdepolitiikka*. Helsinki: Valopaino.

Habermas, Jürgen. 1994. "Citizenship and National Identity," in Bart van Steenbergen, ed., *The Condition of Citizenship*. London: Sage.

Habermas, Jürgen. 1996. "Paradigms of Law," in *Cardosos Law Review*.

Hagfors, Robert. 1999. "The Convergence of Financing Structure 1980–1995," in *Financing Social Protection in Europe*. Helsinki: Ministry of Social Affairs and Health Publications 1999:21.

Halila, Aimo. 1960. "Suomen Voimistelu- ja Urheiluliiton historia. Ensimmäinen osa. 1900–1917," in Halila and Paul Sirmeikkö, *Suomen Voimistelu- ja Urheiluliitto SVUL 1900–1960*. Vammala: Vammalan Kirjapaino.

Halila, Aimo. 1965. "Kunnallinen itsehallinto," in Pentti Renvall, ed., *Suomalaisen kansanvallan kehitys*. Helsinki: Werner Söderström Oy.

Hanell, Tomas, Hallgeir Aalbu, and Jörg Neubaer. 2002. *Regional Development in the Nordic Countries 2002*. Nordregio Report 2002:2.

Harrinvirta, Markku. 2000. *Strategies of Public Sector Reform in the OECD Countries*. The Finnish Society of Sciences and Letters, Commentationes Scientiarum Socialum 57/2000.

Haveri, Arto. 2000. *Kunnallishallinnon muutokset ja niiden arviointi*. Helsinki: Suomen kuntaliitto.

Heikkala, Juha. 1998. *Ajolähtö turvattomiin kotipesiin. Liikunnan järjestökentän muutos 1990-luvun Suomessa*. Acta Universitatis Tamperensis 614. Vammala: Vammalan Kirjapaino.

Heikkilä, Kaisa. 2000. *Suomi ja Naton rauhankumppanuusohjelma*. Helsinki: Pääesikunnan kansainvälisen osaston julkaisuja 2/2000.

Heikkinen, Sakari, and Kai Hoffman. 1982. "Teollisuus ja käsityö," in Jorma Ahvenainen, Erkki Pihkala, and Viljo Rasila, eds., *Suomen taloushistoria 2. Teollistuva Suomi*. Helsinki: Tammi.

Held, David, and Anthony McGrew. 2000. "The Great Globalization Debate: An Introduction," in Held and McGrew, eds., *The Global Transformation Reader. An Introduction to the Globalization Debate*. Cambridge: Polity Press.

Hellsten, Katri, and Olavi Riihinen. 1985. "Arvot ja aatteet yhteiskunnallisessa muutoksessa ja sosiaalipolitiikassa," *Sosiaaliviesti* 6/85.

Helsingin Sanomat daily. 2000–2002.

Hentilä, Seppo. 1992. "Urheilupolitiikasta liikuntapolitiikkaan," in Teijo Pyykkönen, ed., *Suomi uskoi urheiluun.* Helsinki: VAPK-kustannus.

Henttinen, Annastiina. 1999. "Kolmannen tien etsijät," in Markku Kuisma, Henttinen, Sami Karhu, and Maritta Pohls, *Kansan talous. Pellervo ja yhteinen yrittäminen 1899–1999.* Tampere: Tammer-Paino.

Higher Education Policy in Finland. 1996. Ministry of Education. Helsinki: Nykypaino.

Hjerppe, Riitta. 1989. *The Finnish Economy 1860–1985. Growth and Structural Change.* Helsinki: Government Printing Centre.

Hobsbawm, Eric. 1995. *The Age of Extremes. The Short Twentieth Century 1914–1991.* New York: Vintage.

Honkasalo, Markku. 2000. *Suomalainen sotainvalidi.* Keuruu: Otava.

Honkasalo, Markku. 2001. *Suomalainen sotainvalidi. Tilasto-osa.* Helsinki: Siniprint.

Human Development Report 2001. Making New Technologies Work for Human Development. 2001. New York: Oxford University Press.

Hämäläinen, Sirkka. 1998. "Statement on the occasion of the closing of the accounts for 1997." *Bank of Finland Bulletin* 1/72.

Härmälä, Sanna. 2000. "Hallintolainkäyttö," in Marjukka Litmala, ed., *Oikeusolot 2000.* Helsinki: Oikeuspoliittinen tutkimuslaitos.

Härmälä, Sanna, and Jyrki Tala. 2000. "Laillisuusvalvonta ja asiamiesjärjestelmät," in Marjukka Litmala, ed., *Oikeusolot 2000.* Helsinki: Oikeuspolittinen tutkimuslaitos.

Hänninen, Jarmo. 1995. "Uusosuustoimintaliike Suomessa," in Pekka Pättiniemi, ed., *Sosiaalitalous ja paikallinen kehitys.* Helsinki: Helsingin yliopisto. Osuustoimintainstituutti.

Ilmonen, Kaj. 1998. "Uudet ja vanhat yhteiskunnalliset liikkeet," in Ilmonen and Martti Siisiäinen, eds., *Uudet ja vanhat liikkeet.* Tampere: Tammer-Paino.

Ilmonen, Kaj, and Pertti Jokivuori. 1998. "'Kypsän' vaiheen liike jälkiteollisessa yhteiskunnassa," in Ilmonen and Martti Siisiäinen, eds., *Uudet ja vanhat liikkeet.* Tampere: Tammer-Paino.

Ilveskivi, Paula. 2000. *Perusoikeudet sosiaaliturvalainsäädännön toimeenpanossa.* Kansaneläkelaitos. Sosiaali- ja terveysturvan tutkimuksia 57. Vantaa: K-Print.

Inglehart, Ronald. 1997. *Modernization and Postmodernization.* Princeton: Princeton University Press.

Inkilä, Arvo. 1969. *Kansanvalistusseura Suomen vapaassa kansansivistystyössä.* Helsinki: Otava.

Isaksson, Guy-Erik, and Voitto Helander. 2001. *Interpellationer i Norden: Kontroll eller propaganda?.* Åbo: Akademis förlag.

Jaakkola, Magdalena. 2000. "Finnish Attitudes towards Immigrants in 1987–1999." *Yearbook of Population Research in Finland XXXVI.* Helsinki: The Population Research Institute.

Jakobson, Max. 1998. *Finland in the New Europe.* Westport, Connecticut: Praeger.

Jallinoja, Riitta. 1983. *Suomalaisen naisasialiikkeen taistelukaudet.* Juva: Werner Söderström Oy.

Jansson, Jan-Magnus. 1982. "Eduskunta ja toimeenpanovalta," in *Suomen kansanedustus-laitoksen historia XII.* Helsinki: Eduskunnan historiakomitea.

Jansson, Jan-Magnus. 1985. "Language Legislation," in Jaakko Uotila, ed., *The Finnish Legal System.* Helsinki: Finnish Lawyers Publishing Company.

Jensen, Torben K. 2000. "Party Cohesion," in Peter Esaiasson and Knut Heidar, eds., *Beyond Westminster and Congress: The Nordic Experience.* Columbus: Ohio State University Press.

Jokivuori, Pertti, Kimmo Kevätsalo, and Kaj Ilmonen. 1996. *Ay-jäsenen monet kasvot. Tutkimus SAK:n, STTK:n ja Akavan jäsenistä.* Jyväskylä: Jyväskylän yliopiston sosiologian tutkimuksia 60.

Julkunen, Raija. 2001a. "Jälkiekspansiivinen hyvinvointivaltio," *Janus.* Vol 9, 4/2001.

Julkunen, Raija. 2001b. *Suunnanmuutos. 1990-luvun sosiaalipoliittinen reformi Suomessa.* Tampere: Vastapaino.

Juntto, Anneli. 1999. "Asuminen," in Kristiina Andreasson and Vesa Helin, eds., *Suomen vuosisata.* Jyväskylä: Gummerus.

Jutikkala, Eino. 1988. Kuolemalla on aina syynsä. Porvoo: Werner Söderström Oy.

Jutikkala, Eino, with Kauko Pirinen. 1996. *A History of Finland.* Porvoo: Werner Söderström Oy.

Jäntti, Markus, Olli Kangas, and Veli-Matti Ritakallio. 1996. "From Marginalism to Institutionalism," in *Review of Income and Wealth.* Series 42, Number 4.

Järvelin, Jutta. 2001. *Health Care System in Transition. Finland.* Copenhagen: European Observatory on Health Care Systems.

Kaase, Max, and Kenneth Newton. 1995. *Beliefs in Government.* Oxford: Oxford University Press.

Kaase, Max, and Samuel H. Barnes. 1979. "In Conclusion: The Future of Political Protest," in Barnes and Kaase et al., *Political Action.* Beverly Hills: Sage.

Kaase, Max, and Alan Marsh. 1979. "Political Action Repertory: Changes Over Time," in Samuel H. Barnes and Kaase et al., *Political Action.* Beverly Hills: Sage.

Kalela, Jorma, Jaakko Kiander, Ullamaija Kivikuru, Heikki A. Loikkanen, and Jussi Simpura. 2001. "Introduction," in Kalela, Kivikuru, Loikkanen, and Simpura, eds., *Down from the Heavens, Up form the Ashes. The Finnish economic Crisis of the 1990s in the Light Economic Social Research.* Government Institute for Economic Research. Saarijärvi: Gummerus.

Kansalaismielipide ja kunnat. Ilmapuntari 2000. Vammala: Kunnallisalan kehittämissäätiö.

Karisto, Antti, Pentti Takala, and Ilkka Haapola. 1999. *Matkalla nykyaikaan. Elintason, elämäntavan ja sosiaalipolitiikan muutos Suomessa.* Porvoo: Werner Söderström Oy.

Kaukiainen, Yrjö. 1981. "Taloudellinen kasvu ja yhteiskunnan muuttuminen teollistuvassa Suomessa," in Kaukiainen, ed., *När samhället förändras – Kun yhteiskunta muuttuu.* Historiallinen arkisto 76. Helsinki: Suomen Historiallinen Seura.

Kautto, Mikko. 1999. "Is there a Nordic Model of Financing Social Protection?," in *Financing Social Protection in Europe.* Helsinki: Ministry of Social Affairs and Health Publications 1999:21.

Keinänen, Päivi. 1999. "Työttömyys," in Kristiina Andreasson and Vesa Helin, eds., *Suomen vuosisata.* Jyväskylä: Gummerus.

Kekkonen, Jukka. 1999. "The development of the Finnish judicial system since independence," in Jorma Selovuori, ed., *Power and Bureaucracy in Finland 1809–1998.* Helsinki: Prime Minister's Office.

Kekäle, Petri. 1999. *MTS-Tutukimukset 1998.* Helsinki: Maanpuolustustiedotuksen suunnittelukunta.

Kiander, Jaakko, and Jaakko Pehkonen. 1998. "Työttömyyden kasvun syyt," in Matti Pohjola, ed., *Suomalainen työttömyys.* Helsinki: Taloustieto.

Kivimäki, Timo, and Teija Tiilikainen. 1998. "Suomen EU-politiikan haasteet," in Erkki Berndtson and Kivimäki, eds., *Suomen kansainväliset suhteet.* Acta politica 9, Helsingin yliopisto, Yleisen valtio-opin laitos.

Komiteanmietintö 1986:6. 1986. *Aluepolitiikkatoimikunnan mietintö.* Helsinki: Valtion painatuskeskus.

Konttinen, Esa. 1998. "Uusien liikkeiden tuleminen subjektiviteetin puolustamisen kulttuuri-ilmastossa," in Kaj Ilmonen and Martti Siisiäinen, eds., *Uudet ja vanhat liikkeet*. Tampere: Tammer-Paino.

Korpijaakko-Labba, Kaisa. 2000. *Saamelaisten oikeusasemasta Suomessa*. Kautokeino: Sámi instituhatta.

Kuronen, Ilpo. 2002. Suomiko ympäristöasioissa maailman ykkössijalla?," in *Helsingin Sanomat*, March 4, 2002.

Kuusi, Pekka. 1961. *60-luvun sosiaalipolitiikka*. Porvoo: Werner Söderström Oy.

Kytömäki, Juha, and Erja Ruohomaa. 1999. *YLE – a public service for everyone*. The Finnish Broadcasting Company, Audience Report 1999.

Lane, Jan-Erik, and Svante O. Ersson. 1995. *Politics and Society in Western Europe,* 3rd. ed. London: Sage.

Lappalainen, Tuomo. 2000. "Ensimmäiset viisi vuotta," in *Suomi 5 vuotta Euroopan unionissa*. Helsinki: Eurooppa-tiedotus.

Lappi-Seppälä, Tapio, Jyrki Tala, Marjukka Litmanen, and Risto Jaakkola. 1999. *Luottamus tuomioistuimiin*. Helsinki: Oikeuspoliittinen tutkimuslaitos.

Lehtimaja, Lauri. 1999. "Eduskunnan oikeusasiamies perus- ja ihmisoikeuksien valvojana." *Lakimies* 6–7/1999.

Letto-Vanamo, Pia. 2000. "Euroopan unionin oikeus Suomessa," in *Suomi 5 vuotta Euroopan unionissa*. Helsinki: Eurooppa-tiedotus.

Liikanen, Ilkka. 1987. "Kansanvalistajien kansakunta," in Risto Alapuro, Liikanen, Kerstin Smeds, and Henrik Stenius, eds., *Kansa liikkeessä*. Vaasa: Kirjayhtymä.

Lijphart, Arend. 1984. *Democracies*. New Haven and London: Yale University Press.

Lipset, Seymour Martin. 2001. "Cleavages, parties, and democracy," in Lauri Karvonen and Stein Kuhnle, eds., *Party Systems and Voter Alignments Revisited*. London and New York: Routledge.

Linnakylä, Pirjo et al. 2000. *Lukutaito työssä ja arjessa. Aikuisten kansainvälinen lukutaitotutkimus Suomessa*. Jyväskylä: ER-paino.

Litmala, Marjukka. 2000. "Oikeusongelmat," in Litmala, ed., *Oikeusolot 2000*. Helsinki: Oikeuspolittinen tutkimuslaitos.

Litmanen, Tapio. 1998. "Kansainvälinen ydinvoiman vastainen liike ja sen suhde ydinaseiden vastaiseen liikkeeseen," in Kaj Ilmonen and Martti Siisiäinen, eds., *Uudet ja vanhat liikkeet*. Tampere: Tammer-Paino.

Lyytinen, Eino. 1996. "The foundation of Yleisradio, the Finnish Broadcasting Company and the early years of radio in prewar Finalnd," in Rauno Endén, ed., *Yleisradio 1926–1996. A history of broadcasting in Finland*. Yleisradio Oy.

Mair, Peter. 1997. *Party System Change*. Oxford: Oxford University Press.

Mansner, Markku. 1981. *Suomalaista yhteiskuntaa rakentamassa. Suomen Työnantajain Keskusliitto 1907–1940*. Jyväskylä: Gummerus.

March, James G., and Herbert A. Simon. 1958. *Organizations*. New York: John Wiley & Sons.

Martikainen, Tuomo, and Hanna Wass. 2002. "Laskeva äänestysaktiivisuus sukupolvi-ilmiönä." *Politiikka* 1/2002.

Mauranen, Tapani. 1987. "Osuustoiminta – kansanliikettä aatteen ja rahan vuoksi," in Risto Alapuro, Ilkka Liikanen, Kerstin Smeds, and Henrik Stenius, eds., *Kansa liikkeessä*. Helsinki: Kirjayhtymä.

McRae, Kenneth D. 1997. *Conflict and Compromise in Multilingual Societies: Finland*. Waterloo, Ontario: Wilfrid Laurier University Press.

Mestrovic, Stjepan. 1997. *Postemtional Society*. London: Sage.

Milbrath, Lester W., and M.L. Goel. 1977. *Political Participation*. Chicago: Rand McNally.

MTS (Maanpuolustustiedotuksen suunnittelukunta). *Tiedotteita ja katsauksia* 2/2001. Helsinki: Puolustusministeriö.

Myles, John, and Paul Pierson. 2001. "The Comparative Political Economy of Pension reform," in Pierson, ed., *The New Politics of the Welfare State*. Oxford: Oxford University Press.

Myllymäki, Arvo. 1979. *Etujärjestöt, tulopolitiikka ja ylimmät valtioelimet*. Tampere. Finnpublishers.

Myllymäki, Arvo, and Eija Tetri, 2001. *Raha-automaattiyhdistys kansalaispalvelujen rahoittajana*. Vammala: Vammalan kirjapaino.

Myllyntaus, Timo. 1992. "Vaaran laelta toimiston nurkkaan – taloudellinen kehitys ja elämänmuodon muutokset," in Marjatta Rahikainen, ed., *Suuri muutos. Suomalaisen yhteiskunnan kehityspiirteitä*. Vammala: Vammalan Kirjapaino.

Myrdal, Gunnar. 1957. *Economic Development and Under-Developed Regions*. London: Gerald Duckworth & Co.

Myrdal, Gunnar. 1958. *Value in Social Theory*. London: Routledge and Paul Kegan.

Myrskylä, Pekka. 1999. "Elinkeinorakenne," in Kristiina Andreasson and Vesa Helin, eds., *Suomen vuosisata*. Jyväskylä: Gummerus.

Noponen, Martti. 1989. "Kansanedustajan valitsemisprosessi ja poliittinen ura;" and "Kansanedustajan toimi, sen hoitotapa ja kehitys," in Noponen, ed., *Suomen kansanedustusjärjestelmä*. Porvoo: Werner Söderström Oy.

Nordiska arbetsgruppen för regionalpolitisk forskning. 1978. *Nordisk forskning om regionalpolitik i imvandling*. Stockholm: GOTAB.

Nousiainen, Jaakko. 1998. *Suomen poliittinen järjestelmä*. Porvoo: Werner Söderström Oy.

Nousiainen, Jaakko. 2000. "From Semi-Presidentialism to Parliamentary Government: The Political and Constitutional Development in Finland," in Lauri Karvonen and Krister Ståhlberg, eds., *Festschrift for Dag Anckar on his 60th Birthday*. Åbo: Åbo Akademi University Press.

Numminen, Jaakko. 1961. *Suomen nuorisoseuraliikkeen historia I. Vuodet 1881–1905*. Helsinki: Otava.

Numminen, Jaakko. 1999. "The Council of State," in Jorma Selovuori, ed., *Power and Bureaucracy in Finland 1809–1998*. Helsinki: Prime Minister's Office.

Nurmela, Sakari, Juhani Pehkonen, and Risto Sänkiaho. 1997. *Viiltoja suomalaiseen yhteiskuntaan*. Helsinki: Publications of the Office of the Council of State 1997/6.

Nygård, Toivo. 1987. "Poliittisten vastakohtaisuuksien jyrkentyminen sanomalehdistössä," in Päiviö Tommila, ed., *Suomen lehdistön historia 2*. Kuopio: Kustannuskiila.

Nyholm, Pekka, and Carl Hagfors. 1968. *Ryhmäyhtenäisyyden kehityksestä eduskunnassa 1930-1954*. University of Helsinki, Institute of Political Science, Research Report 14.

OECD Economic Outlook 2000. Paris: OECD.

OECD. 2001. *Education Policy Analysis 2001*. Paris: OECD.

Ojanen, Tuomas. 2000. "Tuomioistuimet," in Tapio Raunio and Matti Wiberg, eds., *EU ja Suomi*. Helsinki: Edita.

Oksanen, Matti. 1972. *Kansanedustajan rooli*. Helsinki: Gaudeamus.

Pajarinen, Mika and Pekka Ylä-Anttila. 2001. *Maat kilpailevat investoinneista, teknologia vetää sijoituksia Suomeen*. Helsinki: Elinkeinoelämän tutkimuslaitos, Sarja B 173.

Paloheimo, Heikki. 2000. "Vaaliohjelmat ja ehdokkaiden mielipiteet," in Pertti Pesonen, ed., *Suomen europarlamenttivaalit*. Tampere: Tampere University Press.

Pehkonen, Jaakko. 1998. "Pitkäaikaistyöttömyys," in Matti Pohjola, ed., *Suomalainen työttömyys*. Helsinki: Taloustieto.

Pekkarinen, Jukka, and Juhana Vartiainen. 1993. *Suomen talouspolitiikan pitkä linja*. Porvoo: Werner Söderström Oy.

Pesonen, Pertti. 1973. "Il finanziamento pubblico dei partiti in Finlandia," *Rivista italiana di scienza politica 3*, 491–519.

Pesonen, Pertti. 1974. "Finland: Party Support in a Fragmented System," in Richard Rose, ed., *Electoral Behavior*. New York: The Free Press.

Pesonen, Pertti. 1973b. "Dimensions of Political Cleavage in Multi-Party Systems." *European Journal of Political Research 1*, 109-132.

Pesonen, Pertti. 1982. "Finland: the 'one man-one vote' issue," in Hans Daalder and Edward Shils, eds., *Universities, Politicians and Bureaucrats*. Cambridge: Cambridge University Press.

Pesonen, Pertti. 1985. "Finland: The Country, the People, and the Political System," in Jaakko Uotila, ed., *The Finnish Legal System*. Helsinki: Finnish Lawyers Publishing Company.

Pesonen, Pertti. 1994. "Kansanäänestys ja edustuksellinen demokratia," in Pesonen, ed., *Suomen EU-kansanäänestys 1994*. Helsinki: Ministry for Foreign Affairs.

Pesonen, Pertti. 1995. "The Voters' Choice of Candidate," in Sami Borg and Risto Sänkiaho, eds., *The Finnish Voter*. Helsinki: The Finnish Political Science Association.

Pesonen, Pertti. 1998. "Voting Decisions," in Andreas Todal Jenssen, Pesonen, and Mikael Gilljam, eds., *To Join or Not to Join*. Oslo: Scandinavian University Press.

Pesonen, Pertti, and Risto Sänkiaho. 1979. *Kansalaiset ja kansanvalta*. Porvoo-Helsinki: Werner Söderström Oy.

Pesonen, Pertti, Risto Sänkiaho, and Sami Borg. 1993. *Vaalikansan äänivalta*. Porvoo-Helsinki: Werner Söderström Oy.

Pesonen, Pertti, and A.H. Thomas. 1983. "Coalition Formation in Scandinavia," in Vernon Bogdanor, ed., *Coalition Government in Western Europe*. London: Heinemann.

Piekkola, Hannu. 1996. "Pohjoismainen hyvinvointivaltio kriisissä?" *Talous & yhteiskunta* 2/1996.

Pihkala, Erkki. 2001. *Suomalaiset maailmantaloudessa keskiajalta EU-Suomeen*. Helsinki: Suomalaisen Kirjallisuuden Seura.

Piirainen, Timo. 1992. "Hyvinvointivaltio ja yhteiskunnalliset ristiriidat: kohti postkorporatistista sosiaalipolitiikkaa?," in Olavi Riihinen, ed., *Sosiaalipolitiikka 2017*. Porvoo: Werner Söderström Oy.

Pohjola, Matti. 1998. "Työttömyys suomalaisen yhteiskunnan ongelmana: Johdanto ja kirjan tiivistelmä," in Pohjola, ed., *Suomalainen työttömyys*. Helsinki: Taloustieto.

Political Action: An Eight Nation Study 1973–1976. 1979. Universität zu Köln, Zentralarchiv-Study-No.0765.

Ponton, Geoffrey. 1984. "Pluralist and Elitist Theories of Political Processes," in Anthony Forder, Terry Caslin, Ponton, and Sandra Walklate, *Theories of Welfare*. London: Routledge & Kegan Paul.

Poropudas, Olli, and Raimo Mäkinen. 2001. "90-luvun koulutuspolitiikan taustat ja yleispiirteet," in Mäkinen and Poropudas, eds., *Irtiotto 90-luvun koulutuspolitiikasta*. Turku: Turun yliopiston kasvatustieteellisen tiedekunnan julkaisuja B:67.

Poteri, Riitta. 1998. *Meissä on ytyä! Selvitys valtakunnallisten sosiaali- ja terveysjärjestöjen toiminnasta*. Helsinki: Edita.

Prescott-Allen, Robert. 2001. *The Wellbeing of Nations*. Washington: Island Press.

Pulkkinen, Tuija. 1987. "Kansalaisyhteiskunta ja valtio," in Risto Alapuro, Ilkka Liikanen, Kerstin Smeds, and Henrik Stenius, eds., *Kansa liikkeessä*. Helsinki: Kirjayhtymä.

Pulma, Panu. 1999. "Municipal autonomy, local democracy and the state," in Jorma Selovuori, ed., *Power and Bureaucracy in Finland 1809–1998*. Helsinki: Prime Minister's Office.

Rahkonen, Keijo. 1990. "Jälkiteolliset utopiat," in Olavi Riihinen, ed., *Suomi 2017*. Jyväskylä: Gummerus.

Rajavaara, Marketta, and Mikko Viitanen. 1997. "Toiveena työ, suuntana eläke?," in Rajavaara, ed., *Työtä, eläkettä vai työttömyyttä?*. Helsinki: Kansaneläkelaitos, Sosiaali- ja terveysturvan tutkimuksia 37.

Rasila, Viljo. 1982. "Liberalismin aika," in Jorma Ahvenainen, Erkki Pihkala, and Rasila, eds., *Suomen taloushistoria 2. Teollistuva Suomi*. Helsinki: Tammi.

Raunio, Tapani and Matti Wiberg. 2000. "Johtopäätökset," in Raunio and Wiberg, eds., *EU ja Suomi*. Helsinki:Edita.

Reinans, Sven Alur. 1996. "Den finländska befolkningen i Sverige," in Jarmo Lainio, ed., *Finnarnas historia i Sverige 3. Tid efter 1945*. Jyväskylä: Finska Historiska Samfundet.

Rentola, Kimmo. 1998. "Finnish Communism, O.W.Kuusinen and Their Two Native Countries," in Tauno Saarela and Rentola, eds., *Communism, National and International*. Tampere: Tammer-Paino.

Riihelä, Marja, Risto Sullström, Ilpo Suoniemi, and Matti Tuomala. 2001. "Income Inequality in Finland during the 1990s," in Jorma Kalela, Ullamaija Kivikuru, Heikki A. Loikkanen, and Jussi Simpura, eds., *Down from Heavens, Up from the Ashes*. Government Institute for Economic Research. Saarijärvi: Gummerus.

Riihinen, Olavi. 1965. *Teollistuvan yhteiskunnan alueellinen erilaistuneisuus*. Porvoo: Werner Söderström Oy.

Riihinen, Olavi. 1973. "Kaupungistuminen ja ulkoiset säästötekijät," in Briitta Koskiaho, Matti Manninen, Anja Savisaari, Pentti Junna, and Ritva Torniainen, eds., *Sosiaalipolitiikan arvot, tavoitteet ja käytäntö 1970-luvulla*. Tampere: Tampereen Arpatehtaan Kirjapaino.

Riihinen, Olavi. 1983. "Social Policy Problems in the 1990s," in *Personal Insurance as a Supplement to Social Security*. The Pohjola-Group. Tampere: Tamprint.

Riihinen, Olavi. 1984. "Social Policy in the 1990s", in *Annual Report for 1983 of the Pohjola Group*. Tampere: Tamprint.

Riihinen, Olavi. 1985. "Industrialization and Social Policy," in Riihinen, ed., *Social Policy and Post-Industrial Society*. Basic Report, 13th Regional Symposium on Social Welfare, Turku, Finland, June 9–14, 1985. Helsinki: Yleisjäljennös.

Riihinen, Olavi. 1992. "Sosiaalipolitiikka ja legitimiteetti," in Riihinen, ed., *Sosiaalipolitiikka 2017*. Sitran julkaisusarja 123. Helsinki: Werner Söderström Oy.

Riihinen, Olavi. 1998. "Teknologinen kehitys, työllisyys ja sosiaalinen eriytyminen," in *Sosiaaliturva myöhäisteollisessa murroksessa*. Helsinki: Kansaneläkelaitos, Sosiaali- ja terveysturvan katsauksia 24.

Ringdahl, Kristen and Henry Valen. 1998. "Structural Divisions in the EU Referendums," in Anders Todal Jenssen, Pertti Pesonen and Mikael Gilljam, eds., *To Join or Not to Join*. Oslo: Scandinavian University Press.

Ritakallio, Veli-Matti. 2001. "Multidimensional Poverty in the Aftermath of the Recession: Finland in 1995 and 2000," in Jorma Kalela, Ullamaija Kivikuru, Heikki A. Loikkanen, and Jussi Simpura, eds., *Down form the Heavens, Up from the Ashes*. Government Institute for Economic Research. Saarijärvi: Gummerus.

Rodger, John. 2000. *From Welfare State to Welfare Society*. London: Macmillan.

Rose, Richard. 1974. "Comparability in electoral studies," in Rose, ed., *Electoral Behavior*. New York: The Free Press.

311

Saari, Juho. 1999. "Jatkuvuus vai murros? Sosiaalipolitiikan pitkät linjat ja käännekohdat jälkiteollistuvissa länsimaissa," in Pekka Kosonen and Jussi Simpura, eds., *Sosiaalipolitiikka globalisoituvassa maailmassa.* Helsinki: Gaudeamus.

Salokangas, Raimo. 1987. "Puoluepolitiikka ja uutisjournalismi muuttuvilla lehtimarkkinoilla," in Päiviö Tommila, ed., *Suomen lehdistön historia 2.* Kuopio: Kustannuskiila Oy.

Salonen, Kari, Kimmo Kääriäinen, and Kati Niemelä. 2000. *Kirkko uudelle vuosituhannelle.* Tampere: Kirkon tutkimuslaitos.

Sandberg, Siv. 2000. "Kunnat ja alueet," in Tapio Raunio and Matti Wiberg, eds., *EU ja Suomi.* Helsinki: Edita.

Savolainen, Reino. 1999. "The Finnish system of central government administration," in Jorma Selovuori, ed., *Power and Bureaucracy in Finland 1809–1998.* Helsinki: Prime Minister's Office.

Selovuori, Jorma. 1999. "Provincial administration," in Selovuori, ed., *Power and Bureaucracy in Finland 1809-1998.* Helsinki: Prime Minister's Office.

Seppälä, Risto. 1990. "Metsäsektori – yhäkö Suomen talouden moottori," in Olavi Riihinen, ed., *Suomi 2017.* Jyväskylä: Gummerus.

Shively, W. Phillips. 2003. *Power & Choice. An Intorduction to Political Science,* 8th edition. New York: McGraw-Hill.

Siisiäinen, Martti. 1998. "Uusien ja vanhojen liikkeiden keinovalikoimat," in Kaj Ilmonen and Siisiäinen, eds., *Uudet ja vanhat liikkeet.* Tampere: Vastapaino.

Sillanpää, Lennard. 1994. *Political and Administrative Responses to Sami Self-Determination.* Helsinki: Societas Scientiarum Fennica.

Silvasti, Eero. 2002. "Hyvinvointivaltiosta tuli huoltovaltio," in *Aamulehti,* April 9, 2002.

Singer, Peter, ed. 1994. *A Companion to Ethics Blackwell Companions to Philisophy.* Oxford: Blackwell Publishers.

Sivonen, Pekka. 2001. "Finland and Nato," in Bo Huldt, Teija Tiilikainen, Tapani Vaahtoranta, and Anna Helkama-Rågård, eds., *Finnish and Swedish Security.* Swedish National Defence College.

Social Welfare and Health Care Organizations in Finland. 1999. Helsinki: Erweko Painotuote.

Soikkanen, Hannu. 1961. *Sosialismin tulo Suomeen.* Porvoo: Werner Söderström Oy.

Soikkanen, Hannu. 1966. *Kunnallinen itsehallinto kansanvallan perusta.* Helsinki: Maalaiskuntien Liiton kirjapaino.

Soikkanen, Hannu. 1975. *Kohti kansanvaltaa 1. 1899–1937. Suomen Sosiaalidemokraattinen Puolue 75 vuotta.* Vaasa: Oy Kirjapaino Ab.

Sosiaaliturvan kehitys Suomessa 1950–1977. 1978. Helsinki: Suomen virallinen tilasto XXII:56.

*Sosiaaliturvan suunta 1999–2000.*1999. Helsinki: Sosiaali- ja terveysministeriön julkaisuja 1999:27.

Statistical Yearbook of Finland (SYF) 1953, 1961, 1962, 1963, 1972, 1973, 1981, 1983, 1990, 1991, 1992, 1994, 1996, 1997, 1998, 2000, and 2001. Helsinki: Statistics Finland.

Statistical Yearbook of the Social Insurance Institution, Finland, 2000. 2001. Vammala: Vammalan Kirjapaino.

Statistical Yearbook on Social Welfare and Health Care 2000. 2001. Social Security 2001:1. Saarijärvi: Gummerus.

Sulkunen, Irma. 1986. *Raittius kansalaisuskontona.* Societas Historica Finlandiae, Historiallisia Tutkimuksia 134. Jyväskylä: Gummerus.

Sulkunen, Irma. 1987. "Naiset ja järjestäytyminen ja kaksijakoinen kansalaisuus," in Risto Alapuro, Ilkka Liikanen, Kerstin Smeds, and Henrik Stenius, eds., *Kansa liikkeessä.* Vaasa: Kirjayhtymä.

Sundberg, Jan. 1996. *Partier och partisystem i Finland.* Esbo: Schildts.

Suomen Kuvalehti 4/2002.

Suomen Lehdistö 6/2002.

Suominen, Leena. 1979. *Lapsiperhe Suomessa.* Kolmikantasarja 7. Helsinki: Väestöliitto.

Suominen, Tapani. 1997. *Ehkä teloitamme jonkun. Opiskelijaradikalismi ja vallankumous-fiktio 1960- ja 1970-lukujen Suomessa, Norjassa ja Länsi-Saksassa.* Helsinki: Tammi.

Suonoja, Kyösti. 1992. "Kansalaisten parhaaksi – yhteistuntoa ja politiikkaa. Sosiaali ja terveysministeriö 1939–1992," in Pekka Haatanen and Suonoja, *Suuriruhtinaskunnasta hyvinvointivaltioon. Sosiaali- ja terveysministeriö 75 vuotta.* Helsinki: Valtion painatuskeskus.

Sänkiaho, Risto, and Erika Säynässalo. 1994. "Suomalaisuus, kansainvälisyys ja EU-jäsenyys," in Pertti Pesonen, ed., *Suomen EU-kansanäänestys 1994.* Helsinki: Ministry for Foreign Affairs.

Takala, Hannu, ed 1979. *Poliislakko.* Helsinki: Oikeuspoliittisen tutkimuslaitoksen julkaisuja 30.

Taloudellinen katsaus. 2001. *Valtion talousarvioesitys 2002,* Appendix. Helsinki: HE 115/2001 vp.

Talousneuvosto. 2000. *Alueellinen kehitys ja aluepolitiikka Suomessa.* Työryhmäraportti. Helsinki: Valtioneuvoston kanslian julkaisuja 2000/6.

Taylor, Charles. 1989. "The Liberal-Communitarian Debate," in Nancy Rosenblum, ed., *Liberalism and the Moral life.* Cambridge, MA: Harvard University Press.

Teljo, Jussi. 1949. *Suomen valtioelämän murros 1905–1908.* Porvoo: Werner Söderström Oy.

Tennilä, Liisa. 1999. "Kulutus," in Kristiina Andreasson and Vesa Helin, eds., *Suomen vuosisata.* Jyväskylä: Gummerus.

Topf, Richard. 1995. "Beyond Electoral Participation," in Hans-Dieter Klingemann and Dieter Fuchs, eds., *Citizens and the State.* Oxford: Oxford University Press.

Transparency International. 2001. *The 2001 Corruption Perceptions Index.* http://www.transparency.org/documents/cpi.

Trends. 2001. Helsinki: Tilastokeskus, International Business Statistics.

Tuominen, Marja. 1991. *"Me kaikki ollaan sotilaitten lapsia." Sukupolvihegemonian kriisi 1960-luvun suomalaisessa kulttuurissa.* Helsinki: Otava.

Tuominen, Uuno. 1974. "Ulkopuoliset painostustekijät ja valtiopäivätoiminta," in *Suomen kansanedustuslaitoksen historia IV.* Helsinki: Eduskunnan historiakomitea.

Turpeinen, Oiva. 1987. "Lastensuojelu ja väestökehitys. Lastensuojelun lääkinnöllinen ja sosiaalinen kehitys Suomessa," in Panu Pulma, and Turpeinen, *Suomen lastensuojelun historia.* Kouvola: Kouvolan kirjapaino.

Turpeinen, Oiva. 1997. *Telecommunications since 1796.* Helsinki: Telecom Finland/Edita.

Tweedie, Mrs. Alec E. 1913. *Through Finland in Carts.* London, Edinburgh, Dublin and New York: Thomas Nelson & Sons.

Törnudd, Klaus. 1968. *The Electoral System of Finland.* London: Hugh Evelyn.

Törnudd, Klaus. 1982. "Yleinen mielipide ja eduskuntatyö," in *Suomen Kansanedustus-laitoksen historia XII.* Helsinki: Eduskunnan historiakomitea.

Törnudd, Klaus. 2001. "The makers of Finnish Security Policy," in Bo Huldt, Teija Tiilikainen, Tapani Vaahtoranta, and Anna Helkama-Rågård, eds., *Finnish and Swedish Security.* Swedish National Defence College.

Ulkoasiainministeriö Toimintakertomus 2000. 2001. Helsinki: Ministry for Foreign Affairs.

Uotila, Jaakko. 1985. "Fundamental rights of the citizens," in Uotila, ed., *The Finnish Legal System.* Helsinki: Finnish Lawyers Publishing Company.

Vaarama, Marja, Jaakko Luomahaara, Arja Peiponen, and Päivi Voutilainen. 2002. *Koko kunta ikääntyneiden asialle.* Stakes, raportteja 259. Saarijärvi: Gummerus.

Vaarnas, Kalle. 1976. *Ministerimatrikkeli 1917–1966. Valtioneuvoston historia 1917–1966 IV.* Helsinki: Valtion painatuskeskus.

Valtion talousarvioesitys 2002. Helsinki: HE 115/2001 vp.

Vartia, Pentti and Pekka Ylä-Anttila. 1996. *Kansantalous 2021.* Elinkeinoelämän tutkimuslaitos. Series B 126. SITRA 153. Tampere: Tammer-Paino.

Vartiainen, Perttu. 1998. *Suomalaisen aluepolitiikan kehitysvaiheita.* Helsinki, Sisäasiainministeriö, Aluekehitysosaston julkaisu 6/1998.

Vattula, Kaarina, ed. 1983. *Suomen taloushistoria 3. Historiallinen tilasto.* Helsinki: Tammi.

Venho, Tomi. 1999. "Tutkimus vuoden 1999 eduskuntavaaliehdokkaiden kampanjarahoituksesta," in *Vaalirahoituskomitean mietintö.* Helsinki: Oikeusministeriö.

Virmasalo, Veera. 2000. "Kansallinen mediatutkimus 2000," in *Suomen Lehdistö* 8/2000.

VNS 2/2001 vp. *Suomen turvallisuus- ja puolustuspolitiikka 2001.* Valtioneuvoston selonteko, Valtiopäivät 2001.

Väyrynen, Raimo. 1999. *Globalisaatio ja Suomen poliittinen järjestelmä.* Helsinki: Taloustieto.

Wahlke, John C., et al. 1962. *The Legislative System.* New York: John Wiley.

Wallerstein, Immanuel. 1987. "World-Systems Analysis," in Anthony Giddens and Jonathan H. Turner, eds., *Social Theory Today.* Cambridge: Polity Press.

Wattenberg, Martin P. 2000. "The Decline of Party Mobilization," in Russell J. Dalton and Wattenberg, eds., *Parties without Partisans.* Oxford: Oxford University Press.

Webster, Frank. 2000. "Higher Education," in Gary Browning, Abigail Halcli, and Webster, eds., *Understanding Contemporary Society: Theories of the Present.* London: Sage.

Wiberg, Matti. 1997. "Suomalainen valtionapuvetoinen puoluetukijärjestelmä," in Sami Borg, ed., *Puolueet 1990-luvulla.* Turku: Turun yliopisto, valtio-oppi.

The World Almanac 2001. 2001. Mahwah, New Jersey: World Almanac Books.

The World Competitiveness Yearbook 2001. 2002. IMD, Geneva.

World Press Trends. 2001 and *2002.* Paris: World Association of Newspapers.

World Values Surveys 1981, 1990 and 2000. The Finnish Gallup Institute.

Yearbook of Population Research in Finland 1993. 1993. Vammala: Vammalan Kirjapaino.

Yearbook of Population Research in Finland XXXIII. 1996. Vammala: Vammalan Kirjapaino.

YLE. 2002. *Annual Report 2001.* Helsinki: Yleisradio.

Web pages:

http://www.ciesin.columbia.edu/indicators/ESI

http://www.cif.fi (July 16, 2002)

http://fakta.eduskunta.fi

http://www.intermin.fi/intermin/home.nsf

http://www.mol.fi/tiedotus (February 21, 2002)

http://www.mmm.fi/metsatalous

http://www.research.fi/k tk-menot.fi (March 21, 2002)

http://www.research.fi/k tk-valtio.fi (March 21, 2002)

http://www.slu.fi (July 16, 2002)

http://www.sttk.fi

http://www.tekes.fi/eng/rd/policy (March 20, 2002)

http://www.telegalleria.fi

http://www.tt.fi/english/tarinat.shtml#pkt-asiat

http://www.tul.fi (July 16, 2002)

Index